The Basel Handbook

The Basel Handbook:
A Guide for Financial Practitioners

Edited by Michael K. Ong

Published by Risk Books, a Division of Incisive Media plc

Haymarket House
28–29 Haymarket
London SW1Y 4RX
Tel: +44 (0)20 7484 9700
Fax: +44 (0)20 7484 9800
E-mail: books@riskwaters.com
Sites: www.riskbooks.com
       www.riskwaters.com

Every effort has been made to secure the permission of individual copyright
holders for inclusion.

© Incisive RWG Ltd 2004
© Incisive Media Investments Ltd 2005

Reprinted 2004
Reprinted 2005

ISBN 1 904339 18 2

British Library Cataloguing in Publication Data
A catalogue record for this book is available from the British Library

Managing Editor: Sarah Jenkins
Copy Editor: Andrew John
Copy Editor: Romilly Hambling
Editorial Assistant: Steve Fairman

Typeset by Mizpah Publishing Services, Chennai, India

Printed and bound in Spain by Espacegrafic, Pamplona, Navarra

Contents

SECTION 1: PARAMETERISATION OF THE INTERNAL
RATINGS-BASED APPROACH

SECTION 2: IMPLEMENTATION AND TESTING OF
COMPLIANT IRB SYSTEMS

Foreword

By redefining how banks worldwide calculate regulatory capital and report compliance to regulators and the public, the "New Accord" is intended to improve safety and soundness in the financial system by placing increased emphasis on banks' own internal control and risk management processes and models, the supervisory review process, and market discipline. Its complex recommendations will likely create a variety of regulatory compliance challenges for banks in Europe and around the globe.

The New Accord's risk focus gives banks and financial practitioners new impetus to focus on comprehensive risk management. While the 1988 Capital Accord addressed market and credit risks, Basel II substantially changes the treatment of credit risk and also requires that banks have sufficient capital to cover operational risks. It encourages ongoing improvements in risk assessment and mitigation.

Although many bank leaders have recognised the significance of evolving operational risks, many do not yet perceive them as a distinct class of risks or fully understand the business benefits banks can derive from a comprehensive, consistent approach to operational risk management. Basel II brings new urgency to the issue by asking banks to implement an enterprise-wide risk management framework that encompasses operational risks. As Ulrich Anders and Gerrit Jan van den Brink explain in their chapter, *Implementing a Basel II Scenario-Based AMA for Operational Risk,* "The quantification of operational risks cannot be regarded as a goal in itself. The higher-level goal is an improvement in the management of operational risks" (see p. 356).

The New Accord's risk management requirements are likely to prompt significant changes in the core business of an individual bank as well as in its organisational structure. Under Basel II, the "outputs" of better management of credit and operational risk will be the "inputs" of an economic capital model by which banks can allocate capital to various functions and transactions depending on risk. Aside from new or altered methods that must be employed, the new capital requirements will also drive change in resource needs, processes, and IT system architecture.

As Michel Araten points out in his chapter, *Development and Validation of Key Estimates of Economic Capital Models,* "Today, many banks do not have sufficient historical data in exactly the form required. As a temporary step they can draw on external studies. Going forward, they need to make immediate investments in manpower and systems resources to develop and analyse their own internal experience" (see p.13). To comply with Basel II, banks will have to develop and use various models (risk-specific and for economic capital management) to allocate capital to business activities based on how much risk, and of what type, an individual activity contributes to the bank's portfolio of risks. These models would determine how much capital is required to support the various activities of the bank – a purpose regulatory capital cannot adequately serve, even under the more risk-sensitive calculations of Basel II.

These changes could ultimately pose broad challenges for a bank's board of directors and its senior management, who are charged with new risk management and reporting responsibilities under the New Accord. These senior leaders will need to consider how Basel II compliance could (or should) integrate with other efforts they are making to improve corporate governance.

To be able to implement Basel II sufficiently, most banks will need to rethink their business strategies as well as the risks that underlie them. Indeed, calculating capital requirements under the New Accord requires a bank to implement a comprehensive risk framework across the institution. The risk management improvements that are the intended result may be rewarded by lower capital requirements. However, large implementation projects will likely have wide-ranging effects on a bank's information technology systems, processes, people, and business – beyond the regulatory compliance and finance functions.

Adapting to the New Accord will be more demanding for some institutions than for others, based on factors including current risk management practices, business size, number of geographies, risk types, and specific business, portfolio, and market conditions. Transforming the institution while conducting business as usual is central to this challenge. Such an endeavour can ultimately help banks understand whether they are in the right business and serving or targeting the right customers.

The complexity of the New Accord, as well as its interdependencies with International Financial Reporting Standards and local regulation worldwide, makes implementation of Basel II a highly complex project. For a bank, a project will be driven by the structure of its business, beginning with its strategy and encompassing its risk management and capital calculation methods, business processes, data requirements, and IT systems.

With a structured and disciplined approach, banks can begin to achieve the Basel Committee's intended benefits of enhanced risk management and lower capital requirements. Such changes, in turn, could influence banks' strategies, customer relations, and, over time, their business models. Moreover, Basel II could trigger a wide range of business implications and risk management challenges – not just for banks but for their non-bank competitors, customers, rating agencies, regulators, and, ultimately, the global capital markets.

Jorg Hashagen
Head of KPMG's Basel Initiative

List of Contributors

Scott D. Aguais is director and head of Credit Risk Methodology at Barclays Capital – the investment banking unit of Barclays Bank PLC. He has been involved with credit risk modelling and management for over 15 years. At Barclays Capital, Scott's responsibilities include, developing, validating and managing credit risk models and methodologies for the banking and trading books. Prior to joining Barclays Capital, Scott worked for Algorithmics, KPMG Consulting, AMS and DRI-McGraw-Hill. He holds a PhD in economics from Boston University. Scott speaks and writes extensively on credit risk and jointly with Larry Forest has published substantial research on "MtM" valuation models for loan instruments that analyse embedded options and structure in loans.

Ulrich Anders is head of operational risk for Dresdner Bank Group. He is overseeing the introduction of a comprehensive operational risk management framework. In addition to this, he has been appointed to be head of governance framework for Dresdner Bank. Previously Dr. Anders was employed at Deutsche Bank and ZEW (Centre for European Economic Research). In Deutsche Bank he was engaged in market and operational risk. In ZEW he was responsible for financial market analysis as well as media and press related activities. Dr. Anders has a Masters degree in business engineering and a PhD in statistics and finance both from University of Karlsruhe, and an MBA in general management from the University of Kent at Canterbury.

Michel Araten is senior vice president of the Risk Capital and Research Group of JP MorganChase & Co. His responsibilities include developing and implementing portfolio models for assessing risk capital for global retail, wholesale, and capital markets exposures. He has been an adjunct lecturer at Columbia University, at the Fordham Graduate School of Business, and at the Polytechnic Institute. He holds a PhD in operations research, a MS in industrial engineering, a BS in chemical engineering, and a BA in liberal arts, all from Columbia University. He has been a frequent speaker at risk conferences.

Christian Bluhm is a vice president at HypoVereinsbank's Group Credit Portfolio Management in Munich where he and his team are responsible for the modelling and analytic evaluation of asset-backed securities, especially CDOs. His first involvement in risk/portfolio management was with

Deutsche Bank. Christian has a PhD in mathematics from the University of Erlangen-Nuremberg and was a post-doctoral member of the mathematics department of Cornell University, New York.

Gerrit Jan van den Brink is managing operational risk controller with Dresdner Bank AG. He is responsible for the roll-out of the operational risk framework within Dresdner Bank Group and is heading the Operational Risk Analysis and Advisory Function, in which risk capital is calculated and quarterly reports are composed. He was previously an internal auditor, controller, IT-Manager, CFO and Head of Operations with Rabobank (1988–1999) both in the Netherlands and Germany. Dr. van den Brink is a lecturer in operational risk at the Johann-Wolfgang Goethe University in Frankfurt am Main and has published books on operational risk and operations management topics. He holds a PhD in economics from the Erasmus University of Rotterdam.

Ashish Dev is executive vice president, risk management at KeyCorp in Cleveland, Ohio where he heads up the enterprise risk solutions area. Ashish has been instrumental in building several published/unpublished credit risk models, some of which have directly influenced international regulatory capital adequacy rules for banks. Prior to joining KeyCorp in 1999, Ashish was head of quantitative research and analysis in Bank One. Ashish has a PhD in economics from State University of New York at StonyBrook. He also holds the CFA professional designation.

Donald R. van Deventer is the chairman and chief executive officer of risk management firm Kamakura Corporation, based in Honolulu. Dr. van Deventer, who was named to the RISK Hall of Fame in December 2002, was formerly senior vice president in the investment banking department of Lehman Brothers Tokyo branch and treasurer of First Interstate Bancorp in Los Angeles. Dr. van Deventer is the author of Credit Risk Models and the Basel Accords (with Kenji Imai, 2003), Financial Risk Analytics (also with Kenji Imai, 1996) and Financial Risk Management in Banking (with Dennis Uyemura, 1992). Dr. van Deventer received his PhD in business economics in 1977 from Harvard University.

Diana Diaz-Ledezma is a member of Barclays Capital Credit Risk Methodology team. Before joining Barclays Capital, Diana was a financial analyst at the Central Bank of Mexico and risk manager at one of the largest development banks in Latin America. She holds a doctorate on credit risk modelling and has presented her research at several international finance conferences. Her academic career includes lecturing finance, statistics and mathematics at Cass Business School, London Business School and at the National Autonomous University of Mexico.

Edward A. Duncan is assistant director of European Policy at the International Swaps and Derivatives Association (ISDA). At ISDA his responsibilities include global accounting policy, the European tax committee, and risk management. He is also responsible for co-ordinating the work of the Internal Ratings Working Group, and has worked closely with the Basel Accord Implementation Group, and the FSA's Credit Risk Implementation Advisory Group. Edward A Duncan graduated in economics from the University of Manchester in 1993. He joined the International Swaps and Derivatives Association (ISDA) as assistant director of European Policy in April 2002. He has a diploma in finance from the University of London, and received a diploma certificate in Regulation and Compliance from the Securities Institute.

Lawrence R. Forest, Jr currently works on Basel II implementation as a consulting associate director for Barclays Capital and has worked previously for Algorithmics, KPMG Consulting, AMS, DRI-McGraw-Hill, the Congressional Budget Office, and the Federal Reserve. He holds a PhD in economics from the University of California, Berkeley. Recent publications include: "Implementing a Comprehensive Credit-Risk-Management System: The Case Study of Hanvit Bank," (with Scott Aguais), *Journal of Commercial Lending*, Spring 2001, and "Building a Credit Risk Valuation Framework for Commercial Loans," (with Scott Aguais and Dan Rosen).

Antoine Frachot has been head of the Groupe de Recherche Operationnelle (GRO) since 1999. GRO is the risk analytics division of the Global Risk Management Unit at Crédit Agricole/Crédit Lyonnais. Prior to this, Antoine Frachot was a top civil servant in the macroeconomics and forecasting division of the French Ministry of Economics and Finance. He is the author of many papers on mathematical finance, interest-rate modelling, asset-liability management and operational risk. He is a part-time professor in economics at Ecole Polytechnique and a member of the Professional Risk Managers International Association (PRMIA). Antionne graduated from Ecole Polytechnique and Ecole Nationale de la Statistique et de l'Administration Economique (ENSAE).

Sebastian Fritz is the head of the Risk Analytics and Instruments Department of the Deutsche Bank Group, responsible for the development of rating and scoring methodologies, pricing tools, portfolio models and operational risk methodology. He has worked in Deutsche Bank's credit risk management division since 1997, in positions such as credit risk instruments analyst and head of rating and pricing tool development.

He was previously a research associate at the Gesellschaft fuer Schwerionenforschung mbH, Darmstadt, Germany. Sebastian gained his physics degree with a minor in computer science and biophysics at the University of Hamburg, and his PhD in heavy ion physics at the Johann-Wolfgang-Goethe-University, Frankfurt.

Michael Haubenstock is the director of operational risk management at Capital One, a leading consumer finance company. This role involves working on operational risk self assessment and supporting technologies, the event database, and building key risk indicators and operational risk economic capital. Through 2001, he was a partner in the financial risk management practice at PricewaterhouseCoopers, where he led the practice for operational risk management for financial institutions. Michael has worked with leading domestic and international banks in diverse areas including enterprise risk management, risk policies and methodologies. Michael holds a BS from the University of Pennsylvania, an MS from Washington University and an MBA from New York University.

Simon Hills is a director in the Wholesale and Regulation Team at the British Bankers Association. He is part of the BBA team working on the Basel Accord and its implementation in Europe in the new Risk Based Capital Directive and the FSA's integrated prudential sourcebook. Simon is also responsible for the management of the LIBOR Rate Fixing process and other benchmark developments. He was previously a director at BZW responsible for originating bonds, medium term notes, derivative and tax based transactions. He studied at London Business School gaining an MBA and Imperial College obtaining BSc in biochemistry and more recently completed a Masters' in financial services regulation at Guildhall University.

Esa Jokivuolle currently works as a project supervisor at the Financial Markets Department of the Bank of Finland, and as a lecturer at the Helsinki School of Economics. His interest in Basel II stems from his participation in the European Commission's Working Group on Internal Ratings, from 2000 to 2002. Earlier he worked as a senior quantitative analyst at Leonia plc (now Sampo plc), Helsinki. Publications related to Basel II, all joint with Samu Peura include "Regulatory Capital Volatility", *Risk*, May 2001, "Incorporating Collateral Value Uncertainty in Loss Given Default Estimates and Loan-to-value Ratios", *European Financial Management*, September 2003. Esa earned a PhD in finance in 1996 from University of Illinois at Urbana-Champaign.

Michael Luxenburger is head of credit rating and process systems and is globally responsible for the development of rating and scoring methodologies for Deutsche Bank Group. He is also working on Basel II implementation. He joined Deutsche Bank in 1994 to work on market risk related topics and headed the development team for a global market risk management system. Michael holds a PhD in mathematics and studied in Darmstadt and Paris.

Thomas Miehe is a risk analyst in the Risk Analytics and Instruments Department of the Deutsche Bank Group. He works on the calibration and validation of credit risk parameters, the Basel II implementation and the development of rating methodologies. Thomas joined Deutsche Bank in 2001 after gaining experiences as a trainee in credit risk management, relationship management and structured finance. He studied financial mathematics in Berlin and Cracow.

Olivier Moudoulaud is a research assistant at the Groupe de Recherche Opérationnelle. Olivier graduated from Ecole Nationale de la Statistique et de l'Analyse de l'Information (ENSAI).

Richard Norgate works in the Financial Risk Management Group at KPMG, where he now leads the retail credit risk team. He has worked for a number of clients in the UK and throughout Asia, Australia and Africa on developing credit risk solutions, both within and beyond the remit of Basel. Richard received a PhD in mathematical modelling from Cranfield University in 1998, and in his spare time reviews books for "Financial Engineering News".

Michael K. Ong is professor of finance and director of the finance program at the Stuart Graduate School of Business, Illinois Institute of Technology. He is also executive director of the Center for Financial Markets. Until recently, Dr. Ong was executive vice president and chief risk officer for credit Agricole Indosuez in New York. He had enterprise-wide responsibility for all risk management functions for corporate banking, merchant banking, asset management, capital markets activities, and the Carr Futures Group. Dr. Ong received a BS degree in physics, *cum laude*, from the University of the Philippines and his MA degree in physics, MS degree in applied mathematics, and PhD degree in applied mathematics from the State University of New York at Stony Brook.

Ludger Overbeck holds a professorship of mathematics and its application at the University of Giessen in Germany. His main interests are quantitative methods in finance and risk management and stochastic analysis. Until June 2003 he was head of risk research & development in Deutsche Banks Credit Risk function, located in Frankfurt. Ludger's main responsibilities included development and implementation of the internal group-wide credit portfolio model, the operational risk model and the EC/RAROC-methodology. Ludger holds a PhD in mathematics and habilitations in applied mathematics from the University of Bonn and in economics from the University of Frankfurt.

Tony Peccia is vice president of operational risk and corporate insurance management at the Bank of Montreal. He is responsible for developing, implementing and monitoring the application of emerging best practices in operational risk management, including the proposed new Basel requirements for operational risk practice and regulatory capital. Tony spent eleven years with CIBC in various executive positions, including operational risk management, market risk management, and asset liability management, prior to that he spent ten years at the Royal Bank of Canada holding various positions. Tony has an MBA and a MSc in theoretical physics from McGill University.

Samu Peura is a risk manager at Sampo plc, a Finnish bank and life insurer. He is currently working on the development of group level capital allocation and risk-adjusted performance measurement. Previously he has developed in-house systems and processes for credit portfolio risk measurement and credit pricing. Prior to banking, he was a consultant at McKinsey&Co, and has published in refereed risk management, finance and computational economics journals. Samu holds a doctorate degree in economics from the University of Helsinki.

Martti Purhonen is currently in Corporate Ratings Department at Sampo Bank as a credit analyst. He has been in Sampo Bank's risk management since his graduation. His main tasks have been Sampo Bank's Basel I capital adequacy calculation for market risk and preparation for the Basel II framework on behalf of credit risk issues, including both retail and non-retail side. He graduated from Helsinki University of Technology, with the degree of Master of Science in technology, which was awarded in 1999 from the Department of Mechanical Engineering. Noted publications include "New Evidence on IRB Volatility", Risk, Credit Risk, March 2002.

Andrea Resti is associate professor of mathematical finance at the University of Bergamo, Italy, where he also is managing director of the FinMonitor research institute; he also works as a consultant for the main Italian banking groups and regularly writes in two financial newspapers. In the 1990s, he was a manager at the Banca Commerciale Italiana, one of Italy's leading credit institutions. His research activities focus on credit risk (especially credit VAR models) and the Basel reform process, but also include bank efficiency measurement and bank mergers and acquisitions.

Andrea earned a PhD in financial markets and institutions from the University of Bergamo.

Thierry Roncalli is a senior quantitative analyst at the Groupe de Recherche Opérationnelle (GRO), Crédit Agricole/Crédit Lyonnais, where he works on market risk, portfolio management and operational risk. Prior to this he was a research fellow at the Financial Econometrics Research Centre, City University Business School. He is the author of many articles on quantitative finance, has written two books in French on Gauss programming and has developed the TSM (Time Series and Wavelets) Gauss application. He is associate Professor of economics at the University of Evry and teaches risk management at ENSAI. Thierry holds a PhD in economics from the University of Bordeaux.

Andrea Sironi is full professor of financial markets and institutions at Bocconi University, Milan, where he also holds the positions of director of the research division of SDA Bocconi School of Management, and director of the Master in Risk Management (MARISK). Andrea previously held visiting positions at the research and statistics department of the Federal Reserve Board of Governors, Washington DC and at the Salomon Brothers Center for the study of financial institutions, Stern School of Business, New York University. He has been director of the working group on bank risks at the Italian Deposit Insurance Fund in Rome and is an honorary member of the Italian Financial Risk Management Assocation (AIFIRM). Andrea holds a degree in economics from Bocconi University.

John Thirlwell is executive director of the Operational Risk Research Forum. He was formerly a director of the British Bankers' Association, which he joined in December 1996 from Hill Samuel Bank, where he had been director and head of risk. At the BBA he was responsible for risk issues and on behalf of the banking industry he has been in discussions with regulators concerning the new Basel Capital Accord. He chairs the Financial Services and Insurance Committee of the International Chamber of Commerce in the UK and is a frequent speaker and writer on risk and related issues, including a regular column in *Operational Risk*. John graduated from Oxford University with a degree in English.

Xiaoming Wang is currently a PhD student in economics at the University of Hawaii, Manoa. She has been working as an intern with Kamakura since 2001. Her areas of interest include credit risk modeling, default correlation, and comparative analysis of credit risk models. She is expecting her first publication soon in the Journal of Risk as a co-author with Professor Robert Jarrow and Dr. Don van Deventer. Ms. Wang got her MS in economics in University of International Business and Economics, China, in 2000.

Lawrence J. White is Arthur E. Imperatore professor of economics at New York University's Stern School of Business. Prof. White received the BA from Harvard University (1964), the MSc from the London School of Economics (1965), and the PhD from Harvard University (1969). Prof. White served on the Senior Staff of the President's Council of Economic Advisers and was chairman of the Stern School's Department of Economics. He is the author of numerous books and of articles in leading economics and law journals. Lawrence was also the North American editor of The Journal of Industrial Economics in 1984–1987 and 1990–1995.

Elaine Wong is an associate director at Barclays Capital Credit Risk Methodology team in London. One of her main responsibilities is day-to-day project management of credit risk modelling efforts and model implementation related to Basel II at Barclays Capital. She previously worked in strategic risk management at Dresdner Kleinwort Wasserstein and at the bank of Hawaii, as head of the Country Risk and Credit Risk Analytics departments. She holds a Masters degree in accountancy and has published her research in the International Journal of Accounting. Elaine is also a holder of Chartered Financial Analyst.

Introduction

Michael K. Ong

In June 1999, the Basel Committee on Banking Supervision made its long-anticipated announcement to introduce a new capital adequacy framework to replace the 1988 Accord.[1] Citing a critical need to redesign the antiquated 1988 Accord in light of market innovations and a fundamental shift toward more complexity in the banking industry during the past decade, the Committee declared that:[2,3]

> "The world financial system has witnessed considerable economic turbulence over the last two years and, while these conditions have generally not been focused on G-10 countries directly, the risks that internationally active banks from G-10 countries have had to deal with have become more complex and challenging. This review of the Accord is designed to improve the way regulatory capital requirements reflect underlying risks. It is also designed to better address the financial innovation that has occurred in recent years, as shown, for example, by asset securitisation structures. As a result of this innovation, the current Accord has been less effective in ensuring that capital requirements match a bank's true risk profile. The review is also aimed at recognising the improvements in risk measurement and control that have occurred."

With these broad pronouncements, the Basel Committee immediately set about its task in laying down the fundamental building blocks of what it calls a more "risk-sensitive" capital framework. In July 1999, the Committee quickly released four papers dealing with the management and disclosure of credit risk.[4] In January 2000, supplementary documents regarding market discipline and banks' internal rating systems were published by the Committee.[5] In September 2000, the Committee issued guidance on credit risk management and disclosure.[6]

All of these preparatory documents and so-called consultative papers, mentioned earlier paved the way for the more coherent and comprehensive Basel Committee package released in January 2001 for public comments (also known as the Second Consultative Paper or CP2). The CP2 package consisted of nine parts, parceled amongst 500 pages. The January 2001 announcement christened the proposed package the New Basel Capital Accord, which is now commonly referred to simply as Basel II.

The decidedly more complex (and controversial) new proposal was originally (and unrealistically) intended to be finalised at the end of 2001 after an early round of planned consultation with the financial industry. Accordingly, the Committee envisioned a Basel II implementation date of 2004 among its member jurisdictions. But the proposed revisions quickly encountered stiff opposition, criticism, and scepticism from some industry sectors, in addition to some guarded praise and cautious optimism.

While trumpeting the more coherent and tidier CP2 package in January 2001, William McDonough, Chairman of the Basel Committee and President and Chief Executive Officer of the Federal Reserve Bank of New York, introduced the Basel II proposal, noting,

> "the new framework is intended to align regulatory capital require-
> ments more closely with underlying risks, and to provide banks and
> their supervisors with several options for the assessment of capital
> adequacy".[7]

He added further that:

> "the Committee believes it has laid the groundwork for a flexible
> capital adequacy framework that has the capacity to adapt to changes
> in the financial system and will enhance safety and soundness."

Since the initial announcement in June 1999 to revamp the 1988 Accord and replace it with Basel II, the Basel Committee had engaged the financial industry in countless discussions and consultations. These extensive, and often times contentious, discussions resulted in the more recent Consultative Paper Three (CP3) released in April 2003. There were also numerous data collection and joint regulatory–industry field exercises performed by the so-called Quantitative Impact Study (QIS). The results of the most recent QIS3 impact study were released in May 2003.

CP3 and QIS3 not only attempted to iron out some kinks in previous rounds of consultation with the banking industry, it also set forth the Committee's targeted desire to finalise Basel II by the end of 2003,[8] with an implementation schedule further delayed to the end of 2006.

Following the industry commentary period resulting from the release of the CP3 documents, in August 2003 the Committee published its most serious report to date entitled, "High-level principles for cross-border implementation of the New Accord".[9] The report reiterated the target date of year-end 2006 for the official implementation of Basel II and leg work necessary to initiate its global implementation. The report also emphasised the need for closer cooperation and coordination among supervisors. It outlined a "variety of supervisory responsibilities under the New Accord, including: (1) initial approval and validation of 'advanced' approaches (eg, IRB, AMA) under Pillar 1; (2) the supervisory review process under Pillar 2; and (3) ongoing assessments to verify that banking groups are applying the New Accord properly and that the conditions for 'advanced' approaches continue to be met."

While prudent capital adequacy rules are evolutionary in nature, however, it seems clear from significant developments during 2003 that the major pieces of Basel II are now securely anchored in place and await implementation. It is for this very reason that this book was conceived. My fundamental goal is to present a handbook on Basel II, highlighting some of its most important proposals and complicated issues, while providing guidance to practitioners regarding its implementation. The handbook is intended to be evolutionary as well and will require continual revisions as we approach the final implementation date.

Why revise the 1988 Accord?
The 1988 Accord played a remarkably important role in providing infrastructural support for the integrity and stability of the international financial system. Even though the Accord was only morally and not legally binding, its provisions concerning risk-based capital

adequacy quickly became the reference point for regulation on credit risk, not just in the original G10 member countries of the Accord, but also eventually in over 100 countries throughout the globe.[10]

Unquestionably, throughout the numerous tumultuous market events during the past decade, the 1988 Accord has provided much stability among the internationally active banks by strengthening the capital base of the international financial system. The fact that almost all internationally active banks are sufficiently well capitalised now is a strong testament to the wisdom embedded in the noble goals of the 1988 Accord and the prudence and vigilance with which the regulators throughout the globe enforced them in their own jurisdictions.

However, in spite of its success, the 1988 Accord has a lot of shortcomings, resulting in vocal outcry for fundamental reforms from the major international banking community. The reasons for revising the antiquated and increasingly ineffective 1988 Accord are plentiful. Below I list a few notable ones:

❑ *Distortions of material credit risk in banking provided by financial innovations during the past decade.* The most obvious shortcoming during the past decade has been the regulatory capital arbitrage opportunities provided by financial innovations through asset securitisation vehicles. Asset securitisation has rendered the 1988 Accord's minimum regulatory capital requirement ineffective as a tool for promoting safety and soundness in banking. Through asset securitisations, banks have been able to lower their risk-based capital requirements significantly without actually reducing the material credit risk embedded in their banking portfolios.

❑ *Fundamental need to enhance the risk sensitivity of capital requirements.* The 1988 Accord is an overly simplified approach having only four broad risk-weighting categories for credit risk capital charge and crude distinctions of sovereign risks. Consequently, it cannot provide enough granularity in the measurement and distinction of different levels of credit risk embedded in banking portfolios.

❑ *Failure of the "one-size-fits-all" approach to risk management.* The application of the same criteria to all banks in determining minimum capital requirements does not provide enough incentive for banks to improve their risk management functions.

❑ *Very limited attention given to credit risk mitigation.* Even with the exponential growth in credit derivatives as a risk management tool during the past few years, the 1988 Accord does not recognise offsets in the banking book through credit risk mitigation techniques, in direct contrast to banks' management of their credit risk on a portfolio basis.

❑ *Narrow focus on minimum capital requirement without due emphasis on the risk management processes within banks.* With the exception of the 1996 amendment, to include capital adequacy due to market risk, the 1988 Accord was focused primarily on credit risk capital requirements. But, over the past 15 years, technological advances in information technology have allowed banks to make rapid improvements in their risk management functions covering a far more comprehensive range of risks outside of credit risk and market risk. The 1988 Accord simply did not keep pace with developments in the banking industry,

❑ *Failure to recognise "other risks" such as operational risk by focusing strictly on financial risk.* Although operational risk was discussed during the 1996 market risk amendment, the current capital accord is focused primarily on financial risk. However, during the past decade, events such as the collapse of large financial entities (eg, Barings Bank and LTCM), the World Trade Center tragedy and the ensuing market disruption, the Enron/WorldCom bankruptcies and their ensuing issues surrounding corporate governance and accounting practices, the billion-dollar losses due to rogue trading at AllFirst Bank and other major events have heightened the awareness of risks other than market and credit risks.

Basel II was intended to address most of the shortcomings delineated above. In addition to imposing minimum capital requirements that are more in line with current technological advancement within the financial industry, the revised Accord also strives to incorporate a more enhanced supervisory review process and then overlays it with greater transparency by requiring public disclosure as part of market discipline.

Final thoughts

In their January 2003 white paper on Basel II, G. David and C. Sidler of EDS summed it up best:[11]

> "In the final analysis, Basel II is about *full industrialization* of the global financial industry (banking, in particular); *realigning a bank's activities and businesses* based on the *best risk adjusted return on capital*; and *re-engineering the bank's complete supply chains at least cost, least risk best quality.* The Accord also focuses on *best practice in bank management and leadership* (implementing and embedding the processes of continuous improvement in all areas of bank leadership, management and operations). Finally, Basel II focuses on *leveraging information technology* to manage global risk (market, credit and operations risks); *on transparency; and on optimizing the capital* used in the bank in its entirety."

Indeed, Basel II should not be simply about capital adequacy. It is more about improving risk management within the financial industry by providing the correct incentives for better corporate governance and fostering greater transparency. In fact, Basel II is very important. It provides opportunities, challenges and threats in one full swoop. How the financial industry and its supervisors rise up to these challenges will decide the opportunities for improving the stability and integrity of international banking, and thereby minimise the unavoidable threats that naturally arise in the course of doing business.

1   The Basel Committee on Banking Supervision is a committee of banking supervisory authorities which was established by the central bank Governors of the Group of Ten countries in 1975. It consists of senior representatives of bank supervisory authorities and central banks from Belgium, Canada, France, Germany, Italy, Japan, Luxembourg, the Netherlands, Sweden, Switzerland, the United Kingdom and the United States. It usually meets at the Bank for International Settlements in Basel, where its permanent Secretariat is located.

2   Basel Committee on Banking Supervision (1988), International convergence of capital measurement and capital standards, July.

3   Bank for International Settlements (1999), Basel Committee publications no. 50, June.

4   The four papers are: Sound practices for loan accounting and disclosure; Principles for management of credit risk; Best practices for credit risk disclosure; Supervisor guidance for the managing settlement risk in foreign exchange transactions. Bank for International Settlements (July 27, 1999).

5   The supplementary documents are: A new capital adequacy framework: pillar three, market discipline; Range of practice in banks' internal rating systems. Bank for International Settlements (January 18, 2000).

6   The papers are: Principles for the management of credit risk; Best practices for credit risk disclosure. Bank for International Settlements (September 14, 2000).

7 Bank for International Settlements (2001), The New Basel Capital Accord, January 16.

8 The October 11, 2003, press release by the Committee, however, indicated a mid-year 2004 date for the finalization of Basel II and an implementation date of year-end 2006.

9 Bank for International Settlements (2003), Basel Committee publications no. 100, August.

10 It is estimated that there are currently 110 signatory countries to Basel II.

11 David, G., and Sidler, C. (2003), Impact of the New Basel Accord, January. http://www.eds.com/financial/fc_news_papers_basel.shtml.

Section 1

Parameterisation of the Internal Ratings-Based Approach

Development and Validation of Key Estimates for Capital Models

Michel Araten

JPMorganChase & Co

INTRODUCTION

Economic capital models, as well as Basel II Regulatory Capital Models under the Advanced Internal Ratings Based (AIRB) approach, require, at minimum, estimates of three key parameters. This chapter deals with methods for estimating the values of these parameters from historical data and with approaches for validation of these estimates for Basel II. The three key parameters are:

❑ *Probability of default (PD)*, also known as "expected default frequency", is the default probability for a borrower over a one-year period. It is often associated with, or mapped to, the risk grade or risk rating (RR) of the borrower.

❑ *Loss given default (LGD)*, also known as "loss severity", is the expected amount of loss on a facility provided to the borrower. Loss given default and recovery (given default) are the mirror images of each other as they sum to the amount owed by the borrower at the time of default.

❑ *Exposure at default (EAD)*, also known as "usage given default" (UGD), is the amount the borrower owes at the time of default.

These parameters, when multiplied together (PD × LGD × EAD), give rise to *expected loss*. In conjunction with the maturity estimate of the exposure, they are also used to determine capital for both economic and Basel II regulatory capital models.

DEFINITION OF DEFAULT

Since all of these parameters are based on a default event, the definition of default is a critical starting point. In general, the default event arises from the non-payment of principal or interest. If payment is past due 90 days, proper accounting requires that banks no longer accrue interest on the loan and place the loan on "non-accrual". These loans are sometimes characterised as "non-performing". Borrowers may be in violation of certain covenants in their loan agreements, but that may not be a sufficient condition for classifying them as being in default. However, it is a long-standing practice among financial institutions to place loans on non-accrual in advance of payment default if there is a high degree of certainty that these loans will incur payment default.

The system that records non-accruing loans is often used as the main source of current and historical information on non-accruals and is used in public financial disclosures and reports to regulatory agencies, as well as in internal management reports. Most systems are geared to automatically place loans on non-accrual status according to the loan accounting systems that generate past due reports. As a result, there are accounting-related operational causes for a loan being placed on non-accrual when in actuality neither the bank nor the borrower would consider the loan to be in default. These include minor differences in the calculation of interest payments, crediting of interest or payment to the wrong account, and maturing of the loan with another loan being taken out to replace it without properly crediting the first loan. What is important is to cull out the spurious defaults, which, while correct from a strict accounting view, do not meet the economic intent of the default definition. The danger associated with an overestimation of the incidence of non-accruals and, therefore, of the PD is a corresponding underestimation of the LGD. Ultimately, it will be determined that the LGD on these facilities was zero.

There may also be cases when a facility is structured and secured in such a way that the borrower continues to pay principal and interest on that facility while being in default on other facilities to other lenders, even entering bankruptcy. In such instances, it may be desirable to record the event as a default event though the loan has not been placed on non-accrual, resulting in a LGD of zero. However, this may be a manually intensive adjustment that, given the small incidence of these occurrences, may not be worth making.

PROBABILITY OF DEFAULT AND RISK RATINGS

All AIRB institutions must have a valid risk rating (RR) methodology with a demonstrated philosophy as to the meaning of the RR. That is, the bank must stipulate whether a grade represents the borrower's current condition or the borrower's condition evaluated over a longer period of time that incorporates a business or economic cycle. Emphasis on current condition assessment is known as "point in time" (PIT). PIT estimates are often drawn from current market indicators such as market spreads or from estimates provided by firms such as Risk Metrics (credit grades) and KMV (expected default frequency, or EDF™). The longer-term view is known as "through-the-cycle" (TTC) and is the primary rating philosophy followed by the ratings agencies, who set as a goal that "ratings are intended to be accurate and stable measures of relative credit risk … To measure ratings stability, Moody's tracks the frequency of rating changes, the frequency of … rating changes … [and] … rating reversals."[1] It is very difficult to determine exactly where on the continuum between PIT and TTC a bank bases its ratings. These issues are discussed in a Federal Reserve report by William Treacy and Mark Carey, who feel that banks may be more PIT inclined.[2] Jeremy Taylor of Union Bank, in a recent article in the *RMA Journal*, argues that "[while] banks have been pulled back toward PIT … [and are] … more sensitive to company news … most banks lie somewhere between the extremes."[3]

Although banks may now be moving towards a mark-to-market view of the value of their portfolios, relying more heavily on current market indicators, the majority of banks have rating philosophies that lie somewhat closer to the TTC end. While current conditions do influence ratings, banks are more likely to be relatively quick to downgrade but less likely to upgrade when conditions improve. The bulk of the current historical data that a bank typically possesses is likely to be based on the TTC view. That is also the primary basis for estimation and validation of PDs for Basel II purposes. The Basel II Accord specifies: "banks must use a longer time horizon in assigning ratings … [They] must be consistent with current conditions and those that are likely to occur over a business cycle … ".[4]

To demonstrate the consistency of their risk rating system and to validate the PDs that they associate with their ratings, banks need to conduct a rating migration study similar to what the rating agencies have been doing for a long period of time. Many firms have evolved their rating scale and methodology over time, often as a result of mergers where they have had to reconcile different rating systems employed by predecessor banks. Under these circumstances, it may be quite a challenge to develop a database of ratings history that fairly represents a consistent ratings philosophy.

At JPMorganChase (JPMC), an analysis of the firm's rating and default experience was accomplished through the formation of annual cohorts at the parent/obligor level over a recent six-year period.[5] The number of parents in each rating category was determined at the beginning of each year, and the transitions to other rating categories (including default) at year-end were measured. Aggregation of the transition counts in a given category and computation of the proportions of these transitions out of the total number of starting observations across all cohorts yielded estimates of the transition probabilities for a given category. These are termed one-year average transition matrices. They can also be constructed over longer time horizons.

In developing the ratings migrations, it is important to decide on an appropriate treatment for "withdrawn" ratings. Withdrawn ratings are observed when customers have a rating as of the beginning of a year but no rating nor any exposure at year-end. These are clearly non-defaulters, as a bank would have had a record of their defaulting. They represent a combination of firms that no longer need to borrow or that roll over their debt with another lender. In JPMC's experience, withdrawn grades account for 18% of the transitions; in agency studies the proportion is about 6%. The approach followed here, similar to one used by S&P, is to adjust for withdrawn grades by subtracting all of the "withdrawn" observations from the denominator. Ignoring all beginning ratings that transitioned to a withdrawn status will result in a proportional scaling up of all probabilities. It should be noted that new credit exposures that arrive in the middle of the year and which have a year-end rating are also not included in the analysis. Should a borrower "withdraw" from the bank and subsequently default with another lender, we might attribute this positive outcome to the bank's skilled credit management. However, it is important to separate the assessment of ratings consistency and accuracy from credit management skills.

A migration and default-rate analysis, when broken down by organisational area or type of borrower, may well point out ratings inconsistencies across the bank. Inconsistencies could relate to liberal or conservative biases for public versus private companies, US versus non-US entities and large corporate versus middle-market borrowers. In addition, comparison of ratings migrations by industry can also be made. These are useful for correcting whatever biases may exist in the ratings processes. A bank can assess the ability of its rating system to differentiate defaulters from non-defaulters by developing power curves, called cumulative accuracy profiles (CAP). "The cumulative accuracy profile is constructed by plotting for each rating category, the proportion of defaults accounted for by firms with the same or a lower rating against the proportion of all firms with the same or a lower rating."[6] The closer the curve bows towards the northwest corner of the plot, the more powerful is the rating scheme's ability to distinguish risk. These curves can also be used to compare different rating systems. This comparison requires an identical population of borrowers and periods of times for measuring ratings.

The overall default rates by rating class can be used for validation against Basel II requirements. For example, if a bank sets its PDs by rating class to a blend of PDs derived from historical rating agency experience and current market estimates – say derived from KMV EDF[TM]s – it can compare its historical actual experience against these projections. The bank can construct confidence intervals based on actual default history and determine whether its estimate lies within that band. Care must be taken to interpret confidence intervals for the investment-grade ratings since very few defaults are likely to have occurred.

LOSS GIVEN DEFAULT

To determine the LGD, a bank must be able to accurately identify the borrowers that actually defaulted, the exposures outstanding at the time of default, and the amount and timing of repayments ultimately received. In addition, demographic information pertaining to the borrower, including industry assignment, public or private designation, and geographic domicile, are important for developing LGD estimates that are segmented according to these characteristics. Finally, the structural elements of the defaulted facilities, such as whether the bank's interest is senior or subordinated and whether it has received any collateral, should be noted.

The determination of the default event should follow the same procedures discussed earlier. We also need to examine other issues involved in calculating LGD. These include definition of LGD, exposure measurement, determination of what constitutes resolution, calculation methodology and collateral segmentation.

Most bank records generally focus on chargeoffs and recoveries (reversals of chargeoffs) and are the source of data for calculating an "accounting" LGD or "net chargeoff". However, for both internal and Basel II purposes we need to determine an "economic" LGD. Accounting LGD differs from economic LGD in that it does not take into account the length of the workout period and it does not include certain costs and payments. The simplest measurement of economic LGD would be the market value of an exposure measured shortly after default. For marketable bonds and loans, the rating agencies attempt to report the trading price of a defaulted obligation one month after default. For most bank loans such market information will not be available and a bank will have to calculate the economic LGD from its own internal records. This requires discounting of all net cashflows received at an appropriate discount rate.

Exposure needs to be measured as close as possible to the time of default. For example, if six months prior to default collateral was liquidated due to technical violations of covenants and exposure was thus reduced, the net exposure at the time of default will be the basis for determining LGD. Past due interest should also be added to the exposure amount. If some facilities were granted different seniority status or were given collateral distinct from other facilities and cashflows can be uniquely segregated, then these could be viewed as separate exposures. However, since it is often difficult to determine to which of several defaulting facilities the bank applied recoveries, it may be best to aggregate all defaulting exposures to the same borrower into a single exposure.

In some instances, a bank may advance additional money to the borrower despite the latter being in default simply to enhance the likelihood of receiving payment on its original loan. This may arise in the case of partially completed real estate projects where it is important to complete construction with the original borrower in place to be able to realise any of the bank's principal. These outflows are to be included in the cashflow calculations. Expenses such as those of the workout department, though generally small (approximately 1%), along with legal fees, also need to be incorporated into the outflows.

Most banks do not report cashflow actually received on defaulted loans. However, cashflow can be reconstructed from a combination of periodic reported book values, chargeoffs, and recoveries of chargeoffs. It is not important to distinguish between payments made for principal reduction and for interest owed that the bank chooses to apply to principal. Payment in kind, such as property, equity or warrants may also reduce principal outstanding. These are usually valued conservatively at the time of receipt. If they are liquidated at a later date, one could incorporate their discounted liquidated values based on when they were realised.

Final resolution of a defaulted loan can be deemed to occur in a number of ways. These include when a loan has been returned to an accruing status (even with principal or interest forgiven), when final receipt of all cash payments has been obtained, and when liquidation of property in kind is finalised. In large corporate credits the workout period can be quite lengthy, ranging anywhere up to six years or more, with the average around three years. Waiting to determine a LGD based on the final resolution of a default can severely limit the sample size needed for estimation purposes. In practice, a bank should truncate by two to three years the historical sample period for identifying defaults. This will allow cash receipts to manifest themselves during this truncated period. However, by applying typical recovery patterns to unresolved defaulted loans, one can develop reasonable estimates of ultimate recoveries.

Once cashflows on defaulted loans are reconstructed, they are then discounted at an appropriate discount rate. The discount rate needs to resemble as closely as possible the yield a buyer of distressed assets at the time of default would require to obtain the cashflows projected. It is inappropriate to use the original contract rate of interest as there is substantial risk that cashflows projected at the time of default may not be accurate. In fact, the volatility of LGD is usually quite high. At JPMC, a 15% discount rate was selected to reflect the average yield over time required by buyers of distressed assets. Moody's reported that the long-run average return to defaulted public bonds is 17.4%.[7] A case could well be made that in different parts of the economic cycle the required yield could vary anywhere from 10 to 20%, or even higher.

An 18-year (1982–99) study conducted at JPMC covered 3,761 defaulted loans and resulted in an average economic LGD of 39.8%, with a standard deviation of 35.4%.[8] The sensitivity to the discount rate was such that using a 10% discount rate resulted in an average LGD of 36.2%, and using a 5% discount rate resulted in an average LGD of 31.9%. The average "accounting" LGD or the average net chargeoff rate, determined without any discounting, resulted in a 27% LGD.

The presence of security and the nature of the collateral obtained can be an important distinction in the estimation of LGD. Although historical data on collateral are often not captured, it is important to differentially determine LGD based on collateral. A subset of JPMC's LGD data set (1990–99) where security information was collected was studied. LGDs on unsecured exposures averaged 50.5%, while LGDs on secured exposures averaged 40.9%. A further breakdown of LGD by type of collateral (cash and marketable securities, accounts receivable, inventory, fixed assets, mortgages and blanket liens) was also obtained.

It should be noted that the analysis of the presence of security focuses on whether the exposure is secured at the time of default. In JPMC's experience a large majority of defaulted loans were deemed secured at the time of default. However, a large majority of the loans that it makes are unsecured at the time of origination. It is often the case that once a borrower's credit quality deteriorates, non-payment covenants are triggered and a bank is able to step in to obtain additional collateral prior to default. Thus, in certain circumstances, adjustments to the pure "unsecured" LGD could be made based on the presumption that by the time the borrower defaults, additional security will be obtained and the "secured" LGD average will apply.

Many banks assign LGDs at the time of origination based on the average experience that they have had with different types of borrowers in different legal environments based on certain collateral distinctions. The actual experience of defaulted loans versus their subjectively assigned LGD needs to be compared for Basel II validation purposes. LGD assignments could well change over the life of the loan based on new information, just as rating assignments change. However, the LGD assignment at the time of default needs to be the basis for the comparison against actual experience.

EXPOSURE AT DEFAULT

Exposure measurement for purposes of determining economic loss and capital for loans that are outstanding is conventionally understood to be the face amount owed by the borrower. However, when a bank makes a credit commitment and the borrower draws down less than the entire commitment, the bank has exposure to the undrawn portion of the commitment, in addition to the drawn portion. The loan equivalent (LEQ) of the unused exposure is defined as the expected additional amount the borrower will draw down at the time of default. It should be noted that it is *not* the average utilisation of the unused commitment absent default. That is, we are only interested in the average utilisation conditional upon default. The LEQ is usually expressed as a percentage of the unused commitment. The exposure at default (percent EAD) is thus the sum of the current utilisation expressed as a percentage of the total commitment and the LEQ expressed as a percentage of the commitment times the unused expressed as a percentage of the commitment:

❏ U = Utilisation (current) as a percentage of commitment;
❏ LEQ = Additional utilisation as a percentage of the unused commitment; and
❏ EAD = U + LEQ(100% − U).

Normally, it might be expected that a borrower headed towards default would draw down 100% of its unused commitment. However, the presence of covenants and their violation may provide an opportunity for a bank to cut off the unused commitment, giving rise to fractional LEQs.

There are data-cleansing and methodological issues to be dealt with in calculating LEQ. If there are a number of revolving credit facilities to the same entity, they should be aggregated into a single facility for analysis as borrowers may make an arbitrary decision as to which revolver they draw. Very small unused amounts prior to default should be eliminated since it is not likely that a severely distressed borrower would have been able to draw them down. Including 0% LEQ observations would distort the overall results. There are instances when the borrower may have paid back a portion of the amount outstanding prior to default, resulting in a negative LEQ. Conservatism suggests that these should be floored at 0%. There are also instances when a borrower has drawn down more than its availability at a particular time, principally either because of operational or data errors or because commitments were increased sometime prior to default. Practice is to cap these at 100%. Care must be taken when new revolving credit facilities replace old ones. While there may actually be an opportunity for a bank to eliminate its exposure at the time of the rollover, a more conservative approach is to consider the new revolver a continuation of the old one.

In a published study by Michel Araten and Michael Jacobs, Jr, conducted at JPMC, the bank evaluated its LEQ experience with regard to revolving credits and advised lines to defaulting borrowers over a six-year period ending in December 2000.[9] It analysed 1,021 observations for 399 borrowers classified as sub-standard or worse.[10] The average LEQ was 43%, with a relatively high standard deviation of 41%.[11]

It was also found that the longer the tenor of the exposure, the greater the likelihood that a borrower had drawn down additional amounts of its unfunded commitment. Commitments with longer maturities expose the bank to a longer period of time over which the borrower may experience credit deterioration and have a greater need to borrow.

Another observation was that LEQs appear to increase with better credit quality. This can be rationalised by noting that many investment-grade borrowers have relatively few covenants in their revolving credit agreements that would enable a bank to step in and cut off the unused. In contrast, non-investment-grade borrowers are more closely watched and have tighter covenants.

A regression equation was developed involving both of these variables.[12] The application of the LEQ to individual exposures of a given rating and tenor, t, must be made by considering the relative probability of default in any period i over tenor t. Thus, a weighted average LEQ should be calculated for a particular tenor, with the weights being the relative probabilities of default applied to the LEQs associated with individual periods, i.

If assigned LEQs are a function of both rating and tenor, they will need to be validated at various points in time prior to default against the Basel II requirements.

Other unfunded commitments, such as advised lines, standby financial letters of credit, performance letters of credit and commercial letters of credit, also need to have LEQs assessed.

Advised lines are non-legal commitments to lend, generally renewed annually, and can be cancelled at any time at the bank's discretion. The JPMC study reported an average LEQ of 20%. Standby financial letters of credit are generally viewed as equivalent to guarantees that have an LEQ assignment of 100%. There is little experience or data available on defaulted performance letters of credits and commercial letters of credit. LEQs may have to be assigned judgmentally based on the specific conditions and terms of these facilities.

SUMMARY

The development of key parameters, namely, PDs, LGDs and EADs, for use in economic capital models and their validation for Basel II purposes require careful data handling and analysis. Today, many banks do not have sufficient historical data in exactly the form required. As a temporary step they can draw on published external studies. Going forward, they need to make immediate investments in manpower and systems resources to develop and analyse their own internal experience. This will assist those banks seeking to buttress their capital modelling processes and who wish to qualify for AIRB status under Basel II.

1   Moody's Investors Service (2003). Special comment: measuring the performance of corporate bond ratings, p. 1.
2   Treacy, W., and M. Carey, (1998). Credit risk rating at large US Banks. *Federal Reserve Bulletin*, November, p. 899.

3 Taylor, J. (2003). Risk-grading philosophy: through the cycle versus point in time. *RMA Journal*, November, p. 32.

4 Basel Committee on Banking Supervision (2003). *The New Basel Capital Accord*, p. 73.

5 This study involved 33,000 distinct obligors and almost 100,000 transitions.

6 Moody's Investors Service (2003). Special comment: measuring the performance of corporate bond ratings, p. 9.

7 Moody's Investors Service (2000). The investment performance of bankrupt corporate debt obligations: Moody's Bankrupt Bond Index 2000, p. 1.

8 Negative LGDs resulting from additional income or property values collected were floored at -10% and very large LGDs resulting from additional advances on defaulted loans were capped at 175%.

9 Araten, M., and M. Jacobs, Jr (2001). Loan equivalents for revolving credits and advised lines. *RMA Journal*, May.

10 In this study, the regulatory classification of sub-standard or worse defined the default event as it did not seem likely that the borrower had any availability once this grade was reached and the sample size could be increased.

11 In an updated internal study covering a longer, nine-year period ending in 2002, a similar average LEQ of 43% was determined using sub-standard as the default event. Using the actual default date as the default event, the average LEQ was 45%.

12 LEQ = 48.36 − 3.49(facility grade) + 10.87 (TTD), where facility grade corresponds to 1: AAA/AA−, 2: A+/A−, 3: BBB+/BBB, 4: BBB−/BB+, 5: BB, 6: BB−/B+, 7: B/B+, 8: CCC and TTD is time-to-default or maturity in years.

2

Explaining the Correlation in Basel II: Derivation and Evaluation

Christian Bluhm; Ludger Overbeck*

HypoVereinsbank; University of Giessen

INTRODUCTION

The implementation of correlation in the new regulatory capital framework has its roots in credit portfolio models like Credit-Metrics or the KMV-Model. In such models, correlation quantifies the linear dependence between obligors in a credit portfolio. There are basically two types of correlation applied, namely the *asset correlation*, quantifying the dependence between obligor's asset-value processes, and the *default correlation* as a measure of dependence between binary default events. In the new capital accord, *asset* correlation as an input parameter in the basic benchmark risk weight formula constitutes an important driver of regulatory capital. This motivates a closer look at the correlation concept underlying the current Basel II consultative document.

DERIVATION OF CORRELATIONS IN BASEL II

Current discussion on banking supervision is focused on the new capital adequacy proposals embodied in the consultative paper issued by the Basel Committee on Banking Regulation (henceforth, Basel II – see Basel Committee on Banking Supervision, 2003). From a purely quantitative point of view, the current *8%-rule* that lies at the heart of the regulatory capital requirement, as defined in

*The contents of this chapter reflect the personal views of the authors, in particular it does not represent the opinion of HypoVereinsbank.

the Basel I guidelines of 1988, will be replaced by a capital rule that depends primarily on the creditworthiness of the borrower and some loss given default information. In this context, creditworthiness is determined by the associated credit rating. In the standard approach, the internal rating will be mapped to a default probability set by the regulators, whereas in the internal-ratings-based (IRB) approach the assignments of the probabilities of default (PD) will rely on some internal calibration of the lending financial institution, subject to some qualification criteria. The loss given default (LGD) is the second driver of regulatory capital and will be set either by the regulators, or, in the advanced IRB-approach, by the lending bank.

Besides *PD* and *LGD*, there are two other parameters implemented in the Basel II *benchmark risk weight* (*BRW*) formula. The first one is a so-called maturity (*MAT*) adjustment and the second parameter is correlation (*CORR*). The generic formula provided in the Basel II proposals is of the form

$$BRW(PD, LGD, MAT, CORR)$$
$$= LGD \times Factor(MAT) \times Factor(PD, CORR).$$

In this chapter we shall consider the term *Factor*(*PD*, *CORR*), which is driven by the *asset* correlation *CORR* and the default probability *PD*. The formula underlying the calibration of this factor is borrowed from a one-factor version of an asset value credit portfolio model as implemented by KMV, CreditMetrics and others (see Crosbie, 1999; Finger, 1999; Vasicek, 1987, 1991; and Bluhm, Overbeck and Wagner, 2003, Chapter 2). The original idea behind the asset-value approach is based on the original paper by the Nobel prizewinner for economics, R. Merton (1974).

The formula itself is the *quantile* function of the loss distribution associated with a *one-factor* model. KMV users know this distribution function from the analytic version of the KMV-software Portfolio Manager. A derivation of the formula can be found in a paper by Vasicek (1987, 1991), and its formulation as used in the consultative documents can be found in papers by Gordy (2001). Later in this chapter we will present a derivation of the formula. The underlying assumption is that there exists a single economic factor, the "state of economy", which captures all macroeconomic and systematic risk. Additionally, all idiosyncratic risk is diversified away by the assumption that each rating bucket or *PD* class contains infinitely many borrowers. For this reason, the model is also called an *infinitely granular* one-factor asset-value model.

The correlation parameter now links the default event of a single counterparty with the macroeconomic environment described by just one factor. For example, an asset correlation of 20% means that the correlation of any borrower's asset value variable with the macroeconomic factor equals square root of 20%, such that any two borrowers' asset value variables admit a uniform asset correlation of 20%.

In this chapter, we first explain the derivation of the Basel II correlation concept. We then provide an easy but efficient and quick way to derive asset correlations (see also Bluhm and Overbeck, 2003) from the volatility of default rates. The advantage of our approach is that it does not rely on the ability to describe an obligor's credit risk by means of the distance of an asset value process to the borrower's default point. In fact, many obligors, such as retail customers or sovereigns, or, more generally, non-listed borrowers cannot be described by classical asset value models such as the KMV framework because asset value processes are typically inferred from equity processes that are not available for non-listed companies. On the other side, every firm obviously has some asset value, or, more generally, some *ability-to-pay* (APP) process, reflecting the total wealth compared with the total liabilities of the company. Even retail borrowers admit such a process. It is very useful to have some tool for estimating the correlation between such *latent* APP processes for *all* types of obligor. Moreover, because the only data needed to apply the tool are a history of default rates for the considered class of obligors, and such histories are required in the Basel II framework anyway, an application of our method should be easy to implement for any bank.

For the interpretation of the results one should also keep in mind that a one-factor model does not allow for *economic diversification*. For example, in a one-factor model a downturn of the economy will hit all markets with the same intensity and at the same time. Therefore, diversification benefits are significantly underestimated (see Bluhm and Overbeck, 2003) in the new capital requirement rules, such that one can safely say that the current proposal for the new capital accord does not provide any incentive to optimise the portfolio's risk profile by investing in different "risk segments" such as countries or industries. From a global economic point of view, this is somewhat unfortunate and it will not help to make the financial world a safer place for lending, borrowing and investing in credit-risky securities.

The Basel II correlation settings explained

The level of correlation in the Basel II framework depends on the probability of default, or *PD* (see Basel Committee on Banking Supervision, 2003). The reason behind such a dependency is that quite often smaller firms have higher PDs but are less dependent on the "state of economy". Or, in other words, smaller firms bear more idiosyncratic than systematic risk. For example, in smaller firms the management of the company owner is more important than in large firms, where the firm's economic fate depends more on the market and the economic environment the company belongs to. We will later see that this may be true for investment-grade borrowers but can be incorrect for sub-investment-grade assets.

The formula (see Basel Committee on Banking Supervision, 2003, Paragraph 241) determining the correlation ρ for corporate counterparties is given by,

$$\rho = 0.12 \times \frac{1-\exp(-50 \times PD)}{1-\exp(-50)} + 0.24 \times \left(1 - \frac{1-\exp(-50 \times PD)}{1-\exp(-50)}\right)$$

The form of the equation clearly shows that it is a logarithmic interpolation between a correlation of 12% and 24% with respect to the *PD*. A zero default probability would imply the largest possible correlation, namely 24%, and a *PD* equal to 1 would yield the lowest ρ, namely 12%. The smallest *PD* arising in the Basel II framework is 3 bps, and the correlation for corporates with that default probability equals 23.82%. The lowest correlation in the class of corporate counterparties is 12.000545%, which corresponds to a *DP* of 20%.

The table and chart in Figure 1 illustrate the correlation formula.

For small- and medium-sized enterprises (SME) the correlation formula explained above admits a firm-size adjustment (see Basel

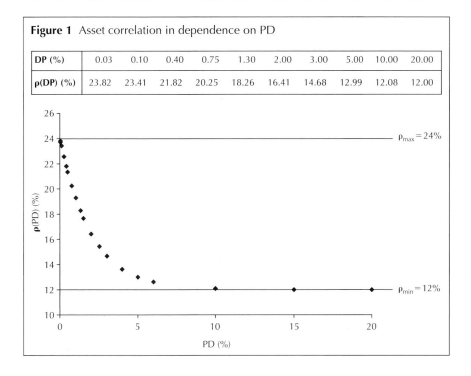

Figure 1 Asset correlation in dependence on PD

DP (%)	0.03	0.10	0.40	0.75	1.30	2.00	3.00	5.00	10.00	20.00
ρ(DP) (%)	23.82	23.41	21.82	20.25	18.26	16.41	14.68	12.99	12.08	12.00

Committee on Banking Supervision, 2003, Paragraph 242) by subtracting the expression

$$0.04 \times \left(1 - \frac{S-5}{45}\right)$$

from the equation for ρ given above, where S equals the total annual sales in millions of euros. The application of this rule is as follows:

❏ If S exceeds 50, no adjustment is necessary.
❏ If S is smaller than 5, the adjustment is the same as for $S = 5$, ie, the asset correlation decreases by 4%. In other words, there is an effective floor at $S = €5$ million.
❏ If S falls between the range of €5 million and €50 million, the formula for firm-size adjustment given above is applied and the correlation is lowered accordingly.

For example, for an SME with S lower than or equal to 5 and a default probability of 3 bps a correlation parameter of 19.82% (ie, 23.82% correlation minus 4% firm-size adjustment) has to be applied, whereas a $DP = 10\%$ would yield a correlation parameter of 8.08% (ie, 12.08% correlation minus 4% firm-size adjustment); see the table in Figure 1.

For correlation treatment of retail exposures, the Basel II framework considers three cases (see Basel Committee on Banking Supervision, 2003 pp. 59–60):

❑ Residential mortgages: correlation equals 15% flat.
❑ Qualifying revolving retail exposures: correlation again is interpolated in a similar fashion as the case for corporates, but with a different minimum correlation (2% instead 12%) and a different maximum correlation (11% instead of 24%). The formula is given as follows:

$$\rho = 0.02 \times \frac{1 - \exp(-50 \times PD)}{1 - \exp(-50)} + 0.11 \times \left(1 - \frac{1 - \exp(-50 \times PD)}{1 - \exp(-50)}\right).$$

In a similar fashion, the correlations for retail exposures now change accordingly to the following table:

DP (%)	0.03	0.10	0.40	0.75	1.30	2.00	3.00	5.00	10.00	20.00
ρ(DP) (%)	10.87	10.56	9.37	8.19	6.70	5.31	4.01	2.74	2.06	2.00

❑ Other retail exposures: correlation is interpolated between 2% and 17%, but with a different coefficient (the "50" in the formula is replaced by "35") so that we obtain:

$$\rho = 0.02 \times \frac{1 - \exp(-35 \times PD)}{1 - \exp(-35)} + 0.17 \times \left(1 - \frac{1 - \exp(-35 \times PD)}{1 - \exp(-35)}\right).$$

This leads to the following table:

DP (%)	0.03	0.10	0.40	0.75	1.30	2.00	3.00	5.00	10.00	20.00
ρ(DP) (%)	16.84	16.48	15.04	13.54	11.52	9.45	7.25	4.61	2.45	2.01

In all considered cases, $Factor(PD, \rho)$ is given by the formula (see Basel Committee on Banking Supervision, 2003, Paragraphs 241, 298, 299, 301):

$$Factor(PD, \rho) = N\left[\frac{1}{\sqrt{1-\rho}} N^{-1}(PD) + \sqrt{\frac{\rho}{1-\rho}} N^{-1}(0.999)\right].$$

In the formula above, the function N denotes the cumulative standard normal distribution function, whereas the N^{-1} refers to its inverse, namely the standard normal quantile function.

Note that in the Basel II consultative document, the correlation parameter is denoted by "R".

The purpose of the following section is to explain the formula for $Factor(PD, \rho)$.

Explanation of Factor(PD, CORR) in the benchmark risk weight formula

We will now explain that $Factor(PD, \rho)$ is the capital-at-risk for a 99.9% confidence level with respect to a one-factor asset value model with infinite granularity. The starting point is a standard uniform Bernoulli mixture model (see, eg, Bluhm, Overbeck and Wagner, 2003, Chapter 2), where joint default probabilities are given by

$$P[L_1 = \delta_1, \ldots, L_m = \delta_m] = \int_0^1 p^{\sum \delta_i}(1-p)^{m-\sum \delta_i} \, dF(p)$$

where L_i describes the "state" (loss or survival) of obligor i and δ_i either shows a "1" in case obligor i defaults or shows a "0" in case obligor i survives. Here, m denotes the number of obligors in the portfolio considered and $k = \sum \delta_i$ describes the number of defaults. The integrand in the above formula is the probability for the occurrence of k-times a "1" and $(m-k)$-times a "0" in m independent Bernoulli trials with a "1"-occurrence probability of p. The "mixture" with respect to the distribution function F transforms the independent Bernoulli trials into correlated Bernoulli trials.

The mixture distribution F can be derived in the following way by a so-called *latent variables* approach, or more in the spirit of

Merton, an asset-value model with only one factor considered at the one-year horizon. More precisely, denote by r_i the asset value of obligor i at the one-year horizon.[1] Then the following representation is assumed to hold:

$$r_i = \sqrt{\rho} \times Y + \sqrt{1-\rho} \times Z_i$$

where Y refers to a single macroeconomic factor, Z_i represents the specific effect or idiosyncratic component of obligor i and ρ denotes the uniform asset correlation assumed in the model. We assume Y, $Z_1,\ldots, Z_m$ to be iid standard normal random variables.

Along with the one-factor representation of r_i comes a decomposition of variance as follows:

$$1 = V[r_i] = \underbrace{V[\sqrt{\rho} \times Y]}_{\text{systematic}} + \underbrace{V[\sqrt{1-\rho} \times Z_i]}_{\text{idiosyncratic}} = \rho + (1-\rho).$$

Comparing this decomposition of variance with standard linear regression theory, we see that ρ equals the so-called coefficient of determination, often shortly referred to as the R-squared of the obligor (compare, for example, with the terminology in the KMV model framework). It quantifies the systematic risk of the considered obligor, because it measures how much of the volatility in the asset value movement at the horizon is due to the volatility of the systematic factor Y. The residual risk then obviously is quantified by $(1 - \rho)$. It varies independently of the systematic variable.

The link between the Bernoulli variables L_i indicating default or survival and the asset value decomposition at the horizon comes from a threshold definition,

$$L_i = 1\{r_i < c_i\} = \begin{cases} 1 & \text{if } r_i < c_i \\ 0 & \text{otherwise} \end{cases}$$

expressing that obligor i defaults if and only if the asset value process r_i at the horizon falls below a critical threshold c_i, the so-called default point (see Crosbie, 1999). Therefore, we can write the (assumed) uniform default probability PD of the obligors in the homogeneous portfolio by

$$PD = P[L_i = 1] = P[r_i < c_i].$$

Because r_i follows a standard normal distribution, we can conclude that based on a uniform PD the thresholds c_i also must be equal to some constant c, yielding

$$c_i = c = N^{-1}[PD]$$

The constant c can be interpreted as a uniform default point for all obligors in the whole portfolio.

The principal form of the formula underlying the quantity $Factor(PD, \rho)$ now already occurs by considering the default probability conditional on the macroeconomic factor $Y = y$ by

$$
\begin{aligned}
g(y) &= P[L_i = 1 | Y = y] \\
&= P[\sqrt{\rho} \times Y + \sqrt{1-\rho} \times Z_i < N^{-1}[PD] | Y = y] \\
&= N\left[\frac{N^{-1}[PD] - \sqrt{\rho} \times y}{\sqrt{1-\rho}}\right]
\end{aligned}
$$

which holds, because Z_i is a standard normal random variable.

Figure 2 provides an interpretation of the formula (see Bluhm, Overbeck and Wagner, 2003).

If the macroeconomic factor Y takes on values on the negative real axis, this indicates a bad state of economy. The lower the Y variable, the worse the economic environment and the higher the default probability conditional on Y. Values of Y on the positive real axis indicate favourable economic conditions. The higher the Y variable, the better the economic conditions and the lower the conditional default probability.

Based on the conditional default probability, the mixture distribution F driving our Bernoulli mixture model can be defined by $F = N \circ g^{-1}$ where N again denotes the standard normal

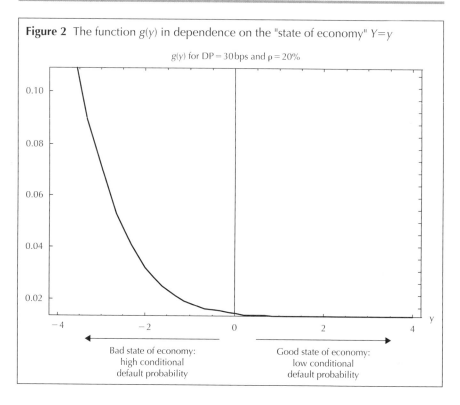

Figure 2 The function g(y) in dependence on the "state of economy" $Y=y$

$g(y)$ for DP = 30 bps and ρ = 20%

Bad state of economy:
high conditional
default probability

Good state of economy:
low conditional
default probability

distribution function. The joint default probabilities are then given by

$$P[L_1 + \cdots + L_m = k] = \binom{m}{k} \int_0^1 g(y)^k (1-g(y))^{m-k} dN(y)$$

because defaults are "exchangeable" here, ie, the homogeneous portfolio model does not distinguish between obligors. It is an "old" insight, going back to a paper by Vasicek (see Vasicek, 1987, 1991; Finger, 1999; Bluhm, Overbeck and Wagner, 2003) of KMV Corporation, that if one increases the number of obligors m in a homogeneous portfolio with a uniform default probability PD and a uniform asset correlation ρ, then the distribution of the portfolio loss converges to a limit distribution with

$$P[L \le x] = P[g(Y) \le x] = N\left[\frac{1}{\sqrt{\rho}}\left(N^{-1}[x]\sqrt{1-\rho} - N^{-1}[PD]\right)\right]$$

where $L = g(Y)$ denotes the percentage portfolio loss of the limit portfolio admitting infinitely many obligors that are uniformly correlated and admit a uniform probability of default PD.[2] The quantile function (see Gordy, 2001; Bluhm, Overbeck and Wagner, 2003, Proposition 2.5.8) n of the variable L with respect to a level of confidence α is given by

$$q_\alpha(L) = N\left[\frac{N^{-1}[PD] + \sqrt{\rho} \times q_\alpha(Y)}{\sqrt{1-\rho}}\right]$$

where $q_\alpha(X)$ denotes the α-quantile of a given random variable X.

Rearranging terms in the formula for the quantile, and writing $N^{-1}(0.999)$ for the α-quantile of the normal random variable Y with $\alpha = 99.9\%$, we conclude that

$$g_\alpha(L) = N\left[\frac{1}{\sqrt{1-\rho}} N^{-1}(PD) + \sqrt{\frac{\rho}{1-\rho}} N^{-1}(0.999)\right] = Factor(PD, \rho).$$

This completely explains the definition of the formula constituting the "heart" of the Basel II benchmark risk weights.

EVALUATION OF CORRELATIONS IN BASEL II

In this section we explain an estimation procedure (see Bluhm and Overbeck, 2003) for asset correlations based on the volatility of default rates time series. First of all we need the formula for the joint default probability (JDP) of two obligors in a uniform portfolio with parameters (PD, ρ),

$$JDP = JDP(PD, \rho) = JDP_{i,j}$$
$$= \frac{1}{2\pi\sqrt{1-\rho^2}} \int_{-\infty}^{N^{-1}[PD]} \int_{-\infty}^{N^{-1}[PD]} \exp\left[-\frac{1}{2}\frac{x_i^2 - 2\rho x_i x_j + x_j^2}{1-\rho^2}\right] dx_i dx_j$$

where the two upper integration limits refer to the uniform default point for a homogeneous portfolio with parameters (PD, ρ).

The explanation of the bivariate normal integral in this context is obvious: the asset values of two obligors at the horizon are jointly normally distributed, and the default point provides the critical threshold up to which the integration has to be done. The *JDP* formula is the main "ingredient" of the formula expressing the variance (see Bluhm, Overbeck and Wagner, 2003, Section 2.7) of the conditional default rates $g(y)$ explained in the previous section. It is given by

$$V[g(Y)] = JDP(PD,\rho) - PD \times PD.$$

Now, this formula provides a natural approach for estimating the asset correlation underlying the considered credit portfolio, because the only unknown parameter in the formula is the asset correlation ρ. In other words, observing a time series of default rates of a credit portfolio admitting a representation or approximation by a uniform portfolio with parameters PD and ρ as explained above, we can estimate[3]

❏ *PD* by the mean value of the time series, and
❏ *V[g(Y)]* by the sample variance of the time series of observed default rates, and then
❏ calculate all terms in the variance formula with ρ being the only unknown parameter.

Solving for ρ will yield an implied asset correlation ρ. The idea underlying this approach can be illustrated by Figure 3, where default rates observed by Moody's (2002) are plotted.

A heuristic description of the approach can be stated as follows: correlation as a dependence measure should be reflected by the up-and-down variation of default rates. The up-and-down variation of default rates can be quantified by the standard deviation or the variance of the time series of default rates. Assuming that a suitable modelling framework is chosen, the correlation number best matching the observed data should yield a reasonable estimate of the correlation underlying the portfolio. We have done this exercise for all rating classes based on Moody's (2002) data.

We followed two approaches when calculating the "best matching" asset correlation for the considered Moody's data:

❏ Approach I takes the historical time series as they are and calculates an implied (best-matching) asset correlation for every rating class.

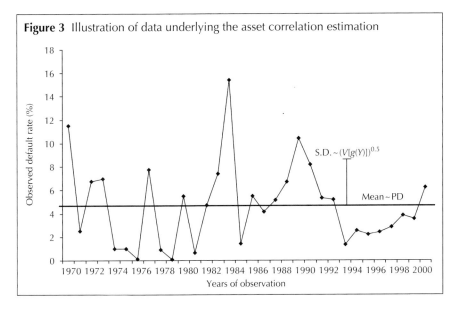

Figure 3 Illustration of data underlying the asset correlation estimation

Table 1 Implied asset correlations according to Approach II

Rating	Mean (%)	S.D.(%)	Implied asset correlation (%)
Aaa	0.005	0.0031	21.17
Aa	0.0030	0.0134	20.17
A	0.0194	0.585	18.80
Baa	0.1263	0.2557	17.23
Ba	0.8228	1.1180	15.90
B	5.3623	4.8879	16.41
Caa	34.9453	21.3696	32.08
Mean	5.8917		20.25

❑ Approach II "smoothes" the means and standard deviations arising from the historical time series by a linear regression on a logarithmic scale. The motivation for a regression analysis is the sparseness of defaults observed for the Aaa rating.

Table 1 shows the implied correlation results using data from Moody's (2002), relying on a regression of the original data (Approach II). Table 2 shows the results based on the original data without regression (Approach I).

The results are quite interesting. First of all we see that the overall magnitude of asset correlations implemented in Basel II is of the

Table 2 Implied asset correlations according to Approach I

Rating	Mean (%)	S.D.(%)	Original asset correlation (%)
Aaa	0.0000	0.0000	not observed
Aa	0.0216	0.1220	31.50
A	0.0138	0.0556	22.89
Baa	0.1528	0.2804	15.95
Ba	1.2056	1.3277	13.00
B	6.5256	4.6553	11.77
Caa	24.7322	21.7857	42.51
Mean	4.6645		22.94

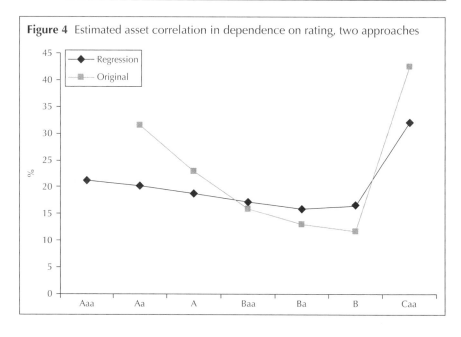

Figure 4 Estimated asset correlation in dependence on rating, two approaches

same order as the correlation numbers we find by following our simple estimation approach. But, secondly, we observe that the implied asset correlation is not necessarily decreasing with decreasing credit quality as demonstrated in Figure 4. As one can see in the chart, the two approaches (with and without regression) yield quite different results. This does not come much as a surprise based on what we said about the data smoothing applied in Approach II.

However, what both approaches show is that correlation first decreases with decreasing PD but then increases again, for sub-investment-grade ratings in case of the regression-based correlations and for Caa in the non-smoothed approach. This observation could be explained by a superposition of several reasons. First, the number of obligors in the rating class Caa is very small, which might lead to some statistical noise. Secondly, under these relatively few obligors in Caa might be some larger firms. Thirdly, the simplification that the parameter ρ is a function of the parameter PD, in which a two-parameter model is collapsed to a one-parameter model, reduces the ability to use information in an optimal way. In many cases the parameters r and PD can both be estimated, as shown in this chapter by time series data. Therefore, the simplification to one parameter often is unnecessary. The fourth reason why the correlation for sub-investment firms increases again is the use of a model with only one economic factor. This fact and its impact on risk management are highlighted in the first paragraph of this chapter. In a paper on systematic risk estimation (see Bluhm and Overbeck, 2003) the estimation procedure explained in this chapter is extended to a two-factor model, yielding some significantly different results.

Obviously, the progression of asset correlations *vis-à-vis* ratings is portfolio-specific and is subject to change when one changes the overall universe of considered companies.

We can, therefore, conclude this chapter with the following statement. Besides the fact that there is no good mathematical reason to convert a two-parameter model into a one-parameter model by implementing a functional relationship between ρ and PD, we also find the reduction is not necessary. In the present chapter it is shown how the correlation can be estimated from time series of default rates. In general, also the estimation and setting of asset correlations in the Basel II context suffer from the basic deficiency of the Basel II proposal, namely the lack of a multi-factor model.

1   Mathematically, r_i denotes the log return of the asset value process at horizon (here usually one year). For simplicity we also call r_i the asset value or asset value process.
2   See, eg, Bluhm, Overbeck and Wagner, 2003, Proposition 2.5.4, for a precise statement and its proof.
3   A mathematically precise derivation can be found in Bluhm and Overbeck, 2003.

BIBLIOGRAPHY

Basel Committee on Banking Supervision, 2003, "The New Basel Capital Accord", Consultative Document, April.

Bluhm, C., L. Overbeck, and C. Wagner, 2003, *An Introduction to Credit Risk Modelling* (Chapman Hall/CRC, Boca Raton FL, USA).

Bluhm, C., and L. Overbeck, 2003, "Systematic Risk in Homogeneous Credit Portfolios", in G. Bol *et al* (eds), *Credit Risk; Measurement, Evaluation and Management, Contributions to Economics* (Physica-Verlag/Springer, Heidelberg, Germany).

Crosbie, P., 1999, "Modelling Default Risk", White Paper of MKMV Corporation, www.mkmv.com

Finger, C. C., 1999, "Conditional Approaches for CreditMetrics Portfolio Distributions", *CreditMetrics Monitor*, April.

Gordy, M., 2001, "A Risk Factor Model Foundation for Ratings-Based Bank Capital Rules", *Draft*, February.

Merton, R., 1974, "On the Pricing of Corporate Debt: The Risk Structure of Interest Rates", *Journal of Finance*, **29,** pp. 449–70.

Moody's Investors Services, 2002, "Default & Recovery Rates of Corporate Bond Issuers", February.

Vasicek, O. A., 1987 and 1991, "Probability of Loss on Loan Portfolio", White Paper of MKMV Corporation, www.mkmv.com

3

Explaining the Credit Risk Elements in Basel II

Simon Hills

British Bankers Association

Modern banking is built on the sensible premise that a large portfolio of loans held together is less risky than holding a single loan on its own. Hence, whilst some borrowers may default, the loss of principal should be more than offset by the interest received from those that do not. Credit risk is the major risk to which banks are exposed – making loans or extending credit is the principal activity of most banks – and it has confounded bankers since the first loan was made.

INTRODUCTION

Credit risk is the risk to a bank's earnings or capital base arising from a borrower's failure to meet the terms of any contractual or other agreement it has with the bank. Credit risk arises from all activities where success depends on counterparty, issuer or borrower performance. It is present at any time that a bank has funds extended, invested, or otherwise committed, to a counterparty, whether reflected on or off the balance sheet. Credit risk arises because, in extending credit, banks have to make judgements about a borrower's creditworthiness. This creditworthiness may decline over time due to poor management or changes in the business climate, such as deteriorating terms of trade, rising inflation, weaker exchange rates or increased competition.

From this representation it can be seen that credit risk arises from a whole host of banking activities, apart from traditional lending – issuing guarantees, portfolio management, derivatives trading, custody and settlement all have credit risk implications.

In order to ensure banks do not fail, banking regulators regularly monitor the lending activities of the banks they supervise. Banks must supply details about exposures to their 20 largest counterparties as well as information on all exposures over 10% of the reporting bank's capital base. But more importantly, regulators require banks to hold capital against the *amount of credit risk exposure* that they hold.

A number of factors impact the credit risk a bank is exposed to, and these are expressed in the following formula:

$$\text{Expected loss (EL)} = \text{exposure at default (EAD)} \\ \times \text{probability of default (PD)} \\ \times \text{loss given default (LGD)}$$

Exposure at default (EAD) is the amount that the borrower legally owes to the bank at the time of default – it may not be the entire amount of the facility the bank has granted to the borrower. For instance, a borrower with a revolving facility, under which any outstandings go up and down depending on the borrower's cash flow need, could fail at a point when not all of the facility has been drawn down.

Probability of default (PD) is the expected probability that a borrower will default on the debt obligation before its maturity. It is generally estimated by reviewing the historical default record of other loans with similar characteristics.

Loss given default (LGD) recognises that banks often take collateral or hold credit derivatives as a credit risk mitigant, such that the actual loss may not be 100% of the EAD.

BASEL I

In July 1988 the Basel Committee on Banking Supervision released a set of recommendations aimed at introducing minimum levels of capital for internationally active banks. This was partly motivated by the desire to ensure a level playing field between banks from different countries. For example, at that time, Japanese banks held significantly less capital against a non-Japanese bank with similar credit risk, with the result that they could price their loans more cheaply.

These Basel proposals were not legal requirements in their own right. Rather they were expressions of good practice in which the 100 or so supervisors from around the world who signed up to them agreed to use their best efforts to implement in their own countries, either by changes to legislation or to their regulatory practice. In Europe, for instance, they were implemented through the Capital Adequacy Directive (CAD).

The Basel Committee recommended that core capital of at least 8% should be maintained against a bank's portfolio of exposures. Different categories of exposure were allocated different risk weightings – for example, holdings of government bonds carried a 0% risk weighting, whereas loans to corporates carried a 100% weighting, regardless of the underlying credit quality of the borrower concerned.

The original Basel Accord acknowledged that the different risk weightings employed – 0%, 10%, 20%, 50% or 100% – were simplistic in their treatment. Counter-intuitively, a secured loan to a AAA-rated company carried the same 100% risk weighting as an unsecured loan to a BBB-rated issuer, resulting in banks selling down exposures to better quality credits, to release capital but holding lower-rated, riskier ones, which tended to yield more but consume the same amount of capital. Not surprisingly the banks arbitraged the rules to maximise return on capital! But the approach of the original Basel Accord was generally recognised at the time as a good compromise. The technology of credit risk measurement was not sufficiently developed at the time to permit more finely-tuned capital requirements, and there was an overarching need to set harmonised minimum capital requirements in the face of a long-term decline in bank capital levels.

Since then, however, the process of allocating capital to a particular loan has become more sophisticated with many banks using an internal ratings approach. Business loans may be scored on a 1 to 10 scale, with 1 being the equivalent of an AAA credit and 10 being a loan that is in the process of being "written off".

Some banks have gone further and used historical loss data to estimate the mean and variance of losses on each grade of loan so that a loss probability distribution can be established. This can then be used to manage the overall lending portfolio so that the bank itself (as a proxy for a portfolio of loans) maintains a target rating on its own market debt.

BASEL II

In 1999, the Basel Committee decided to instigate a thorough review of the capital adequacy regime that would bring the 1988 capital requirements up-to-date, in light of the structural, portfolio and management changes that have impacted international banking over the past 15 years.

The Consultative Papers issued between June 1999 and mid 2003 have sought to meet the Basel Committee's objective of moving from a prescriptive approach to one involving more supervisory discretion. They also recognise the advances in the science of credit risk management and provide incentives by allowing users of more sophisticated credit risk management techniques to hold less capital. The rising use of credit derivatives – which allow a bank to limit its exposure to a particular borrower, industry or country in exchange for the payment of a small, regular fee to the counterparty taking on the default risk – is but one example of new techniques that have been developed. Others include a greater use of collateralisation and securitisation.

Basel II proposes three different approaches to calculating capital:

❏ The *standardised approach*, which is Basel I with more refined risk buckets. It also allows banks to use external ratings in some circumstances and gives some benefit for credit risk mitigation.
❏ The *foundation Internal Ratings Based (IRB) approach*, which is a methodology permitting a bank to use its own internal risk rating system, including its own calculation of PD, but with the LGD factor provided by supervisors.
❏ The *advanced IRB Approach*, which bases capital calculations on a bank's own supervisory–validated models, including bank-calculated PDs and LGDs.

The standardised approach

This entails general rules and re-defined risk weights as explained below

Table 1 The standardised approach risk weightings

Claim		Assessment					
		AAA to AA−	A+ to A−	BBB+ to BBB−	BB+ to B−	Below B−	Unrated
Sovereigns (if export credit agencies)		0% (1)	20% (2)	50% (3)	100% (4–6)	150% (7)	100%
Banks	Option 1[1]	20%	50%	100%	100%	150%	100%
	Option 2[2]	20% (20%)[3]	50% (20%)[3]	50% (20%)[3]	100% (50%)[3]	150% (150%)[3]	50% (20%)[3]
Corporates		20%	50%	100%	BB+ to BB− 100%	Below BB− 150%	100%

[1]Risk weighting based on risk weighting of sovereign in which the bank is incorporated (but one category is less favourable).
[2]Risk weighting based on the assessment of the individual bank.
[3]Claims on banks of a short original maturity, less than three months, would generally receive a weighting that is one category more favourable than the usual risk weight on the bank's claim.

The chart above indicates the risk weightings that will apply to different categories of borrowers, depending on their rating bucket.

Compared to Basel I, sovereign and bank risk weightings will no longer depend on whether the sovereign (or in the case of banks, its country of incorporation) is a member of the OECD. This removal of the sovereign ceiling is welcomed by lenders to non-sovereign, emerging market borrowers, as it removes the disincentive to lend to strong corporate credits in weak countries.

Externally weighted corporates will no longer share the same 100% risk weight, but where a borrower's creditworthiness is rated by an external agency deemed to be acceptable by the supervising national authority, the risk weight will depend on that rating. However, under the standardised approach, it is at the national's discretion to permit banks to risk weight all corporate exposures at 100%, rather than base the weighting on external ratings.

Where counterparties have a low external rating (below B− for sovereigns and banks, and below BB− for corporates and securitisations), the maximum weighting is increased from 100% to 150%. Under the standardised approach, the risk weight allocations for past due loans will be based on the level of specific provision raised. This is more risk sensitive and more equitable than an earlier proposal under which non-performing assets more than 90 days past due would be weighted at 150%, but this will be more complex to administer.

Exposures that the supervisor considers to be retail claims for supervisory purposes will be risk weighted at 75%. In order to be classified as retail under Basel II, the exposure must:

❑ be to an individual or small business;
❑ be of a specific product type, for instance a credit card, personal loan or small business facility;
❑ exceed no more than 0.2% of the overall regulatory retail portfolio; and
❑ not exceed 1 million Euro to any one counterparty.

Under the standardised approach, the risk weighting for residential mortgages is 35%, which is a substantial reduction from 50% under Basel I. This is likely to make an important difference to the amount of capital a retail bank will have to hold against its retail portfolio.

It does not appear that the standardised approach will have that much of an impact on the overall capital that smaller, uncomplicated banks hold as they generally have fewer sovereign exposures. Also, smaller banks generally do not lend to rated corporates and have exposures to banks that are mainly short-term claims on well rated institutions. The reduction in risk weights for well rated corporate and securitisation transactions will give smaller banks the ability to diversify their portfolios at a lower capital cost than under Basel I.

Procyclicality

What the impact on a bank's regulatory capital position might be in the event of an economic downturn is less clear. It may be that a bank's capital position will deteriorate more quickly than under the current approach as, for the first time, an objective test for the recognition of an impaired credit quality has been introduced – the ninety days past due test. This contrasts with the current treatment where no capital hit is taken *until* the bank's own management decide to raise a specific provision against the exposure. Furthermore, a downgrading of an external rating will result in *more* capital being required even if the obligor continues to perform well and no specific provision is been made. This issue of procyclicality arises because a bank is required to raise more capital following a downturn in economic conditions, this affects ratings generally not necessarily because of any weakening in the banks own specific credit portfolio. Any such deterioration may coincide with a period during which it is difficult for banks to raise capital cost-effectively, so the only alternative would be for banks to reduce the supply of lending. To the extent that this action may tend to amplify the economic cycle, this clearly provides a threat to the stability of the financial system as a whole.

Role of ECAI and implementation considerations

The standardised approach relies heavily on external ratings provided by the so-called external credit assessment institutions (ECAIs) and recognises that, for the most part, ratings agencies have performed well in benchmarking a borrower's credit default risk.

The use of ECAIs in Basel II to establish regulatory capital raises a number of policy issues, including:

❏ the reliability of ratings as indicators of default risk;
❏ the consistency of ratings across agencies and countries and across time, raising the spectre of credit rating inflation;
❏ the possible abuse of the ratings process itself through "rate-shopping" for higher ratings; and
❏ the relationship between ratings of external rating agencies and banks' internal ratings.

Recognising this, the Basel Committee has decided to leave it to individual national supervisors to determine whether a particular rating agency is objective, independent and has the credibility and resources to carry out a high quality assessment, before banks are permitted to use its rating for capital allocation purposes. The precise way in which this will be done remains to be seen and is a topic on the Accord Implementation Group's agenda.

Credit risk mitigation

Banks use a number of techniques to mitigate credit risk, through collateralisation, through guarantees or by the use of credit derivatives. The benefit that this brings to banks has been recognised and a wider range of credit risk mitigants are now permitted than under Basel I.

Collateral

There are two approaches to the treatment of collateral. The simple approach is similar to the 1988 Accord whereby the risk weighting of the collateral is substituted for the risk weighting of the counterparty, subject to a 20% floor. It is likely to be suitable for banks that are not sufficiently involved in collateralisation transactions to justify the development of transaction-by-transaction haircuts.

The comprehensive approach is based on applying haircuts to protect against price volatility. Haircuts are supplied either by the supervisor or (subject to qualitative and quantitative criteria) can be the bank's internally generated haircuts. The adjusted market value of collateral is then offset against the value of the gross exposure to arrive at an adjusted exposure that is multiplied by the counterparty's risk weighting.

Both approaches recognise a wider range of collateral than the 1988 Accord, which was limited to government securities issued by Zone A sovereigns or cash. Included in the current list are:

❏ cash on deposit;
❏ securities rated BB− or above, issued by sovereigns and public sector entities;
❏ corporate securities rated at least BBB−;
❏ equities included in the main index; and
❏ gold.

In addition, the comprehensive approach recognises equities not in the main index but traded on a recognised exchange, some unrated bank bonds, collective investment schemes and mutual funds.

In order to obtain any benefit from its collateral management programme, a bank must meet three standards, relating to:

❏ the legal certainty of the documentation used;

❑ the requirement that credit risk mitigation assets must bear a low correlation with the assets they are collateralising; and

❑ the robustness of their collateral management policies.

As an alternative to standard or their own estimate haircuts, banks can use value-at-risk (VAR) modelling to reflect the volatility of the exposure and the collateral for repos covered by bilateral netting agreements.

Guarantees and credit derivatives

The proposals in relation to guarantees and on balance sheet netting widen the range of eligible guarantors or credit derivative providers by recognising credit protection given by sovereigns or banks with a lower risk weight than the borrower, as well as other entities rated A− or better. This last category would include protection provided by parents, subsidiaries or affiliates of the obligor, when they have a lower risk weight – these changes have been welcomed by banks.

But the proposals take a more cautious approach to measuring the benefit of the guarantee or credit derivative. In the future, the present principle of substitution – whereby the risk weight of the guarantor replaces that of the borrower – will be diluted as the risk weight applied to the guaranteed exposure will not be the guarantor's risk weight, but rather a weighted average of the guarantors risk weight *and* that of the underlying borrower.

Banks will wish to consider the beneficial capital impact of including a wider range of eligible guarantors or credit derivative providers, which may be offset by the negative changes in the measurement approach.

The internal ratings based (IRB) approach

The Basel Committee's contemplation that internal ratings could be used in the capital allocation process tacitly acknowledged the progress made over the intervening 10 years in the measurement and management of credit risk. It acknowledged that banks with sophisticated internal ratings approaches to credit risk assessment should be allowed to apply them to some of their portfolios, but subject to external validation criteria. These are likely to depend on how individual regulators decide to implement Basel II in their jurisdictions.

Under the IRB approach, banks must categorise banking book exposure into five broad classes of assets with different underlying risk characteristics. These are:

❏ corporate;
❏ sovereign;
❏ bank;
❏ retail; and
❏ equity

Within the retail asset class banks are required to separately identify three sub-classes of exposure – retail mortgages, revolving retail exposures (such as credit cards) and other retail.

The corporate asset class is further broken down into small and medium sized enterprise (SME) lending, and five subclasses of specialised lending:

❏ project finance;
❏ object finance;
❏ commodities finance;
❏ income producing real estate; and
❏ high-volatility real estate.

Most of a bank's credit portfolio will be risk weighted using a single formula, although this will be modified for equity, retail and project finance portfolios.

The formula derives risk weights from a continuous function based on the obligor's probability of Default (PD) and the exposure's Loss Given Default (LGD). Previously an add-on factor – the granularity adjustment – which penalised banks with undiversified credit portfolios, had been superimposed. But it was removed when it was realised that the increased complexity that the granularity adjustment introduced did not in fact increase a bank's capital very significantly.

Under the foundation IRB approach, banks use their own PD estimates, with LGD being supplied by the supervisor, whereas under the advanced approach, they can use their own PD and LGD estimates and use internal credit migration modelling techniques.

The actual formulae used to calculate risk-weighted assets are shown below:

$$\text{Correlation (R)} = 0.12 \times \frac{1 - \exp(-50 \times PD)}{1 - \exp(-50)}$$

$$+ 0.24 \times \frac{1 - \exp(-50 \times PD)}{1 - \exp(-50)}$$

Maturity adjustment (b) = $(0.08451 - 0.05898 \times \log(PD))^{\uparrow 2}$

Capital requirement (K)
  = LGD × $N[(1 - R)^{\uparrow 0.5} \times G(PD) + (R/(1 - R))^{\uparrow 0.5} \times G(0.999)]$
  × $(1 - 1.5 \times b(PD))^{\uparrow 1} \times (1 + (M - 2.5) \times b(PD))$

Risk-weighted assets (RWA) = K × 12.50 × EAD

$$\text{Effective maturity (EM)} = \frac{\sum_{t} t * CFt}{\sum_{t} t * CFt}$$

As will be readily appreciated, the IRB risk-weighting functions are complex and inaccessible to all but the most mathematically adept, although the key risk component inputs, PD, LGD, EAD and EM are intuitively easier to comprehend.

❑ *Probability of default* (PD) is based on the bank's own estimate, subject in some cases to a floor. For bank and corporate exposures, the PD is the greater of either the one-year PD associated with the internal borrower grade to which an exposure has been assigned, or 0.03%. For sovereign PDs, there is no floor.
❑ A *loss given default* (LGD) estimate must be provided for each corporate, sovereign or bank exposure, using either the foundation IRB or advanced approach.

Under the foundation IRB approach, corporate, sovereign or bank exposure not secured by recognised collateral is assigned a 45% LGD, whereas subordinated claims on similar asset classes are assigned a 75% LGD. Under the advanced approach, banks use their own estimated of LGD as long as they are able to meet the minimum requirements for the derivation of LGD estimates.

❑ *Exposure at default* (EAD) is the amount legally owed to the bank – ie, gross of any partial write-offs or specific provisions.

For off-balance sheet items, exposure is calculated as the committed, but undrawn, credit line multiplied by a credit conversion factor (CCF). There are two approaches to CCF estimation – foundation or advanced – the more basic of which uses CCFs supplied by supervisors, whereas banks on the advanced approach can use their own internal estimates.

❑ *Effective maturity* (M) is deemed to be 2.5 years under the foundation approach. Banks on the advanced approach are required to make a specific maturity adjustment. This is the greater of 1-year and the remaining effective maturity in years as defined below, but subject to a 5-year ceiling.

The role of collateral

Collateral considered under the foundation IRB approaches is treated in the same way as under the comprehensive methodology as in the standardised approach, but the range of eligible collateral is increased. This collateral includes receivables, real estate and "other eligible IRB collateral" classes, providing that there is a liquid, publicly available, market in the securities that are taken as collateral. Where such other collateral is taken, an asset-class specific LGD is assigned, depending on the degree of collateralisation of the exposure concerned. Under the advanced IRB approach banks are permitted to use their own LGD estimates.

Provisions

The IRB approach allows banks to recognise general provisions as offsets to the (EL) of risk weighted assets in a particular class, but only to the extent where they do not exceed EL. Where provisions, taken against defaulted assets only, exceed the EL capital charge of that defaulted asset, the excess may be applied against the EL capital charge against other defaulted assets in the same asset class. This reallocation of excess provisions adds to the complexity of an already complex IRB approach.

More importantly, however, any provisions exceeding the EL capital charge on non-defaulted assets may not be set off against capital charges. This limitation results in a perverse outcome for the prudent bank that raises conservative provisions. Once all available EL offsets have been used, surplus provisions become a deduction from Tier 1 capital (as they are a charge to profit and loss) without any benefit in reduced risk-weighted assets. This may have a particular impact on provisioning policy in times of economic downturn when it may be more difficult for banks to raise new capital at the very time they need it.

What are the minimum qualifications for the IRB approach and how can banks comply with these requirements?
Before a bank can use internal estimates of PD and/or LGD it must meet strict regulatory criteria that establish minimum requirements in relation to the banks' use of the IRB approach and its ongoing compliance with them. Basel II lists minimum requirements in 11 different categories, which are designed to enable the bank to demonstrate to its supervisor that its risk management system is able to rank, order and quantify risk in a consistent, reliable and valid way. The different categories relate to:

❑ composition of minimum requirements;
❑ compliance with minimum requirements;
❑ rating system design;
❑ risk rating operations;
❑ corporate governance and oversight;
❑ use of internal ratings;
❑ risk quantification;
❑ validation of internal estimates;
❑ supervisory LGD and EAD estimates;
❑ capital charge calculation for equity exposures; and
❑ disclosure requirements.

Implementing the IRB approach
Although the Basel II proposals are not yet finalised, banks are already some way down the road in deciding how they will implement them. The IRB approach is data greedy and, in order to take the full benefit of the new risk based capital proposals, banks will have to demonstrate to their supervisors that they have sufficient, valid historic data on which to base their PD, LGD and EAD estimates. The largest banks are likely to spend upwards of US$100 million each in implementing Basel II with the result that the industry as a whole is expected to spend billions of dollars over the next three or four years to ensure they are ready to meet regulatory demands.

While the BIS's Accord Implementation Group has released six high level principles that regulators should abide by when implementing Basel II in their own jurisdiction, these are focused on how home and host regulators should cooperate in their joint supervision of cross-border banking groups. Only a few regulators have yet gone deeper into articulating how they envisage practical, day-to-day implementation happening.

In the summer of 2003, the UK's Financial Service's Authority (FSA) published a Consultation Paper that started its dialogue with industry practitioners on how the revised Basel Accord (and the Risk-Based Capital Directive which will be the European legislation turning Basel II into law) should be implemented.

The FSA will base its implementation on a number of principles:

❑ senior management within the bank bears the prime responsibility for ensuring the IRB approach is implemented properly;
❑ banks can choose whether to implement the IRB approach, but if they stay on the standardised approach, the FSA may impose extra capital under Pillar II;
❑ the FSA will be flexible in its interpretation of standards and transparent in disclosing which banks are on which approach; and
❑ promotion of the concept of lead supervision when working with other national regulators and standards will be applied in an internationally consistent way.

The FSA's work so far has focused on *qualifying criteria, validation* and *technical clarification*. In addition, it provides a framework for corporate governance issues associated with Board level oversight of usage of the advanced approach and how it delegates responsibility to senior management.

Qualifying criteria

Before a bank will be permitted to move to the IRB approach and use its own estimates as input into the regulatory capital calculation, they must demonstrate they are central to the way in which a firm manages and measures its risk, rather than being merely an add-on to satisfy the regulator to obtain a lower capital charge. This "use test" requirement will expect that the use of the bank's own estimates of PD, LGD, and EAD should be an integral part of its risk and business management culture. For example, a bank will submit a self-assessment "scorecard" demonstrating compliance with the "use test" and its relation to the bank's core credit processes such as : credit approval and the setting of limits and provisioning. The bank will attempt to confirm its commitment to the "use test" by its adoption of these techniques in broader areas such as strategy, profitability and performance measurement and demonstrate that these will be supported by appropriate technology and skills infrastructures.

A further qualifying criteria is that before adopting the IRB approach, banks will be required to run parallel IRB calculations with the standardised approach (or Basel I if they are planning to move to IRB by the end of 2006) in order that the regulator can gauge, ahead of time, what the likely impact on a bank's capital will be.

Validation

Banks will be required to demonstrate that the estimates they are using as IRB inputs are reliable and provide a meaningful differentiation of risk, again through completion of a self-assessment scorecard.

This validation work will be based on statistical analysis of the rating system and be performed on all portfolios and in some depth on significant portfolios. The aim of the validation is to assess the accuracy of the overall output of the rating system, not just to check the inputs into it, and it will be performed in conjunction with staff independent of the credit risk management function.

Where external models or external data are used in the banks' risk measurement system, it must complete, with the model vendor, a grid providing information on model design, any known limitations and the degree of ongoing support the vendor will provide.

It is expected that validation work will be undertaken on at least an annual basis and once completed, considered by senior management who will identify any requirements to refine the rating system.

Technical clarification

The final area on which banks will have to do work before being permitted to use the advanced approach relates to technical clarification of, for instance, the definition of default and the approach to stress testing.

The refinement of the default definition is necessary as the Basel II proposals as they stand at the moment leave it open to interpretation. The starting point is that a default has occurred if a bank considers the obligor will be unable to repay in full without resorting to security, or if the borrower is 90 days past due. But by its nature the definition of default is complex, and it is unlikely that rules will be able to cover every eventuality. Some of the issues that remain open include the definition of "obligor", which is particularly relevant where the borrower is part of a group, and the treatment of obligor, versus obligation in the retail portfolio – where it is recognised that an individual could be in default under a personal loan or credit card, but still current on their mortgage borrowing. In the retail portfolio, there is also national discretion to extend the past due timeframe from 90 to 180 days for some products where late payment can be demonstrated not to result in an actual loss to the bank.

Stress testing is an area of much concern among banks, particularly in relation to the procyclicality that the Basel II proposals potentially introduce. Capital requirements for IRB banks may increase sharply as credit quality deteriorates, leading to a much greater variation in capital ratios than is currently the case due to fluctuations in the economic cycle. Firms are required, therefore, to stress test their regulatory capital estimates in order to ensure they have an adequate capital buffer, built up in good times to reduce the impact of rising capital requirements in more difficult times.

Whilst the FSA's proposals represent some welcome early thinking on the topic of implementation, the industry is concerned that they are too prescriptive as a "one size fits all", defining a single "best practice". This will require banks to demonstrate that their approach, if different to the standard, is not wrong rather than recognising that there can be more than one way of managing credit risk.

CONCLUSIONS

Basel II acknowledges that credit risk management techniques have improved greatly since the first Accord in 1988 and incentivises banks to manage risk better by rewarding them with lower capital charges. However, the revision to the Accord that has emerged is extremely complex and will require very substantial investment by banks as they put in place appropriate systems to manage data on credit performance and validate credit management processes for the supervisor. Whilst banks welcome the move from a prescriptive approach under Basel I to a more conceptual framework, they understand that the smooth implementation of the new Accord over the next three years will be very dependent on working closely with regulators to ensure that their proposals build on current credit risk management practice, rather than creating a totally separate structure for regulatory capital purposes. Only time will tell if this can be achieved.

4

Loss Given Default and Recovery Risk: From Basel II Standards to Effective Risk Management Tools

Andrea Resti*; **Andrea Sironi****

Bergamo University; Luigi Bocconi University

INTRODUCTION

One of the main objectives pursued by the Basel Committee's proposals to reform the capital adequacy framework (originally developed in 1988) is to narrow the gap between regulatory capital requirement and the economic capital produced by banks' own internal models. This gap is indeed perceived to be the main reason behind regulatory capital arbitrage transactions. Following this objective, the committee introduced the internal ratings-based (IRB) approach as a way of estimating a bank's credit risk capital requirement. According to this approach, four main variables affect the credit risk of a financial asset. They are: (i) the probability of default of the borrower (PD); (ii) its "loss given default" (LGD), that is, the percentage of a loan that is actually lost, after accounting for all recoveries on the defaulted exposure; (iii) the exposure at default (EAD); and (iv) its maturity (M). Moreover, although not explicitly mentioned, loss given default affects also the standardised approach. In fact, some facilities and collaterals are granted a reduction in the capital requirements because they are thought to imply higher recoveries.

*Andrea Resti is associate professor of mathematical finance, Department of Mathematics and Statistics, Bergamo University, Italy.
**Andrea Sironi is professor of financial markets and institutions, Luigi Bocconi University, Milan, Italy.

While significant attention has historically been devoted by the credit risk literature to the estimation of the first component (PD), much less attention has been dedicated to the estimation of LGD and to the relationship between PD and LGD. This is mainly the consequence of two related factors. First, credit pricing models and risk management applications tended to focus on the systematic risk components of credit risk, as these are the only ones that attract risk premia. Second, credit risk models traditionally assumed recovery rates (RR) to be dependent on individual features (eg, collateral or seniority) that do not respond to systematic factors, and to be independent of PD. As a consequence, these models focused on systematic risk in defaults and paid much less attention to the subject of collateral value and recovery rates in the event of default.

More generally, one could argue that recovery risk has been somewhat overlooked (eg, in the first credit VAR models that were released in the second half of the 1990s) because it is seen as a "second-order" risk, that "bites" only if default has actually materialised.[1]

Evidence from many countries in recent years suggests, however, that collateral values and recovery rates can be volatile. Moreover, they tend to go down just when the number of defaults goes up in economic downturns (see Altman, 2001; Hamilton, Gupton and Berthault, 2001). Still, little quantitative analysis has appeared during the 1980s and the 1990s to assist bond portfolio managers and banks in setting sufficient collateral haircuts, estimating recovery rates as well as pricing debt with stochastic collateral values.[2] Most credit risk models have indeed been based on static loss assumptions with, at best, a single average recovery rate used for all unsecured loans and another single average used for all unsecured loans. These simplifying assumptions are particularly relevant given the high standard deviations and fat tails of the empirical distributions of recovery rates.[3]

This traditional focus on default analysis has been partly reversed by the significant increase in the number of studies dedicated to the subject of LGD estimation and the relationship between PD and LGD that appeared during the last four years (see Fridson, Garman and Okashima, 2000; Gupton, Gates and Carty, 2000; Jokivuolle and Peura, 2000; Altman, Resti and Sironi, 2001; Frye, 2000a, 2000b and 2000c; Jarrow, 2001). This is partly the consequence of the parallel increase in default rates and decrease of recovery rates registered during the 1999–2002 period in the international bond markets.

Following this increased attention to LGD analysis, this chapter looks at this variable not only from a regulatory perspective but also from an effective risk management perspective. The second section presents a definition of LGD and looks at the treatment of this risk variable in the standard, foundation and advanced approaches of the proposed revision to the Basel Accord (henceforth Basel II). The third section is devoted to the problem of estimating LGD for corporate bonds. It presents the available empirical evidence and the implications of seniority and guarantees, and it highlights the main results of previous studies. The fourth section looks at the estimation of LGDs for bank loans, analysing the methodological framework and the effect of delays on the economic value of recoveries. Finally, the fifth section focuses on the link between PD and LGD, highlighting the empirical evidence and the effects of this link in the estimation of expected and unexpected losses of a portfolio of credit exposures. It also looks at the effects of procyclicality, an issue that has often been discussed by the regulatory community and by the Basel Committee itself. The sixth section concludes this chapter.

THE REGULATORY FRAMEWORK

LGD can be defined as the share of a defaulted exposure that will never be recovered by the lender. Note that recoveries have to be assessed in an economic sense rather than from a mere accounting perspective: when measuring them (*ex post*) or estimating them (*ex ante*), all relevant factors that may reduce the final economic value of the recovered part of the exposure must be taken into account. This includes the discount effect associated with the time span between the emergence of the default and the actual recovery, but also the various direct and indirect administrative costs associated with collecting information on the exposure.

Accounting data, then, are just a starting point for the computation of the true loss rates. The efficiency levels (in terms of costs and time) of the bank's workout department may affect LGD quite significantly, and must be reflected in the estimates used to assess recovery risks on future defaulters. This means that any improvement in the recovery procedures leading to a reduction in empirical LGDs may lead to lower capital requirements for the following years, as far as supported by sound empirical evidence.

Recoveries tend to be different for the various facility types issued by a bank. They vary according to the value of the facility and the degree of stability of any collateral associated with the exposure. This implies that, in order to build a good set of in-house LGD estimates, a bank must set up an enterprise-wide, well-organised and complex database that is well rooted in its corporate history.

The measurement and estimation of LGDs, therefore, does not represent an easy task. Accordingly, the Basel Committee has designed three different approaches to LGD measurement.[4] From the simplest to the most complex (but also most flexible) one, these are: the *standardised approach*, the *foundation approach* and the *advanced approach*. They are described separately in Panels 1 through 3.

PANEL 1 THE STANDARDISED APPROACH

LGD is not explicitly quoted in the section of the Basel Accord dealing with the standardised approach. Yet, better recovery expectations help explain the most favourable treatment designed for some specific portfolios and collaterals.

LGD estimations enter the standardised approach in two ways. First, some specific portfolios of exposures are granted a more favourable treatment. Second, some widely used financial instruments, the value of which can easily be marked-to-market, are accepted as a risk mitigant that can reduce total capital requirements. Those two complementary approaches are shortly summarised below.

The portfolios commanding lower risk weights comprise exposures secured by residential property and by commercial real estate. The former – loans collateralised by mortgages on residential property that is or will be occupied by the borrower or that is rented – will be risk-weighted at 35% (compared with a 75% weight for other exposures to individuals included in the so-called "retail portfolio"). Such a discount on regulatory capital can be justified in several ways. To begin with, families applying for a mortgage may have been considered less prone to default than individuals using credit cards, instalment loans and other retail facilities. Moreover, since the redemption plan of a mortgage is fixed, no exposure risk is present on such products.[5] These arguments are without a doubt correct, yet the low risk weight assigned to residential mortgages is also driven by a more favourable recovery experience on this kind of loan.[6] Turning to loans secured by

---

commercial real estate, the Basel Accord states that they may, under exceptional circumstances, receive a lower capital requirement than unsecured corporate exposures. The risk weight may be as low as 50% (compared with 100% for unrated corporate loans), although this represents a minimum threshold, and not a standard value. Since no specific limitations are imposed on the exposure type and the borrower's PD for this discount to be applicable, the presence of a lower risk weight seems to be motivated mainly by LGD considerations.

The impact of financial collateral on credit risk can be quantified in two different ways: the so-called simple and comprehensive approaches.[7] In the simple approach, the portion of the exposure covered by recognised collateral receives the risk weight applicable to the collateral itself, not to the original borrower, subject to a floor, usually, of 20%. In the comprehensive approach, no capital requirement is applied to the collateralised portion of the exposure, but the value of the collateral (C) must be reduced by a haircut (H_C), reflecting the risk that the market value of the financial instrument may decrease before it is revaluated or remargined. This explains why haircuts tend to be different based on the historical volatility of the various securities pledged as collateral, and need to be scaled up as the actual number of days between remargining or revaluation dates increases (see Table 1). Once the appropriate haircut is chosen, the adjusted exposure E^*, net of the risk-mitigation effect of the collateral (that is, the residual amount, if any, on which the capital requirement must be computed) can be calculated as follows:

$$E^* = \max[0, E - C\,(1 - H_C)] \qquad\qquad (1)$$

where E is the original exposure.

Table 1 Haircuts (%) for different collaterals

Collateral	Rating	Maturity	Revaluation/ remargining period (days)		
			10	**30**	**90**
Sovereign bonds	AAA to AA−	Below 1 year	0.5	0.7	1.4
		1–5 years	2.0	2.8	5.7
		Beyond 5 years	4.0	5.7	11.3
	A+ to BBB−	Below 1 year	1.0	1.4	2.8
		1–5 years	3.0	4.2	8.5
		Beyond 5 years	6.0	8.5	17.0
	BB+ to BB−	Any	15.0	21.2	42.4
Corporate bonds	AAA to AA−	Below 1 year	1.0	1.4	2.8
		1–5 years	4.0	5.7	11.3
		Beyond 5 years	8.0	11.3	22.6

Table 1 (continued)

Collateral	Rating	Maturity	Revaluation/ remargining period (days)		
			10	30	90
	A+ to BBB−	Below 1 year	2.0	2.8	5.7
	and unrated	1–5 years	6.0	8.5	17.0
	bank bonds	Beyond 5 years	12.0	17.0	33.9
Equities included in main index			15.0	21.2	42.4
Other listed equities			25.0	35.4	70.7
Gold			15.0	21.2	42.4
Cash (in the same currency)			0.0	0.0	0.0
Currency mismatch			8	11.3	22.6

Note that, in case the loan is not issued in cash (eg, in the case of securities lending), its value may increase over time. This, too, might cause the collateral to become inadequate for the exposure to be fully secured. In such cases, a haircut H_E must be added to the current value of the exposure. Moreover, if a currency mismatch is present between collateral and exposure, the value of the former must be further reduced, through another haircut (H_{FX}), to account for foreign exchange risk. The adjusted exposure then becomes[8]

$$E^* = \max[0, E(1 + H_E) - C(1 - H_C - H_{FX})] \qquad (2)$$

PANEL 2 "FOUNDATION IRB APPROACH"
The haircut system is widely used also in the "foundation" approach of IRB. In this case, however, the haircuts are not applied to the value of the exposure, but to LGDs in a direct and explicit way.

In the foundation approach, the "basic" loss given default is fixed at 45% for all senior, unsecured exposures. This value must be raised to 75% for subordinated exposures, but can be adjusted downwards when some recognised collateral is pledged against the loan. However, this reduction cannot be based on a bank's internal models or past experience. Instead, a set of rules has been introduced that quantify the effect of financial and non-financial collaterals.

As far as financial instruments are concerned, the formula for the computation of the adjusted LGD (denoted by LGD^*) is the following

$$LGD^* = 45\% \cdot \max\left[0, 1 + H_E - \frac{C}{E}\left(1 - H_C - H_{FX}\right)\right] \qquad (3)$$

where all symbols retain the same meaning as before.[9] Note that, as in the standardised approach, LGD is increased if the loan is not issued in cash (and consists of financial instruments with a haircut H_E greater than zero), while the coverage ratio C/E of collateral to original exposure is reduced according to the haircut of the collateral and the currency mismatch haircut, if present.

As concerns non-financial assets, three different categories of collateral are accepted. These are receivables, real estate (both commercial and residential), and other collateral (including physical capital, but excluding any assets acquired by the bank as a result of a loan default).[10]

For these collaterals (also called "IRB" collaterals, since they are eligible only for banks implementing the internal ratings-based approach) the haircuts are replaced by a system of minimum and maximum thresholds (T_{min} and T_{max}) that help compute the adjusted LGD as follows:

$$LGD^* = 45\% - \max\left(0, \frac{\min\left(C/E, T_{max}\right) - T_{min}}{T_{max} - T_{min}}\right)\left(45\% - LGD_{min}\right) \quad (4)$$

where LGD_{min} indicates the minimum value that can be attained by the adjusted LGD, when the term in the first parenthesis is 1.

The values for LGD_{min} and the thresholds are reported in Table 2. Using these values we show, through an example, how equation (4) works: a 100-million-dollar loan (E) secured by a building with a current value (C) of 105 million dollars, would have an adjusted LGD^* of:

$$LGD^* = 45\% - \max\left(0, \frac{\min\left(\frac{105}{100}, 140\%\right) - 35\%}{140\% - 35\%}\right)\left(45\% - 35\%\right)$$

$$= 45\% - \max\left(0, \frac{105\% - 35\%}{105\%}\right) \cdot 10\% = 45\% - \frac{2}{3} \cdot 10\% \cong 38.3\%$$

Table 2 Key parameters for the computation of LGD when IRB collaterals are available

Type of IRB collateral	T_{min} (%)	T_{max} (%)	LGD_{min} (%)
Receivables	0	125	35
Commercial and residential real estate	30	140	35
Other collateral	30	140	40

PANEL 3 "ADVANCED IRB APPROACH"

Banks adopting the advanced IRB approach will be allowed to use their own estimates of LGDs, provided they can demonstrate to the regulatory supervisors that their internal models are conceptually sound and historically consistent with their past experience. To demonstrate this, data on historical recovery rates must be collected and archived. This includes data on the different components of the recoveries experienced on defaulted exposures, for instance, amounts recovered, source of recovery (eg, collaterals and guarantees, type of liquidation and bankruptcy procedure), time period elapsed before the actual recovery, and administrative costs. Note that all relevant information must be retained on a single-facility basis. Aggregated cashflows recovered from a given defaulted borrower must therefore be broken down, giving separate evidence to the partial recoveries associated with different loans issued to the same counterparty.

The Basel Committee also requires that the LGD estimates produced by banks be long-run estimates, accounting for the possible correlation between recovery rates and default frequencies (see also the fourth section in this chapter). This implies that estimates must be based on the average economic loss of all observed defaults in the bank's database.

Table 3 LGDs: simple versus weighted averages

Year	Default rate (%)	Loss given default (%)
1	1	20
2	3	30
3	7	45
4	3	40
5	2	20
Simple average	3	31
Weighted average		36.6

To see how this "default-weighted average" works, consider the data in Table 3. Note that the simple mean of average annual loss rates would be 31%. However, this would not account for the fact that defaults are clustered during times of economic distress, like Year 3, for example, and that LGDs (at least in the case of the data in Table 2) tend to be correlated with default rates. Hence, a simple average (also called "time-weighted average", as every year counts as one) may materially understate the severity of true historical losses. It is thus necessary to weight annual LGD rates by the respective default rates, getting a default-weighted average of 36.6%.

The default-weighted average might be replaced by an even more conservative estimate if the bank feels that an economic downturn is approaching. In this case, the long-run weighted average, although unbiased in the long term, might not be adequate to represent the expected loss rate conditional on a recession. Estimates that are appropriate for an economic downturn (eg, the 45% LGD, the third value in Table 3) should then be used. Alternatively, banks that have sophisticated LGD models in place might consider worst-case scenarios for the macroeconomic factors driving the recovery rates. For example a bank that, based on internal data concerning past recessions, has established a sound econometric link between LGDs on the retail portfolio and housing prices might simulate a sharp drop in the real estate and increase expected LGDs accordingly.

The link between LGD and the expected frequency of default also needs to be addressed on a single-borrower basis. Any dependence between the risk of the borrower and that of the collateral must be assessed and incorporated into the LGD estimates in a conservative manner.[11] Any currency mismatch between the underlying obligation and the collateral must be considered and translated into an increase in the expected LGD.

A remarkable difference between the foundation and the advanced approach to LGD lies in the fact that, while in the former all computations are directly based on the current value of the collateral, the advanced approach explicitly states that all collateral values must be evaluated *in the light of historical recovery rates*. This means that, if the bank's past workout performance denotes some degree of inability to quickly gain full control of the collateral and liquidate it, this must be incorporated into the LGD estimates on future defaults. Moreover, banks should ascertain that their current requirements for collateral management (eg, the level of legal certainty and the effectiveness of all operational procedures) are at least in line with those in place when past LGDs were measured. A set of minimum standards should also be set for collateral to be accepted as a source of LGD reduction.

As past evidence plays a pivotal role in the reliability of internal LGD estimates, a minimum amount of historical data is required for a bank before being allowed to use the advanced approach. Such a minimum observation period should ideally cover at least one complete economic cycle. In the case of loans to corporates, banks and sovereigns, it must never be shorter than seven years. As for retail exposures, five years of data might be considered enough. If, however, due to legal or organisational changes, recent data offer a better representation of future loss rates, they might be given more weight than older ones in the analysis of historical LGDs.

Retail portfolios
No foundation approach is available in the case of retail portfolios, and the advanced approach must be adopted by all banks using internal

ratings. Moreover, the Basel Committee states that exposure risks on retail loans with uncertain future drawdown (such as credit cards) may be incorporated into LGD estimates, accounting for the expectation of additional drawings prior to default. In other words, when a bank does not reflect risk on undrawn lines in its EAD estimates, it must reflect this in its LGD estimates. For example, if the bank expects that exposure at default on a retail pool will be 20% higher than current usage, LGD can be increased accordingly (eg, from 50% to 60%) to account for exposure risks without having to establish a formal system of credit conversion factors on undrawn credit lines.

THE ESTIMATION OF LGDs FOR CORPORATE BONDS

Two main methodologies exist for estimating recovery rates. The first one is based on the ratio between the present value, at the time of default, of all payments made on a defaulted debt instrument, and the face value (plus any accrued interest) of this instrument. Analytically, this can be expressed as follows:

$$LGD = 1 - \sum_{t=1}^{T} \frac{\dfrac{\left(FR_t - AC_t\right)}{EAD}}{\left(1+r\right)^t} \qquad (5)$$

where:

- FR_t represents the face (nominal) value of recoveries at time t;
- AC_t represents the amount of costs (legal costs, administrative costs, etc) associated with the recovery process at time t;
- EAD represents the exposure at default;
- r represents the discount rate; and
- t represents time, and T is the last date associated with a recovery inflow.

Assume an investor holds a position in a senior secured bond with a market value of €1 million. Assume that, given its seniority and security, a total recovery amount of €750,000 in five years' time is expected in case of default, with total costs of €50,000 euro. For simplicity, assume that both the recoveries and the costs are entirely obtained and paid at the end of the fifth year. Assuming a 4% discount rate, the value of LGD would be:

$$LGD = \frac{\dfrac{(750{,}000 - 50{,}000)}{1{,}000{,}000}}{(1+0.04)^5} = 40.78\%$$

Three main problems are connected to this method: (i) an appropriate discount rate must be estimated; (ii) a price must be estimated for some instruments, such as equity, residual debt enhancement or even physical assets, that are frequently used as means of repayment by defaulted obligors and that may lack a liquid secondary market to get independent market values; and (iii) the time period from default to final recovery may be very long, thereby negatively affecting the availability of data.

Because of these problems, a second methodology based on the trading price of the defaulted instrument is often used. This method is available for some debt instruments only, such as bonds and large syndicated loans, as standard bank loans lack a secondary market. While the first methodology (present value of post-default repayments) is based on actual recovered amounts and gives rise to *ex post* measures of recovery rates, the second one (trading prices after default) reflects market expectations of future recoveries.

The available empirical evidence on recovery rates for corporate bonds is generally based on the second methodology described above. While the number of empirical studies on recovery rates has increased since the second half of the 1990s, they are still rather limited. Robust estimates of recovery rates can be obtained only if a large number of defaults occur. Given the relatively rare occurrence of default events, this also means that the estimates of recovery rates tend to be based on relatively small empirical samples. In addition to this, since most of the default events involved speculative-grade bonds, estimates of recovery rates for investment grade bonds tend to be rare.

Table 4 reports the results in terms of mean recovery rates – by seniority and security – obtained by four of the main empirical studies based on corporate bond defaults data. All empirical studies confirm that the recovery rate is a direct function of the seniority of the defaulted bond and an indirect function of its degree of

Table 4 Comparison of mean recovery rates from different empirical studies

Study	Senior secured (%)	Senior unsecured (%)	Senior subordinated (%)	Subordinated (%)
Fons (1994)	65	48	40	30
Altman & Kishore (1996)	58	48	34	31
Van de Castle & Keisman (1999)	66	49	37	26
Hu & Perraudin (2002)	53	50	38	33

Table 5 Recovery rates on defaulted bonds

Seniority class	Number of defaults	Mean recovery (%)	Std dev (%)
Senior secured	85	57.89	22.99
Senior unsecured	221	47.65	26.71
Senior subordinated	177	34.38	25.08
Subordinated	214	31.34	22.42
Junior subordinated	–	–	–

Source: Altman & Kishore, 1996

subordination. Results also tend to be rather similar in terms of average recovery rates.

Despite these similar results, which would appear encouraging when one wants to estimate the recovery rate of a bond exposure, two important problems must be highlighted. First, a significant cross-section variability of recovery rates is typically reported by the empirical studies. Table 5 reports more details on one of the above studies, the one by Altman and Kishore, and shows the high standard deviation that characterises recovery rates of bonds with different seniority and subordination. This is indeed always higher than 20%.[12]

Second, recovery rates tend to be unstable over time. Table 6 shows default rate data from 1982 to 2001, as well as the weighted average annual recovery rates and the default loss rate (last column). The sample includes annual averages from about 1,300 defaulted bonds drawn from a database constructed and maintained by

Table 6 Default rates, recovery rates and losses

Year	Par value outstanding (a) (US$ millions)	Par value of defaults (b) (US$ millions)	Default rate (%)	Weighted price after default (recovery rate)	Weighted coupon (%)	Default loss (c) (%)
2001	649,000	63,609	9.80	25.5	9.18	7.76
2000	597,200	30,295	5.07	26.4	8.54	3.95
1999	567,400	23,532	4.15	27.9	10.55	3.21
1998	465,500	7,464	1.60	35.9	9.46	1.10
1997	335,400	4,200	1.25	54.2	11.87	0.65
1996	271,000	3,336	1.23	51.9	8.92	0.65
1995	240,000	4,551	1.90	40.6	11.83	1.24
1994	235,000	3,418	1.45	39.4	10.25	0.96
1993	206,907	2,287	1.11	56.6	12.98	0.56
1992	163,000	5,545	3.40	50.1	12.32	1.91
1991	183,600	18,862	10.27	36.0	11.59	7.16
1990	181,000	18,354	10.14	23.4	12.94	8.42
1989	189,258	8,110	4.29	38.3	13.40	2.93
1988	148,187	3,944	2.66	43.6	11.91	1.66
1987	129,557	1,736	1.34	62.0	12.07	0.59
1986	90,243	3,156	3.50	34.5	10.61	2.48
1985	58,088	992	1.71	45.9	13.69	1.04
1984	40,939	344	0.84	48.6	12.23	0.48
1983	27,492	301	1.09	55.7	10.11	0.54
1982	18,109	577	3.19	38.6	9.61	2.11
Weighted average			4.19	37.2	10.60	3.16

Notes: (a) measured at mid-year, excludes defaulted issues; (b) does not include Texaco's bankruptcy in 1987; (c) includes lost coupon as well as principal loss.
Source: Altman, Brady, Resti, Sironi (2003)

Table 7 Average recovery rates by issuer industry

Industry	Average (%)	Volatility (%)	Number of defaults (%)
Transportation	38.6	27.4	72
Industrial	40.5	24.4	728
Insurance	39.8	21.4	12
Banking	22.6	16.6	25
Public utility	69.6	21.8	57
Finance	45.6	31.2	11
Thrifts	25.6	26.3	20
Securities	15.4	2.0	2
Real estate	25.7	17.2	8
Other non-bank	24.8	15.4	15
Sovereign	56.8	27.4	8

Source: Hu and Perraudin (2002)

the NYU Salomon Center, under the direction of Edward Altman. Note that the average annual recovery is 41.8% (weighted average is 37.2%). However, its value ranges from a minimum of 25.5% (2001) to a maximum of 62% (1987) during this 20-year sample. This variability is a clear evidence of what is generally called "recovery risk", ie, the risk that the *ex post* recovery rate of a bond portfolio is different from what has been originally estimated (*ex ante*).

Finally, it must be stressed that bonds' recovery rates may be industry-specific. Indeed, the business activity of a company dictates the nature of its assets. Other things being equal, firms with more tangible and liquid assets should allow higher recovery rates to their creditors in case of default. Table 7, based on Moody's data, reports average recovery rates by industry of the issuer. Note that these values tend to be significantly different between industries.

THE ESTIMATION OF LGDs FOR BANK LOANS
Past empirical studies
The first study on bank loan recovery rates released by Moody's is due to Carty and Lieberman (1996) and presents two alternative approaches: (1) prices recorded on the market for large syndicated loans soon after default, (2) estimates based on the discounted

Table 8 Recovery estimates on bank loans

Type of loans	N.	Mean (%)	Median (%)	Min (%)	Max (%)	Std dev (%)
Secured (AR)	178	86.7	100.0	7.4	128.7	22.8
Unsecured (AR)	19	79.4	90.0	23.6	100.4	26.6
Secured (MP)	72	72.8	79.75	15.00	98.00	20.97

Source: Carty (1998)

cashflows associated with recoveries occurred after default. The former approach leads to an average recovery rate (on a sample of 58 loans) of 71% and a median of 77%. In the latter, the mean is close to 79%, while the median value is 92%.

The study is subsequently updated by Carty (1998) where secured and unsecured loans are treated separately. For the former, estimates based on actual recoveries (AR) are contrasted with market prices (MP). The main results are summarised in Table 8.

Based on market prices one month after the default, Gupton, Gates and Carty (2000) find mean recovery rates of 69.5% for secured loans, 52.1% for unsecured ones. The same methodology is used by Hamilton (2002) on a sample of secured bank loans, finding an average recovery of 71.3%.

Van de Castle and Keisman (1999) report the results of a study based on about 1,200 defaulted exposures, of which 258 are bank loans. Recovery-rate estimates are based on secondary market prices, adjusted to account for debt/equity and other debt/asset swaps. The average RR is 84.5%. The authors also develop a simple regression model to test the effect on recoveries of different collateral types and of the seniority levels.

Methodological framework for typical bank loans

Although market prices may be available for large syndicated loans, the LGD of most bank loans usually cannot be estimated based on secondary market values, as most distressed exposures tend to stay on the originating bank's books until the recovery process is over. Hence, past data represent the primary source of information on the expected recovery rate of a defaulted loan. Such data must be analysed according to an "economic" definition of

LGDs (see the second section), which also considers all administrative and financial costs connected with the recovery process. Such a definition leads to the following formula:

$$RR = \frac{DNR}{EAD} = \frac{FR}{EAD} \cdot \frac{FR - AC}{FR} \cdot (1+r)^{-T} \tag{6}$$

where RR is the actual recovery rate on a defaulted exposure; DNR is the discounted net value of the recovery, that is, the present value at the time of default of all recovered amounts, net of all costs; EAD is the exposure at default; FR is the face value of the recovered amount, as recorded in the bank's accounting data; AC are the administrative costs connected with the workout procedure on the defaulted exposure; r is a discount rate; and T is the duration of the recovery process.[13] Some components of equation (6) require further clarifications.

The face value of the recovery must comprise any fees collected from the defaulted borrower, including fees from late payment. However, such fees – together with any unpaid late fees included in the bank's income statement – must be added also to the original exposure at default.

Administrative costs should encompass all direct and indirect expenses faced by the bank to collect any payments on the defaulted loan (including the cost of external legal advisers). Note that the factor $(FR - AC)/FR$ describes the incidence of administrative costs per recovered dollar, while the analysis of past data can provide some precious insight into it. The estimation of LGDs on future defaults might also be based on the market price of the recovery services provided by some specialised provider. Actually, since most large banking groups tend to use a dedicated unit (the so-called "bad bank") for the workout of their distressed loans, the internal transfer prices charged by this unit might be used as a guideline to estimate the future impact of administrative costs. For example, if the recovery fees were expressed as a constant share of the recovered amount (ie, if $AC = k\ FR$), then $(FR - AC)/FR$ would simplify to $(1 - k)$.

The discount rate r, to be used in the computation of the present value of FR at the time of default, might be based on historical values, that is, on average market rates observed between the default and the end of the workout process. However, this would clearly lead to a backward-looking measure, which would not account for the present (and future) market conditions. When estimating LGDs on future bad loans, a bank is concerned with the interest rates that might prevail on the market after a new default has surfaced. Since a bank's PDs usually imply a one-year risk horizon, estimated LGDs actually refer to defaults that might emerge one year later. If these considerations are correct, then the use of past interest rates would clearly be irrational and unjustified. Instead, in computing the present value of the recoveries on future defaults, one-year forward interest rates should be used as a quick forecast of the future spot rates. For example, if the expected duration of the recovery process is T years, a T-year forward rate for investments starting one year later ($_1r_T$) should be computed by means of the following formula, which relies on non-arbitrage arguments (see, eg, Hull, 2002):

$$_1r_T = \frac{\left(1+r_{T+1}\right)^{T+1}}{1+r_1} - 1 \tag{7}$$

where r_n denotes the spot rate associated with an n-year maturity. An example of forward rates derived from the current spot curve is shown in Figure 1.[14]

Finally, the duration of the workout process, T, should be computed in a financial sense, accounting for the existence of any intermediate flows. In the case of distressed bank loans, in fact, recoveries might take place only gradually, and different amounts of money might be cashed in at different moments in time. The same might happen with exposures, if the original exposure at default is subsequently adjusted because of late-payment fees, or because some further amount has to be loaded onto the borrower's account (eg, some unpaid discounted receivables). In such cases, the total exposure at default – on which the recovery rate must be computed – will be given by the sum of all partial loadings.

Figure 2 shows an example of multiple loadings and recoveries. The obligor originally defaulted for 100 dollars, but some further 10 dollars were debited on his/her account two months later. The bank managed to recover 35 dollars at the end of the first year, and

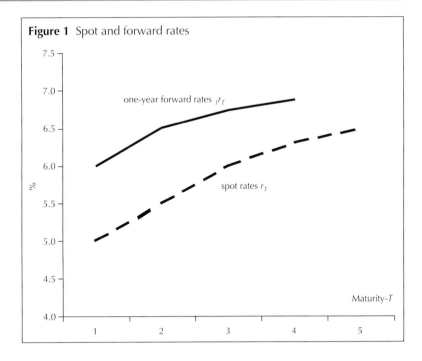

Figure 1 Spot and forward rates

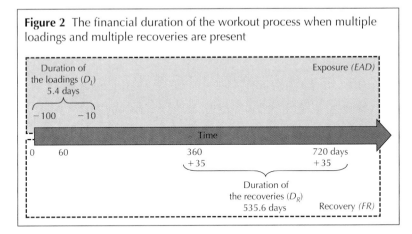

Figure 2 The financial duration of the workout process when multiple loadings and multiple recoveries are present

another 35 dollars at the end of year two. So 110 represents the total EAD, and 70 is the face value of the recovery (FR), according to the bank's accounting books. Although the recovery process seemingly took two years, this would clearly overstate its financial duration.

Actually, since not all loadings (x^-) took place at the beginning of the workout period, the default must not be situated at time zero, but at some intermediate date between 0 and 60 days. Using a flat yield curve and a flat interest rate r of 5% for all maturities, one can easily compute the Macaulay duration of the loadings (D_L):

$$D_L = \frac{\sum_{t=0}^{T} t x_t^- (1+i)^{-t}}{\sum_{t=0}^{T} x_t^- (1+i)^{-t}}$$

$$= \frac{0 \cdot 100 (1+5\%)^{-0/360} + 60.10 (1+5\%)^{-10/360}}{100 (1+5\%)^{-0/360} + 10 (1+5\%)^{-10/360}}$$

$$\cong 5.4 \text{ days}$$

Similarly, the financial duration D_R associated with the total recovery (FR) is not two years; rather, it must be computed as a weighted mean of the maturities associated with the two inflows (x^+). Using Macaulay's formula we obtain:

$$D_R = \frac{\sum_{t=0}^{T} t x_t^+ (1+i)^{-t}}{\sum_{t=0}^{T} x_t^+ (1+i)^{-t}}$$

$$= \frac{360 \cdot 35 (1+5\%)^{-360/360} + 720 \cdot 35 (1+5\%)^{-720/360}}{35 (1+5\%)^{-360/360} + 35 (1+5\%)^{-720/360}}$$

$$\cong 535.6 \text{ days}$$

The financial duration of the workout process, T, to be used equation (6), is then given by

$$T = D_L - D_C = 535.6 - 5.4 = 530.2 \text{ days}^{15}$$

From past data to LGD estimates

Suppose a database of LGDs has been compiled according to the methodology above, based on past data and on some assumptions

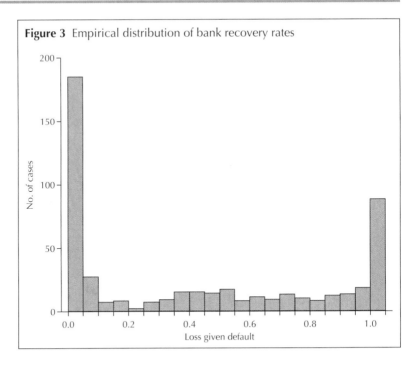

Figure 3 Empirical distribution of bank recovery rates

on future interest rates. The empirical frequency distribution of those values must then be described and summarised by means of some key indicators that will be used to estimate LGDs on potential future defaults.

In principle, one might compute the mean of such a distribution and use it as a rough-and-ready appraisal of future LGDs. However, risk managers usually should not be interested in mean values since only the *deviations from the expected value* represent risk in a strict sense. Moreover, in the case of recovery rates and LGDs the mean happens to be a very poor indicator, as most values tend to cluster near zero and one. This is shown in Figure 3, which is based on the actual data of a medium-sized European bank. In such a U-shaped distribution, the probability of observing values which are close to the mean is dramatically low.

One way to deal with this problem is to use conditional means instead of just one overall average value. The bank should break down the database of past LGDs by identifying some clusters that share similar characteristics and for which the "within" variance in empirical recovery rates is relatively low. Cluster means would

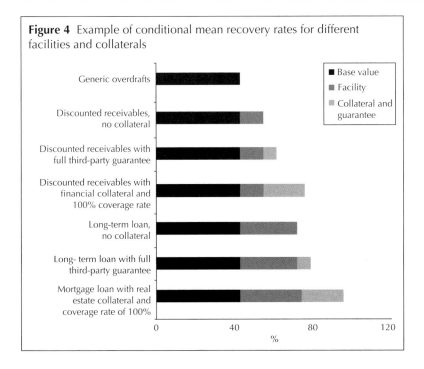

Figure 4 Example of conditional mean recovery rates for different facilities and collaterals

then offer a more reliable approximation of the expected loss rates on different loans.[16]

Such conditional means $\mu(\mathbf{x})$ can be estimated through linear or non-linear least squares, based on a vector $\mathbf{x}$ describing the most significant features of each facility in the LGD database. Those features should include the facility type (eg, overdrafts, discounted receivables, long-term loans), the type of collateral (eg, financial instruments, real estate, physical capital) and its coverage rate, the presence of any guarantees (eg, a guarantee from the borrower's parent company, which might induce him/her to pay back a significant share of the defaulted exposure), and all other factors that are statistically significant in explaining empirical differences among past recovery rates.

The $\mu(\mathbf{x})$ can be expressed as a linear function of the x_is. In this case, the effects on LGD of different factors (eg, of a given facility type and a full collateralisation through Treasury bonds) will be additive, and the conditional average LGD will simply be the sum of the unconditional value plus a set of adjustments (see Figure 4

Table 9 The interaction between exposure and recovery risks: an example

Facilities	(a) Current exposures (US dollars)	(b) Expected EAD per dollar of current exposure (%)	(c) Expected exposure at default (US dollars)	(d) Conditional mean LGD (%)
Discounted receivables	300	54	162	44.8
Five-year mortgage loan	100	100	100	4.1
Overdraft (no collateral)	250	155	387.5	56.8
Total	650		649.5	

for an example). The contributions of the different loan character-istics to the expected recovery rate will then be transparent and easy to assess. However, since a linear function can take any value between minus and plus infinity, conditional means might happen to suggest a loss rate greater than 100%, or even a negative LGD. This clearly counterintuitive behaviour can be avoided if a non-linear function, bounded between 0 and 1 (like the logistic function, or the normal cumulative density function), is used to represent the link between the loan features and $\mu(\mathbf{x})$.

A final caveat is with regard to the fact that LGD values should always be evaluated in the light of a bank's estimates of risk expos-ures. Table 9 reports an example of how those two sets of figures might interact in affecting the overall loss rate associated with a default. Column (a) shows the current exposures associated with the various facilities issued to a borrower, one year before the potential default. Column (b) shows the ratio between EADs and current exposures: discounted receivables tend to decrease (since the borrower's sales slow down as default approaches, and fewer invoices and commercial documents are available for discount), while long-term loans remain virtually unchanged and overdrafts increase significantly (due to a more intense use of loan commit-ments). Column (c) shows the potential exposures at default (com-puted as the product between (a) and (b)). Column (d) reports an estimate of conditional LGDs for the different facilities, based on past empirical data. The average LGD can be computed based on current exposures (a) or, more correctly, on the expected facility mix at default (c). The former approach leads to a value (43%) that is considerably lower than the real one (46%). This shows that even a correct set of LGD estimates might lead to a wrong perception of recovery risk if exposure volatility is not accounted for. Note that in this example total exposure is unchanged, so that no exposure risk seems to emerge, at least on an aggregate basis.

THE LINK BETWEEN PDS AND LGDs
Theoretical framework
As clearly highlighted by the Basel Committee proposals concerning the internal ratings-based (IRB) approach to capital requirements, the key inputs to determine a credit exposure expected loss (EL) and unexpected loss (UL) are represented by the probability of default (PD), the loss given default (LGD) and the exposure at default (EAD).

Each of these three components is stochastic. This is true even for the PD, as its value (although it can be seen as the mean of a binomial variable taking value 1 when the obligor defaults, 0 otherwise) may change over time, depending on the state of the economy, as well as on any change in the idiosyncratic risk of the borrower.

Thus, the expected loss of a credit exposure can be expressed as the product of the means for these three variables:

$$EL = E(EAD) \cdot E(PD) \cdot E(LGD) \tag{8}$$

where $E(\cdot)$ denotes expectations.

Note that, if RR denotes the recovery rate, then:

$$E(LGD) = 1 - E(RR) \tag{9}$$

Moreover, assuming a fixed exposure of €1, the UL can be estimated as follows:

$$UL = \sqrt{\sigma_{PD}^2 \cdot \left[E(LGD)\right]^2 + \left[E(PD)\right]^2 \cdot \sigma_{LGD}^2 + \sigma_{PD}^2 \cdot \sigma_{LGD}^2}. \tag{10}$$

where σ_{LGD}^2 is the variance of the loss given default rate, and σ_{PD}^2 is the variance of the PD.

It is important to note that both equations (8) and (10) are based on the assumption of independence between PD and LGD. Indeed, equation (8) holds only if the three components are not correlated. In fact, the mean of the product of two (or more) random variables equals the product of their means if and only if their correlation is zero. Equation (10) is also based on the assumption that PD and LGD are independent, which implies more specifically that they have no common systematic factor.[17] Testing for the correlation between default and recovery rates is therefore crucial to assess the correctness of the above formulae on which most empirical estimations of both unexpected loss and credit value at risk are based.

Current credit risk models treat PD and LGD as two independent stochastic variables.[18] This is equivalent to considering them as functions of different factors. Indeed, default rates mainly depend on the economic and financial conditions of the issuer/borrower, which in turn are a function of firm specific factors (eg, management, leverage, profitability, liquidity, etc), industry-specific factors (earnings prospects, competition, regulation, barriers to entry, etc) and general economic-cycle conditions. On the other side, recovery rates are well documented to be mainly a function of specific factors such as seniority and security in debt instruments (see Table 4).

Common systematic factors affecting both default rates and recovery rates may exist. These factors can be macroeconomic factors (eg, business failure rates, actual foreign-exchange rate, stock market activity and the economic cycle in general) and firms' asset-value expectations. Indeed, several reasons behind a negative correlation between default and recovery rates can be identified.

❑ *Chain effects*: If default rates increase due to an economic downturn and part of the assets of the defaulting companies are represented by claims/credits to other companies, then a decrease in recovery rates would also follow.
❑ *Financial assets and interest rates*: If the collateral for some specific debt instruments is based on financial assets (eg, fixed-income securities) and default rates increase following a rise in interest rates, then a corresponding decrease in recovery rates could occur.
❑ *Real estate and interest rates*: If the collateral for debt instruments is based on real estate, then an increase in default rates caused

by a recession could be accompanied by a decrease in real estate prices and in recovery rates.

❑ *Industry-specific effects*: If default rates increases in specific industries are caused by decreases in sales/turnover due to product substitution (as it happens, eg, in high-tech or pharmaceutical companies), then a decrease in the value of inventories could also follow. This would in turn lead to a decrease in recovery rates.

These are just a few of the possible reasons behind a negative correlation between default rates and recovery rates. Indeed, recent available empirical evidence indicates that recovery rates for defaulted bonds are correlated with macroeconomic conditions and the aggregate risk of default. Since 1980 recovery rates have decreased at the beginning of business-cycle contractions, as in 1981 and 1990, and increased during economic expansions, as in the mid-eighties and mid-nineties. Even more significant are the data concerning the last four years, from 1999 to 2002, when bond default rates increased and recovery rates significantly decreased (see Table 5).

Following this empirical evidence, new approaches explicitly modelling and empirically investigating the relationship between PD and RR have been developed during the last few years. These include Frye (2000a and 2000b); Jokivuolle and Peura (2000); Jarrow (2001); Altman, Resti and Sironi (2001); Hu and Perraudin (2002) and Bakshi *et al* (2001). Their results are briefly summarised in Panel 4.

Implications for expected and unexpected loss

The most widely used credit pricing and VAR models are based on the assumption of independence between PD and LGD, and treat RR either as a constant parameter or as a stochastic variable independent from PD. In the latter case, RR volatility is assumed to represent an idiosyncratic risk that can be eliminated through adequate portfolio diversification. If, instead, recoveries were treated as correlated with defaults, then their variability would represent a systematic risk factor and should attract a risk premium.

Altman, Resti and Sironi (2001) empirically estimated the effect of a negative correlation between PD and LGD through a simulation

Table 10 Main results of the LGD simulation

	LGD modelled according to approach			% Error*
	(a)	(b)	(c)	
Expected loss	46.26	45.81	59.85	29.4
Standard error	98.17	97.84	127.16	29.5
95% VAR	189.91	187.96	244.86	28.9
99% VAR	435.41	437.08	564.46	29.6
99.5% VAR	549.05	545.83	710.15	29.3
99.9% VAR	809.22	814.52	1053.13	30.1

*Computed as [(c) − (a)]/(a)
Source: Altman, Resti and Sironi (2001)

exercise. They estimated *EL, UL* and value at risk (VAR) of a credit portfolio according to three alternative assumptions: (a) a deterministic (fixed) recovery rate; (b) recovery rates that are stochastic, yet uncorrelated with the probability of default; (c) stochastic RRs, negatively correlated with default probabilities. Introducing this third hypothesis prompts a significant increase (30%) both in risk measures (unexpected losses) and in the expected cost of defaults.

Table 10 shows the main outcomes of this simulation exercise. The first three columns of data show loss and risk indicators obtained under the three approaches discussed above. The last column quantifies the increase in those indicators when we move from the "quiet" world, where no recovery risk is present, to the more "dangerous" one, where default and recovery risk tend to move together. All VAR measures (regardless of the confidence interval chosen), as well as the standard deviation, look considerably underestimated when recovery risk is overlooked.

Note that not only unexpected losses (ie, the standard error and percentiles), but also expected losses, tend to increase materially when shifting from column (a) to (c). This looks especially important since expected losses are generally thought to be computed correctly by multiplying the (long-term) average PD by the expected LGD (see equation (9)). The numbers in Table 10 suggest that such a straightforward practice might not be correct and may seriously understate the actual loss.[19]

Implications for the procyclicality effect

The existence of a negative correlation between default rates and recovery rates also has relevant implications for the issue of procyclicality. Procyclicality involves the impact of the rating distribution of bank portfolios on regulatory capital. Since average ratings and default rates are sensitive to business cycle effects, the new internal ratings-based regulatory capital may be more dependent on the cycle, increasing capital charges, and limiting credit supply right when the economy is slowing.

Since banks adopting the so-called "advanced" IRB approach are free to estimate their own severity rates, they might tend to adjust these estimates according to the economic cycle. As default rates increase and ratings worsen, LGDs could be revised upwards, making Basel capital even more procyclical than expected.

The impact of such a mechanism has been empirically assessed by Resti (2002) through a simulation exercise based on the evolution of a portfolio of 250 bank loans over a 20-year period. He assumed an initial arbitrary rating composition of the loan portfolio and simulated the changes of the bank's portfolio mix according to S&P transition matrices for the period 1980–2000. He measured capital requirements according to both the "corporate" curve presented in the so-called "Consultative Paper 2" or CP2 (Basel Committee on Bank Supervision, 2001a) and the new corporate curve circulated in November 2001 (Basel Committee on Bank Supervision, 2001b).

The simulation showed that when LGDs are free to fluctuate with default rates, the procyclicality effect increases significantly, both for the CP2 curve and the November 2001 curve. Thus, if a positive correlation between default and recovery exists, the procyclicality effects might be even more severe than expected.[20]

PANEL 4 "EVIDENCE OF PD AND LGD CORRELATION"

The model by Frye draws on the conditional approach suggested by Finger (1999) and Gordy (2000). A single systematic factor – the state of the economy – may cause defaults to rise and RRs to decline. The correlation between these two variables, therefore, derives from their common dependence on the systematic factor. The intuition behind Frye's theoretical model is relatively simple: if a borrower defaults on a loan, a bank's recovery may depend on the value of the loan collateral.

The value of the collateral, like the value of other assets, depends on economic conditions. If the economy experiences a recession, RRs may decrease just as default rates tend to increase. This gives rise to a negative correlation between default rates and RRs. The model originally developed by Frye (2000a) implied recovery from an equation that determines collateral. His evidence is consistent with the most recent US bond market data, indicating a simultaneous increase in default rates and LGDs in 1999–2001.[21] Frye's (2000b and 2000c) empirical analysis allows him to conclude that, in a severe economic downturn, bond recoveries might decline 20–25 percentage points from their normal-year average. Loan recoveries may decline by a similar amount, but from a higher level.

Jarrow (2001) presents a new methodology for estimating RRs and PDs implicit in both debt and equity prices. As in Frye (2000a and 2000b), RRs and PDs are correlated and depend on the state of the economy. However, Jarrow's methodology explicitly incorporates equity prices in the estimation procedure, allowing the separate identification of RRs and PDs and the use of an expanded and relevant dataset. In addition, the methodology explicitly incorporates a liquidity premium, which is considered essential in the light of the high variability in the yield spreads between risky debt and US Treasury securities.

A rather different approach was proposed by Jokivuolle and Peura (2000). The authors present a model for bank loans in which collateral value is correlated with the PD. They use the option pricing framework for modelling risky debt – the borrowing firm's total asset value determines the event of default. However, the firm's asset value does not determine the RR. Rather, the collateral value is, in turn, assumed to be the only stochastic element determining recovery. Because of this assumption, the model can be implemented using an exogenous PD, so that the firm's asset value parameters need not be estimated. Assuming a positive correlation between a firm's asset value and collateral value, the authors obtain a similar result to that of Frye (2000a), that actual default rates and recovery rates have an inverse relationship.

Using Moody's historical bond market data, Hu and Perraudin (2002) examine the dependence between recovery rates and default rates. They first standardise the quarterly recovery data in order to filter out the volatility of recovery rates given by the variation over time in the pool of borrowers rated by Moody's. They find that correlations between quarterly recovery rates and default rates for bonds issued by US-domiciled obligors are 0.22 for post-1982 data (1983–2000) and 0.19 for the 1971–2000 period. Using extreme value theory and other non-parametric techniques, they also examine the impact of this negative correlation on credit VAR measures and find that the increase is statistically significant when confidence levels exceed 99%.

Bakshi *et al* (2001) enhance the models presented above to allow for a flexible correlation between the risk-free rate, the default probability and the recovery rate. Based on some preliminary evidence published by rating agencies, they force recovery rates to be negatively associated with default probability. They find some strong support for this hypothesis through the analysis of a sample of BBB-rated corporate bonds. More precisely, their empirical results show that, on average, a 4% worsening in the (risk-neutral) hazard rate is associated with a 1% decline in (risk-neutral) recovery rates.

Altman, Brady, Resti and Sironi (2003) empirically investigate the determinants of bonds' recovery rates and find a negative correlation between default rates and RRs. However, they find that a single systematic risk factor – ie, the performance of the economy – is less predictive than the above-mentioned theoretical models would suggest. They rather emphasise the role played by supply and demand of defaulted bonds in determining aggregate recovery rates. Their econometric univariate and multivariate models assign a key role to the supply of defaulted bonds and show that this variable, together with variables that proxy the size of the high-yield-bond market, explains a substantial proportion of the variance in bond recovery rates aggregated across all seniority and collateral levels.

CONCLUDING REMARKS

LGD represents a key variable for risk managers, affecting the loss profile of a portfolio of credit exposures. While the Basel Committee has developed a rather comprehensive and multi-faceted treatment of this variable in its New Basel Capital Accord (NBCA), leading to relevant implications for capital requirements, the new regulatory framework is not enough to gain a full insight, nor does it provide an appropriate understanding of recovery risk.

Indeed, a credit portfolio manager should be able to: (i) estimate the expected LGDs of the credit exposures of its portfolio based on conditional means; (ii) measure the recovery risk associated with the variability of this stochastic variable; and (iii) understand the relationship between LGD and other risk factors such as PD and EAD.

In this chapter, we tried to assess these problems by analysing the regulatory perspective, the available empirical evidence on LGDs, and the methodological issues associated with their measurement. We started by presenting a definition of LGD and examined the treatment of this risk variable in the standard, foundation and advanced approaches of the NBCA. We then focused on the problem of the LGD estimation. We reported some empirical evidence on past studies, both for corporate bonds and bank loans, and we illustrated the main alternative methodologies that can be (and have been) adopted.

As far as bonds are concerned, we focused on the effects of seniority and subordination, and highlighted the high cross-sectional and temporal variability in the data, a finding that it signals a significant "recovery risk" around the mean. Regarding bank loans, we focused our attention on the methodological problems connected to the estimation of LGD, highlighting the effect of delays on the economic value of recoveries.

We finally moved to the relationship between LGD and other risk factors. On one side, we showed that even a correct set of LGD estimates might lead to a wrong perception of recovery risk if exposure volatility is not accounted for. We also reviewed the growing empirical evidence concerning the correlation between default and recovery rates and analysed the effects that this link exerts on the estimation of expected and unexpected losses of a portfolio. We also looked at the effects of this correlation on procyclicality, an issue that has often been discussed by the regulatory community and by the Basel Committee itself, and concluded that this problem would be exacerbated by the link between PD and LGD.

1   In Creditrisk+ (Credit Suisse Financial, Products, 1997) recoveries are treated as deterministic (meaning that a 100-dollar loan with an expected recovery of 50% can be converted into a 50-dollar loan with fixed, zero recovery). The Creditmetrics methodology (see Gupton, Finger and Bhatia, 1997) simply suggests to generate values for recovery rates from a beta distribution, with mean and variance taken from the historical experience of the bond market; yet, no specific effort is devoted to the analysis of the factors explaining the variance across recovery rates experienced on different facilities, or when different types of collateral had been pledged by the borrower.

2   A collateral haircut is equivalent to a limit on the loan to value ratio, ie, the maximum amount of loan that can be granted against a given amount of collateral in order to retain the risk of the loan at a desired level. Haircuts are present in the Basel Committee's proposals to reform the capital adequacy framework (see the second section).

3   See Van de Castle and Keisman (1999 and 2000) and the fourth section in this chapter for empirical evidence on this point.

4 All references to the new Basel regulation refer to the so-called Third Consultative Package (Basel Committee on Banking Supervision, 2003), the most recent draft available when this chapter was prepared.

5 By "exposure risk" we mean the risk that the exposure at the time of default is higher than what was originally estimated by the bank. Exposure risk comes from the fact that for some kind of credit products, such as credit lines, EAD is a stochastic variable.

6 The (implied) link between the lower capital requirement on residential mortgages and the expected LGD on those loans is made apparent by the fact that, for the reduced weight to be applicable, the Accord requires the existence of a substantial margin of additional security over the amount of the loan. This clearly evokes the "haircut" mechanism (see below) that is explicitly used to adjust the effect on LGD of financial collaterals.

7 Eligible financial collaterals include: cash and deposits issued by the lending bank; gold; bonds with a rating of at least BB– for sovereigns (at least BBB or other issuers); listed senior bonds issued by a bank that is considered of "investment grade" by the supervisors and the recognised external credit assessment institutions; equities included in a main index or (in the comprehensive approach only) listed on a recognised stock exchange; unit trusts and mutual funds having a daily quoted price and investing in the above-mentioned instruments.

8 Note that, for repo-style transactions with core market participants, the haircut may be set to zero, provided that: both the exposure and the collateral are cash or a sovereign security qualifying for a 0% risk weight; no currency mismatch exists between the exposure and the collateral; the transaction is overnight or marked-to-market and remargined daily; the collateral can be liquidated within four days if the counterparty fails to remargin; the transaction is settled across a proven settlement system and governed by standard documentation (specifying that, if the counterparty fails on its obligations, then the transaction is immediately terminable and the collateral can immediately be seized and liquidated).

9 Eligible collaterals are the same as in the standardised approach (see Note 7).

10 Note that the borrower's risk must not be directly dependent on the performance of the property (in other words, the repayment of the facility must not be materially linked to the cash flows generated by the real estate serving as collateral); similarly, the value of the collateral pledged must not be materially dependent on the performance of the borrower. Moreover, the collateral has to be revaluated at least once a year, based on a market fair price.

11 This correlation risk has been addressed also in the foundation approach, by ruling that collaterals be not acceptable if their value is significantly linked to the borrower's creditworthiness (see Note 10).

12 Note that, in case the recovery rate probability distribution were a uniform (rectangular) one, meaning that all values from 0% to 100% of the recovery rate have the same probability to occur, its standard deviation would be approximately equal to 29%. The reported standard deviation results therefore imply a high degree of uncertainty concerning the expected recovery rate.

13 This equation draws upon the seminal work by Altman (1977) and represents an alternative way to express equation (5).

14 One might wonder what spot curves (risk-free or risk-adjusted) should be used in the computation of forward rates. In our opinion, if the uncertainty on the actual recovery rate on future defaults is already accounted for by other tools (namely, by estimating the whole probability distribution of all possible values of FR/EAD and T, and not just their expected values), then the use of risk-adjusted rates would be overly conservative, and the risk-free curve would represent a more adequate solution. If, however (as it happens in most banks), FR/EAD and T are estimated based on mean values (usually conditional on facility type and collateral), then a risk-adjusted curve (eg, for speculative-grade bonds) looks advisable and more consistent with the goals of a "risk-averted" model.

15 Note that the recovery rate based on an exposure (EAD) of 110, a nominal recovery (FR) of 70 and a duration (T) of 530.2 days is identical to the recovery rate computed by discounting the single cash flows in Figure 3, that is:

$$RR = \frac{\sum_{t=0}^{T} x_t^+ (1+i)^{-t}}{\sum_{t=0}^{T} x_t^- (1+i)^{-t}} = \frac{35(1+5\%)^{-360/360} + 35(1+5\%)^{-720/360}}{100(1+5\%)^{-0/360} + 10(1+5\%)^{-60/360}} = \frac{65}{109.0} \cong 59.2\%$$

16 The distribution of the residuals around cluster means might also be estimated, if each cluster contains a large enough number of observations. Due to the U-shaped probability distribution of LGDs and recovery rates, beta distributions have often been used (see, eg, Gupton, Finger and Bhatia, 1997; Crouhy *et al*, 2001); non-parametric beta kernel methods have also been suggested (Renault and Scaillet, 2003) to estimate the probability distribution without imposing too much structure on the data.

17 If this were not the case, then the covariance between the two variables should also be considered and the resulting UL would be higher in case of positive correlation. Note that a positive correlation between PD and LGD is equivalent to a negative correlation between default rates and recovery rates.

18 See Altman, Resti and Sironi (2001) for a detailed analysis of the way alternative credit risk models treat the relationship between PD and LGD.

19 Another noteworthy result is that no significant differences arise when moving from column (a) to (b): in other words, when recovery rates are considered stochastic, but independent on each other, the law of large numbers ensures that all uncorrelated risks can be effectively disposed of.

20 Moreover, simulation results showed that the procyclicality effect is driven more by up- and downgrades, rather than by default rates; in other words, adjustments in credit supply needed to comply with capital requirements seem to respond mainly to changes in the structure of weighted assets, and only to a minor extent to actual credit losses.

21 Hamilton, Gupton and Berthault (2001) provide clear empirical evidence of this phenomenon.

BIBLIOGRAPHY

Altman, E., B. Brady, A. Resti, and A. Sironi, 2003, "The Relationship Between Default and Recovery Rates: Theory, Empirical Evidence and Implications", *Journal of Business*, forthcoming.

Altman, E. I., 1977, "Some Estimates of the Cost of Lending Errors for Commercial Banks", *Journal of Commercial Bank Lending*, **60**, pp. 51–68.

Altman, E. I., 2001, "Altman High Yield Bond and Default Study", Salomon Smith Barney, US Fixed Income High Yield Report, July.

Altman, E., A. Resti, and A. Sironi, 2001, "Analysing and Explaining Default Recovery Rates", unpublished Research Report, ISDA.

Altman, E. I., and V. M. Kishore, 1996, "Almost Everything You Wanted to Know About Recoveries on Defaulted Bonds", *Financial Analysts Journal*, November/December.

Bakshi, G., D. Madan, and F. Zhang, 2001, "Understanding the Role of Recovery in Default Risk Models: Empirical Comparisons and Implied Recovery Rates", Finance and Economics Discussion Series, 2001-37, Federal Reserve Board of Governors, Washington D.C.

Basel Committee on Banking Supervision, 2001a, "The Basel Capital Accord", Consultative Paper, Bank for International Settlements, January.

Basel Committee on Banking Supervision, 2001b, "Potential Modifications to the Committee's Proposals", Bank for International Settlements, Basel, November.

Basel Committee on Banking Supervision, 2003, "Consultative Document – The New Basel Capital Accord", Mimeo, Bank for International Settlements, April.

Carty, L. V., and D. Lieberman, 1996, "Defaulted Bank Loan Recoveries", Special Report, Moody's Investors Service, November.

Carty, L. V., 1998, "Defaulted Bank Loan Recoveries", Special Report, Moody's Investors Service, June.

Credit Suisse Financial Products, 1997, "CreditRisk+. A Credit Risk Management Framework", Technical Document.

Crouhy, M., D. Galai, and R. Mark, 2001, *Risk Management* (New York: McGraw-Hill).

Finger, C., 1999, "Conditional Approaches for CreditMetrics Portfolio Distributions", *CreditMetrics Monitor*, April.

Fons, J., 1994, "Using Default Rates to Model the Term Structure of Credit Risk", *Financial Analysts Journal*, September–October, 25–32.

Fridson, M. S., C. M. Garman, and K. Okashima, 2000, "Recovery Rates: The Search for Meaning", Merril Lynch & Co, High Yield Strategy.

Frye, J., 2000a, "Collateral Damage", *Risk*, pp. 91–4, April.

Frye, J., 2000b, "Collateral Damage Detected", Federal Reserve Bank of Chicago, Working Paper, *Emerging Issues Series*, pp. 1–14, October.

Frye, J., 2000c, "Depressing Recoveries", *Risk*, November.

Gordy, M., 2000, "A Comparative Anatomy of Credit Risk Models", *Journal of Banking and Finance*, pp. 119–49, January.

Gupton, G. M., D. Gates, and L. V. Carty, 2000, "Bank Loan Loss Given Default", Moody's Investors Service, Global Credit Research, November.

Gupton, G. M., C. C. Finger, and M. Bhatia, 1997, "CreditMetrics – Technical Document" (New York: JP Morgan).

Hamilton, D. T., 2002, "Default and Recovery Rates of Corporate Bond Issuers", Moody's Investors Service, February.

Hamilton, D. T., G. M. Gupton, and A. Berthault, 2001, "Default and Recovery Rates of Corporate Bond Issuers: 2000", Moody's Investors Service, February.

Hull, J. C., 2002, *Options, Futures, and Other Derivatives* (4th edn) (New York: Prentice-Hall, Finance Series).

Hu, Y.-T., and W. Perraudin, 2002, "The Dependence of Recovery Rates and Defaults", BirkBeck College, mimeo, February.

Jarrow, R. A., 2001, "Default Parameter Estimation Using Market Prices", *Financial Analysts Journal*, **57(5)**, pp. 75–92.

Jokivuolle, E., and S. Peura, 2000, "A Model for Estimating Recovery Rates and Collateral Haircuts for Bank Loans", Bank of Finland Discussion Papers 2.

Renault, O., and O. Scaillet, 2003, "On the way to recovery: A nonparametric bias free estimation of recovery rate densities", Hautes Études Commerciales, Genève DP 2003.10.

Resti, A., 2002, *The New Basel Capital Accord: Structure, possible Changes, micro- and macro-economic Effects* (Brussels: Centre for European Policy Studies).

Van de Castle, K., and D. Keisman, 1999, "Recovering Your Money: Insights Into Losses From Defaults", Standard & Poor's *CreditWeek*, 16 June.

Van de Castle, K., and D. Keisman, 2000, "Suddenly Structure Mattered: Insights into Recoveries of Defaulted ", Standard & Poor's *Corporate Ratings*, 24 May.

Section 2

Implementation and Testing of Compliant IRB Systems

5

Implementation of an IRB Compliant Rating System

Sebastian Fritz, Michael Luxenburger and Thomas Miehe

Deutsche Bank Group

INTRODUCTION

Numerous publications exist regarding Basel II and the related issue on credit rating, but they concentrate on very specific topics. Our objective in this chapter is to compile all aspects that are relevant to the implementation of a rating system, which is compliant with Basel II. We start with general considerations on the assessment horizon, data quality and default definition, describe several measures for the separation power, and the assignment of probabilities of default (PD).[1]

We then elaborate how to derive rating methodologies based on econometric approaches, expert systems and hybrid systems. Using these techniques, we then explain how to derive ratings for retail, corporate, bank, (sub-) sovereign exposure and specialised lending.[2]

A separate section describes the additional risk components such as exposure at default (EAD) and loss given default (LGD) and how to come up with a calibration and validation for the advanced approach.

Finally, an approach on how to structure a Basel II implementation project is outlined. This includes sections for the validation on different aggregate levels in terms of expected loss (EL), risk parameters, rating, score, etc. The nomenclature we used here and the bibliography are listed at the end of the chapter.

When we talk about rating in this chapter, we define it as the (objective) assessment of the present and the future economic situation (solvency, for instance) of customers. This assessment is often designated in a letter code, eg, AAA, BB, etc.

However, different rating levels have to be distinguished by:

❑ individual solvency (result: rating-class and expected default probability);
❑ product- or collateral-specific solvency (result: expected loss); and
❑ portfolio dependent solvency (result: unexpected loss).

Many banks already use rating systems, since an objective assessment of the client's default risk is a prerequisite of what follows:

1. Who can decide on the transaction? (credit authority);
2. What amount should be extended? (expected loss and economic capital);
3. At what margin should the loan be granted? (expected loss and economic capital);
4. How can the loan be monitored? (changes in score, expected loss, economic capital);
5. How should the loan be accounted for? (credit reserves);
6. How can potential concentrations be measured? (economic capital);
7. How can loan portfolios be managed? (securitisations);
8. Is there any more credit-related business with that client? (marketing and sales support).

One can therefore clearly say that, irrespective of the Basel II process, ratings have become a central part of modern credit risk management within banks.

Why Basel II?

Basel II is designed to extend and refine the current regulatory approach (Basel I) used in measuring credit and operational risk.

Its main goals are:

❑ to maintain the current level of capital in the financial system while creating incentives for a risk-sensitive management; and
❑ to reduce the possibility for regulatory capital arbitrage.

In addition, Basel II used a one factor credit risk model to calibrate risk weights which should result in a stronger convergence between regulatory and economic capital.[3]

The Basel II framework is based on external (standard approach) or internal ratings (foundation and advanced approach). In this chapter we will describe our view of the ingredients needed to comply with the Basel II advanced approach.

RATING DEVELOPMENT AND VALIDATION TECHNIQUES
Introduction
Assessment horizon
The assessment horizon is the time period that is considered in a risk assessment, rating decision or credit decision. Traditionally, it is equivalent to the lifetime of either specific transactions or customer relations with credit exposure (or the suitable part of it in case of long-term exposures). Ideally, it should be at least as long as the minimum commitment period (ie, until the bank can exit). In reality, a one year time horizon is chosen for most ratings (typical time span in which the bank re-rates the client).

The PD is a measure of the expected probability that a default occurs. In order to avoid confusion regarding the exact meaning of the PD, we have to distinguish between the following definitions:

❑ One-year PD: Expected probability that the default occurs within the next twelve months. It is strictly related to the rating of, for example, the counterparty or a specific deal.
❑ Cumulative or multi-year PD for k years: Expected probability that the default occurs within the next k years. One common approach to model these PDs is the introduction of a migration matrix to account for the possibility that the rating can change over time. However, the migration matrix method comprises questionable assumptions, eg, that the applied matrix

represents the migration pattern for any given year (time homo-geneity). In addition, this approach assumes that the migration pattern is Markovian, which empirically does not hold true, specifically for the migration matrices published by external rating agencies. As an alternative, one could also introduce a maturity adjustment factor that depends linearly on the maturity and non-linearly on the PD (as it is done in the Basel II formula).

❏ PD for time periods of up to one year: expected probability that the default occurs within $n < 12$ months. One common approach to model these PDs is to introduce a so-called *time adjustment factor* (TAF). For capital calculation purposes one typ-ically uses a TAF that takes the replacement of assets with tenors less than one year into account. The corresponding PD is then calculated by multiplying the one-year PD by TAF and the tenor as a fraction of a year.

❏ Conditional (forward) PD for year k: expected probability that the default will occur exactly during year k.

On one hand, the one-year horizon is the common approach for planning purposes, ie, for the calculation of EL and EC, based on the financial year as the "natural" period and definitions imposed by the regulators. It usually is also accepted as a reasonable time to react and reduce or exit exposure. The one-year horizon obviously uses one-year PDs for the EL calculation.

On the other hand, the credit decision, ie, the decision to add an exposure to the portfolio, has to be based on an estimate of the credit quality over the total lifetime. For pricing purposes EL and EC over the lifetime of a transaction have to be calculated to esti-mate the profitability of a transaction. The lifetime EL is also used to determine the required credit approval level. This multi-year approach requires multi-year PDs for every rating class.

The different time horizon of these two approaches might imply some inconsistencies. Optimising the one-year PD might lead to the fact that multi-year effects are not taken into account. Taking into account all effects until maturity might lead to the fact that the discriminatory power of the one-year PD gets worse.

As a typical example of that effect, we would like to mention commercial real estate financing. Empirical default frequencies in the first year after application are usually zero. However, the commercial real estate loans carry a different (ie, much higher) credit risk on a five-year time horizon.

Different rating approaches
There exists a variety of approaches to find and weigh relevant information for assessing the creditworthiness of a counterparty. They can be categorised into *non-standardised* and *standardised* approaches.

As an example of a non-standardised approach, the five common Cs of credit analysis are described by:

❑ character (reputation of a firm);
❑ capital (leverage);
❑ capacity (volatility of earnings);
❑ collateral; and
❑ cycle (especially for cycle-dependent industries).

There is no fixed predetermined set of criteria the analyst recognises. The criteria might be different for every individual counterparty.

This approach is easy to implement and depends on the know-how of the analyst. On the flip side, development is both expensive and time-consuming, and the resulting analysis is not founded on a sound statistical basis. In addition, the quality depends only on the analyst's know-how. Such non-standardised approaches are usually used by credit rating agencies. Although regulators seem to accept this approach, we will not describe the development of such a rating methodology in detail.

Standardised approaches determine relevant factors that discriminate between "good" and "bad" firms in each single segment. In a second step, these factors are weighted and combined. These factors and weighted combinations form the basis for each rating analysis. The standardised approach itself is separated into expert systems and econometric techniques.

For expert systems, the peculiarity of each criterion is assessed by a credit analyst based on certain guidelines. Thus, these rating methodologies still carry some subjectivity.

Econometric techniques are developed by using statistics. In most cases, they are based on so-called hard facts (eg, financial data, marital status, etc.). However, it may sometimes be necessary to allow some rules to be overruled due to the fact that the credit officer might have additional relevant information not covered by the econometric model prediction.

Data quality and default definition

The Basel Committee on Banking Supervision (Basel Committee on Banking Supervision, 2003) defines default on a counterparty level, whereas some default criteria are monitored on a transaction level. In principle, two events trigger the default of a counterparty. They are:

❏ the obligor is unable to make a timely payment of its credit obligations to the banking group in full; or
❏ the obligor is past due for more than a fixed set of days on any material credit obligation to the banking group.

Indicators for the inability to pay include:

❏ The bank puts the credit obligation on non-accrual status.
❏ The bank makes a charge-off or account-specific provision.
❏ The bank sells the credit obligation at a material credit-related economic loss (distressed sale).
❏ The bank consents to a distressed restructuring of the credit obligation (also known as troubled debt restructuring (TDR)).
❏ The bank has filed for the obligor's bankruptcy.
❏ The obligor has sought or has been placed in bankruptcy or similar protection.

One should keep in mind that a bank's internal historical default data might not be based on the current Basel II definition of default. Furthermore, this default definition might not be appropriate for some business areas such as project finance and structural loans.[4]

In addition, some of the default criteria are subjective. The process to assign a specific provision might change over time based on a modification of policies or even change of accounting standards. Therefore, risk provisions might not be comparable directly for different years and probably not at all for different banks. Thus, the first step for rating development is the generation of a proper default history.

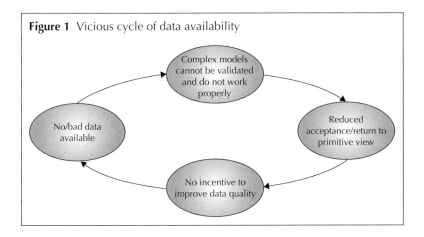

Figure 1 Vicious cycle of data availability

The vicious cycle

This so called vicious cycle is defined as the following:

Without data or with poor data quality complex models cannot be validated. Without validation, models do not work properly and the acceptance by the business areas is reduced. So, there is no incentive to improve data quality (see Figure 1).

Even if longer time series of data are available, some quantities requiring a lot of data (eg, correlations) or describing rare events (eg, joint default probabilities) cannot be validated to a satisfactory level.

The possibilities to break that cycle are management intervention and one-off data collection or the modification of systems and processes such that additional data can be captured on a timely basis. Whereas the latter approach might be costly (changes to legacy systems!) and will take some time (many transactions have to be captured in the amended system), the first approach will deliver data within a short timeframe but will not help to continuously capture additional information as they arrive.

Measures for separation power

Development and validation of a rating system can be separated into two steps: analysis of the separation power and assignment of a PD (or EL ratio or UL ratio). For the separation power, the following measures are common.

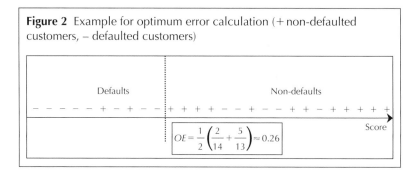

Figure 2 Example for optimum error calculation (+ non-defaulted customers, – defaulted customers)

1. Optimum error

The optimum error (*OE*) is the minimum of the average classification error of the sample obtained at the so-called optimal cut-off score:

$$OE = \frac{1}{2}\left(\frac{non\_defaults\_incorrect}{all\_non\_defaults} + \frac{defaults\_incorrect}{all\_defaults}\right)$$

where *non_defaults_incorrect* and *defaults_incorrect* denote the number of non-defaulted customers classified as defaulted and the number of defaulted customers classified as non-defaulted, respectively. The number *defaults_incorrect* represents a type I error and *non_defaults_incorrect* represents a type II error. The closer *OE* is to zero, the better the defaulting customers are separated from non-defaulting ones.

This measure makes no model assumptions as to the score distributions of the sample. However, the value of *non_defaults_incorrect* is hardly determinable, since usually all applications classified as defaulted are rejected and, thus, the future behaviour cannot be observed. Note that this measure can only be used for rating methodologies with more than two classes if all rating classes are put into a default and non-default class (eg, AAA−B−> Non-default, CCC and below −> default).

2. Alpha/beta error (or discriminant classification error)

Based on the cut-off score of a discriminant analysis (eg, provided by the so-called Mahalanobis distance) the classification error of both defaulted and non-defaulted customers can be calculated.

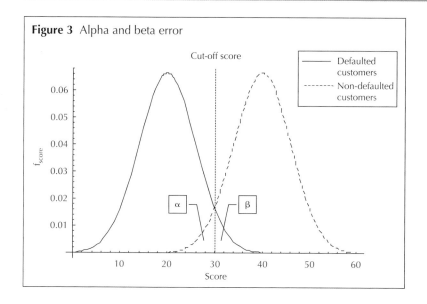

Figure 3 Alpha and beta error

We denote the percentage of defaulted customers classified as non-defaulted by α, and the percentage of non-defaulted customers classified as defaulted by β. The discriminant classification error (*DCE*) is then calculated by:

$$DCE = \frac{\alpha + \beta}{2} \in [0,1]$$

The closer *DCE* is to zero, the better the defaulting customers are separated from non-defaulting ones.

There are two drawbacks. It is assumed that the sample is normally distributed and the classification error β is hardly determinable (see the explanation for "Optimum error" above). Similar to the optimum error, this measure can only be used for rating methodologies with more than two classes if mapped into two classes.

3. Gini-coefficient

The Gini-coefficient describes the normalised area between the Lorenz-curve and the diagonal. The sample is sorted by observations

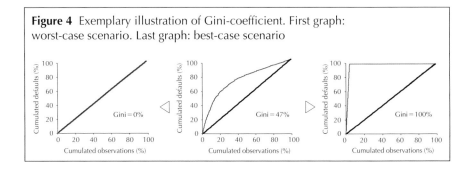

Figure 4 Exemplary illustration of Gini-coefficient. First graph: worst-case scenario. Last graph: best-case scenario

(score or rating classes). In case discrete observations are given, this area is calculated in the following way:

$$A = \frac{\sum_{i=1}^{n} \left(obs_{\text{cum},n} - obs_{\text{cum},i} \right) \cdot bad_i}{obs_{\text{cum},n} \sum_{i=1}^{n} bad_i}$$

where *bad* denotes the number of defaulted customers and obs_{cum} is defined as:

$$obs_{\text{cum},i} = \sum_{j=1}^{i} obs_j.$$

The Gini-coefficient is then calculated by

$$Gini = |2A - 1|.$$

The range of the continuous Gini-coefficient is [0,1]. The closer the Gini-coefficient is to one, the better are defaulted customers separated from non-defaulting ones. For the continuous framework refer Fritz, Popken and Wagner (2002).

4. Coefficient of concordance
For the calculation of the Gini-coefficient the cumulated defaulted customers are plotted against the cumulated observations in the

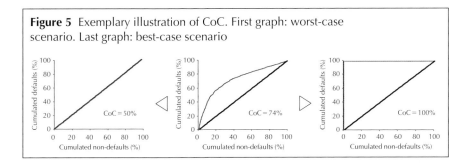

Figure 5 Exemplary illustration of CoC. First graph: worst-case scenario. Last graph: best-case scenario

definition of the Lorenz-curve. As an alternative the cumulated defaults can be plotted against the cumulated non-defaulted observations. This leads to the calculation of the so-called Coefficient of Concordance (CoC):

$$CoC = \frac{\sum_{i=1}^{n} \left(good_{\text{cum},n} - good_{\text{cum},i} \right) \cdot bad_i}{good_{\text{cum},n} \sum_{i=1}^{n} bad_i}$$

with *good* denotes the number of non-defaulted customers and $good_{\text{cum}}$ is given by:

$$good_{\text{cum},i} = \sum_{j=1}^{i} good_j$$

The range of the CoC is [0.1]. The closer the CoC is to one, the better are defaulted customers separated from non-defaulting ones. For CoC below 0.5, the ordering is in the wrong direction, ie, the bad counterparties get a good score value.

The CoC, as well as the Gini-coefficient, can be calculated if the dependent variable is binary (ie, default or non-default). However, there are samples with limited default but rank information like external ratings instead. Hence, the dependent variable is not binary any more. In such circumstances prognosis power can be described as the availability of the rating model to meet the given ordering (eg, by external ratings). We describe a measure for rank correlation, hereafter called modified CoC ($mCoC$), quantifying such a prognosis power.

Let N denote the number of pairs (i,j) where i and j denote two observations with different response, ie, $external(i) <> external(j)$. We introduce the following classification:

❑ $internal(i) < internal(j)$ and $external(i) < external(j)$: (i,j) is called concordant,
❑ $internal(i) < internal(j)$ and $external(i) > external(j)$: (i,j) is called discordant,
❑ $internal(i) = internal(j)$ and $external(i) <> external(j)$: (i,j) is called tie.

Let N, N_c and N_t denote the number of total, concordant and tie pairs, respectively. Then the modified CoC is calculated by:

$$mCoC = \frac{N_c + 0.5 \cdot N_t}{N}$$

The range of the $mCoC$ is $[0,1]$. The closer $mCoC$ is to one, the better the internal output meets the external one over all customers. One can question whether the factor 0.5 in the nominator is appropriate. The idea behind that factor (primarily for the CoC) is that, in case of the same internal score/rating, one tosses a coin and bases the decision on that result. However, since average PDs are not around 50%, the replacement of 0.5 by the average PD is more appropriate. We omit to deduce a more appropriate treatment of tie pairs in case of a dependent variable with more than two values.

5. Brier score

Glenn W. Brier (see Brier, 1950) introduced a verification score or to be more precise a verification error for weather forecasts defined by

$$err_{Brier} = \frac{1}{n} \sum_{j=1}^{r} \sum_{i=1}^{n} \left(p_{ij} - \delta_{ij} \right)^2$$

where n denotes the number of observations, r is the number of categories in which observations can occur, and p_{ij} is the probability that the observation i will occur in category j. The binary variable δ_{ij} takes the value 1 (observation i occurred in category j) or 0 (observation i did not occur in category j). The smaller the Brier score, the better the forecasts: $err_{Brier} = 0$ is the result of perfect forecasting, whereas the worst possible forecasting results in $err_{Brier} = 2$.

In the context of credit risk this score can be simplified. Considering only two categories, "default" and "non-default", leads to:

$$err_{Brier} = \frac{2}{n} \sum_{i=1}^{n} \left(p_i - \delta_i \right)^2$$

where n denotes the number of customers within the portfolio under consideration, and p_i is the default probability of the rating class the customer i is assigned to. We set $\delta_i = 1$ if customer i defaulted, and $\delta_i = 0$, if not. Taking the total default probability P of the portfolio instead of individual p_i, the expected Brier score is calculated by:

$$E\left[err_{Brier} \right] = E\left[\frac{2}{n} \sum_{i=1}^{n} \left(P - \delta_i \right)^2 \right] = 2\left(P - P^2 \right) \xrightarrow[P \to 0 \, \vee \, P \to 1]{} 0$$

This is a drawback of the Brier score. For most of the credit portfolios, total default probabilities are rather small. Using them instead of individual default probabilities results in small Brier scores already. This reduces the effectiveness of the Brier score.

In addition, this measure has a more general drawback. It compares a default probability of a rating class taking values in the interval [0,1] with a binary variable depending on the default or non-default (and nothing in between) of single customers. This is a kind of "apples and oranges" comparison. A more appropriate approach is to compare the default probability of a rating class with the observed default frequency (ODF) of this class. This leads to a modification of the Brier score:

$$err_{Brier}^{mod} = \frac{2}{n} \sum_{i=1}^{m} \left(p_i - ODF_i \right)^2$$

where m denotes the number of rating classes under consideration. Please note that this modification is nothing more than the mean square error of forecast times two.

6. Wilks' lambda

Let $i \in \{0,1\}$ denote the group of non-defaulted and defaulted customers, respectively. To each customer $j \in \{1, \dots, n_i\}$ a $score_{ij}$ is assigned. The sum of squares between these two groups ($ss_{between}$) and the sum of squares within each of these groups (ss_{within}) are calculated in the following way:

$$ss_{between} = \sum_{i=0}^{1} n_i \left(\overline{score_i} - \overline{score} \right)^2 \text{ and}$$

$$ss_{within} = \sum_{i=0}^{1} \sum_{j=1}^{n_i} \left(score_{ij} - \overline{score_i} \right)^2$$

where

$$\overline{score} = \frac{1}{n} \sum_{i=0}^{1} \sum_{j=1}^{n_i} score_{ij} \text{ and } \overline{score_i} = \frac{1}{n_i} \sum_{j=1}^{n_i} score_{ij} \text{ for } i \in \{0,1\}$$

Wilks' lambda Λ_{Wilks} is defined by:

$$\Lambda_{Wilks} = \frac{ss_{within}}{ss_{between}}$$

The closer Wilks' lambda Λ_{Wilks} is to zero, the better the defaulting customers are separated from non-defaulting ones. One major drawback: it is assumed that both groups are normally distributed.

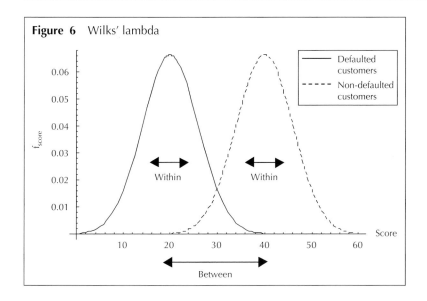

Figure 6 Wilks' lambda

7. Information value
A similar measure to Wilks' lambda is called information value (IV). It is defined as:

$$IV = \frac{\mu_G - \mu_B}{\sigma_G \sigma_B}$$

where μ and σ are mean and standard deviation for non-defaulted (good) and defaulted (bad) clients, respectively. As with Wilks' lambda, normality is assumed here.

WHICH RATINGS FOR WHICH SEGMENT
Ratings based on econometric approaches
Due to the normally large number of customers, statistical methods are well suited for the development of rating systems for retail customers. Therefore, a large variety of economic approaches to the development of retail scorecards exists, ranging from simple linear discriminant analysis or logistic regression to kernel density methods, generalised additive methods or neural networks. For a brief overview on these methods, refer to Fritz, Popken and Wagner (2002).

As an example case for scorecard development, this section focuses on the logistic regression that is one of the standard approaches. The logistic regression directly models the default probability as a function of the input variables $(x_1, x_2, \ldots, x_p) = x \in \mathfrak{R}^p$.

To simplify the notation, we define for each observation i a variable $y^{(i)}$:

$$y^{(i)} = \begin{cases} 1 : i \in B \\ 0 : i \in G \end{cases} \tag{1}$$

where B and G denote the set of defaulted (bad) and non-defaulted (good) customers.

The probability of observation i being in set B or in set G is denoted by $\pi^{(i)} = p(B|x^{(i)})$ and $1 - \pi^{(i)} = p(G|x^{(i)})$, respectively. Assuming that the observations are independent, the probability (likelihood) of the observed situation of the training sample T is then given by

$$L = \prod_{i \in T} (\pi^{(i)})^{y^{(i)}} \cdot (1 - \pi^{(i)})^{1 - y^{(i)}} \tag{2}$$

In the next step for defining a model, we would like the probabilities $\pi^{(i)}$ to depend on the vector of observed variables

$$\pi^{(i)} = \beta^T x^{(i)} \tag{3}$$

where $\beta \in \mathfrak{R}^p$ is a vector of regression coefficients. One problem with this model is that the range of the left-hand side of (3) is limited to [0,1] while the predictor on the right-hand side can take any real value. Therefore, the right-hand side is transformed using a monotonous function $h : \mathfrak{R} \rightarrow [0,1]$

$$\pi^{(i)} = h(\beta^T x^{(i)}) \tag{4}$$

or, equivalently,

$$g(\pi^{(i)}) = \beta^T x^{(i)}, \; g = h^{-1} \tag{5}$$

with $g(h(\eta)) = \eta$ for all $\eta \in \mathfrak{R}$. g is called a *link function*. Typical choices for g are the logit-function

$$g(\pi^{(i)}) = \log\left(\frac{\pi^{(i)}}{1-\pi^{(i)}}\right), \; h(\eta) = \frac{1}{1+\exp(-\eta)} \qquad (6)$$

and the probit function

$$g(\pi^{(i)}) = \Phi^{-1}(\pi^{(i)}), \; \Phi(\eta) = (2\pi)^{-1/2} \int\limits_{-\infty}^{\eta} \exp(-t^2/2) \; dt.$$

Given a link function g, the parameters β are constructed such that the probability of the observed response situation is maximised. Therefore, in (2) $\pi^{(i)}$ is replaced by (4) and the parameters β are chosen such that the logarithm of the likelihood

$$\log L = \sum_{i \leq n} y^{(i)} \log(h(\beta^T x^{(i)})) + (1-y^{(i)}) \log(1-h(\beta^T x^{(i)}))$$

is maximised. This technique is called maximum likelihood estimation. The score value for an observation i resulting from the generalised linear model is then given by

$$score^{(i)} = \beta^T x^{(i)} \qquad (7)$$

where $x^{(i)}$ denotes the values of the input variables for observation i and β is the vector of regression parameters. Combining (4), (6) and (7) leads to a default probability estimate for observation i

$$\pi^{(i)} = h(\beta^T x^{(i)}) = h(score^{(i)}) = \frac{1}{1+\exp(-score^{(i)})} \qquad (8)$$

For more theoretical background information please refer to Fahrmeier, Hamerle and Tutz (1996).

Retail scorecards

As described in the previous section, a typical retail scorecard consists of a linear combination of certain input variables to a score value that is then often transformed into a default probability (see next section). The input variables can be derived from different information areas and sources such as:

❏ socio-demographic data (age, marital status, job position, region, etc);
❏ financial information (income, liabilities, instalments, assets, etc);
❏ account data (limit, average balance, credits, debits, etc); and
❏ external data (credit history, credit cards, default events, etc).

Sometimes loan-type products and collateral characteristics are included in the scorecard. This may result in different default probability if the same customers apply for two different loan products (eg, a mortgage and an instalment loan). One should therefore try to use only client-specific and not loan-specific information (such as collateral) for PD scorecards and then estimate the LGD component separately.

One can distinguish between application and behaviour score. The application scorecard uses data that is typically available at the time of the loan application. This is often socio-demographic data, financial information from the customer and external data. On the other hand, the behaviour score is based on data that are regularly updated, such as the account data and maybe some external (eg, credit registries) or socio-demographic data. As application and behaviour scores might estimate different default probabilities for the same customer, the separation of application and behaviour score might lead to inconsistent results. We, therefore, favour a smooth transition from application to behaviour score as proposed in Fritz, Popken and Wagner (2002). However, if only an application score is available, the score to PD transformation has to depend on the vintage of the application. Several years after application, the application score usually differentiates good and bad customers only to a low extent. This mapping (score, vintage) to PD can be used to derive the average PD of a sub-portfolio. For retail sub-portfolios with a high rollover frequency (eg, for products with tenor of three to six months), the future PD distribution of the portfolio has to be estimated. This clearly has to take into account credit policy, current risk appetite of the institution and other circumstances that influence credit decisions.

The issues mentioned above are also valid for small and medium enterprises' (SME) scorecards and, to a lesser extent, for corporate score systems.

Assignment of PDs
The assignment of a default probability to each rating class is called calibration. Initially the sample has to be arranged in increasing or decreasing score order. Then it has to be divided into buckets (rating classes). This can be based on one of the following criteria: each bucket contains a fixed number or portion of customers or each bucket has a predefined score range.

The easiest way to assign default probabilities to each rating class is known as direct calibration. For each bucket the observed default frequency (ODF) is calculated. Let all_k denote the total number of customers in rating class $k \in \{1, \dots, n\}$, where $defaults_k$ denotes the number of defaulted customers in this rating class. If $all_k > 0$, then

$$ODF_k = \frac{defaults_k}{all_k}, \text{else } ODF_k = 0, \quad \forall k \in \{1, \dots, n\}$$

and finally:

$$PD_k = ODF_k, \quad \forall k \in \{1, \dots, n\}$$

The direct calibration might have undesirable properties such as non-monotonicity of the ODFs.

One can determine so-called implied default probabilities (IPD) by regression to avoid or mitigate the above-mentioned effects and to smooth the ODF distribution. Usually an exponential regression is appropriate. However, a linear or piecewise combination of both regression types might be useful as well. As an example, the calculation of an exponential fit is given below:

$$IPD_k^{exp} = intercept_{exp} \cdot slope_{exp}^k, \quad \forall k \in \{1, \dots, n\}$$

where

$$slope_{exp} = \exp\left(\frac{n \cdot \sum_{k=1}^{n} k \cdot \ln\left(ODF_k\right) - \sum_{k=1}^{n} k \cdot \sum_{k=1}^{n} \ln\left(ODF_k\right)}{n \cdot \sum_{k=1}^{n} k^2 - \left(\sum_{k=1}^{n} k\right)^2}\right)$$

$$intercept_{exp} = \exp\left(\frac{\sum_{k=1}^{n} \ln\left(ODF_k\right) - \ln\left(slope_{exp}\right) \cdot \sum_{k=1}^{n} k}{n}\right)$$

As above:

$$PD_k = IPD_k, \quad \forall k \in \{1, \ldots, n\}$$

If a sufficient number of data that is typically available one can directly transform each score to a probability of default. A suitable methodology is the so-called kernel density estimator (KDE) approach. Roughly speaking, based on the estimated smooth non-parametric density distribution of both good (*density_good*) and bad customers (*density_bad*), the default rate is defined by:

$$PD(score) = \frac{density\_bad\,(score)}{density\_bad\,(score) + density\_good\,(score)}$$

For more information on the KDE approach, see Fritz, Popken and Wagner (2002).

Ratings based on expert judgement
Rating sheet development
Rating sheets are used for counterparty types where insufficient historical data is available to develop scores or if standardised approaches do not deliver the appropriate results. The typical counterparty types for which rating sheets are used are financial

institutions and multinational corporates. This approach might be utilised as well for sovereigns and SMEs. The typical approach for developing an "expert" rating sheet is described in the following.

Selection of application field. It has to be made clear for which counterparties the new rating sheet will be utilised. Therefore, the counterparty type may be defined via its industry or NACE (*nomenclature des activités économiques dans la Communauté européenne*) code. Border cases (eg, shall the bank subsidiary of a corporate be rated using the methodology for banks, corporates or a subsidiary analysis?) have clearly to be specified.

Selection of criteria with experts. New criteria and guideline for scoring of these rating criteria are developed by in-house experts (eg, credit analysts and account officers). The guideline shall be used to help in understanding the criteria more precisely. The counterparty rated should generally be compared to the global universe of counterparties in the credit portfolio, rather than just its immediate peers in the same country or region.

Number of values per criterion. In general, the number of values per criteria should be an even number to avoid the assessment of an "average" value. In case of an even value, the credit officer has to decide whether the tendency is rather "good" or rather "bad" with regard to a single criterion. The number of possible values might vary for each attribute, but a fixed number of attributes (four or six) should be preferred. Note that a high number of values for a single attribute usually only pretends to increase the separation power.

Optional: Rating of a set of representative counterparties by experts. The working group may assess a small set of representative counterparties. This list can help in assigning the right qualitative description such as "very good", "below average", etc to the criteria for the counterparty on a global basis. It is also intended as a tool to ensure consistency across all future users.

Selection of a test sample of counterparties. The test universe – determined by the group of experts – consists of a representative number of counterparties evenly distributed geographically and across credit ratings.

Rating of test sample by responsible credit officers. The credit officers have to assign and record a holistic counterparty PD rating (ie, the expert judgement of the rating) to each of the counterparties of the test group they are responsible for. The rating shall represent credit officers' actual opinion on the counterparty. In addition, they have to fill in external ratings for benchmarking purposes, if available. With the help of a guidelines sheet, a new rating form template and the sample group, they are asked to input scores for each rating criterion. No total scores are shown in the form since they will be a result of calibration. Possible assignments to each rating criterion are:

❑ very good/excellent;
❑ satisfactory;
❑ higher risk/less satisfactory; and
❑ poor.

A general problem is the treatment of unknown information. A treatment similar to category "poor" is often too conservative, if the information cannot be retrieved (eg, assessment of IT systems for a small bank).

Optional: additional judgement of credit officers on relative weights of the categories of criteria. Based on the credit officers' own view of which category they consider to be relatively more important, they may have to assign a percentage weighting for each of the major categories. These proposals can support the calibration process.

Assignment of weights and combination of criteria. As the simplest approach, weights are assigned linearly for each criterion (eg, "very good/excellent" = 0 points, "satisfactory" = 1 point, "higher risk" = 2 points, "poor" = 3 points or a fixed multiple of these values). Any other functional behaviour (eg, exponential or logarithmic) can be modelled as well. However, the chosen function has to be justified. We do not recommend an arbitrary (monotonous) assignment of points to each value of a criterion since calibration gets more complicated and "overfitting" is likely.

In order to reduce the calculation time, the weights may have a restricted minimum/maximum value. Note that negative weights might not be understood and accepted by the users of the rating sheet. We therefore recommend allowing only non-negative weights.

Regarding the combination of different criteria, a linear combination is common. One can also think of a more complex combination of the single criteria, eg, a combination of fuzzy sets.[5] Again, there should be a rationale for complex combinations.

To achieve optimal weights and an optimal combination of the criteria, the calculation and analysis of ratios, such as *mCoC* described earlier, is required.

Calibration of rating sheet. Based on the optimal combination of the criteria, a mapping to PD ratings has to be established. One approach is to select the borders between the rating grades such that the linear and/or square deviation between expert judgement and theoretical rating (ie, output of the rating sheet) is minimal also considering the selectivity via CoC. Please note that the bands mapped to the same rating should be similar regarding their width, otherwise the probability that a certain rating occurs will be negatively affected.

The PD calibration as described in "Assignment of PDs" above, is not usually feasible for expert systems. On one hand, insufficient defaults are available in historical time series; on the other hand, an objective rating assessment cannot be expected. Imagine asking a credit officer to rate a defaulted customer based on information one year prior to default, the assessment will clearly be biased.

Final adjustments. The "optimal" weightings and mapping table might be modified in order to reflect expectations more appropriately and to avoid any bias resulting from the test group. Therefore, in the course of the development, restrictions can be made such as:

❏ The calculated mathematical optimum for the weightings might yield some criteria with very high weights and some other criteria with a near to zero weight. This might not meet expert opinion, which might require a more balanced weighting for the criteria (for example points distributed evenly between the criteria or not exceeding any maximum points per criterion) which shall lead an acceptable, close to the mathematical, optimum. This can be achieved, for example, by introducing additional conditions such as maximum weight or ratio between maximal and minimal not to exceed a certain value.

❏ The calculated mathematical optimum for a rating sheet's mapping table can yield to completely different bandwidths for the different rating grades: eg, the first rating grade will be derived from 0 to 10 points, the second rating grade from 11 to 27 points, the third rating grade from 28 to 30 points and so on. More smooth bandwidths for the mapping point scores → PD rating can be desired, which yield a result close to the mathematical optimum.

❑ A group of counterparties can be left out of the test group as they do not fit into the scheme. However, it has to be decided whether the risk of these counterparties has been incorrectly assessed by the responsible credit officer or whether the application of the rating sheet has to be restricted.

❑ A criterion/category of questions can be left out as it turns out to have insufficient selectivity.

Rating of validation sample by responsible credit officers. The credit officers have to repeat the rating procedure for a set of additional counterparties in order to validate the results. In case of negative validation the whole process has to be repeated.

Overruling. Note that the outcome of the rating sheet can be overruled by the credit officer. A guideline has to be established regarding the accepted number of deviating rating grades. The overruled rating can deviate from the theoretical rating, to what extent a justification for the overruling is required, and which credit authority is required. This guideline might not necessarily be specific for a single rating sheet but can be applied to all rating sheets.

Ready to use. If verified, the new rating sheet, including calibration results (eg, criteria, weights, mapping tables), has to be presented to senior credit officers and approval committees.

Continuous validation. In order to keep the quality of a rating sheet in spite of changing market conditions, it has to be validated against external ratings, overruling and through comparison with empirical defaults, if applicable.

Hereafter, we describe typical sources of information and criteria, which should be taken into account for the different rating classes. Please note that the listing is not complete with regard to asset/counterparty classes and criteria used.

Corporates

Definition: The asset class *corporates* refers to large corporations. Middle market or small and medium-sized borrowers are not included.

Which data should be used? The following data can be used for a rating tool for corporates:

❑ spread of financial statement;
❑ share price;
❑ public announcements;
❑ (confidential) information about management strategies; and
❑ industry reviews, peer comparison, and assessment of market position.

A typical rating system Based on the sources mentioned above, the following criteria can be used to assess the credit worthiness of a corporate counterparty:

❑ Operating environment (medium- to long-term industry outlook, special risks).
❑ Business and financial condition (quality of product offering, marketing strength, market standing/competition, dependencies, revenue development, ability to generate profits, long-term earnings outlook, internal cashflow generation after working capital, external cashflow generation, access to capital markets, debt to capitalisation ratio).
❑ Management transparency (long-term management strategy, quality of operational management, management structure, continuity plans and succession, business planning).

Subsidiary analysis. Multi-national corporation subsidiaries can be categorised as either inner circle or standalone subsidiaries.[6] For inner-circle subsidiaries, the analysis is based on the parent's PD rating and, depending on the grade of support by the parent, is leading to a downgrading by a fixed number of rating grades. A standalone analysis is required if: the parent states will not support the subsidiary; the parent has a track record of walking away from its subsidiaries or not honouring its commitments; the parent may not have adequate resources to support the subsidiary; the subsidiary is an intermediate (or sub-) holding company or a single operative company where it does not have a relationship with (or comfort from) the parent. A subsidiary analysis is a separate methodology. Downgrades from the parent company can depend on additional criteria such as country, industry or size classifications.

Figure 7 Example for a corporate rating sheet

EXAMPLE RATING SHEET (CORPORATES)

Name of group/borrower:
Domicile country:
Country rating:
Credit officer:
Rating date:

Ext. Ratings
S&P:
Moody's:
Fitch IBCA:

	- NO INTERMEDIATE SCORES ALLOWED -				SCORES	
	Very good/ excellent	Satisfactory	Higher risk/ less satisfactory	Unknown/ poor	(previous)	new
I. Market position						
Criterion 1		x			1	1
Criterion 2	x				1	0
Criterion 3		x			1	1
Criterion 4			x		2	2
Criterion 5				x	4	6
Criterion 6		x			0	3
Section total						13
Section rating						"6"
II. Financial condition						
Criterion 1		x			1	1
Criterion 2		x			1	1
Criterion 3	x				0	0
Criterion 4		x			1	1
Criterion 5			x		2	2
Criterion 6		x			1	1
Criterion 7	x				2	0
Section total						6
Section rating						"2"
III. Management & transparency						
Criterion 1		x			2	2
Criterion 2	x				0	0
Criterion 3	x				0	0
Criterion 4			x		1	2
Criterion 5				x	4	6
Section total						10
Section rating						"6"

Internal calculated risk scoring result (from above)	Total numerical score	24	29
	Counterparty (CP) PD rating	"3"	"4"

Financial institutions

Definition: The asset class *financial institutions* covers banks, life insurance companies, non-life insurance companies, families of funds, broker dealers, hedge funds, exchanges and clearinghouses.

Which data should be used? The following data can be used as rating tools for financial institutions:

❑ spread of financial statement;
❑ share price;
❑ public announcements;
❑ information from regulators;
❑ confidential information about management strategies; and

❏ industry reviews, peer comparison, and assessment of market position.

A typical rating system Based on the sources mentioned above, the following criteria can be used to assess the creditworthiness of a financial institution:

❏ Portfolio (loan portfolio structure and diversification, loan quality and performance, investment portfolio quality).
❏ Funding and capital (funding structure, capitalisation, recourse to external financing).
❏ Management and strategy (clarity and suitability of strategic planning, implementation and performance of strategies, market positioning and competitive strength, quality of IT infrastructure).
❏ Profitability profile (return figures, earnings stability, revenue diversification, profitability prospects).
❏ External factors (franchise value, ability and willingness of state/sovereign to support, regulatory transparency).

Subsidiary analysis. As described above for corporates. In addition, downgrades depend on the country where the subsidiary is located. Countries can be classified reflecting the inherent regulatory risk: strong regulation, medium regulation and low regulation. The downgrade follows a comparison of the regulation strength of the parent versus the subsidiary.

Sovereigns and sub-sovereigns

Definition: The asset class *sovereign* covers states that administer their own governments and are not dependent upon, or subject to, another power. The asset class *sub-sovereign* covers exposures to sub-national entities (eg, federal states, regions or municipalities) that are not totally independent of their sovereign but enjoy a certain autonomy (different in each country and depending on the legislation of the sovereign) and bear some responsibilities delivering public services.

National and sub-national entities are important borrowers on an international scale. Rating agencies have developed ratings for the long- and short-term debt for all national and many sub-nationals that have access to the financial markets.

Which data should be used?
❏ financial and budgetary information;
❏ statistical information about population and firms; and
❏ macroeconomic outlook.

A typical rating system The following criteria can be used to assess the credit worthiness of a sub-sovereign:

❏ The legal environment of each sub-sovereign has to be considered. The intergovernmental system stability and the legislation of a country are essential. Peace, order and monetary stability are major factors for both sovereigns and sub-nationals while the fiscal legislation limiting the risk has a direct impact on the solvency and reliability of the sub-sovereigns (ie, vertical and horizontal equalisation systems such as in Germany are very safe). Furthermore, it has to be verified whether the sovereign is able and willing to support its sub-sovereign and what degree of autonomy the sub-sovereign has (taking into account its level of responsibility for services, investments and borrowing authority). The examination of the fiscal power and the transfers of revenues coming from the sovereign government give information about the way of financing these services. The rigour and consistency of budgetary and fiscal policies over several administrations, and the controls over the quality and modernity of budgets and accountings are the last aspects, which have to be analysed.
❏ General macroeconomic information has to be analysed. Demographic aspects such as the structure of the population (eg, size, density, growth and age) and unemployment rates give information about expected fiscal revenues and expenses (both current and future) and over likely social pressure. The structure of the economy plays an essential role (eg, size of gross domestic product (GDP) and its trends, ratio of GDP per inhabitant). The examination of the geographical situation, the resources and the infrastructure completes the analysis of the economic power and its potential.
❏ Financial aspects have to be assessed: budget performance, operating profit, liquidity situation and debt level are very important points for the rating of the sub-sovereign. It is partially the budget of the sovereign and the sovereign debt that

give information about the weight of the sub-sovereign in a country. A positive or balanced budget and a low debt level are important indicators for the wealth of a region or municipality. Sometimes they reflect also the local legislation (ie, German municipalities must have a balanced budget).

Other segments

According to Consultative Paper 3, specialised lending is subdivided into the following asset classes: project finance, object finance, commodities finance, income-producing real estate and high-volatility commercial real estate.

Depending on the sub-category, information on the ability to generate revenues (such as price development and volatility in case of commodities financing), the risks involved in the project, property or object and, to a lower extent, the borrower have to be taken into account.

Note that we clearly have to separate the collateral position for specialised lending. The fact that a borrower has pledged a property or not does not influence the capability of a property to generate cash flows and thus has not necessarily an effect on the PD. However, in case of non-recourse financing, the willingness of the borrower to pay the debt might be higher if the property is pledged.

We do not see the necessity to link rating sheet development to the classification of CP3.

Project finance

Definition: The asset class *project finance* covers complex and expensive installations such as power plants, chemical processing plants, mines, transportation infrastructure, environment and telecommunications infrastructure.

Typically, the lender looks primarily to the revenues generated by a single project, both as the source of repayment and as collateral for the exposure.

The following criteria can be used to assess the credit worthiness of a project:

❑ Corporate and commercial risks (in terms of the sponsors, contractual parties, operator, fundamental economics, interest and FX risk, and financial strength).

❏ Project risks (eg, technology, completion target and cost over-run, feedstock and reserves, market risk, and environmental issues). Typically, during construction of the project the rating will be lower taking into account the construction risk.

Commercial real estate

Definition: The asset class *commercial real estate* covers exposures for financing commercial properties such as: office, residential, hotels, land, healthcare, industrial/storage, portfolios.

Generally, they are managed through a borrower or a group of borrowers, which can be private individuals, corporates or special purpose vehicles (SPV).

The following approach can be used:

❏ Analysis of the financed property. General information about a property (which can be diversified, eg, office and residential under one roof) and specific information about each of the diversified aspects are used. Both analyses cover complementary information about the standing of the property, competition and financial aspects. Each specific use has a weight in the use-specific rating corresponding to its part in the global rental income. Global property rating and specific-use property rating are calculated separately and are afterwards merged into a property rating factor without risk-enhancing features.

❏ Risk-enhancing features such as contamination and completion risk and cost certainty in the construction process are taken into account.

❏ The analysis of the borrower itself is required. Even if the financing is non-recourse, the borrower might be able and willing to support a single property through cashflows resulting from other projects. Ratings for private individuals or corporates are used for this section.

❏ A combined risk factor is derived based on the risk assessment of both property and borrower. The combination of both might depend on the financial capabilities, experience and reputation of the borrower and whether the financing is non-recourse or not.

Commercial mortgage-backed securities

Definition: The asset class *commercial-mortgage-backed securities* (CMBS) covers real estate loans secured by commercially used properties. These loans are packaged and (180 days maximum) sold to investors as part of a pool in a CMBS transaction.

For calibration purposes, experts' opinions on a significant sample across the typical spectrum found in the portfolio should be used. Additionally, default information on all historical loans originated by the bank that were securitised as part of CMBS pools can be used.

The following criteria can be used to assess the credit worthiness of a CMBS:

❑ Financial ratios as used customarily by market participants in the CMBS market.
❑ Qualitative information about the property (including feature of the object and market characteristics).

Default rates can be extracted from market information to calibrate the mean rating of the calibration sample.

Asset-backed securities
Definition: Asset-backed securities (ABS) transactions are securitisations of clients' assets. Credit rating for ABS deals means rating the exposure in line with the credit risk of an ABS arising from liquidity lines, cash collateral or derivatives.

Due to the scarce information about historical defaults, a typical sample of deals representing a significant share of the transactions in a typical business year is rated using expert opinions.

The following criteria can be used to assess the credit worthiness of an ABS:

❑ The parties associated with the ABS transaction: seller and different levels of services and the counterparties that are specific to each transaction.
❑ The quality of assets in the asset pool.

Ratings based on hybrid approaches
Small and medium enterprises
Definition: Small and medium enterprises (SME) are either self-employed people or small firms with sales typically in the single or tens of million euros, which are typically regional in focus.

Which data should be used? The following data can be used for a rating tool for SMEs:

❏ spread of financial statement;
❏ current account information;
❏ information about management strategies; and
❏ industry reviews, regional reviews and external assessment of market position.

Definition and characteristics

As indicated by the nomenclature and the nature of its segmentation, customers defined as small and medium enterprises are mostly driven by size indicators (see also Basel Committee on Banking Supervision, 2003). Focus is, therefore, on the "medium" or "in-between" status, often referred to as the SME gap. The target of using size indicators for segmentation is to achieve homogeneity with regard to customer, process and risk characteristics.

Table 1 The SME gap

	Segment	Business customers	SME portfolio	Global corporates
Size indicator	Sales/turnover Exposure	<1.5 Mill. €	≤200 Mill. € ≤25 Mill. €	>200 Mill. € >25 Mill. €
Homogeneity	Process	Standardised process	←——→	Individual analysis
		Automised ratings	←——→	External ratings available
	Financing	One bank	←——→	Syndication
		Single risk taker	←——→	Capital market access
	Data	Focus on hard facts	←——→	Transparent information (fillings, analyst meeting, forecasts, etc.)
		Automated interfaces	←——→	Manual spreading, etc.
Diversification	Customer	Market/product/ industry/regional concentration	←——→	Market/product/ industry/regional diversification
	Bank	Customer diversification/ regional concentration	←——→	Customer concentration/ regional diversification

The above matrix gives an overview of size indicators and homo-geneity criteria.

Data

For SME portfolios we differentiate hard facts and soft facts as top-level classification of available data. Information sectors are further differentiated by source or content of information:

Hard facts

❑ financial statements;
❑ account data;
❑ regional data; and
❑ industry sector data.

Soft facts

❑ management evaluation;
❑ market evaluation;
❑ SWOT (strengths, weaknesses, opportunities and threats) analysis; and
❑ balance-sheet forecasts and scenarios.

Hybrid system

A reliable estimate of the default probability of a customer or appli-cant should be based on data from different information sectors – financial (balance sheet) information, account data, external credit bureau data and so on. Technical and maintenance requirements are such that it is often helpful to develop separate score functions for each information sector and to combine the resulting scores into a final default probability estimate. This modular approach can also improve the transparency and acceptability of the score sys-tem. Figure 8 gives an overview of a hybrid system (grey-coloured fields describe a potential process for the medium segment of the SME portfolio with a combination of automated scores and analyst questionnaires).

Such a hybrid approach allows for process scalability with regard to customer needs, risk assessment, automation and efficiency. Information and module availability, manual effort to retrieve information and segment strategy then drive the module combination.

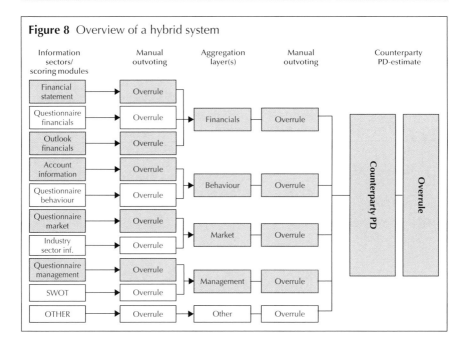

Figure 8 Overview of a hybrid system

As we are more interested in an estimate of the customer's default probability than in the score value itself, each module result is translated into a default probability and then processed through the next layer. The manual overruling represents an optional part of the system, which can be switched off when not necessary.

Example
For SME portfolios a standard process is the combination of financial statement rating, behaviour score and qualitative evaluation of market and management evaluation by the analyst. All results of the sub-modules are translated into a probability of default estimate for combination.

Module 1: Financial statement rating Financial statement information is spread into the internal database either manually by the analyst or using interfaces to external data providers, eg, via the eXtensible Business Reporting Language (XBRL) standard (for more information on XBRL, please refer to www.xbrl.org). Within the module customers are segmented into a small number of industry sectors and sales volume categories. This allows for score

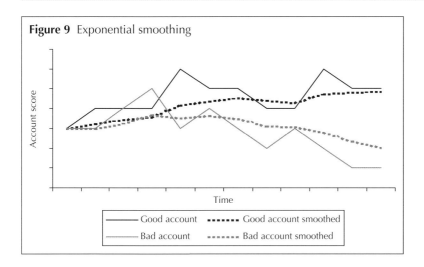

Figure 9 Exponential smoothing

optimisation with regard to industry- and size-specific financial statement ratios. The methodology applied might be a linear discriminant analysis. Ratios include evaluations of the balance sheet structure, the profit-and-loss and the cash-flow situation.

Module 2: Behaviour score based on account data Account data are important up-to-date information on the customer. They are usually of good quality and available electronically. A behaviour score should be based on ratios generated by the variables describing all aspects necessary for account management, eg, account balance information, turnover, utilisation, overdrafts.

Before defining ratios, it is recommended that the account variables d be smoothed by an exponential smoothing function, such as the following:

$$d_{\text{smoothed}}(t) = (1-\alpha) \cdot d(t) + \alpha \cdot d_{\text{smoothed}}(t-1), \text{ with } 0 < \alpha < 1$$

Smoothing mitigates non-systemic fluctuations and helps to identify trends in the account-dependent creditworthiness of the customer. This is illustrated in Figure 9. Afterwards the ratios based on the smoothed variables serve as input parameters for the uni- and multivariate analysis. For further details on the development of a scoring model based on account data, see Fritz and Hosemann (2000).

Module 3: Rating sheet for "market and competition" For scoring competitiveness, a questionnaire evaluating certain markets and competition characteristics of the company is presented to the analyst. Focus is on getting a picture of the company's position in line with common SWOT and product life cycle analysis concepts.

Module 4: Rating sheet for "management quality" Analogous to the rating sheet for "market and competition", management quality is scored. Focus is on total quality management, professionalism and management personality, transparency and control.

OTHER RISK-RELATED COMPONENTS
Exposure data
The exposure at default (EAD) is the expected outstanding amount in the event of the counterparty's default. The basis for the EAD is the outstanding and the external limit booked in the official process systems. However, the expected outstanding amount might vary for specific products. Therefore, the EAD has to be calibrated on a transaction level from historical default information.

Lending products with full utilisation
The part of loans that are by definition fully drawn (eg, bullet or amortising loans) has generally no chance to further increase his exposure in excess of the set transaction limit. Hence, in the event of default, the exposure for such transactions is given by the current outstanding (ie, book value of the loan).

$$EAD = outstanding$$

Lending products with variable utilisation
Lending products such as overdraft, revolving line of credit and commercial paper backups are characterised by an external limit and an average of the utilisation of the month (*outstanding*) under consideration. It can be expected that a counterparty close to default tends to increase its utilisation, while the bank will work against this by reducing available limits. Therefore, it becomes necessary to recognise a portion of the unutilised or free limit in the EAD.

EAD is calculated as the outstanding plus a percentage of the free limit expressed by the credit conversion factor (CCF).

$$EAD = outstanding + CCF \cdot freelimit$$

where *freelimit* is defined as the maximum of 0 and the difference between external limit and utilisation:

$$freelimit = \max\{0; limit - outstanding\}$$

Under consideration of accrued interest (*accrued_interest*) and workout costs (*workout_costs*^{unsec}; ie, discounted to date of default, internal and external costs associated with the income from workout for receivables resulting from this transaction without costs generated by liquidation of related collateral or payments of guarantors), additional add-on factors have to be introduced:

$$EAD = AIF \cdot COF \cdot (outstanding + CCF \cdot freelimit)$$

where *AIF* denotes the accrued interest factor, and *COF* is the cost (of workout) factor.

In order to calibrate the CCF parameters, defaulted customers need to be identified. The outstandings and external limits of these customers at the default time d and the preceding year $d - 1$ needs also to be collected.

$$CCF = \max\left\{0; \frac{outstanding_d - outstanding_{d-1}}{limit_{d-1} - outstanding_{d-1}}\right\}$$

can be calculated if the denominator is non-negative. This usually reduces the number of datasets available for calibration purposes if quite a substantial number of lines is fully utilised one year prior to default. Note that unwanted effects can be observed if the denominator is negative or close to zero.

Then, for a predefined segment y, all CCFs of the related transactions have to be averaged:

$$CCF_y = \frac{1}{N_y} \cdot \sum_{i=1}^{N_y} CCF_i$$

where N_y denotes the number of all transactions in the segment under consideration within a one-year period. The CCF may be calibrated dependent on customer segment, customer rating and product segment. More specifically, the facilities with covenants (restricting the drawing in case of worsening financials or external ratings) have to be treated separately.

Note that, by definition, the empirical CCF might even be above one if the limit is increased and, thus, the outstanding at time d can be above the limit at time $d - 1$. That can be observed, for example, if a bank wants to prevent a default by increasing the working capital line. If the CCF were not set at a floor of zero, there would also be negative CCFs if the outstanding decreases prior to default. This can be observed if the limit and outstanding are actively cut.

The calibration of AIF and COF can be based on the following empirical values:

$$AIF = \frac{outstanding_d + accrued\_interest}{outstanding_d}$$

$$COF = \frac{outstanding_d + workout\_costs^{unsec}}{outstanding_d}$$

Then, as described above, the average of AIF and COF, respectively, has to be calculated for the segment under consideration.

For some customers and products, the information available on historic internal losses may not be sufficient. Expert judgements and external data analysis need to be used as well.

Guarantees

Certain products such as guarantees can be categorised as low-risk business compared with cash loans. One can observe that not every drawn guarantee will be utilised by the beneficiary in case of default of the counterparty. This can be reflected by a reduction of the exposure at default as follows:

$$EAD_{guarantee} = usage \cdot (outstanding + CCF \cdot (limit^{guarantee} - outstanding))$$

$$EAD_{guarantee} = AIF \cdot COF \cdot \big(usage \cdot \big(outstanding$$
$$+ CCF \cdot \big(limit^{guarantee} - outstanding\big)\big)\big)$$

The "usage" can be calibrated for different guarantee types by an investigation of the utilised guarantee amount (ie, the drawn guarantee amount not expired nor returned) of defaulted customer compared to the drawn guarantee amount.

$$usage = \frac{guarantee\_amount^{utilised}}{guarantee\_amount^{drawn}}$$

Traded products
For traded products, *EAD* is determined by the average future exposure for a given year in the future:

$$AFE_s = \mathop{E}_{\omega \in \Omega,\, t \in [s-1,s]} \Big[\max\{0,\, MtM_{t,\omega}\} \Big]$$

where the expectation is taken over the time period $[s-1,s]$ and the state space Ω. *MtM* denotes the mark-to-market value for the traded product under consideration.

This measure is much more appropriate than the current credit exposure, ie, the positive portion of its current market or mark-to-model value. This amount does not reflect the risk involved in such transactions properly, as no volatility of the market value is taken into account. Note that, in case of a negative market value, the credit risk involved in that transaction is zero but not negative.

Loss data
The loss given default (LGD) is generally defined as

$$LGD = 100\% - \frac{recovery\_amount}{EAD} = 100\% - recovery\_rate$$

where *recovery_amount* denotes the amount the bank is likely to recover if the obligor has defaulted. It has to be denominated in the

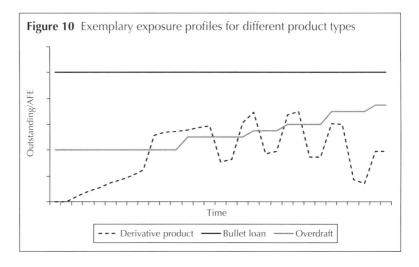

Figure 10 Exemplary exposure profiles for different product types

same currency as the EAD. Recovery rates are usually either high or low depending on whether the exposure is collateralised or not. Hence, it is appropriate to distinguish between the collateralised (EAD_{sec}) and uncollateralised portion (EAD_{unsec}) of the expected exposure at default and measure the recovery rates for each of those portions. Therefore, we can separate the LGD into LGD_{sec} and LGD_{unsec}. This leads to a more differentiated calculation of the expected loss amount at default:

$$LGD \cdot EAD = LGD_{sec} \cdot EAD_{sec} + LGD_{unsec} \cdot EAD_{unsec}$$

LGD_{sec} should differ by collateral type and collateral country of risk. For validation purposes it should be possible to select all collateral with finalised recovery process for calibration. An outline of the different calibration techniques applicable to differing collateral types is given in the following sections.

Specific (liquid) collateral
One should note that direct costs of workout (liquidation costs) are already subtracted from recoveries. We have to validate LGD_{sec} as well as the haircuts used to determine the liquidation value of the collateral, ie, the collateral value post-haircut. First of all, LGD_{sec} on

a single collateral level is calculated for a one-year period:

$$LGD_{sec} = \max\left\{0\%;\ 100\% - \frac{recovery\_amount\_sec}{\min\{nominal\_value_{d-1},\ collateral\_value\_post\_haircut_{d-1}\}}\right\}$$

where $recovery\_amount\_sec$ denotes all payments generated by liquidation of the collateral or all payments of the guarantor discounted to the date of default; $nominal\_value_{d-1}$ denotes the fixed amount of claims to the collateral provider(s) if it is expressed in the collateral agreement one year prior to default (also called: contract value, guarantee amount), and, $collateral\_value\_post\_haircut_{d-1}$ denotes the estimated liquidation value one year prior to default (also called liquidation value).

Furthermore, the appropriateness of applied haircuts has to be validated as well:

$$haircut\_cal = \frac{recovery\_amount\_sec}{collateral\_value\_pre\_haircut_{d-1}}$$

where $collateral\_value\_pre\_haircut_{d-1}$ denotes estimated market value one year prior to default (also called market value). Note that since the haircut rather reflects that the market value of the collateral falls below the collateral value post haircut only in eg, 10% of all cases, the validation of haircuts should use the according quantile of the empirical distribution. Then, for a predefined type c of collateral, all LGD_{sec} of the related collateral have to be averaged for the one-year period under consideration:

$$LGD_{sec,c} = \frac{1}{N_c} \cdot \sum_{i=1}^{N_c} LGD_{sec,i}$$

where N_c denotes the number of all pieces of collateral of the type c under consideration.

For guarantees and indemnities the formula stated above has to be modified:

$$LGD_{sec} = \max\left\{0\%;\ 100\% - \frac{recovery\_amount\_sec}{\min\{amount\_to\_secure,\ nominal\_value/coverage\_level\}}\right\}$$

where *amount_to_secure* denotes the aggregated nominal amount (at date of default) of all transactions secured by this collateral minus aggregated recovery of all other collateral assigned to these transactions. Furthermore, *coverage_level* denotes the percentage of exposure that is covered by this collateral.

Note that this information might be used for guarantees instead of using joint default probabilities (JDP) between counterparty and guarantor. As alternative, different LGD_{sec} can be assigned to different classes of guarantees depending on $PD_{counterparty}$, $PD_{guarantor}$ and asset correlation.

Treatment of overcollateralisation

Among others, the following reduction of the LGD_{sec} for collateral values exceeding 100% of the applicable exposure at default are possible:

$$LGD_{sec\_over}[coll, \sigma, EAD] = g(\sigma) \cdot EAD^{f(\sigma)} \cdot coll^{-f(\sigma)} + LGD_{sec\_min}$$

$$LGD_{sec\_over}[coll, EAD] = \frac{LGD_{sec} \cdot EAD + (coll - EAD) \cdot LGD_{sec\_min}}{coll}$$

with $coll = collateral\_value\_post\_haircut$ for collateral and $coll = nominal\_value$ for guarantees and where $g(\sigma)$ and $f(\sigma)$ denote monotonous functions depending on the volatility σ of the collateral.

In both proposals, an LGD_{sec_min} as a lower bound needs to be defined. Furthermore, the hyperbolic function $g(\sigma) \cdot EAD^{f(\sigma)} \cdot coll^{-f(\sigma)}$ needs to be specified. In the case where sufficient data is not available, these parameters should be set following expert consultation.

LGD_{unsec} refers to the loss given default to be expected for the unsecured part of a facility. This parameter should differ by counterparty type and country. On facility level seniority has to be taken into account in addition. The LGD_{unsec} parameter has to be calibrated on counterparty level and then aggregated to a counterparty class level (eg, type/country). Calibration techniques differ by levels of aggregation with details listed in the following paragraph.

Counterparty level
First, empirical LGD_{unsec} on counterparty level is calculated for a one-year period:

$$LGD_{unsec} = \max\left\{0\%;\ 100\% - \frac{recovery\_amount\_unsec}{EAD - \sum_i recovery\_amount\_sec_i}\right\}$$

where i denotes the index for collateral assigned to this counterparty and *recovery_amount_unsec* denotes the cumulated amount resulting of an applied work-out process (without payments generated by the liquidation of collateral) discounted to default date. An algorithm for the distribution of LGD_{unsec} to facility level should be in place in case facilities assigned to the counterparty have different seniority.

Counterparty class level
After the determination of LGD_{unsec} on counterparty level, LGD_{unsec} on counterparty class level has to be calculated for the one-year time period:

$$LGD_{unsec,\,cpy} = \frac{1}{N_{cpy}} \cdot \sum_{i=1}^{N_{cpy}} LGD_{unsec,\,i}$$

where N_{cpy} denotes the number of all counterparties assigned to the counterparty class *cpy* under consideration.

HOW TO STRUCTURE A BASEL II CREDIT RISK IMPLEMENTATION PROJECT

Generally, the implementation project can be separated into the following processes:

❑ data-collection process;
❑ reporting process;
❑ parameter-validation process; and
❑ methodology-validation process.

This is shown in the following figure.

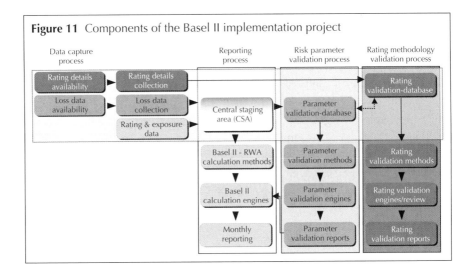

Figure 11 Components of the Basel II implementation project

Reporting process

Capital reporting processes based on transaction-level information are already implemented in many banks, either to comply with current BIS rules or to allocate capital via an economic model. If the second holds true, the Basel II reporting process can be based on the internal economic capital process since the main ingredients, PD, LGD and EAD on client/transaction level are needed for both.

If a bank starts from scratch, the situation might be easier. But the biggest problem for data collection as well as capital reporting is to have an integral data-collection process and database such that each client/customer group is uniquely defined and can be identified for each transaction so that a correct aggregation of transactions on group level can be accomplished.

It should be clear that such a reporting process can be established and maintained only if different departments, such as risk management, risk reporting and IT, in a bank work closely together. A separate Basel II implementation team not embedded in the existing structures and processes is not likely to succeed.

Parameter-validation process

The parameter validation process has to validate PD, LGD and EAD. However, parameters used for Basel II reporting should not be turned down based on statistical tests alone but on a combination of those as well as expert judgements.

Parameter validation routines should run in parallel to the reporting routines (ie, monthly). However, the evaluation of such results should rather be done once every six months or once per year. We are currently in the process of making first experiences with an acceptable regulatory validation process for all parameters ie, PD, LGD and EAD. But one thing can already be said today: each validation process needs senior management buy-in. In other words, a Basel II project needs a steering committee of senior managers (chief risk officer, chief credit risk officer, chief risk controller, senior business representatives) in order to get the buy-in needed for such an important project for a bank.

Validation of ratings

The rating quality strongly influences the output quality of internal and regulatory credit risk models under Basel II. This refers to the calibrated default probability as well as to the assignment of customers to rating classes in a given rating methodology. To assess quality and prevent quality deterioration at an early stage, ratings need to be validated. Possible reasons for quality deterioration are systematic changes of input factors (eg, change from payment by cheque to electronic transfer) or changes in the structure of the portfolio. Furthermore, senior management, auditors and regulators require a constant quality reassurance. One important aspect of the validation standards for banks applying for the IRB approaches of Basel II is to meet the criteria that will be required by the regulators (see Basel Committee on Banking Supervision, 2003): "Banks must have a robust system in place to validate the accuracy and consistency of rating systems, processes and the estimation of all relevant risk components. A bank must demonstrate to its supervisor that the internal validation process enables it to assess the performance of internal rating and risk estimation systems consistently and meaningfully."

The frequency of validation generally depends on the business cycle, the turnover frequency of assets in the portfolio, the relative significance of the segment under consideration. Ratings should be reviewed at least annually. An appropriate validation cycle for rating models consists of two to three years at most (for more details on the validation of rating methodologies please refer to section

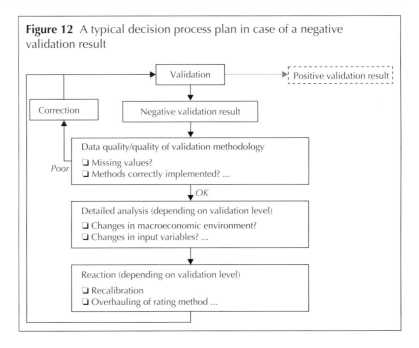

Figure 12 A typical decision process plan in case of a negative validation result

"Methodology validation process" below). However, one should always be prepared for an ad hoc review (eg, in cases when the portfolio structure changes significantly).

If the validation results in a negative outcome (eg, significant difference between observed and estimated values) the quality of the analysed data and the implementation of the validation methodology have to be checked. In case this "pre-scanning" explains the unsatisfactory validation result, problems have to be solved (eg, improvement of data quality) and the validation is carried out again. Otherwise the analysis must be extended and based on the result of the analysis, some actions might have to be taken. Possible reactions include the overhauling of the PD calibration (recalibration), a follow-up validation (and overhauling) of the rating methodology, etc. This process can be supported by a detailed decision process plan. A simplified example is illustrated in Figure 12. Validation methodologies, validation results and reactions have to be documented.

We would like to stress at that point that the introduction of amended methodologies should be feasible within a short time-frame. This implies the necessity for a modular IT implementation.

Methodology validation process

Generally, the methodology validation process can be separated into four different steps and applied on four different layers:

1. portfolio at the EL level;
2. rating class at the PD level;
3. score level; and
4. criteria level

A detailed description can be found in Fritz, Popken and Wagner (2002).

Validation on expected loss level

The EL is calculated on transaction level and aggregated on portfolio level. It is very common to compare the aggregated EL with write-offs. Due to the time lag between EL and write-offs it is difficult to define an appropriate measure for EL validation.

EL versus write-offs

❏ For each counterparty, the EL at time t is calculated. The user selects the portfolio. Afterwards the EL is aggregated on a port-folio level.

❏ For the portfolio selected the aggregated amount of write-offs resulting from defaults within one year is calculated. If this information is not available, a so-called "release-factor" can be introduced describing the average release of specific provisions (see below).

❏ Time series for write-offs as well as EL are developed by calculating these amounts for each year within a predefined time interval.

Determination of a release factor For a portfolio and time period selected, a ratio *release_factor* is calculated. Only those counterparties are considered with the following properties:

❏ a risk provision was made within the given time period (or time sub-period) or it had existed at the beginning of this period; and
❏ a write-off or release was made within the given time period or time sub-period.

These counterparties are used to calculate the following ratio for each one-year period within the predefined time interval:

$$release\_factor_{\text{portfolio}} = 100\% - \frac{m}{n}$$

where for a given portfolio m denotes the number of counterparties with risk provisions and write-offs and n denotes the number of counterparties with risk provisions.

When analysing time series of specific provisions, write-offs, and EL, one has to overcome the following problems:

❑ the reasons for changes in expected loss (amount or ratio);
❑ consideration of time lag between provisioning, default and write-offs;
❑ the reasons for changes in write-offs (amount or ratio);
❑ the appropriateness of expected loss with respect to write-offs, eg, on an average basis;
❑ the appropriateness of other parameters, eg, loss given default, exposure at default; and
❑ the possibility that specific provisions and write-offs incorporate unexpected loss features.

Validation on rating level
Regarding rating at the *PD* level, one can and should check for the following questions:

1. Is the monotonicity and curvature of the slope of the rating or PD curve acceptable?
2. Do quality measures, eg, Gini-coefficient or optimal error, deliver sufficient results?
3. Do the rating classes differ significantly from each other in terms of default rate? Would it, especially for small portfolios, be sensible to aggregate several rating classes to only one?
4. Is the confidence level appropriately chosen?
5. What are the effects of the business cycle?
6. Are there systematic changes in the input variables to the rating scheme (eg, companies more frequently using off balance-sheet financing that influence the leverage etc)?
7. What is the effect of the bank's deliberate change in target clientele (different customer/risk groups)?

8. Are deviations in default rates within the statistical noise?
9. Are the deviations systematic (all changes of the same sign) or unsystematic?
10. Does the rating have to be re-calibrated?
11. Should the rating scheme be overhauled?
12. How volatile is the rating scheme in terms of migration and is this plausible from the input factors of the scheme?
13. Is the maximum of the diagonals larger than other entries on the same row? If not, what is the explanation?
14. Is the migration matrix, up to statistical fluctuations, monotonous from both sides of the diagonal? What are the reasons for a violation of monotonicity?
15. Are there large shifts in the distribution of the rating? Are the shifts systematic, ie, is either of the triangle matrices dominating (in terms of overall entries) the other? What is the reason for any systematic shifts (eg, macroeconomic change in bank's strategy or credit approval process)?
16. Is an external rating available for a major part of the analysed portfolio?
17. Can the default definition of the external rating provider be mapped to the internal default definition?
18. Are the external default frequencies compatible with the internal rating classes?
19. To what extent are changes of the internal rating (in terms of probability of default) congruent with changes in the external ratings?

Validation on score level
On the score level, one needs to check on the following questions:

1. Is the quality (in terms of Gini-coefficient or others) still acceptable?
2. Is the current default rate function $PD(Score)$ that is used in subsequent risk assessment tools still applicable?
3. What are sensible score intervals if the default rates per rating class are to stay constant?
4. What are sensible score intervals if the frequency distribution over the rating classes is to stay constant?
5. Are there violations to the monotonicity of the default rate that are not explicable by statistical fluctuations? What is their nature?

Validation on criteria level

On the criteria level, one should check for the following questions:

1. Is the separation power of the individual criterion sufficient?
2. Is there an alternative for the selected criterion?
3. Can the criterion (or the set of criteria) be replaced by external information?
4. Has the separation power of the individual criterion decreased and, if yes, why?
5. Is the assessment horizon of the criterion appropriate?

Introduction into credit process

Advanced methodologies are useless if not introduced into a bank's regular day-to-day process. Therefore, all affected parties (credit officers, relationship manager, risk control, IT) have to be involved right from the beginning. Otherwise, new methodologies might not be accepted, cannot be implemented in time or integrated into systems and workflow, or, worse, cannot be integrated at all. Just imagine that after the finalisation of a methodology it turns out that numerous users cannot be trained in adequate time or that the application of the methodology is very time-consuming.

One of the least considered facts is the implication of a methodological change. One has to consider that possibly the following decisions or processes are linked to ratings, expected loss, or capital figures: credit decisions, credit authority, specific risk provisions, general value adjustment, portfolio strategies, limit allocation, capital allocation, diversification, pricing. Thus, one has to carefully analyse all requirements of the new methodology being introduced.

---

1 The separation power (also called discriminative power) describes how well a rating model discriminates between defaulting and non-defaulting customers.
2 The asset-class sub-sovereign includes federal states, regions and municipalities.
3 See also, eg, Basel Committee on Banking Supervision, 2001, p. 11: "The regulatory capital requirement (ie, Basel I) has been in conflict with increasingly sophisticated internal measures of economic capital."
4 We call a loan a structural loan, if the loan is granted against the pledging of collateral and the collateral agreement allows the bank to immediately (ie, within a few days) close out the collateral with near zero risk.
5 Ie, each value of a criterion is interpreted as a fuzzy set in the mathematical sense.
6 "Inner circle" subsidiaries are those subsidiaries where a parental support is likely, eg, due to a written legally binding statement of support of the parent or, eg, if the subsidiary is engaged in activities consistent with the major businesses of its parent.

BIBLIOGRAPHY

Basel Committee on Banking Supervision, 2001, "The New Basel Capital Accord: An explanatory note".

Basel Committee on Banking Supervision, 2003, "The New Basel Capital Accord. Consultative Document".

Brier, G., 1950, "Verification of Forecasts Expressed in Terms of Probability", *Monthly Weather Review*, **(78)1**, pp. 1–3.

Fahrmeir, L., A. Hamerle, and G. Tutz, 1996, *Multivariate Statistische Verfahren* (Berlin: De Gruyter Verlag).

Fritz, S. G., and D. Hosemann, 2000 "Restructuring the Credit Process: Behaviour Scoring for German Corporates", *Int. J. Intell Sy. Acc Fin Mgmt*, **9**, pp. 9–21.

Fritz, S. G., L. Popken, and C. Wagner, 2002, "Scoring and Validating Techniques for Credit Risk Rating Systems", *Credit Ratings-Methodologies, Rationale and Default Risk*, Michael K. Ong (ed) (London: Risk Books).

NOMENCLATURE

In the preceding chapter, we made use of the following nomenclature:

ABS	asset-backed securities
AIF	accrued-interest factor
BIS	Bank for International Settlement
CCF	credit conversion factor (also called loan equivalent factor)
CMBS	commercial mortgage-backed securities
COF	cost of workout factor
EAD	exposure at default
EL	expected loss
EC	economic capital
IPD	implied probability of default (probabilities of default derived from ODFs by using regression techniques)
LGD	loss given default
NACE	industry classification code, European Union standard
ODF	observed default frequency
PD	probability of default
SME	small- and medium-sized enterprises
SPV	special-purpose vehicle
SWOT analysis	strengths, weaknesses, opportunities and threats analysis
TAF	time adjustment factor
TDR	troubled debt restructuring
XBRL	eXtensible Business Reporting Language

6

Stress Tests of Banks' Regulatory Capital Adequacy: Application to Tier 1 Capital

Esa Jokivuolle; Samu Peura*

Bank of Finland; Sampo Plc

ABSTRACT

The internal ratings-based capital requirements of the new Basel Accord will expose banks to potentially significant variation in their minimum capital requirements due to ratings evolution. Banks can accommodate the volatility in the minimum capital requirement through holding sufficient precautionary buffer capital over the regulatory minimum. The Basel Committee (2003) itself has suggested that banks apply stress tests to determine the size of the required buffers. In previous work (see Peura and Jokivuolle, 2003) we have presented a credit VAR based framework for performing such stress tests. In this chapter we apply the framework to banks' Tier 1 capital. We also contrast the measures of capital implied by our approach with measures of economic capital. We suggest that our approach could provide banks with useful guidance in setting their Tier 1 capitalisation targets.

INTRODUCTION

The internal ratings-based capital regimes of the new Basel Accord (henceforth, Basel II) will expose banks to potentially significant

*We thank our colleagues for many useful discussions. However, the views expressed here are solely ours and do not reflect the views of the Bank of Finland or Sampo Plc.

variation in their minimum capital requirements due to ratings evolution. This variation and its consequences, often referred to as the procyclicality of risk-sensitive capital requirements (see Erwin and Wilde, 2001), are a concern for both banks themselves and for financial regulators alike. Individual banks will face an increasing challenge to steer their capital adequacy over time in order to meet the requirements of the regulator and the markets.

Many people in the industry have suggested that banks can accommodate the volatility in the minimum capital requirement through an adjustment of their capital buffers over the regulatory minimum requirements (eg, Borio, Furfine and Lowe, 2001, and Lowe, 2002). It appears that this recommendation has also been adopted by the Basel Committee itself, which suggests banks to conduct stress tests of capital adequacy as a means of determining the size of the capital buffers.[1] The idea in these stress tests would be to consider the extent to which a bank could see its actual capital erode, and its minimum capital requirement increase, during a period of severe credit deterioration. Such stress tests have been presented, for example, by Erwin and Wilde (2001) and Catarineu-Rabell, Jackson and Tsomocos (2002), in the form of deterministic scenarios corresponding to some historical period of credit distress.

In this chapter, we use the framework of Peura and Jokivuolle (2003; see also Jokivuolle and Peura, 2001) to conduct analogous stress tests in a stochastic value-at-risk (VAR) framework and to extend their results. We ask how much capital a bank needs in order to be protected, at some desired statistical confidence level, against shocks to its actual capital and to its minimum capital requirement. The required capital buffer in this approach is a solution to a VAR-type criterion associated with regulatory capital adequacy. The simulation-based approach utilises the information in historical transition matrices to produce a complete description of the dynamics of a bank's capital buffer, and as such is not dependent on any single, deterministically specified stress scenario.

Our model of bank capital dynamics is an extension of a credit risk model of the CreditMetrics type (J. P. Morgan, 1997). We add minimum capital formulae and bank income dynamics into a credit portfolio model, which generates rating changes and defaults so as to generate a model of the joint evolution of both actual bank capital and the bank's minimum capital. Actual capital (in the absence of mark-to-market accounting) is driven by bank income and credit losses, whereas capital requirements are driven by ratings transitions. As in Peura and Jokivuolle (2003), we also introduce an underlying conditioning variable that represents the state of the business cycle. The business cycle variable follows a two-state Markov process, and the ratings transition probabilities for each period are conditioned on the state of the business cycle. The multi-period simulations are measured in quarters, which is somewhat non-standard in credit risk contexts but well grounded, since most banks report their capital adequacy to their regulators on a quarterly basis.

This chapter refines the analyses in Peura and Jokivuolle (2003) in a number of ways. We reconsider the choice of business cycle scenarios in our simulations. The estimate of average bank profitability is now anchored to actual bank data. We also provide sensitivity results of the capital buffer with respect to the time horizon of the analysis, and suggest that the time horizon is best interpreted as the bank's recapitalisation horizon.

Most importantly, in this chapter we perform the analysis in terms of Tier 1 capital relative to its minimum requirement of four per cent of risk-weighted assets. In Peura and Jokivuolle (2003) we measured capital buffers in excess of the total capital requirement of eight per cent, making no distinction between Tier 1 and Tier 2 capital. Tier 2 capital may comprise at most a half of total capital, and, thus, the total regulatory minimum requirement of eight per cent is automatically violated once Tier 1 capital has fallen below its four per cent minimum. Therefore, it can be argued that Tier 1 is the more relevant measure of bank capitalisation. Moreover, we believe that the minimum requirement of Tier 1 capital, plus the extra buffer, can be directly compared with standard measures of economic capital, in order to assess which of these constitutes the binding capital constraint to banks.

As far as we are aware, the Basel Committee has not explicitly discussed the role of the capital buffers as a factor influencing the total level of capital in the banking system after the reform. The Quantitative Impact Study (QIS) conducted by the Basel Committee alone does not provide sufficient information on how the overall level of capital is likely to change in the reform. The extra buffers should also be taken into account. The issue is also related to the alignment of regulatory minimum capital requirements with banks' economic capital. Simply equating the regulatory minimum requirement with economic capital (which appears to be the stated aim of Basel II) does not necessarily produce the desired outcome if the extra buffers that banks will choose to hold are not counted in.

The chapter is organised as follows. Panel 1 reviews the framework for determination of regulatory capital buffers. The second section presents the specific model for ratings evolution and business cycle dynamics, and describes the parameterisation used in this chapter. The third section presents our new results on Tier 1 capital buffers and on their sensitivity to key model parameters. The fourth section compares regulatory capital buffers against economic capital, and the fifth section concludes.

PANEL 1 A FRAMEWORK FOR CAPITAL ADEQUACY ANALYSIS

In this panel we review the framework for capital adequacy simulations presented in Peura and Jokivuolle (2003). We think of a bank with assets composed of illiquid loans. The bank is subject to the regulatory minimum capital requirement

$$E_t \geq R_t \qquad (1)$$

where E is the banks' Tier 1 book equity and R is the regulatory minimum capital requirement on Tier 1 capital, ie, four per cent of the bank's risk-weighted assets.[2]

The regulatory capital requirement (1) is monitored quarterly, and hence time in our model is measured in quarterly increments. We define bank capital buffer B as the excess of Tier 1 equity over the minimum Tier 1 requirement

$$B_t = E_t - R_t. \qquad (2)$$

Bank Tier 1 capital dynamics, ignoring dividends and capital issues, satisfies

$$E_{t+1} = E_t + I_{t+1} - L_{t+1} \qquad (3)$$

where we use I to denote bank income (net of all operating costs but before credit losses), and L to denote the bank's credit losses. Since our focus is on conservative, stress-oriented risk measurement, we find it reasonable to assume that dividends and new equity issues are ignored over the horizon of the analysis.

Combining (2) and (3), we can express bank Tier 1 capital buffer at time t as

$$B_t = B_0 + \sum_{s=1}^{t} I_s - \sum_{s=1}^{t} L_s - (R_t - R_0). \tag{4}$$

This implies that capital buffer at time t is obtained by adding bank profits to and deducting credit losses and the net increase in the regulatory minimum capital requirement from the initial capital buffer. In particular, R_t in our analysis is the capital charge of the bank's initial portfolio evaluated based on time t ratings of the assets in the portfolio, less the capital relief due to any expirations and defaults of assets up to time t.

Our stress test for bank regulatory capital adequacy is the following. We require that the capital buffer defined by (4) remain positive for each quarter over a stress horizon T, at a confidence level that is no lower than a given number, say α. In other words, we introduce the VAR-type regulatory capital requirement

$$P\left[\min_{0 \leq t \leq T} B_t \geq 0\right] \geq \alpha \tag{5}$$

where α is a confidence level such as ninety-nine per cent and T is a fixed horizon (in quarters). Because the capital buffer for each t is increasing in the initial capital buffer B_0, there is a minimum value $\hat{B}_0$ satisfying (5),

$$\hat{B}_0 = \inf\left\{B_0 : P\left[\min_{0 \leq t \leq T} B_t \geq 0\right] \geq \alpha\right\} \tag{6}$$

We refer to formula (6) as the bank's regulatory capital buffer constraint.

We also define the bank's *economic capital* quite consistently with the standard usage of the term, but acknowledging the bank's profit flow and the periodic surveillance in our multi-period setting, as a solution to the VAR criterion

$$P\left[\min_{0 \leq t \leq T} E_t \geq 0\right] \geq \beta \Leftrightarrow P\left[\min_{0 \leq t \leq T} (B_t + R_t) \geq 0\right] \geq \beta \tag{7}$$

Here, the confidence level associated with solvency is denoted by β, and the equivalence follows from applying the definition of the buffer (2). The minimum initial capital buffer satisfying the economic capital constraint (7) can be formulated analogously to (6) as

$$\tilde{B}_0 = \inf\left\{B_0 : P\left[\min_{0 \leq t \leq T} E_t \geq 0\right] \geq \beta\right\} \tag{8}$$

Which one of the two constraints, (6) or (8), is binding? Comparison of (5) and (7) shows that, when $\alpha = \beta$, the regulatory buffer constraint

(6) is always binding over the economic capital constraint (8) (since $R_t \geq 0$). We would, however, expect the confidence level applied to regulatory capital adequacy, α, to be lower than the confidence level applied to solvency, β, in which case (6) need not be generally binding over (8).[3] We illustrate these both constraints in Figure 1.

Figure 1 Regulatory capital buffer constraint and economic capital constraint

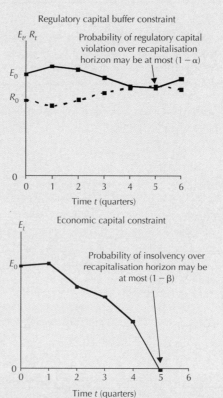

Regulatory capital buffer constraint

E_t, R_t

Probability of regulatory capital violation over recapitalisation horizon may be at most $(1 - \alpha)$

E_0

R_0

0

Time t (quarters)

Economic capital constraint

E_t

Probability of insolvency over recapitalisation horizon may be at most $(1 - \beta)$

E_0

0

Time t (quarters)

The regulatory capital buffer constraint (6) requires that the initial capital buffer $E_0 - R_0$ must be sufficiently high so that the probability of violating the regulatory minimum capital requirement over the bank's recapitalisation horizon is at most $1 - \alpha$, when regulatory capital adequacy is measured periodically. A standard economic capital constraint (8) requires that the initial capital must be sufficiently high so that the probability of bank insolvency (negative net worth) over the bank's recapitalisation horizon is at most $1 - \beta$. The regulatory minimum capital requirement plays no role in the measurement of economic capital.

Assuming that (6) determines the bank's Tier 1 capital buffer, initial Tier 1 capital will be $E_0 = R_0 + \hat{B}_0$, and Tier 1 capital ratio can be expressed as

$$\left(1 + \frac{\hat{B}_0}{R_0}\right) 4\% \qquad (9)$$

Our reported capital buffers and capital ratios in Section 3 are based on formulae (6) and (9).

The confidence level α in our framework is an exogenously chosen parameter. In a fully optimising model of the bank, such as Barrios and Blanco (2003), Estrella (2001), Furfine (2001), Milne and Whalley (2001) or Peura and Keppo (2003), this confidence level would be effectively determined from the trade-offs that influence the bank's choice of capital. α would be influenced by factors such as the costs and penalties associated with regulatory capital violation, the capital market frictions that affect the recapitalisation of the bank, the sensitivity of the bank's funding cost to the amount of capital held by the bank, and the availability of growth options to the bank. Also, regulators' concerns regarding the viability of bank capitalisation would be reflected in α through the Pillar 2 of the new Basel Accord.

Within our risk-management-oriented framework, the parameter α may be calibrated based on information on actual bank capital ratios. Given a bank's portfolio and its capital ratio, there is an implied value of α, which makes the capital ratio (9) solved from the model equal to the observed capital ratio. We perform this type of calibration of α below.

BUSINESS CYCLE DYNAMICS AND PARAMETERISATION

The framework presented in Panel 1 leaves considerable room for the specification of bank capital dynamics. In all but the most trivial specifications, the capital buffers will have to be solved numerically from (6). In this section we describe our model of bank capital dynamics, which is the same as that presented in Peura and Jokivuolle (2003).

A bank's capital dynamics as in (4) depends on the dynamics for bank income, credit losses, and the minimum capital charge. We simulate these three components based on a model of rating transitions that is an extension of the CreditMetrics™ framework (J.P. Morgan, 1997). Rating transitions determine the evolution of the minimum capital charge. Defaults, which determine credit losses, are just special cases of rating transitions. Bank income in our model is assumed to accrue solely from non-defaulted loans.

Our model of rating transitions is a one-factor version of the CreditMetrics framework (see eg, Gordy, 2000), extended with an underlying conditioning variable, which is interpreted as business cycle state. The CreditMetrics model takes a single-transition probability matrix of ratings as given. We assume that the transition matrix is conditioned on a business cycle variable, which is a two-state, time-homogeneous Markov chain whose possible states are referred to as "expansion" and "recession". The transition matrix associated with the recession state is expected to display higher volatility in rating changes, and higher default probabilities, than is the transition matrix associated with the expansion state. Models of ratings dynamics of this type have been suggested by Bangia *et al* (2002). Figure 2 illustrates the rating transition model.

Our simulation is in quarterly time increments. Credit portfolio models are typically implemented as one-period simulations with an annual horizon, but we find the quarterly time interval compelling because banks typically report their capital adequacy

Figure 2 Rating transition model with underlying business cycle variable

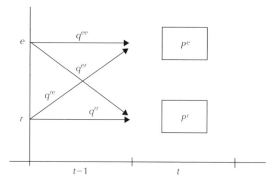

The business cycle variable is a time-homogeneous Markov chain with two possible states, "expansion" (e) and "recession" (r). Each quarter t, a new business cycle state is first simulated according to the switching probabilities q, conditional on the business cycle state in the previous quarter. The state of the business cycle determines the rating transition probability matrix P applied to simulate rating transitions over the same quarter. At the first quarter, we simulate the business cycle state conditional on its assumed value over the last observed quarter.

to their regulators quarterly. Both the regime transition probabilities and the rating transition probabilities that we use are quarterly
probabilities estimated based on US data. The regime-switching
matrix for the underlying business cycle variable is from Table 5.2
in Bangia *et al* (2002). This is based on NBER business cycle data
over the postwar period. The conditional rating transition matrices
the expansion and the recession states are from Table 5.1 in Bangia
et al (2002). These are based on S&P data on US corporate ratings
over the period 1981–98. We set asset correlations between all
obligors equal to twenty per cent, which is broadly in line with the
assumptions underlying the Basel II IRB formulae.

PANEL 2 SAMPLE TEST PORTFOLIOS

In this panel, we form two illustrative test portfolios, "high quality"
and "average quality", based on the credit-quality distributions of US
banks reported in Gordy (2000). These are reproduced in Table 1. The
table also shows the annual unconditional default probabilities,
calculated based on the same data as the conditional transition
matrices. These annual default probabilities are used in the Basel II risk
weight formulae.

Each portfolio contains one hundred equal-sized loans.[4] The loans
are bullet loans with a maturity that in all cases at least equals the
VAR horizon *T* (the amount by which a loan maturity exceeds *T* has
no effect on our results). The loans are *ex ante* identical in all other

Table 1 Average bank portfolios

S&P grade	Default probability (%)	US average quality (%)	US high quality (%)
AAA	0.00	3	4
AA	0.00	5	6
A	0.04	13	29
BBB	0.24	29	36
BB	1.01	35	21
B	5.45	12	3
CCC	23.69	3	1
Expected default rate		1.79	0.71

The quality distribution of the US portfolios is from Federal Reserve Board survey, as
reported in Gordy (2000).
Default probabilities are annual default frequencies from S&P data 1981–98.

respects except the initial obligor rating. We normalise the nominal exposure for each portfolio to 100. All our simulations are based on the assumption that no new assets are bought, and no existing assets are sold, over the VAR horizon. This assumption is not descriptive of actual bank portfolio dynamics. However, the size of the capital buffers is determined by portfolio dynamics over multi-period recessions, and in such circumstances the assumption of no new business is likely to be much closer to reality.

A credit loss in our model occurs when a loan defaults, ie, its rating ends up in the default state. Consistent with the Basel II IRB formulae, we assume a (non-stochastic) LGD of forty-five per cent across all exposures in the portfolio.

Bank income in our model is proportional to the time 0 (unconditional) expected annual credit loss from the loan. This proportion is constant across all loans in the portfolio. Our base case estimate of this parameter is 3.0.[5] The exact formulae for bank income and credit loss dynamics can be found in Peura and Jokivuolle (2003, Section 4).

Our base-case VAR horizon is 1.5 years, which should be interpreted as the recapitalisation horizon of banks' under a recessionary environment.[6] Given all the other parameters fixed at their reported values, our simulation results (see Figure 4) suggest that the implied value of the confidence level α that yields bank capital ratios of observed magnitude is roughly ninety-nine per cent. Our sensitivity analyses are based on this base-case value.

We will consider three different business cycle scenarios in our simulations. In an "expansion" scenario, we assume that the previous (last observed) quarter was an expansion, and therefore condition the simulation of the business cycle state for the first quarter on the expansion state. In a "recession" scenario, we analogously assume that the previous quarter was a recession. In the third scenario, termed "long recession", we assume that a recession will last throughout the simulation horizon.

RESULTS

Table 2 shows our main results on the behaviour of capital buffers in the current Basel regime relative to the Basel II IRB regime.

Table 2 Minimum Tier 1 capital and capital buffers

Portfolio quality	Business cycle scenario	Current Basel regime				Basel II IRB regime			
		Tier 1 minimum	Tier 1 buffer	Minimum + buffer	Tier 1 ratio (%)	Tier 1 minimum	Tier 1 buffer	Minimum + buffer	Tier 1 ratio (%)
High	Expansion	4.0	1.3	5.3	5.3	2.0	1.7	3.7	7.4
	Recession	4.0	1.4	5.4	5.4	2.0	1.8	3.8	7.6
	Long recession	4.0	2.2	6.2	6.2	2.0	2.8	4.8	9.6
Average	Expansion	4.0	1.9	5.9	5.9	3.3	2.2	5.4	6.6
	Recession	4.0	2.1	6.1	6.1	3.3	2.4	5.7	6.9
	Long recession	4.0	3.5	7.5	7.5	3.3	3.9	7.2	8.8

Capital buffer calculated from (6) at the 99% confidence level. $T = 1.5$ years, bank profitability multiplier $\theta = 3$. Portfolio nominal exposure is 100.

We base our interpretation of Table 2 mainly on the results of the "long recession" scenarios, since this scenario mimics a recession that lasts for several quarters and is the only truly conservative of the three scenarios. We observe in particular that the difference in buffers between the "expansion" and the "recession" scenarios is quite insignificant. A clear difference in buffers can be found only between these and the "long recession" scenario. This indicates that, if we use empirical conditional transition probabilities for the evolution of both the business cycle state and the ratings, it does not make much difference (in a long-horizon simulation) whether we actually condition on the initial business cycle state or not.

We make the following conclusions based on Table 2:

1. Minimum capital requirements on both high- and average-quality credit portfolios are reduced in Basel II. The reduction is largest for the high quality portfolio, up to fifty per cent.

2. The required Tier 1 capital buffer increases in the Basel II regime, both for the high- and the average-quality portfolio. The buffer more than doubles the capital need over the regulatory minimum. In relative terms, the required capital buffer for the high-quality portfolio increases most. This is because the high-quality portfolio has relatively more room for ratings downgrades (see Peura and Jokivuolle, 2003, for a detailed discussion on this).

3. Total Tier 1 capital, ie, minimum capital plus the buffer, of the high-quality portfolio is reduced, while that of the average-quality portfolio remains roughly at its current level. In the case of the average-quality portfolio, the increase in the size of the buffer largely consumes the capital saving from lower minimum requirements.

4. Capital ratios increase throughout, since the size of the buffer goes up while the minimum requirement goes down. Yet the informativeness of this ratio deteriorates because the denominator of the ratio now strongly depends on the asset quality distribution of the bank. In particular, in the IRB regime the Tier 1 capital ratios of high-quality portfolios are higher than those of low-quality portfolios, reflecting the relatively, but not absolutely, larger size of the buffer of the former. Interbank comparisons may have to be based on absolute capital amounts or the leverage ratios.

The first three conclusions are also illustrated in Figure 3.

The effect of the confidence level α on Tier 1 capital under the current Basel regime is shown in Figure 4. The figure shows that a typical large G10 bank's Tier 1 capital ratio, seven per cent

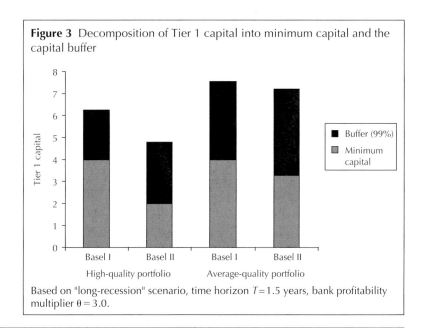

Figure 3 Decomposition of Tier 1 capital into minimum capital and the capital buffer

Based on "long-recession" scenario, time horizon $T = 1.5$ years, bank profitability multiplier $\theta = 3.0$.

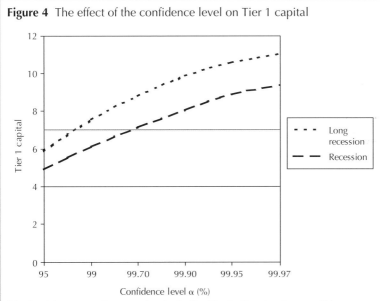

Figure 4 The effect of the confidence level on Tier 1 capital

Tier 1 minimum requirement plus the buffer. The buffer at a given confidence level is the difference between the dotted curve and the horizontal solid line, which depicts the four per cent minimum requirement. Calculations under the current Basel regime, based on the average-quality portfolio, time horizon $T = 1.5$ years, bank profitability multiplier $\theta = 3.0$. The grey line indicates the typical target Tier 1 capital ratio of large G10 banks, seven per cent.

(see Jackson *et al*, 2002), is roughly in line with a confidence level of ninety-nine per cent. This is based on the assumption that the regulatory capital buffer constraint is indeed the binding capital constraint of a typical bank and that this capitalisation decision is made with respect to the "long-recession" scenario. This warrants our using the ninety-nine per cent confidence level as our base-case value.

Figure 5 shows the effect of bank profitability, measured by the income multiplier θ, on required Tier 1 capital. A higher bank income allows for less capital. Tier 1 capital decreases by roughly 0.6 and 0.7 per cent of risk-weighted assets for each one unit increase in the income multiplier, in the current Basel regime and in the Basel II IRB regime, respectively.

Figure 6 shows the effect of the VAR horizon T on Tier 1 capital. A one-year increase in the VAR horizon raises the desired capital

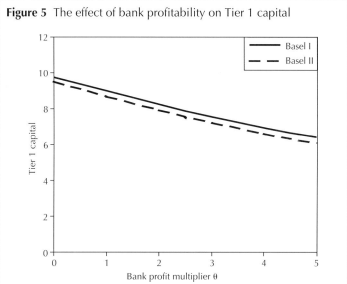

Figure 5 The effect of bank profitability on Tier 1 capital

Tier 1 minimum requirement plus the buffer. Based on the average-quality portfolio, "long-recession" scenario, time horizon $T = 1.5$ years, confidence level $\alpha = 99$ per cent.

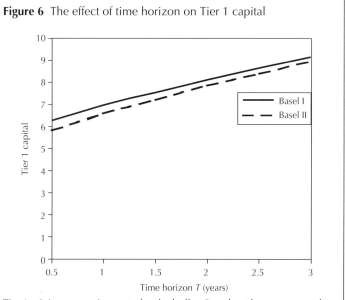

Figure 6 The effect of time horizon on Tier 1 capital

Tier 1 minimum requirement plus the buffer. Based on the average-quality portfolio, "long-recession" scenario, bank profitability multiplier $\theta = 3.0$, confidence level $\alpha = 99$ per cent.

ratio by roughly 1.2 percentage points under the current Basel regime, and by roughly 1.5 percentage points under the Basel II IRB regime.

ECONOMIC CAPITAL VERSUS REGULATORY CAPITAL BUFFER CONSTRAINT

Figure 7 shows a comparison of economic capital against the regulatory capital buffer requirement. Here economic capital has been calculated from (8) based on a confidence level of 99.95 per cent, which is in line with an AA-rating target over the 1.5-year horizon.[7] The regulatory minimum capital plus the additional buffer has been calculated from (6) based on a 99 per cent confidence level. The comparison indicates that economic capital and the regulatory minimum plus the buffer are closely aligned for both the high-quality and the average-quality portfolios under the IRB Approach of Basel II. It is hard to tell whether this is a mere coincidence because the Basel Committee has not been explicit about the role of the additional buffers in aligning regulatory requirements with economic capital. In fact, the alignment of economic capital and regulatory capital would look much worse if we ignored the buffers (the minimum Tier 1 requirements being 2.0 and 3.3,

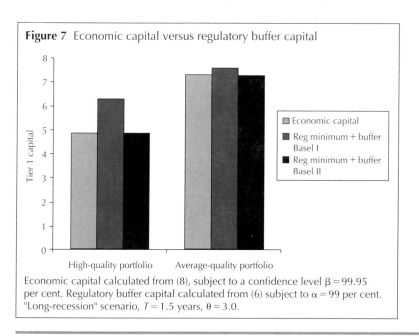

Figure 7 Economic capital versus regulatory buffer capital

Economic capital calculated from (8), subject to a confidence level $\beta = 99.95$ per cent. Regulatory buffer capital calculated from (6) subject to $\alpha = 99$ per cent. "Long-recession" scenario, $T = 1.5$ years, $\theta = 3.0$.

respectively (see Table 2), for the high- and average-quality portfolios in Figure 7).

Under the current Basel regime, the regulatory minimum plus the buffer clearly exceeds economic capital for the high-quality portfolio. This would suggest that, at least for high-quality banks, the regulatory capital buffer constraint is the binding constraint on Tier 1 capital. This is supported by evidence from Jackson, Perraudin and Sapporta (2002), who find that extremely high confidence levels for solvency, in excess of 99.99 per cent, are required to align high-quality banks' economic capital to their actual Tier 1 capital.

It is difficult to distinguish, though, whether a bank's capital choice is determined by its economic capital constraint or by its regulatory capital requirement. Our analysis of the relationship of the two is complicated by the significant uncertainty concerning the realistic level of the confidence level α, although the value of 99.95 per cent for β appears to be something of an industry standard. Limited empirical evidence suggests that in practice either constraint can be binding (Barrios and Blanco, 2003).

CONCLUSIONS

Our analysis has been illustrative in nature, and a practitioner interested in implementing the framework might want to pay more attention to several details of the model. Loss-given default (LGD), which we have assumed constant, could be made countercyclical consistent with the empirical evidence in Allen and Saunders (2002) and Altman, Resti and Sironi (2002). Asset correlations could be made dependent on the state of the business cycle, consistent with evidence in Das *et al.* (2002). The specification of the bank's profit flow could be varied to match more accurately the bank's actual loan pricing as well as income from other sources. We have also ignored the capital charge for operational risk in our analysis of Basel II. The charge for operational risk will feed to the minimum requirement, but, due to its lower volatility relative to the credit risk charge, is not likely to influence the size of the required buffer significantly.

In summary, we believe that our approach is a valuable complement to economic capital as a capital management tool. This is because our approach:

❏ incorporates regulatory minimum requirements and their volatility under the IRB approaches of Basel II; and

❏ has the potential to explain banks', even high-quality banks', observed levels of Tier 1 capitalisation.

Economic capital often appears as an incomplete solution for setting Tier 1 capital targets because it does not consider regulatory capital constraints at all. Economic capital, as it is typically measured, also fails in the second task in the case of high-quality banks in particular, unless exceptionally high confidence levels are allowed for (as demonstrated in Jackson, Perraudin and Sapporta, 2002).

1 Basel Committee (2002) states that "to help address potential concerns about the cyclicality of the IRB approaches, the Committee agreed that meaningfully conservative credit risk stress testing by banks should be a requirement under the IRB approaches as a means of ensuring that banks hold a sufficient capital buffer under Pillar Two of the new Accord".

2 The Tier 1 interpretation of capital is the only departure in this section from Peura and Jokivuolle (2003).

3 The argument here is simply that the costs of insolvency are supposedly higher than costs incurred from (temporary) violation of the regulatory minimum capital constraint.

4 Casual evidence suggests that the largest concentrations in bank credit portfolios typically exceed one per cent of portfolio nominal exposure, yet typical portfolios contain exposures with up to tens of thousands of different obligors. We suggest that a portfolio with one hundred equal-sized exposures is a good proxy for the degree of diversification in actual bank portfolios.

5 The average bank portfolio in Table 1 has expected losses 0.8 per cent (of risk weighted assets), based on a forty-five per cent LGD assumption. The average return (on risk-weighted assets) across US commercial banks is roughly 1.5 per cent. These imply that the average income (before credit losses) is roughly three times the expected losses.

6 This choice is supported by NBER data on the US recession lengths from the past decades. The longest recessions in the mid-1970s and in the early 1980s lasted for roughly five quarters.

7 The standard VAR horizon for calculating economic capital is one year when mark-to-market methodology is used. The fact that our credit portfolio risk calculations are done in the default mode is balanced by the longer simulation horizon, 1.5 years.

BIBLIOGRAPHY

Allen, L., and A. Saunders, 2002, "A Survey of Cyclical Effects in Credit Risk Measurement Models", BIS, Working Papers 126.

Altman, E. I., A. Resti, and A. Sironi, 2002, "The Link Between Default and Recovery Rates: Effects on the Procyclicality of Regulatory Capital Ratios". BIS, Working Papers 113.

Bangia, A., F., et al, 2002, "Ratings Migration and the Business Cycle, with Application to Credit Portfolio Stress Testing", *Journal of Banking and Finance*, **26**, pp. 445–74.

Barrios, V. E., and J. M. Blanco, 2003, "The Effectiveness of Bank Capital Adequacy Regulation: A Theoretical and Empirical Approach", *Journal of Banking and Finance*, **27**, pp. 1935–58.

Basel Committee on Banking Supervision, 2002, press release, Bank for International Settlements, 10 June.

Basel Committee on Banking Supervision, 2003, "The New Basel Capital Accord", third consultative paper, Bank for International Settlements, April.

Borio, C., C. Furfine, and P. Lowe, 2001, "Procyclicality of the Financial System and Financial Stability: Issues and Policy Options", Bank for International Settlements, Papers No 1, March.

Catarineu-Rabell, E., P. Jackson, and D. Tsomocos, 2002, "Procyclicality and the New Basel Accord – Banks' Choice of Loan Rating System", unpublished manuscript.

Das, S. R., et al, 2002, "Correlated Default Risk", unpublished manuscript.

Erwin, W., and T. Wilde, 2001, "Pro-cyclicality in the New Basel Accord", *Risk*, October.

Estrella, A., 2001, "The Cyclical Behaviour of Optimal Bank Capital", working paper, Federal Reserve Bank of New York, New York.

Furfine, C., 2001, "Bank Portfolio Allocation: The Impact of Capital Requirements, Regulatory Monitoring, and Economic Conditions", *Journal of Financial Services Research*, **20(1)**, pp. 33–56.

Gordy, M. B., 2000, "A Comparative Anatomy of Credit Risk Models", *Journal of Banking and Finance*, **24**, pp. 119–49.

Jackson, P., W. Perraudin, and V. Sapporta, 2002, "Regulatory and 'Economic' Solvency Standards for Internationally Active Banks", *Journal of Banking and Finance*, **26**, 953–76.

Jokivuolle, E., and S. Peura, 2001, "Regulatory Capital Volatility", *Risk*, May.

Morgan J. P., 1997, "CreditMetrics", Technical Document. J. P. Morgan, New York.

Lowe, P., 2002, "Credit Risk Measurement and Procyclicality", paper presented at a conference on banking supervision at the Crossroads, Bank of Netherlands, April.

Milne., A., and E. Whalley, 2001, "Bank Capital Regulation and Incentives for Risk-taking", Working Paper, City University Business School, London.

Nickell, P., W. Perraudin, and S. Varotto, 2000, "Stability of Ratings Transitions", *Journal of Banking and Finance*, **24**, 203–27.

Peura, S., and E. Jokivuolle, 2003, "Simulation Based Stress Tests of Banks' Regulatory Capital Adequacy", forthcoming in the *Journal of Banking and Finance*.

Peura, S., and J. Keppo, 2003, "Optimal Bank Capital with Costly Recapitalisation", unpublished manuscript, available at http://www.ssrn.com.

7

Advanced Credit Model Performance Testing to Meet Basel Requirements*

Donald R. van Deventer; Xiaoming Wang

Kamakura Corporation; Kamakura Corporation and University of Hawaii

INTRODUCTION

In Geneva in December 2002, Robert Merton was asked for his advice for financial institutions using the 1974 Merton model to manage credit risk.[1] After a long pause, Professor Merton replied, "Well, the first thing you have to remember is that the model is twenty-eight years old." The persistence of the usage of Merton model by major financial institutions and its obvious influence on the proposed New Capital Accord (henceforth, Basel II) by the Basel Committee on Banking Supervision is a testimony to the powerful intuitive appeal of the model.

Compared to other areas of human endeavour, it is striking that the 1974 technology, with modest extensions, is still regarded by so many as the state of the art.[2] In the semiconductor industry, for example, it is inconceivable that one would prefer a 1974 chip design over the current state of the art. In cross-country skiing, no one would use the 1973 standard classical style in a freestyle race over the skating technique that is obviously faster. In game playing, almost no one

*The authors would like to thank their colleagues at Kamakura Corporation for many helpful comments, particularly Mark Mesler, who provided the data warehouse on which the model performance tests within are based. Robert Jarrow's comments and advice have been invaluable over the eight years of his association with Kamakura Corporation, including his comments on this chapter. Private conversations with Eric Falkenstein and Jorge Sobehart, both formerly of Moody's Investors Service, have also provided many insights. The authors alone are responsible for any errors which may remain in what follows.

would sacrifice the magnificent computer graphics and speed of today's games for the chequers of 1974. Is the continuing prominence of the Merton model a rare example of an intellectual breakthrough that has stood an extraordinary test of time, or should we be more worried, as Robert Merton said, that the model is 28 years old? The purpose of this chapter is to provide a framework for answering that question and to provide some concrete answers.

The primary reasons why there is so little evidence on the performance of credit models fall into two categories. The first is the considerable expense and expertise needed, both in terms of finance and computer science, to assemble the data and computer coding to provide a consistent methodology for testing credit models in a way that the proposed Basel II requires. Van Deventer and Imai (2003) note that the Basel II requires that banks must prove to their regulatory supervisors that the credit models they use perform "consistently and meaningfully" (see Bank for International Settlements, 2001, Section 302, p. 55). Typically, the only institutions who have the capability to assemble these kinds of databases are extremely large financial institutions and commercial vendors of default probabilities. Prior to the commercialisation of default probabilities by Moody's KMV, studies of default were based on a very small number of defaulting observations. Falkenstein and Boral (2000) cite academic papers by Altman (1968) (33 defaults), Altman (1977) (53 defaults), and Blum (1974) (115 defaults) to illustrate the relatively small sample sizes used to draw inferences about bankruptcy probabilities prior to 1999. By way of contrast, Kamakura Corporation's commercial default database includes more than 1,600 failed company observations and its research database, which spans a longer period, contains more than 2,000 failed companies.

For major financial institutions that have incurred the expense of a large default database, the results of model testing are highly valuable and represent a significant competitive advantage over other financial institutions who do not have the results of credit model performance tests. For example, there is a large community of arbitrage investors actively trading against users of the Merton default probabilities when the arbitrage investors perceive the signals sent by the Merton model to be incorrect.

Among the vendor community, the majority of vendors offer a single-default-probability model. This presents a dilemma for potential consumers of commercial default probabilities. A vendor of a single type of credit model has two reasons not to publish quantitative tests of performance. The first reason is that the tests may prove that the model is inferior and ultimately may adversely affect the vendor's commercial prospects. Perhaps for this reason, most vendors require clients to sign licence agreements that forbid the clients from publicising any results of the vendor's model performance. The second reason is more subtle. Even if quantitative performance tests are good, the fact that the vendor offers only one model means that the vendor's tests will be perceived by many as biased in favour of the model that the vendor offers.

Four former employees of Moody's Investors Service have set the standard for quantitative model test disclosure in a series of papers: Andrew Boral, Eric Falkenstein, Sean Keenan and Jorge Sobehart. The authors respect the important contributions of Boral, Falkenstein, Keenan and Sobehart to the integrity of the default-probability generation and testing process.

The need for such tests is reflected in the frequently heard comments of default-probability users who display a naïveté with respect to credit models that will ultimately result in their failure to meet the credit model testing requirements of Basel II. We present some samples in Panel 1 that illustrate the need for better understanding of credit model testing.

PANEL 1 MISUNDERSTANDINGS ABOUT CREDIT MODEL TESTING

A commonly heard comment on credit model performance goes like this: "I like Model A because it showed a better early warning of the default of Companies X, Y and Z."

Many users of default probabilities make two critical mistakes in assessing default-probability model performance. They choose a very small sample (in this case three companies) to assess model performance and use a naïve criterion for good performance. Assessing model performance on only three companies or 50 or even 100 among 8,000 to 10,000 in the total universe of US corporates needlessly exposes the banker to: (a) an incorrect conclusion just because of the noise in the small sample; and (b) the risk of data mining by the default-probability vendor, who (like a magician doing card tricks) can steer the banker to the three or 50 or 100 examples that show the model in the best light. A

---

test of the whole sample eliminates these risks. Bankers should demand this of both internal models and models purchased from third parties.

The second problem this banker's quote has is the performance criterion. The implications of his comment are twofold:

- ❏ I can ignore all false predictions of default and give them zero weight in my decision.
- ❏ If Model A has higher default probabilities than Model B on a troubled credit, then Model A must be better than Model B.

Both of these implications should be grounds for a failing grade by banking supervisors. The first comment, ignoring all false positives, is sometimes justified by saying, "I sold Company A's bonds when its default probabilities hit 20% and saved my bank from a loss of US $1.7 million, and I don't care if other companies that don't default have 20% default probabilities because I would never buy a bond with a 20% default probability anyway." Why, then, did the bank have the bond of Company A in its portfolio? And what about the bonds that were sold when default probabilities rose, only to have the bank miss out on gains in the bond's price that occurred after the sale. Without knowledge of the gains avoided, as well as the losses avoided, the banker has shown a striking "selection bias" in favour of the model he is currently using. This selection bias will result in any model being judged good by a true believer. We give some examples below.

The second implication exposes the banker and the vendor to a temptation that can be detected by the tests we discuss below. The vendor can make any model show "better early warning" than any other model simply by raising the default probabilities. If the vendor of Model B wants to win this banker's business, all he has to do is multiply all of his default probabilities by 6 or add an arbitrary scale factor to make his default probabilities higher than Model A. The banker making this quote would not be able to detect this moral hazard because he does not use the testing regime mentioned below.

Eric Falkenstein and Andrew Boral (2000, p. 46) of Moody's Investors Service address this issue directly:

> Some vendors have been known to generate very high default rates, and we would suggest the following test to assess those predictions. First, take a set of historical data and group it into 50 equally populated buckets (using percentile breakpoints of 2%, 4%, ... 100%). Then consider the mean default prediction on the x-axis with the actual, subsequent bad rate on the y-axis. More often than not, models will have a relation that is somewhat less than 45% (ie, slope <1), especially at these very high risk groupings. This implies that the model purports more power than it actually has, and more importantly, it is miscalibrated and should be adjusted.

We present a second type of test to detect this kind of bias in credit modelling below. If a model has a bias to levels higher than actual default rates, it is inappropriate for Basel II use because it will be inaccurate for pricing, hedging, valuation and portfolio-loss simulation.

Another quotation illustrates a similar point of view that is inconsistent with Basel II compliance in credit modelling: "That credit model vendor is very popular because they have correctly predicted 10,000 of the last 10,500 small business defaults."

Again, this comment ignores false predictions of default and assigns zero costs to false predictions of default. If any banker truly had that orientation, the Basel II credit supervision process would root them out with a vengeance because the authors hereby propose a credit model at zero cost that outperforms the commercial model referred to above.

100% Accurate Prediction of Small Business Defaults: Default Probability for All Small Businesses is 100%.

This naïve model correctly predicts 10,500 of the last 10,500 defaults. It is free in the sense that assigning a 100% default probability to everyone requires no expense or third-party vendor since anyone can say the default probability for everyone is 100%. And, as with the banker quoted above, it is consistent with a zero weight on the prediction of false positive. When pressed, most financial institutions admit that false positives are important. As one major financial institution comments, one model "correctly predicted 1,000 of the last three defaults".

Once this is admitted, there is a reasonable basis for testing credit models.

THE TWO COMPONENTS OF CREDIT MODEL PERFORMANCE

Basel II requires that financial institutions have the capability to test credit model performance and internal ratings to ensure that they consistently and meaningfully measure credit risk. There are two principal measures of credit risk model performance. The first is a measure of the correctness of the ordinal ranking of the companies by riskiness. For this measure, we use the so-called receiver operating characteristics (ROC) accuracy ratio, whose calculation is reviewed briefly in the next section. The second is a measure of the consistency of the predicted default probability with the actual default probability, which Falkenstein and Boral (2000) call "calibration". This test is necessary to ensure the accuracy of the model for pricing, hedging, valuation and portfolio simulation. Just as important, it is necessary to detect a tendency for a model to bias default probabilities to the high side as Falkenstein and Boral note, which overstates the predictive power of a model by the naïve criterion of the first quote in the introduction.

We discuss each of these tests in turn in the next two sections and present results for three types of credit model on a common database of 1.3 million monthly observations for US companies from 1989 to 2003 maintained by Kamakura Corporation as part of its Kamakura Risk Information Services default probability database product. As of this writing, Kamakura Corporation reports default probabilities for three types of model:

Reduced-form credit models
KDP-jc, Kamakura Default Probabilities from an advanced form of the Jarrow-Chava (2002) approach. KDP-jc is based on explicit estimation of default probabilities using logistic regression on a historical default database in a way consistent with the Jarrow (2001) reduced-form model. The model uses six basic inputs, which are transformed to twelve explanatory variables, including financial ratios, equity market data, macro factors and two other variables.

Structural credit models
KDP-ms, Kamakura Default Probabilities using the "best" Merton approach with proprietary mapping to actual default experience by Kamakura.

Hybrid credit models
KDP-jm, Kamakura Default Probabilities combining the Jarrow and Merton approaches in a hybrid model within the logistic regression framework. The KDP-ms Merton default probability is added as an additional explanatory variable to the Jarrow-Chava variables in KDP-jc to form KDP-jm.

We present the performance results for each model in the ordinal ranking of companies by riskiness in the next section.

MEASURING ORDINAL RANKING OF COMPANIES BY CREDIT RISK

The standard statistic for measuring the ordinal ranking of companies by credit riskiness is the ROC accuracy ratio. The ROC accuracy ratio is closely related to, but different from, the cumulative accuracy profiles used by Sobehart, Keenan and Stein (2000), formerly at Moody's Investors Service and now at Citigroup, in numerous publications in recent years.

The receiver operating characteristics (ROC) curve was originally developed in order to measure the signal-to-noise ratio in radio receivers. The ROC curve has become increasingly popular as a measure of model performance in fields ranging from medicine to finance. It is typically used to measure the performance of a model that is used to predict which of two states will occur (sick or not sick, defaulted or not defaulted). Van Deventer and Imai (2003) go into extensive detail on the meaning and derivation of the ROC accuracy ratio, which is a quantitative measure of model performance.

In short, the ROC accuracy ratio is derived in the following way:

❑ Calculate the theoretical default probability for the entire universe of companies in a historical database that includes both defaulted and non-defaulted companies.
❑ Form all possible pairs of companies such that the pair includes one defaulted "company" and one non-defaulted "company". To be very precise, one pair would be the December 2001 defaulted observation for Enron and the October 1987 observation for General Motors, which did not default in that month. Another pair would include defaulted Enron, December 2001, and non-defaulted Enron, November 2001, and so on.
❑ If the default-probability technology correctly rates the defaulted company as more risky, we award one point to the pair.
❑ If the default-probability technology results in a tie, we give half a point.
❑ If the default-probability technology is incorrect, we give zero points.
❑ We then add up all the points for all of the pairs, and divide by the number of pairs.[3]

The results are intuitive and extremely clear on model rankings:

❑ A perfect model scores 1.00 or 100% accuracy, ranking every single one of the defaulting companies as more risky than every non-defaulting company.
❑ A worthless model scores 0.50 or 50%, because this is a score that could be achieved by flipping a coin.
❑ A score in the 90% range is extremely good.
❑ A score in the 80% range is very good – and so on.

Van Deventer and Imai provide worked examples to illustrate the application of the ROC accuracy ratio technique. The ROC accuracy ratio can be equivalently summarised in one sentence: "It is the average percentile ranking of the defaulting companies in the universe of non-defaulting observations."

We turn now to the Jarrow-Chava (2002a, 2002b) database, which we shall use to apply the ROC accuracy ratio technology. The Jarrow-Chava database spans all listed companies in the United States from 1963 to 1998.

The predictive ROC accuracy ratio: techniques and results

Chapter 6 in van Deventer and Imai (2003) summarises the database compiled by Jarrow and Chava (2002a, 2002b). The database includes monthly observations on all listed companies in the United States from 1963 to 1998. There were a total of 17,460 companies that existed for at least some part of this period, and 1,461 of these companies defaulted. The gross number of observations in this database is more than 1.9 million. The effective number of observations for which all relevant data are available is 1.4 million, and there are 979 defaults included. A variation of this database and a more advanced form of the Jarrow-Chava model are sold commercially by Kamakura Corporation as part of its Kamakura Risk Information Services product line.

Other researchers have used annual data, including the work of Sobehart and colleagues noted above. Annual data have been used in the past because of the researchers' interest in long-term bankruptcy prediction. One of the purposes of this chapter is to show how monthly data can be used for exactly the same purpose, and to show how accuracy changes as the prediction period grows longer.

The basic Jarrow-Chava model uses logistic regression technology to combine equity market and accounting data for default probability prediction. Jarrow and Chava provide a framework that shows that these default-probability estimates are consistent with the best practice reduced form credit models of Jarrow (2001) and Duffie and Singleton (1999). They estimate the probability of default based on five basic variables:

❏ net-income-to-total-assets ratio;
❏ total-liabilities-to-total-assets ratio;

❑ relative size, ratio of total firm equity market value divided by total NYSE and AMEX equity value;
❑ excess return, the monthly return on the firm minus the monthly value-weighted CRSP NYSE/Amex index return; and
❑ stock's volatility of previous month's daily prices.

While there are many variations on this approach that score higher from an accuracy point of view, we report here on the basic Jarrow-Chava formulation discussed in detail in Chapter 6 of van Deventer and Imai. All default probabilities reported in this chapter have been converted from the default intensities produced by Jarrow-Chava to the one-year probabilities of default for each company.

We turn now to the ROC accuracy ratios for the Jarrow-Chava reduced-form modelling approach using the basic Jarrow-Chava variables over the 1963–98 period.

The predictive capability of the Jarrow-Chava reduced-form model default probabilities

Basel II is reasonably tentative in its consideration of default-probability models because of a lack of information regarding the predictive capabilities of the models. This section shows that the technology for measuring predictive capability is transparent and straightforward. We show that the reduced-form modelling approach has a high degree of accuracy even when predicting from a distant horizon.

Van Deventer and Imai (2003) report in Chapter 6 that the basic Jarrow-Chava reduced-form model specification scores a very high 0.9274 ROC accuracy ratio over the 1963–98 period using 1.4 million monthly observations and more than 1.3 billion pairs of defaulted and non-defaulted companies. These results compare very favourably (although a direct comparison can only be made on common data sets) with results found by other researchers and noted by van Deventer and Imai.

The 0.9274 accuracy ratio for the Jarrow-Chava reduced-form models means the following: in the month they defaulted, the default probabilities for the 979 defaulting companies in the database were higher than 92.74% of all of the default probabilities for all non-defaulting companies over the 1963–98 period. Of course, results on different data sets and different time periods will vary.

This time period goes as far back in history as possible since daily stock price data are not available for US companies prior to 1963.

The standard calculation for the ROC accuracy ratio is always based on the default measure in the period of default (which could be a month if using monthly data, or a year if using yearly data). In order to address Basel and financial institutions' management questions about the "early-warning" capability of default-probability models, we need to consider the accuracy of credit models earlier than from the perspective of the period in which default occurs.

We know that, in their distant past, companies that defaulted were at some point the same as other companies and their default probabilities were probably no different from those of otherwise similar companies. In other words, if we took their default probability in that benign era and used that to calculate the ROC accuracy ratio, we would expect to see an accuracy ratio of 0.50 or 50%, because at that point in their history the companies are just "average" and so are their default probabilities.

Therefore, our objective is to see how far in advance of default the ROC accuracy ratio for the defaulting companies rises from the 50% level on its way to 92.74% in the month of default.

MEASURING THE PREDICTIVE ROC ACCURACY RATIO

We calculate the time series of predictive ROC accuracy ratios in the following way:

❏ We again form all possible pairs of one defaulted company and one non-defaulted company. Instead of defining the "default date" and associated default probability for Enron as December 2001, however, we step back one month prior to default and use the November time period for Enron as the default date and the November 2001 default probability as the "one-month predictive" default probability.
❏ We calculate the ROC accuracy ratio on this basis.
❏ We lengthen the prediction period by one more month again.
❏ We recalculate which default probability we will use in the ROC comparison for each of the 979 defaulted companies (in the second iteration, we will use the October 2001 default probability for Enron, not November).

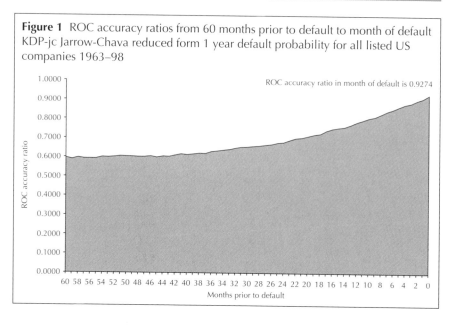

Figure 1 ROC accuracy ratios from 60 months prior to default to month of default KDP-jc Jarrow-Chava reduced form 1 year default probability for all listed US companies 1963–98

❏ We repeat the process until we have studied the predictive period of interest and have calculated the predictive ROC accuracy ratio for each date.

Figure 1 shows that the ROC accuracy ratio is well above the 50% level for the basic Jarrow-Chava default probability series even five years prior to default over the 1.3 billion pairs of default probability comparisons. The ROC accuracy ratio rises steadily as default comes closer and closer.

The rise in the predictive ROC accuracy ratio is easier to see in tabular form. Twelve months prior to default, the accuracy ratio is 78.54%. Two years prior to default, the predictive accuracy ratio is 67.97%, which means the default probabilities for the companies that would ultimately default were already higher than 67.97% of all non-defaulting companies in all time periods. Three years prior to default, the accuracy ratio was still at 63%, and five years before default it was 59.65%. Was this 59.65% estimate of the ROC accuracy ratio statistically different from the 50% accuracy ratio that we would expect if the defaulting companies were so far from default that they were "just average"? The answer is yes – because of the 1.3–1.4 billion comparisons we are making to determine the accuracy ratio, the standard deviation on our estimate of the accuracy

Figure 2 Predictive ROC accuracy ratio of KDP-jc, 1963–98, listed US companies

Months prior to bankruptcy	ROC accuracy ratio	Number of observations	Number of defaults	Number of comparisons	Standard deviation of estimated ROC accuracy ratio	Number of standard deviation from 0.5 ROC accuracy ratio
60	0.5965	1,346,701	979	1,317,461,838	0.0000135	7,140
59	0.5902	1,347,633	979	1,318,374,266	0.0000135	6,659
58	0.5973	1,348,564	979	1,319,285,715	0.0000135	7,206
57	0.5932	1,349,496	979	1,320,198,143	0.0000135	6,894
56	0.5928	1,350,430	979	1,321,112,529	0.0000135	6,865
55	0.5933	1,351,365	979	1,322,027,894	0.0000135	6,906
54	0.6009	1,352,301	979	1,322,944,238	0.0000135	7,494
53	0.5999	1,353,239	979	1,323,862,540	0.0000135	7,419
52	0.6023	1,354,175	979	1,324,778,884	0.0000134	7,608
51	0.6059	1,355,109	979	1,325,693,270	0.0000134	7,891
50	0.6047	1,356,046	979	1,326,610,593	0.0000134	7,800
49	0.6037	1,356,983	979	1,327,527,916	0.0000134	7,725
48	0.6024	1,357,921	979	1,328,446,218	0.0000134	7,626
47	0.6024	1,358,860	979	1,329,365,499	0.0000134	7,629
46	0.6053	1,359,799	979	1,330,284,780	0.0000134	7,857
45	0.5993	1,360,739	979	1,331,205,040	0.0000134	7,393
44	0.6044	1,361,682	979	1,332,128,237	0.0000134	7,793
43	0.6039	1,362,625	979	1,333,051,434	0.0000134	7,756
42	0.6108	1,363,569	979	1,333,975,610	0.0000133	8,300
41	0.6174	1,364,513	979	1,334,899,786	0.0000133	8,825
40	0.6141	1,365,457	979	1,335,823,962	0.0000133	8,566
39	0.6169	1,366,402	979	1,336,749,117	0.0000133	8,792
38	0.6211	1,367,348	979	1,337,675,251	0.0000133	9,130
37	0.6202	1,368,295	979	1,338,602,364	0.0000133	9,061
36	0.6300	1,369,243	979	1,339,530,456	0.0000132	9,855
35	0.6335	1,370,193	979	1,340,460,506	0.0000132	10,144
34	0.6384	1,371,143	979	1,341,390,556	0.0000131	10,550
33	0.6413	1,372,096	979	1,342,323,543	0.0000131	10,794
32	0.6489	1,373,049	979	1,343,256,530	0.0000130	11,433
31	0.6536	1,374,003	979	1,344,190,496	0.0000130	11,835
30	0.6549	1,374,957	979	1,345,124,462	0.0000130	11,950
29	0.6582	1,375,912	979	1,346,059,407	0.0000129	12,237
28	0.6604	1,376,870	979	1,346,997,289	0.0000129	12,431
27	0.6650	1,377,828	979	1,347,935,171	0.0000129	12,835
26	0.6688	1,378,786	979	1,348,873,053	0.0000128	13,172
25	0.6763	1,379,746	979	1,349,812,893	0.0000127	13,844
24	0.6797	1,380,705	979	1,350,751,754	0.0000127	14,155
23	0.6906	1,381,664	979	1,351,690,615	0.0000126	15,160
22	0.7002	1,382,624	979	1,352,630,455	0.0000125	16,070
21	0.7038	1,383,585	979	1,353,571,274	0.0000124	16,422
20	0.7109	1,384,546	979	1,354,512,093	0.0000123	17,121
19	0.7201	1,385,509	979	1,355,454,870	0.0000122	18,049
18	0.7247	1,386,474	979	1,356,399,605	0.0000121	18,527

Figure 2 (continued)

17	0.7400	1,387,438	979	1,357,343,361	0.0000119	20,158
16	0.7502	1,388,404	979	1,358,289,075	0.0000117	21,301
15	0.7557	1,389,371	979	1,359,235,768	0.0000117	21,940
14	0.7594	1,390,337	979	1,360,181,482	0.0000116	22,381
13	0.7709	1,391,307	979	1,361,131,112	0.0000114	23,782
12	0.7854	1,392,278	979	1,362,081,721	0.0000111	25,656
11	0.7951	1,393,251	979	1,363,034,288	0.0000109	26,992
10	0.8063	1,394,226	979	1,363,988,813	0.0000107	28,625
9	0.8133	1,395,201	979	1,364,943,338	0.0000105	29,704
8	0.8270	1,396,176	979	1,365,897,863	0.0000102	31,951
7	0.8412	1,397,152	979	1,366,853,367	0.0000099	34,514
6	0.8520	1,398,129	979	1,367,809,850	0.0000096	36,661
5	0.8653	1,399,106	979	1,368,766,333	0.0000092	39,587
4	0.8776	1,400,083	979	1,369,722,816	0.0000089	42,639
3	0.8851	1,401,061	979	1,370,680,278	0.0000086	44,708
2	0.8992	1,402,039	979	1,371,637,740	0.0000081	49,108
1	0.9098	1,403,017	979	1,372,595,202	0.0000077	52,999
0	0.9274	1,403,898	979	1,373,457,701	0.0000070	61,044

ratio is very small and, at the five-year time horizon, we are more than 7,000 standard deviations from the 50% mark.

Put another way, defaulting companies have default probabilities higher than 60% of all companies 54 months before default. They have default probabilities higher than 70% of all companies 22 months prior to default. They have default probabilities higher than 80% of all companies 10 months before default. By the month of default, again, they have default probabilities higher than 92.74% of all non-defaulting companies over all time periods.

This is an impressive showing for the Jarrow-Chava reduced-form default probabilities over one of the largest commercially available default databases in the United States, with 1.4 million monthly observations. Of course these monthly observations can be converted to annual observations for comparative annual analysis as well.

These concrete results can be used directly by financial institutions to meet the requirements for the internal ratings-based approach in the New Capital Accords proposed by the Basel Committee on Banking Supervision. The results are based on statistical approaches that are standard in mathematical statistics and standard in fields from electronics to medicine to finance. Moreover, the statistical significance of the results can also be determined and replicated by financial institutions themselves who purchase the default database or use their own proprietary databases.

MAPPING THE MERTON MODEL TO ACTUAL DEFAULTS AND THE IMPACT ON ROC ACCURACY RATIO

In comparing different versions of the Merton credit model, one of the key issues is the "mapping of theoretical default probabilities to actual default experience". Different users of the Merton model do this in varying ways, but almost all users of the Merton model have one characteristic in common: the theoretical Merton default probabilities are mapped to actual default experience in a way that changes the absolute level of the default probabilities but not the ordinal ranking of the companies in the universe.

This has a very important implication for the ROC accuracy ratios of the Merton model: the methodology used for mapping theoretical default probabilities to actual default experience will not change the ROC accuracy ratio for the Merton model if it preserves the ordinal ranking of companies by riskiness.

Stating it more simply, the ROC accuracy ratio measures only ordinal accuracy, not calibration or consistency between expected and actual defaults. This point is obvious but often overlooked by naïve users who believe that the mapping methodology improves accuracy. As far as the ROC accuracy ratio goes, this belief is without foundation. The only benefit to a better mapping technology is shown below in measuring the consistency between actual and expected defaults. This is a different issue from measuring the accuracy of the ordinal ranking of companies.

REDUCED-FORM MODEL VERSUS MERTON MODEL PERFORMANCE

To date, other than in papers by the four alumni of Moody's mentioned above, there have been very few studies of credit model performance on a common platform of historical defaults and at various forecasting horizons. In this section, we turn to that task. We compare the accuracy of the ordinal ranking of credit risk for three credit models distributed by the Kamakura Corporation:

Reduced-form credit model
KDP-jc, Kamakura Default Probabilities from an advanced form of the Jarrow-Chava (2002) approach. The model uses six basic inputs, which are transformed to twelve explanatory variables, including financial ratios, equity market data, macro factors and two other variables.

Structural credit models
KDP-ms, Kamakura Default Probabilities using the "best" Merton approach with proprietary mapping to actual default experience by Kamakura.

Hybrid credit models
KDP-jm, Kamakura Default Probabilities combining the Jarrow and Merton approaches in a hybrid model within the logistic regression framework. The KDP-ms Merton default probability is added as an additional explanatory variable to the Jarrow-Chava variables in KDP-jc to form KDP-jm.

Figure 3 shows the ROC accuracy ratios for version 2.2 of all three of the models based on data from 1989 to July 2003. The chart

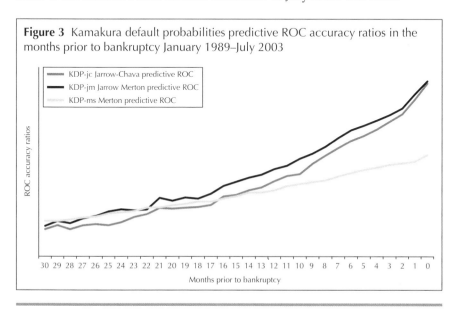

Figure 3 Kamakura default probabilities predictive ROC accuracy ratios in the months prior to bankruptcy January 1989–July 2003

shows clearly that the accuracy of the credit-risk ranking of both the KDP-jc Jarrow-Chava reduced-form model and the hybrid KDP-jm model is superior to that of the KDP-ms Merton model for all forecasting horizons of 15 months and less prior to default. By the month of default, the performance differential is in excess of 15%, a very large difference over the 1.3 million-sample size of default probabilities. In the 15–30-month forecasting horizon, the KDP-jm Jarrow-Merton hybrid model and the KDP-ms Merton model are close in accuracy, with the KDP-jc Jarrow-Chava model slightly less accurate.

With this kind of precision in ranking of models by accuracy for any user-defined forecasting horizon, there should be no question about the superiority of Model A versus Model B when it comes to the Basel II requirements for credit model testing.

PERFORMANCE OF NAÏVE MODELS AS A PERFORMANCE BENCHMARK FOR THE MERTON MODEL

As noted in the introduction, oftentimes a naïve model outperforms a seemingly more elegant model. It is very important that users of credit models test performance of their "favourite" model versus naïve models, both to better assess the accuracy of their favourite model and to determine what amount of financial resources should be invested in the favourite model.

As we saw in earlier sections

❑ no mapping of the Merton theoretical default probabilities to actual defaults changes the ROC accuracy ratio; and

❑ testing the accuracy of ordinal ranking of companies by riskiness should be based on a common historical default database and measured using the ROC accuracy ratio.

In model testing for its version 2.2 default probability release, Kamakura tested its three credit models listed in the previous section against a large number of financial ratios used as a single variable predictor of credit risk. We fitted a logistic regression to each of the financial ratios, one at a time, and measured the ROC accuracy ratios from the resulting logistic regressions. The results are well known to sophisticated users of the Merton and other credit models but have never been previously tested:

❏ Seven of the financial ratios tested had ROC accuracy ratios superior to the accuracy ratio for the Merton model.
❏ Both the KDP-jc advanced Jarrow-Chava model and the KDP-jm Jarrow-Merton hybrid model had ROC accuracy ratios far superior to any financial ratio on a stand-alone basis.

This is a striking conclusion, but it is well known in the industry and consistent with Robert Merton's concern about the age of the Merton model. Needless to say, many of the seven financial ratios are available free on popular financial websites, which calls into question the wisdom of a large investment in a competing credit measure that is less successful. Users of popular credit models and the Basel Committee on Banking Supervision clearly need to be aware of performance versus naïve credit models such as those we have examined here.

We turn now to another measure of model performance.

CONSISTENCY OF ESTIMATED AND ACTUAL DEFAULTS

Falkenstein and Boral (2000) correctly emphasise the need to do more than measure the correctness of the ordinal ranking of companies by riskiness. One needs to determine whether a model is correctly "calibrated". In the words of Falkenstein and Boral, that is whether the model has default probabilities that are biased high or low. As noted in the example in the introduction, a naïve user of credit models can be convinced a model has superior performance just because it gives higher default probabilities for some subset of a sample. A test of consistency between actual and expected defaults is needed to see whether this difference in default probability levels is consistent with actual default experience or just an *ad hoc* adjustment or noise.

A simple example is enough to show why this comparison of actual and expected defaults has to be done period by period, not just over the sample as a whole.

Consider the following example:

❏ Assume we know the actual average probability of default for all listed companies in the United States from 1963 to 1998 and that all companies in the US have this probability of default.

❑ Assume that this default probability is constant over the period 1963–98 (an assumption common to many CDO modelling approaches).

❑ Assume that there is no correlation between the default probabilities of any two companies (another common assumption in CDO modelling).

How consistent would the actual number of defaults and the expected number of defaults have been given these assumptions?

We take the following steps:

1. Based on the number of companies that are listed in the US at the start of each year, we calculate the confidence intervals on the high and low numbers of default that should occur in that year if our assumption that there is zero correlation is true.

2. We then compare the actual number of defaults to our confidence interval.

3. When we do this analysis, we know the following:

   a. Over the entire period 1963–98, our expected number of defaults will exactly match the US total (which is a much better performance than we would get in forecasting CDO defaults).

   b. We can calculate the 99.5% number of defaults.

   c. We can calculate the 0.5% number of defaults.

   d. If our credit-modelling assumptions are good, we will have a high degree of consistency between actual and expected defaults, falling out of the confidence interval only 1% of the time.

Figure 4 shows the results of the forecasting exercise described above.

As Figure 4 shows, even though we correctly forecast the 1,120 bankruptcies that occurred in the United States over the 1963–98, we were dramatically wrong on timing and our assumption that there is no correlation among listed companies in the United States seems to be seriously wrong. Over almost all of the 40-year period, we are at or below the 0.5% percentile level or over the 99.5% percentile level when it comes to actual number of bankruptcies – we are

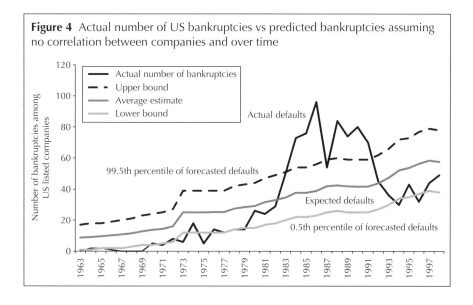

Figure 4 Actual number of US bankruptcies vs predicted bankruptcies assuming no correlation between companies and over time

out of the 99% range of probability much of the time. We can measure how often in Figure 5.

Figure 5 shows that, in 18 of the 36 years studied, exactly half the time, actual defaults were outside 99% confidence interval in our simulation, even though on average we predicted exactly the right number of defaults over the 36 years. This shows that model calibration over time, not just over a "one-period" sample, is very important. We turn to a methodology for doing that in the next section.

A QUANTITATIVE TEST OF CONSISTENCY BETWEEN EXPECTED AND ACTUAL DEFAULTS

Along with the ROC accuracy ratio, one of the key measures of model performance is the consistency between the expected number of defaults (according to a given credit model) and the actual number of defaults that results. Robert Jarrow has established that, conditional on the values of the Jarrow-Chava input variables, the default probabilities of each company are independent.[4] A similar argument applies for the Merton model conditional on the values of company assets being given at any point in time. Figure 6 uses this fact to compare the expected number of defaults with the actual number of defaults for all three models produced by Kamakura for the US universe.

173

Figure 5 Actual bankruptcies in the United States 1963–1998 compared to expected defaults when bankruptcy risk is uncorrelated

Year	Number of listed companies in USA			Simulated number of defaults using average US default probability and assuming no correlation among US companies				
	Not Bankrupt	Bankrupt	Total	Actual number of bankruptcies	Lower bound at 0.5th percentile	Expected number of defaults at 50th percentile	Upper bound at 99.5th percentile	Outside of 99% probability range?
1963	1,252	0	1,252	0	1	8.8	17	yes
1964	1,297	2	1,299	2	1	9.1	18	
1965	1,373	2	1,375	2	2	9.7	18	
1966	1,449	1	1,450	1	2	10.2	19	yes
1967	1,545	0	1,545	0	2	10.8	20	yes
1968	1,645	0	1,645	0	3	11.5	21	yes
1969	1,821	0	1,821	0	4	12.8	23	yes
1970	1,949	5	1,954	5	4	13.7	24	
1971	2,042	4	2,046	4	5	14.4	25	yes
1972	2,277	8	2,285	8	6	16.0	27	
1973	3,560	6	3,566	6	12	25.0	39	yes
1974	3,532	18	3,550	18	12	24.9	39	
1975	3,543	5	3,548	5	12	24.9	39	yes
1976	3,563	14	3,577	14	12	25.1	39	
1977	3,567	12	3,579	12	12	25.1	39	
1978	3,905	14	3,919	14	14	27.5	42	
1979	4,036	14	4,050	14	15	28.4	43	yes
1980	4,133	26	4,159	26	15	29.2	44	
1981	4,493	24	4,517	24	17	31.7	47	
1982	4,669	29	4,698	29	18	33.0	49	
1983	4,885	50	4,935	50	20	34.6	51	
1984	5,302	73	5,375	73	22	37.7	54	yes
1985	5,299	76	5,375	76	22	37.7	54	yes
1986	5,448	96	5,544	96	23	38.9	56	yes
1987	5,913	54	5,967	54	25	41.9	59	
1988	5,959	84	6,043	84	26	42.4	60	yes
1989	5,890	74	5,964	74	25	41.9	59	yes
1990	5,850	80	5,930	80	25	41.6	59	yes
1991	5,870	70	5,940	70	25	41.7	59	yes
1992	6,195	45	6,240	45	27	43.8	62	
1993	6,717	36	6,753	36	30	47.4	66	
1994	7,401	30	7,431	30	34	52.2	72	yes
1995	7,616	43	7,659	43	35	53.8	73	
1996	8,001	32	8,033	32	37	56.4	77	yes
1997	8,281	44	8,325	44	39	58.4	79	
1998	8,154	49	8,203	49	38	57.6	78	
Grand total*		1,120	1,59,551	1,120	622	1,120	1,650	18

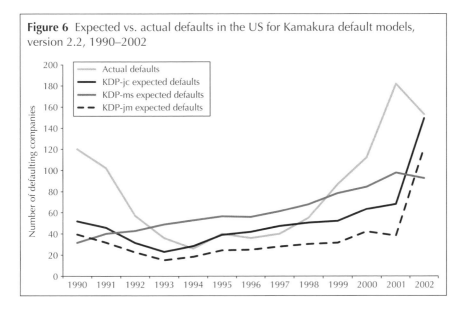

Figure 6 Expected vs. actual defaults in the US for Kamakura default models, version 2.2, 1990–2002

The light tinted line shows the actual number of defaults in the US universe from 1990 to 2002. The dramatic rise and fall and rise in the number of defaults is strong evidence of correlation among default probabilities due to common dependence on macro factors driving default, as explained in van Deventer and Imai (2003). The black line is the expected number of defaults according to the KDP-jc Jarrow-Chava reduced-form default probability. It does a good job of capturing the rise and fall and rise in defaults, although it is biased slightly low. If graphed on the basis of the average default probability in the universe, the results would show the well-known autocorrelation in the observed default rate.

The bottom (dashed) line is the expected number of defaults in the KDP-jm Jarrow Merton hybrid model. This model also captures the credit cycle but it has a stronger bias towards the low end than the KDP-jc model, which is one reason why many analysts prefer the KDP-jc default probability.

The KDP-ms Merton Structure model's expected defaults is the grey line, which tends not to capture the peaks and valleys of defaults over the credit cycle. Expected defaults are nearly a straight line, although the KDP-ms default probabilities on average produce a higher level of defaults over the 1990–2002 period than the other two models do. This tendency is aggravated if a model

175

vendor tends to cap its Merton default probabilities at an arbitrary level that is held constant over the business cycle.

Clearly, the Merton model misses the peaks and valleys of the credit cycle. This is counterintuitive to many, who argue that stock prices will be low when times are bad and default rates are high. The truth is somewhat different, as confirmed by logistic regression linking stock prices indices and default. Stock prices are leading indicators of good times and bad times, as many researchers over the last four decades have found. When times are at their worst and defaults at their peak, stock indices will have already risen in anticipation of good times ahead. The US economy in mid-2003 is a perfect example, with defaults at an all-time high and stock price indices at their highest level in 18 months.

The reduced-form models capture this timing difference, but the Merton model does not. As a result, it is "out of synch" by about half of a credit cycle, which is why it misses the peaks and valleys of default. We measure this quantitatively in the next section.

RANKING THE MODELS BY THEIR POWER TO PREDICT THE ACTUAL NUMBER OF DEFAULTS

It is helpful to quantify the models' ability to predict the actual number of defaults. Most ability measures come from running a regression that predicts the actual number of defaults as a function of the expected number of defaults derived from the model.

We can run the regression Actual defaults = A + B (Expected defaults) for each model.

The reason for running this model is to quantify the stability of its errors. If the predicted number of defaults is always too low by 10 defaults, the regression parameter A will adjust to pick this up. If the model's bias is a consistent proportion of the total, then the coefficient B will pick it up. If the errors of the model are unpredictable, the adjusted R^2 of the regression will measure that precisely.

A superior model has the following characteristics:

❑ It explains a higher percentage of the variation in actual defaults and the adjusted R^2 will be higher.
❑ It has a higher t-score on the expected number of defaults, the explanatory variable in the regression that predicts actual defaults as a function of expected defaults.

❑ It has a lower standard deviation of the difference between the actual defaults and predicted defaults that come from this regression analysis.

❑ It has a coefficient of expected defaults closest to one.

These measures of significance are mathematically related. We look at the models' performance using these measures for the version 2.2 Kamakura Default Probabilities for defaults from 1990–2002.

Explanatory power

The adjusted R^2 in a linear regression is a popular measure of the explanatory power of a linear regression. As shown in Table 1, the KDP-jc Jarrow-Chava model explains more of the variation in actual defaults. The results are based on the regression model we discussed above: Actual defaults = A + B (expected defaults), where A and B are the coefficients determined by the linear regression.

The KDP-jc model explains 43.48% of the variation in actual defaults, compared with 34.96% and 24.75% for the KDP-jm Hybrid and KDP-ms Merton structural models.

Statistical significance (t-score) of expected defaults

When the linear regressions linking actual and expected defaults are run for all three models, the KDP-jc Jarrow-Chava model again was shown to be the best performer. Expected defaults for KDP-jc had a t-score of 3.20, which means the coefficient on expected defaults in the regression was 3.20 standard deviations from zero – the larger the t-score, the better.

Table 1 Actual defaults measured as a function of predicted defaults by the model
Actual defaults = A + B × Expected defaults

Adjusted R^2 of the regression of actual defaults as a function of predicted defaults
Ranked from best to worst

	Adusted R^2
KDP-jc Jarrow-Chava Model	43.48%
KDP-jm Jarrow-Merton Hybrid Model	34.96%
KDP-ms Merton-Structural Model	24.75%

Table 2 Actual defaults measured as a function of predicted defaults by the model
Actual defaults = A + B × Expected defaults

T-score of KDP expected defaults in regression of actual defaults as a function of predicted defaults
Ranked from best to worst

	T-score
KDP-jc Jarrow-Chava Model	3.20
KDP-jm Jarrow-Merton Hybrid Model	2.73
KDP-ms Merton-Structural Model	2.22

Table 3 Actual defaults measured as a function of predicted defaults by the model
Actual Defaults = A + B × Expected Defaults

Standard deviation of difference between expected number of defaults and actual number of defaults
Ranked from best to worst

	Standard deviation
KDP-jc Jarrow-Chava Model	37.61
KDP-jm Jarrow-Merton Hybrid Model	40.34
KDP-ms Merton Structural Model	43.40

The Jarrow-Merton KDP-jm ranked second with 2.73 standard deviations, and the KDP-ms Merton structural model ranked last with 2.22 standard deviations.

Standard deviation of errors in predicting actual defaults from expected defaults

Another measure of performance is the ability to predict actual defaults from expected defaults. The model that has the smallest standard deviation of the errors in doing so is the best performer (although this test is mathematically related to the test on explanatory power above). The Jarrow-Chava model again shows the smallest standard deviation in predicting the actual number of defaults, with a standard deviation of 37 defaults a year.

Table 4 Coefficient of expected number of defaults in regression
Ranked from best to worst

	Coefficient
KDP-jc Jarrow-Chava Model	1.10
KDP-jm Jarrow-Merton Hybrid Model	1.18
KDP-ms Merton Structural Model	1.35

Coefficient on expected number of defaults

The final performance measure for predicting actual defaults comes from the coefficient on expected defaults, which comes from the model. A coefficient of 1.0 is a model where the expected number of defaults has no bias. A coefficient substantially different from 1 indicates a model that has a larger bias.

Table 4 shows, interestingly, that the KDP-jc has the coefficient closest to one, with a 1.10 coefficient. The rise-fall-rise in the credit cycle produced by KDP-jc expected defaults needed less adjustment than the Merton model, which ended up at 1.35.

All of these related tests confirm a consistent finding: actual defaults and expected defaults are more closely related when using reduced-form and hybrid models than when using the Merton model alone.

IMPLICATIONS OF MODEL TESTING FOR BASEL COMPLIANCE AND PRACTICAL USE OF CREDIT MODELS

As Robert Merton pointed out in the opening quotation, the Merton model is now more than 28 years old. It remains popular in industry and regulatory circles, but for the first time there is a well-established scientific basis for measuring the performance of credit models on the same historical default data in two key dimensions:

❑ ordinal ranking of firms by credit riskiness; and
❑ consistency of actual and expected defaults.

Before such tests became available, many well-intentioned bankers were unable to correctly assess credit model performance because of a lack of data and, as noted by Falkenstein and Boral, a tendency for some models to produce higher default probabilities than actual default experience could justify.

This bias is harmful in two respects. Unless the tests outlined in this chapter are performed, it can result in an inaccurate ranking of model performance. More importantly, if this bias is not detected, all calculations using such a model would produce inaccurate pricing, valuation, hedging and portfolio-loss simulation. This compounding of effects is contrary to the principles laid out in Basel II, even though the Basel Committee clearly had the legacy of the older Merton model in mind when drafting its proposals.

A scientific approach to testing multiple models reveals that reduced-form and hybrid models offer superior performance by both the criteria listed above. Furthermore, at least seven financial ratios are more accurate in ranking companies by riskiness than the Merton model for every monotonic mapping of theoretical default probabilities to actual default experience. Practical bankers and skilled regulators need accurate model test results to generate value added for their shareholders.

1   Professor Merton's comments were made at a major risk-management conference before an audience of approximately 400 risk-management experts.

2   An example is the extension of the Merton credit model to incorporate random interest rates by Shimko, Tejima and van Deventer (1993), who combined other Robert Merton insights from the 1970s with his credit model. Other examples are minor modifications of the Merton credit model to allow for early hitting of the default barrier and various methodologies for the estimation of the volatility of company assets in the model.

3   This calculation can involve a very large number of pairs. The current commercial database at Kamakura Corporation involves the comparison of 1.4 billion pairs of observations, but on a modern personal computer as of this writing processing time for the exact calculation is slightly over one hour. Processing time using a very close approximation is less than one minute.

4   They are independent because the macro factors in the logistic regression are the sole drivers of correlation among default probabilities. See Jarrow, Lando and Yu (2003) for proof of this point.

BIBLIOGRAPHY

Altman, E., 1968, "Financial Ratios, Discriminant Analysis, and the Prediction of Corporate Bankruptcy", *Journal of Finance*, **23**.

Altman, E., R. Haldeman, and P. Narayanan, 1977, "ZETA Analysis: A New Model to Identify Bankruptcy Risk of Corporations", *Journal of Banking and Finance*, pp. 29–55.

Basel Committee on Banking Supervision, 2001, "Consultative Document: The New Capital Accords", monograph (Basel: Bank for International Settlements).

Black, F., and M. Scholes, 1973, "The Pricing of Options and Corporate Liabilities", *Journal of Political Economy*, **81**, pp. 399–418.

Blum, M., 1974, "Failing Company Discriminant Analysis", *Journal of Accounting Research*, Spring.

Duffie D., and K. Singleton, 1999, "Modelling Term Structures of Defaultable Bonds", *Review of Financial Studies*, **12(4)**, pp. 197–226.

Falkenstein, E., and A. Boral, 2000, "RiskCalc for Private Companies: Moody's Default Model", Moody's Investors Service Memorandum.

Hosmer, D. W., and S. Lemeshow, 2000, *Applied Logistic Regression* (New York: John Wiley & Sons).

Jarrow, R., 2001, "Default Parameter Estimation Using Market Prices", *Financial Analysts Journal*, September/October.

Jarrow, R., and S. Chava, 2002a, "Bankruptcy Prediction with Industry Effects", Working Paper, Cornell University.

Jarrow, R., and S. Chava, 2002b, "A Comparison of Explicit versus Implicit Estimates of Default Probabilities", Working Paper, Cornell University.

Jarrow, R., D. Lando, and F. Yu, 2003, "Default Risk and Diversification: Theory and Applications", Working Paper, Cornell University.

Jarrow, R., D. van Deventer, and X. Wang, 2002, "A Robust Test of Merton's Structural Model for Credit Risk" *Journal of Risk*, forthcoming.

Merton, R. C., 1974, "On the Pricing of Corporate Debt: The Risk Structure of Interest Rates", *Journal of Finance*, **29**, pp. 449–70.

Shimko, D., H., Tejima, and D. van Deventer, 1993, "The Pricing of Risky Debt when Interest Rates are Stochastic", *Journal of Fixed Income*, September, pp. 58–66.

Sobehart, J., S. Keenan, and R. Stein, 2000, "Validation Methodologies for Default Risk Models", *Credit*, May, pp. 51–6

Shumway, T., 2001, "Forecasting Bankruptcy More Accurately: A Simple Hazard Model", *Journal of Business*, **74(1)**.

Van Deventer, D., and K. Imai, 1996, *Financial Risk Analytics: A Term Structure Model Approach for Banking, Insurance, and Investment Management* (McGraw Hill).

Van Deventer, D., and K. Imai, 2003, *Credit Risk Models and the Basel Accords: The Merton Model and Reduced-Form Models*, (New York: John Wiley & Sons).

Van Deventer, D., and X. Wang, 2002, "Basel II and Lessons from Enron: The Consistency of the Merton Credit Model with Observable Credit Spreads and Equity Prices", Working Paper, Kamakura Corporation.

Van Deventer, D., and X. Wang, 2003, "Measuring Predictive Capability of Credit Models Under the Basel Capital Accords: Conseco and Results from the United States, 1963–1998", Working Paper, Kamakura Corporation.

8

*Point-in-Time Versus Through-the-Cycle Ratings**

Scott D. Aguais; Lawrence R. Forest, Jr; Elaine Y. L. Wong; Diana Diaz-Ledezma

Barclays Capital

To qualify for the advanced internal ratings-based (AIRB) status under the Basel II Capital Accord, "internationally active banks" ("banks") must document the validity not only of their probability of default (PD) estimates but also of the loss given default (LGD) and exposure at default (EAD) measures that they plan to use as alternatives to the foundation internal ratings-based (FIRB) assumptions.[1] The PD, LGD and EAD building blocks are central to most aspects of credit risk management – structuring, monitoring, pricing transactions, establishing loan loss provisions and assessing credit portfolio risk. The likely reduction in regulatory capital

*The authors would like to acknowledge the many Basel and credit risk-related discussions they have had with various members of the Barclays Risk Management Team over the last year. The authors also want to thank Tim Thompson, Julian Shaw and Brian Ranson for helpful comments. KMV also deserves thanks for providing an historical data set of five-year KMV EDF term structures for all of their counterparties. Finally, we thank Zoran Stanisavljevic, for his unending credit data management support for our credit research and modelling efforts. All errors remain the responsibility of the authors. The views and opinions expressed in this chapter are those of the authors and do not necessarily reflect the views and opinions of Barclays Bank PLC.

arising from qualifying for the AIRB status increases the incentives for banks to improve these fundamental measures used in credit risk management.

Banks' internal ratings provide the PD indicators under the IRB approach. These ratings typically summarise information coming from internal financial analyses, vendor credit models and agency ratings. Some of these sources focus on the current situation and others attempt to look at likely developments over several years. Basel's third consultative paper (CP3), as well as other documents, refers to these contrasting approaches as point-in-time (PIT) and through-the-cycle (TTC).

The goal of this chapter is to:

❑ provide operational definitions of PIT and TTC ratings by focusing on the horizon involved in the credit assessment;
❑ introduce an approach for translating agency ratings at different points in the cycle to one-year (PIT) PDs; and
❑ describe tests and initial empirical results measuring the accuracy of existing ratings as either PIT or TTC indicators of default risk.

By defining the relevant horizon for PIT or TTC, we support a definition that can then be empirically tested as to the accuracy of a rating's default prediction. By converting agency ratings into PIT representations of one-year default rates, we provide an approach for integrating PIT ratings (such as one-year KMV EDFs) with agency ratings.[2] Finally, by focusing specifically on what makes a rating system PIT or TTC, we hope to provide a foundation for assessing and validating credit ratings.

A BRIEF REVIEW OF INTERNAL CREDIT RATINGS

A key focus in the credit risk literature over the last five to ten years has been on default prediction and the development of internal rating measures of borrower creditworthiness. Before turning to the issue of PIT versus TTC, we highlight some of the salient characteristics required of sound internal credit rating systems to provide some context for the PIT/TTC discussion to follow.

Banks use internal ratings as critical inputs in approving and pricing loans, establishing reserves, setting limits and managing the portfolio of credit exposures. For banks to perform these functions well, internal credit ratings must discriminate accurately between borrowers with greater and lesser chances of defaulting over the varying time frames used in the analysis.

From an enterprise perspective, credit risk comes in many different colours, styles and shapes, and is traditionally managed in "silos". For example, large banks have different types of obligors – retail customers, large corporate borrowers, SMEs and sovereigns – requiring varying approaches for estimating creditworthiness. See, for example, Aguais and Rosen (2001), who outline an enterprise credit risk management framework that recognises the need for different approaches across the banking enterprise.

Looking back on the evolution of internal ratings, earlier non-statistical approaches focused primarily on deriving ordinal rankings of risk executed on a "yes-or-no" basis. Credit officers used qualitative factors and, later, financial data in assessing a borrower's willingness and ability to repay a credit obligation. As statistical and behavioural credit-scoring models were being developed for consumer markets, fundamental credit analysis was becoming more quantitative for corporate borrowers.

Focusing on approaches applied to the corporate sector, the evolution from qualitative to quantitative (and then ordinal to cardinal) has followed a natural progression. Ed Altman's (1968) approach for the Z-score stands out as one of the first statistical approaches. In the early 1990s KMV Corporation provided one of the first commercially available models based on the Merton framework for predicting one-year PDs (also known as expected default frequency, or EDF). See Ranson (2002), Chapter 3, for a review of some of the evolving approaches to risk rating and default measurement.[3]

With regard to Basel II today, there are some basic characteristics that broadly define a successful internal risk rating system. To start, ratings systems need to distinguish different levels of credit risk with enough resolution (granularity) that the bank avoids adverse selection in competing for customers. In addition, the ratings system must imply default risk measures that are cardinal (ie, numeric), as in KMV EDFs, and not just ordinal. Thus, for each separate internal risk rating, whether labelled BB+, 3– or whatever, one must be able to identify an acceptably narrow range of values (eg, 50 to 75 bps) for the corresponding PD over one or more standard horizons. The different ratings need to span the entire credit risk range consisting of from 0 to 100%. Rating systems that are derived from statistical default modelling typically satisfy these criteria.

Banks also use ratings in the pricing of illiquid, credit-risky instruments. Thus, a bank may also need each ratings level to reference a benchmark credit spread or, equivalently, a risk-neutral PD at one or more maturities.[4] Credit spreads, in principle, could involve ratings somewhat different from those related to PDs. Suppose that companies A and B have the same one-year PD, but that A's PD has a greater propensity to increase in recessions. The two companies would share the same one-year rating related to a real-world default risk, but A's one-year rating related to risk-neutral risk would be inferior to B's. In practice, however, analysts customarily use the same rating in gauging real-world and risk-neutral PDs. The state of the art has not progressed far enough to permit differentiation between real-world and risk-neutral ratings.

With regard to the horizon for calibrating an internal ratings system, banks most often evaluate their ratings systems over one-year intervals. However, credit exposures often have maturities greater than one year and proper pricing and portfolio management usually involves analysis over longer horizons. This makes it important to consider the possibility of distinct PIT and TTC ratings.

POINT-IN-TIME VS. THROUGH-THE-CYCLE RATINGS – AN OVERVIEW

History of the terminology

In the January 2001 Consultative Document on the proposed IRB Approach for the New Basel Capital Accord, the Basel Committee on Banking Supervision (Basel, 2001) provides a formal distinction between PIT and TTC credit ratings. While it doesn't define the two terms explicitly, Basel evidently believes that there are PIT ratings that measure default risk over a short horizon of perhaps a year, and there are TTC ratings that measure it over a longer horizon of perhaps five or more years.

Specifically, paragraph 53, p. 12, of the 2001 Consultative Document for the Internal Ratings-Based Approach says:

> 53. Some banks distinguish their rating system on the basis of whether it estimates the probability of a borrower's default on a "point in time" or "through the cycle" approach. In a "point in time"

process, an internal rating reflects an assessment of the borrower's current condition and/or most likely future condition over the course of the chosen time horizon. As such, the internal rating changes as the borrower's condition changes over the course of the credit/business cycle. In contrast, a "through the cycle" process requires assessment of the borrower's riskiness bases on a worst-case, "bottom of the cycle scenario" (i.e., its condition under stress). In this case, a borrower's rating would tend to stay the same over the course of the credit/business cycle.[5]

While the January 2001 Basel consultative document discusses PIT and TTC approaches more broadly, the first Basel reference seems to be a year earlier, in January 2000. In the Basel Committee's discussion paper describing a G-10 survey of internal ratings systems (Basel, 2000), the PIT/TTC distinction is first referenced under a discussion of risk-rating time horizons. The comments made there are simple, but consistent with the January 2001 comments made above. In addition, the paper raises concerns expressed by some banks during the survey of potential inconsistencies created when mapping between external agency ratings (usually thought of as TTC) and internal PIT ratings.

So the general debate surrounding PIT versus TTC in the context of Basel II was initiated. But where do these terms for PIT and TTC actually come from?[6] Since agency ratings provided early examples of TTC ratings, it is natural that early references to "through-the-cycle" ratings first appeared in Moody's and S&P discussions of their approach to corporate ratings. One of the first examples of through-the-cycle ratings discussions can be found in a November 1995 Moody's report on the copper industry (Moody's, 1995).[7] In 1996 a discussion appearing in S&P's *Corporate Ratings Criteria* entitled, "Factoring cyclicality into corporate ratings" provides S&P's perspective on the TTC issue:

> Standard & Poor's credit ratings are meant to be forward-looking; that is, their time horizon extends as far as is analytically foreseeable. Accordingly, the anticipated ups and downs of business cycles – whether industry specific or related to the general economy – should be factored into the credit rating all along. This approach is in keeping with Standard & Poor's belief that the value of its rating products is greatest when its ratings focus on the long-term, and do not fluctuate with near-term performance. Ratings should never be a

mere snapshot of the present situation. There are two models for how cyclicality is incorporated in credit ratings. Sometimes, ratings are held constant throughout the cycle. Alternatively, the rating does vary – but within a relatively narrow band. ... The ideal is to rate "through the cycle".[8]

Following on the rating agencies discussions, the first use of the "point-in-time" terminology can be found in an analysis and survey of large US bank's risk-rating systems conducted by two researchers from the Federal Reserve, William Treacy and Mark Carey (1998).[9] In this 1998 article, the first reference to point-in-time ratings seems to have been born in a juxtaposition of PIT and TTC ratings approaches. They write that "Rating the current condition [of the borrower] is consistent with the fact that rating criteria at banks do not seem to be updated to take account of the current phase of the business cycle. Banks we interviewed do vary somewhat in the time period they have in mind producing ratings, with about 25 percent rating the borrower's risk over a one-year period, 25 percent rating over a longer period, such as the life of the loan, and the remaining 50 percent having a specific period in mind. ... In contrast to bank practice, both Moody's and S&P rate through the cycle."[10]

Examining the concepts of PIT and TTC

Having developed the history of the PIT/TTC terminology, we will now examine these concepts in more detail. We start by providing working definitions. We then identify conditions under which one can meaningfully distinguish between PIT and TTC ratings. Finally, we introduce the idea of testing the extent to which existing ratings can be regarded as good PIT or TTC indicators.

We start with a working definition of PIT and TTC ratings. Consider the following: A PIT rating measures default risk over a short horizon, often a year or less. A TTC rating measures it over a horizon long enough for business-cycle effects largely to vanish. As one convention, one could regard default risk over a period of five or more years as TTC.

With this definition, we can easily imagine a company's PIT and TTC ratings differing. Suppose we expect a company's creditworthiness to trend up or down *atypically* over several years. In this case, its PIT and TTC ratings would differ, with the disparity reflecting the anticipated but unusual evolution in the company's status.

Observe that we have not said that the pending developments reflect the general business cycle. A rating with a long horizon needs to account for all of the things that may occur over several years, not only the business cycle. In making decisions on multi-year exposures, a bank can't afford to ignore any of the events that seem likely or just possible over an extended period. Thus, we should probably think of TTC as denoting "long term" and PIT "short term."

While we can always imagine separate PIT and TTC ratings, the distinction may be unimportant in practice. We need to consider the following question: *When does a TTC rating provide information not already in a PIT one?*

In answering this, it is easier to describe when a TTC rating provides *no* additional information. Suppose that the relationship between short- and long-term default risks is always the same – say a one-year PD of x invariably implies a five-year PD of $f(x)$. Then the TTC rating is redundant, since the PIT rating already implies it. (Alternatively, we could regard the PIT rating as redundant, implied by the TTC one.) However, if the relationship between short- and long-term default risk varies across firms or time – meaning that a one-year PD of x implies a five-year PD of $f(x) \pm z$, where z is an economically significant random variable – then the TTC rating could add information beyond that already provided by the PIT one. In the example, the TTC rating would add information if it helped predict z.

We could also express this by saying that the PIT $-$ TTC distinction does not matter unless at least two factors influence credit risk. To grasp this point, consider the analogous situation for interest rates. In a single-factor interest rate model, the short rate provides all the information needed to determine the entire yield curve. In other words, the short rate serves not only as a definitive indicator of where interest rates are and will be shortly (PIT) but also as a best predictor of where they might be over any extended time interval (TTC). If, however, it takes more than one factor to describe the predictable patterns in rates, one often selects a long-term interest rate (TTC) as a second factor that, together with the short rate, explains the entire yield curve.

For credit, this point becomes most transparent when applied to spreads. Imagine modelling credit spreads in the same way as interest rates and suppose that one needs values for two risk factors to establish a full term structure. In this case, one could think of the PIT rating as determining the one-year spread and the TTC rating as determining the five-year one, and those two spreads together as establishing the full term structure. However, if spreads derive from a one-factor model, then only one of the two ratings would suffice to pin down the entire term structure. If the term structure arises from a three-factor model, one would need even more information than ratings at two different horizons.

So, the concept of distinct PIT and TTC ratings makes sense if one needs at least two risk factors to explain a typical company's credit risk term structure (see Panel 1 for an example). We think a meticulous modelling of default term structures would involve more than one factor, so we continue to talk of PIT and TTC ratings. However, before rushing to develop a two-part rating system, a bank must ask whether, with the information now available, it would significantly improve the accuracy of its credit evaluations and the quality of its credit decisions to justify the effort. For the most part, we think not. Basel II looks ahead to having banks validate one-factor ratings systems. For most banks, two-factor systems have not yet reached the drawing board. Some day we think they will.

PANEL 1 EXAMPLES OF SINGLE- AND TWO-FACTOR CREDIT MODELS

Consider some of the following credit models for ratings. We start with the single-factor case:

Let $j \; \varepsilon \; \{1, 2, ..., D\}$ represent a *PIT* rating in which 1 indicates the best credit state and D the worst, default. Let j_t be the rating value at time t. Assume, further, that if we know j_t, then we can determine the rating's *probability distribution* at any future time $t+n$ by applying the fixed transition matrix T as follows,

$$D(j_{t+n} \mid j_t) = T^n u(j_t)$$

$$j_{t+n} \equiv credit\ state\ at\ time\ t+n$$

$$D(j_{t+n} \mid j_t) \equiv (p(1_{t+n} \mid j_t), ..., p(D_{t+n} \mid j_t))'$$

$$p(j_{t+n} \mid j_t) \equiv probability\ of\ reaching \qquad\qquad (1)$$

$$j_{t+n}\ at\ time\ t+n\ starting\ from\ j_t\ at\ time\ t$$

$$u(j_t) \equiv (0, ..., 0, \underset{\underset{j_t^{th}slot}{\uparrow}}{1}, 0, ..., 0)'$$

As shown in Equation (1), if we know j_t, we need no further information to evaluate creditworthiness at any future time $t+n$. Given the assumption of a fixed transition matrix at all times, the relevant distribution of future creditworthiness $D(j_{t+n}|j_t)$ in the case of each possible rating is predicted entirely from knowledge of the current PIT rating j_t. No *TTC* rating can add any useful information. The single PIT rating j_t tells us all we can know about a borrower's future credit status, so we may regard it also as the best *TTC* rating.

Next consider a two-factor model of credit risk. Suppose that we can explain random changes over time in the transition matrix with a factor z. Since the z affects transition rates for all borrowers, it is a systematic factor related to general economic conditions. Thus, $T(z_t)$ represents the transition matrix applicable at time t as influenced by the value z_t of the factor at that time. Assume further that the z factor evolves according to the mean-reverting process depicted below

$$z_{t+1} = bz_t + \sqrt{1-b^2}\,\varepsilon_t \qquad (2)$$
$$0 < b < 1$$
$$\varepsilon_t \sim \Phi(0,1)$$

$\Phi(m,s) \equiv$ *normal cdf with mean m and standard deviation d*

Such a process yields time series that can exhibit cycles (see Figure 1). Here, we obtain the probability distributions $D(j_{t+n}|j_t,z_t)$ that describe credit risk at each future time $t + n$ by the integration below

$$D(j_{t+n}\,|\,j_t, z_t) = \left[\int_{-\infty}^{\infty} \dots \int_{-\infty}^{\infty} \prod_{i=1}^{n} T(z_{t+i})\,\phi\,(z_{t+1}, \dots, z_{t+n}\,|\,z_t)\,dz_{t+1}\dots dz_{t+n}\right] u(j_t) \quad (3)$$

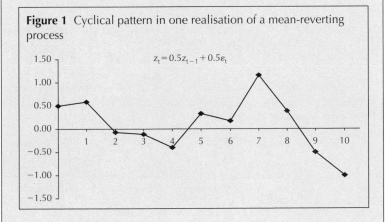

Figure 1 Cyclical pattern in one realisation of a mean-reverting process

$z_t = 0.5z_{t-1} + 0.5\varepsilon_t$

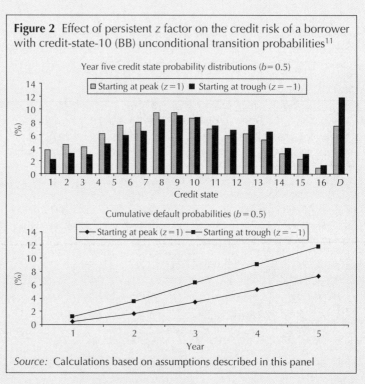

Figure 2 Effect of persistent z factor on the credit risk of a borrower with credit-state-10 (BB) unconditional transition probabilities[11]

Year five credit state probability distributions ($b=0.5$)

□ Starting at peak ($z=1$) ■ Starting at trough ($z=-1$)

Credit state

Cumulative default probabilities ($b=0.5$)

◆ Starting at peak ($z=1$) ■ Starting at trough ($z=-1$)

Year

Source: Calculations based on assumptions described in this panel

We use Equation (2) in determining the density ϕ. The Formula (3) indicates that the credit state distributions depend jointly on the initial credit state j_t and the starting value of the systematic factor z_t. We observe, however, that if $b = 0$ in Equation (2), then z_t offers no information useful in predicting z_{t+i} for $i = 1$, 2 and so on, and this case reverts to the single factor model. However, if the z factor displays "persistence" (meaning $b > 0$), then we obtain different distributions of future credit states for different initial values of z_t (see, Figure 2).

Suppose in the above example we set the PIT rating to the credit state with an unconditional, first-year EDF that most closely matches the first-year EDF of the borrower. If overall credit conditions were strong in our model as indicated by $z = 1$, the first-year EDF of the borrower would be about 50 bps, corresponding to a PIT rating of 5 (approximately A− in the S&P rating scale). If, on the other hand, credit conditions were weak as indicated by $z = -1$, the first-year EDF would be about 120 bps, corresponding to a PIT rating of 10 (*approximately* BB/BB−).

Alternatively, suppose we use the cumulative five-year EDF in determining a TTC rating. Looking ahead from a good credit environment ($z = 1$), we would foresee a five-year EDF of 740 bps, corresponding to a TTC rating of 9 (*approximately* BB+). Looking forward from a difficult environment ($z = -1$), we would anticipate a five-year cumulative EDF of 1,178 bps, corresponding a TTC rating of 11 (*approximately* BB–).

To see the point of this illustration, consider performing the same mappings in the case of the single factor model in which the transition matrix stays fixed at *T*. Here, regardless of the state of the economy, we always would map to the borrower's initial credit state (10 is approximately BB in the illustration) at every horizon.

This example motivates two conclusions. Given a two-factor credit risk, we need two indicators such as a separate short- (PIT) and long-term (TTC) rating in estimating the credit-risk term structure. Further, if the factor describing credit trends exhibits mean-reversion, then the TTC rating would likely vary less than the PIT one.

In closing this panel, we note that in the case of a two-factor credit risk, we would likely need complementary two-factor models describing the risk-neutral and the real-world processes. Analysts sometimes avoid the complexity of estimating both processes simultaneously, working instead only with the one needed for the purpose at hand. This seems like a dubious practice, since at times the best regarded real-world and risk-neutral analyses imply something implausible about the market's relative weighting of returns in recessions and booms.

We now consider the question whether one can classify any of the existing ratings systems as PIT or TTC. We often observe KMV's one-year EDFs described as PIT and agency ratings as TTC and wonder if this is a valid description. Those who believe so observe that (1) the one-year EDF has a PIT horizon; (2) the rating agencies describe their long-term ratings as involving an analysis of conditions over several years; and (3) the agency ratings exhibit considerably less volatility than KMV EDFs. However, one can counter with two observations. If, as is often assumed in pricing and portfolio modelling, credit risk reflects a series of independent shocks, then the long-term rating need not be less volatile than the short-term one. Additionally, the relatively low volatility of agency ratings could simply reflect errors – as would occur if the ratings are merely rank-ordered – or the relatively high volatility of KMV EDFs could reflect errors – as would occur if stock prices were "excessively volatile" compared with more fundamental factors revealed in credit events. Indeed, those who presume that a TTC rating must be less volatile than a PIT rating evidently believe that credit risk exhibits mean-reversion. However, we are unaware of any evidence that justifies this view.

Rather than trying to classify ratings systems *a priori* as PIT or TTC, we are instead seeking to answer the following question: *Which rating, or which combination of existing ratings and other indicators, provides the best predictions of default events over a one-year horizon and which provides the best predictions over a five-year horizon?*

A good PIT rating system could outperform a poor TTC one in trials over a five-year horizon. In this case, we would accept the PIT system as a better TTC indicator. In the end, predictive power matters.

We now turn to two related matters. In the next section, we describe a process of developing dynamic mappings of agency ratings to one-year PDs. In the section after that we describe some ongoing testing of the accuracy of KMV EDFs and agency ratings as default predictors over both one- and five-year horizons. These empirical tests consider the concepts of PIT and TTC as relating to the horizon over which the default rate prediction accuracy is best. Since our internal ratings derive in part from those two sources, we see this effort as integral to the process of establishing the validity of our internal ratings.

USING A SINGLE CREDIT FACTOR FRAMEWORK IN MAPPING AGENCY RATINGS TO ONE-YEAR PIT PDS

As overall credit conditions improve or deteriorate, agency ratings move up and down, but less so than default rates. We reach this conclusion after observing that the default rates, spreads and median KMV EDFs for each agency rating exhibit cyclical variations. This implies that to estimate one-year default losses accurately for the purposes of setting appropriate reserves, one must use dynamic mappings of agency ratings to default rates. We describe an approach for accomplishing that next.

A "static map" always translates a particular rating to the same PD at each relevant horizon as determined from historical average experience (see Table 1).

A "dynamic map" translates ratings to PDs that vary with the credit cycle. In adjusting for the cycle, we start with the static map, which we regard as establishing the unconditional default rates for

Table 1 Illustration of static mappings of Moody's grades to PDs

	Moody's mappings*	
Grade	1-year PD (%)	5-year PD (%)
Aaa	0.000	0.11
Aa	0.015	0.33
A1	0.036	0.51
A2	0.039	0.74
A3	0.040	1.01
Baa1	0.132	1.88
Baa2	0.150	2.73
Baa3	0.367	4.89
Ba1	0.642	8.05
Ba2	0.876	11.61
Ba3	2.550	19.51
B1	3.702	25.06
B2	8.391	35.23
B3	11.957	44.43
Caa	15.926	50.48
Ca	19.576	57.36

*Derived from data in the most recent default-rate study published by Moody's (2003). The above values reflect the smoothing that arises in fitting a transition matrix to the historical average default term structures for the different grades and then producing the mappings from that matrix.

each grade. We then use a single-factor CreditMetrics model to determine default rates conditional on the state of the credit cycle.[12,13]

In applying this approach, we begin by estimating monthly series of latent factor values for each major (alpha, not alphanumeric) agency grade. This involves comparing the monthly, median, KMV one-year EDFs for each major grade with the respective historical average values of those medians. The latent factor values arise from back-solving the CreditMetrics model. For that purpose, we determine the default point for each grade by applying the inverse normal distribution function to the historical average median EDF for each grade. We estimate the correlation parameter for each grade simultaneously with the extraction of latent factors. We set the correlation parameter for each grade so that the extracted factor values have a mean near zero and standard deviation close to one.

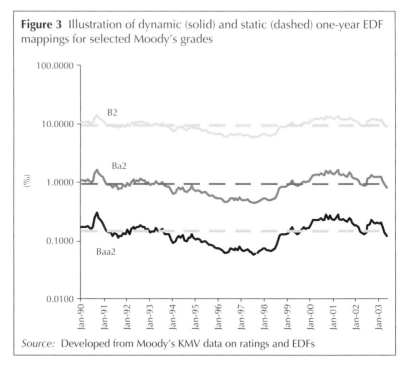

Figure 3 Illustration of dynamic (solid) and static (dashed) one-year EDF mappings for selected Moody's grades

Source: Developed from Moody's KMV data on ratings and EDFs

We next average the latent factors across the major grades, thereby obtaining a single, summary series measuring the credit cycle. We now determine the default points for all of an agency's (alphanumeric) grades by applying the inverse normal function to the long-run PDs in the static map. By substituting the series of single-factor values into the CreditMetrics model, with the correlation parameter set to the average estimated in the factor extractions above, we obtain monthly PDs for each grade adjusted for current credit conditions. (See Panel 2 for a more detailed description of this dynamic mapping approach.) This approach can produce quite different PD translations over time (see Figure 3).

> **PANEL 2 DESCRIPTION OF THE APPROACH FOR UPDATING AGENCY MAPPINGS TO ONE-YEAR PDS**
>
> To update the mappings of agency ratings to one-year PDs, we use the CreditMetrics single-factor modelling approach intrinsic to the Basel II proposals and widely adopted by many credit portfolio models.

We assume, in effect, that today's PIT default probability for each of an agency's ratings arises from the current realisation of a single risk factor measuring the credit cycle. By using only one factor, we impose a uniform, business cycle view across each of an agency's ratings. In this way, we avoid sampling errors that could arise if we were to attempt a more detailed, multi-factor approach based on our limited data.

The approach involves the following steps:

1. Derive the value of a latent risk factor for each of an agency's major risk grades by comparing the current, median, KMV one-year EDF for that grade with its long-run historical average. Specifically, we calibrate the CreditMetrics model for a grade to the long-term average EDF, using a correlation factor that yields factor realisations with a mean close to 0 and a standard deviation near 1. For each month, we back-solve the model for the factor value that generates the current, median KMV EDF for that grade. We use the following formula:

$$Z_{gt} = \frac{\Phi^{-1}(EDF_g) - \sqrt{1-\rho}\,\Phi^{-1}(EDF_{gt})}{\sqrt{\rho}}$$

$Z_{gt} \equiv$ factor value for grade g in period t $\Phi \equiv$ standard normal cdf

$\rho \equiv$ correlation coefficient $EDF_g \equiv$ long-run average EDF for grade g

$EDF_{gt} \equiv$ EDF for grade g in period t

For both S&P and Moody's, we derive factor values for each major grade except CCC (Caa-C). In these cases, KMV's capping of EDFs at 20% biases the estimates and make them invalid for this exercise.

2. Obtain a single, monthly credit-cycle series for the agency by averaging the distinct, monthly latent factor values for each of the agency's major grades. We use the following formula:

$$Z_t = \frac{\sum_{g=1}^{N} Z_{gt}}{N}$$

$Z_t \equiv$ overall average credit-cycle factor value for the agency

$N \equiv$ number of major agency grades used in the analysis

3. Apply the monthly values of this credit cycle index within the CreditMetrics single-factor model, thereby obtaining *PIT* EDFs consistent with this view for each of the agency's ratings. We use the

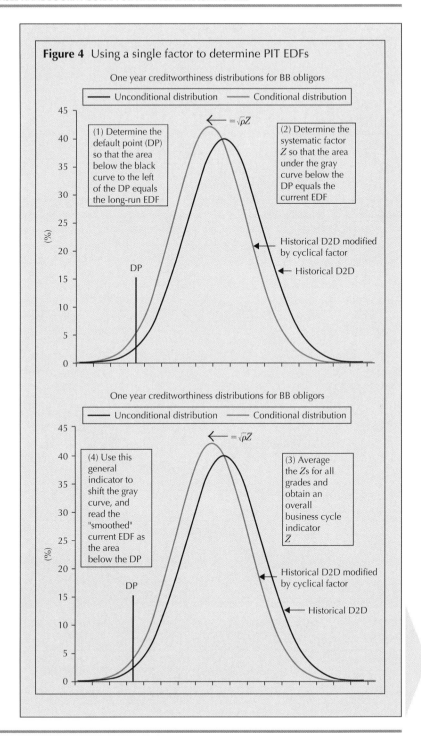

Figure 4 Using a single factor to determine PIT EDFs

One year creditworthiness distributions for BB obligors

—— Unconditional distribution —— Conditional distribution

(1) Determine the default point (DP) so that the area below the black curve to the left of the DP equals the long-run EDF

$\longleftarrow\ = \sqrt{\rho}Z$

(2) Determine the systematic factor Z so that the area under the gray curve below the DP equals the current EDF

Historical D2D modified by cyclical factor

←— Historical D2D

DP

One year creditworthiness distributions for BB obligors

—— Unconditional distribution —— Conditional distribution

$\longleftarrow\ = \sqrt{\rho}Z$

(4) Use this general indicator to shift the gray curve, and read the "smoothed" current EDF as the area below the DP

(3) Average the Zs for all grades and obtain an overall business cycle indicator $\bar{Z}$

Historical D2D modified by cyclical factor

←— Historical D2D

DP

following formula:

$$PD_{gt} = \Phi\left(\frac{\Phi^{-1}(PD_g) - \sqrt{\rho}Z_t}{\sqrt{1-\rho}} \right)$$

$PD_{gt} \equiv$ estimated PD for grade g in period t $\Phi \equiv$ standard normal cdf
$\rho \equiv$ correlation coefficient $PD_g \equiv$ long-run average PD for grade g
$Z_t \equiv$ average factor value for period t

We use PDs here rather than EDFs to denote one-year default rates. This indicates that we are using historical averages and deriving *PIT* values consistent with an agency's experience. The long-run average PDs for many agency grades differ substantially from the long-run average EDFs for those same grades. Thus, we are implicitly tying the agency mappings to actual agency experience.

We summarise this approach in Figure 4.

In using this dynamic mapping approach, we take the one or more agency grades for a company and translate them to PDs using the current mapping. In effect, we retain the rank ordering of default risk determined by agency ratings but attach a default-rate calibration drawn from using KMV data. Thus, the resulting one-year PDs represent a hybrid of agency and KMV information.

A FRAMEWORK FOR ASSESSING AND VALIDATING CREDIT RATINGS

Under the proposed Basel II, banks need to ensure that their credit ratings accurately predict PDs. To support these efforts, there is a growing literature on credit model validation.

Several analysts have worked on evaluating credit ratings focusing on ways of gauging goodness of fit both in- and out-of-sample for discrete variables such as the default/no-default realisations. The rating agencies and credit-scoring firms have long presented power curves – plots of (percent bad, percent good) points at different exclusion thresholds – in illustrating the performance of their indicators in discriminating between good and bad outcomes. Alternatively, van Deventer and Wang (2004) (Chapter 7 in this book) examine the properties of ROC curves and related metrics for judging such predictive performance.

Studies by Stein (2003) and Kurbat and Korablev (2002) look at skewness in small default samples and its effect on tests of the accuracy of default models and ratings. Friedman and Sandow (2003) present a utility-based rationale for using likelihood ratios in judging predictive performance. Most work in this area has focused almost exclusively on goodness of fit, paying little attention to the conceptual soundness of the underlying model. However, KMV in many places has presented an extensive theoretical rationale for its empirical approach.[14]

We view the process of validating credit ratings and the other key Basel II components (LGD and EAD) of credit risk quantification as involving both a theoretical and an empirical component. We see a model, ratings or otherwise, as "valid" only if one can give affirmative answers to both of the following questions:

❏ Is the model conceptually sound, so that, under conditions of ample data for estimation, one would expect it to provide reliable predictions?
❏ Is the model as currently implemented demonstrably reliable, as indicated by statistical tests of significance and precision?

These two conditions mirror academic and industry research journals' acceptance criteria for recognition of research results.

To make a case for statistical significance and precision, typically one must:

❏ show that all of the model coefficient estimates fall within the range of plausible values and achieve significance as indicated by t-statistics or analogous measures;
❏ give evidence that the model is robust by obtaining close to the same parameter values in estimating over varying samples or time periods; and
❏ demonstrate by means of both in- and out-of-sample (including "out-of-time"[15]) simulations that the estimated model produces results superior to an applicable naïve model, such as one that forecasts values as remaining constant or falling on a trend line.

In cases of limited data, statistical tests may have little power. Thus, with new models or old ones newly applied in areas with scarce data for estimation and testing, the first criterion often weighs heavily in evaluating validity. Observe that this condition provides some assurance that a model will perform well in forecasting outside the range of past experience. With enough data, however, one needs to verify this with out-of-sample and out-of-time simulations.

We are currently refining the documentation of new and existing models as part of the validation process. We now turn to some empirical tests that are being conducted on the *components* which go into our internal ratings. Presumably, if the components pass muster and we can show that the process of using these components in establishing a single best rating is sound, our internal ratings will also pass muster as well.

Whether a ratings system is accurate enough to be considered good enough or "valid" for some purpose, such as under Basel II, usually involves human judgment. We can compare the accuracy of different ratings systems reasonably and objectively but often cannot say with strict objectivity what level of accuracy corresponds to validity. Thus, we use the following criterion in this chapter:

> In several places in its consultative papers Basel endorses the use of agency ratings.[16] Therefore, if we find that another rating system outperforms agency ratings in predicting defaults, we will take that as indicating that the other rating system is valid for use in implementing the IRB approach.

In following up on this, we are currently conducting empirical testing designed to address the following question: Which of the following best predicts defaults over a horizon of one year and over a horizon of five years?

❑ KMV one- or five-year EDFs;
❑ KMV one- or five-year EDFs grouped and given group-average EDFs;
❑ S&P ratings mapped statically to one- and five-year EDFs;
❑ Moody's ratings mapped statically to one- and five-year) EDFs;
❑ S&P ratings mapped dynamically to one- and five-year EDFs;
❑ Moody's ratings mapped dynamically to one- and five-year EDFs; and
❑ weighted averages of the above.

These tests will help us determine the best credit ratings over one- and five-year horizons. This will also help us evaluate the advantage of having separate PIT and TTC ratings.

We are measuring accuracy in each case by using the log-likelihood of the default/no-default outcomes, conditional on the particular rating system or combination of systems used in gauging default risk. We are also assessing rank-ordering performance using Lorenz curves and the related metrics.

We compute the log-likelihood, LL, across companies and time for the jth rating system as follows:

$$LL_j = ln\left(\prod_i (1-PD_{ij})^{1-D_{it}} PD_{ij}^{D_i} \right) \qquad (4)$$

$$= \sum_i D_i ln(PD_{ij}) + (1-D_i)ln(1-PD_{ij})$$

$j \equiv$ *index of the rating system*
$ln \equiv$ *natural logarithm*
$i \equiv$ *index of the observation*
$PD_{ij} \equiv$ *PD predicted by the rating system j for the observation i*
$D_i \equiv$ *default indicator for the ith observation* $(1 = default, 0 = no default)$

Friedman and Sandov (2003) provide a theoretical rationale based on utility functions for using the log-likelihood measures in choosing among competing models. They show that rank-ordering measures, such as the Gini coefficient, have no justification for their use. A ratings system could rank order perfectly yet bankrupt a lender due to poor calibration. The likelihood measures account for both rank-ordering and calibration accuracy. Nonetheless, we will also examine the pure rank-ordering performance of the different ratings.

Preliminary assessment and validation results for PIT and
TTC ratings
Our initial tests support the previous findings (Crosbie and Bohn, 2002) that KMV one-year EDFs predict default at a one-year horizon better than agency ratings (see Tables 2–5 and Figures 5–8). This result comes out most strongly in the use of regression analysis in finding the combined measure that explains best (as gauged by maximum likelihood) the observed default and no-default outcomes. The best blended indicator drawing on KMV and Moody's data assigns weights of 84% to the KMV EDF, 16% to the dynamically

Table 2 Likelihood values for Moody's and KMV default predictors

Horizon	Intervals	Moody's		KMV	
		Static mapping	Dynamic mapping	Binned	Full resolution
1 year	Jan 90 to Jan 91 to Jan 02 to Jan 03	−1,120	−1,100	−1,013	−1,007
5 years	Jan 90 to Jan 95 to Jan 98 to Jan 03	−1,562	−1,582	−1,651	−1,645

Source: Moody's/KMV for Moody's ratings and defaults and Credit Monitor EDFs
a. "Static" denotes a Moody's rating mapped to a PD using a historical average default rate.
b. "Dynamic" denotes a Moody's rating mapped using cyclically varying default rate using the procedure explained in Panel 2.

Table 3 Likelihood values for S&P and KMV default predictors

Horizon	Intervals	S&P		KMV	
		Static mapping	Dynamic mapping	Binned	Full resolution
1 year	Jan 90 to Jan 91 to Jan 02 to Jan 03	−963	−935	−884	−831
5 years	Jan 90 to Jan 95 to Jan 98 to Jan 03	−1,141	−1,161	−1,253	−1,251

Source: S&P for S&P ratings and defaults and Moody's/KMV for Credit Monitor EDFs

Table 4 Maximum likelihood estimates of optimal weights on Moody's and KMV indicators for default prediction

Horizon	Moody's		KMV
	Static mapping	Dynamic mapping	Full resolution
1 year	0.00	0.16	0.84
5 years	0.46	0.00	0.54

Source: Moody's/KMV for Moody's ratings and defaults and Credit Monitor EDFs

Table 5 Maximum likelihood estimates of optimal weights on S&P and KMV indicators for default prediction

Horizon	S&P		KMV
	Static mapping	Dynamic mapping	Full resolution
1 year	0.00	0.15	0.85
5 years	0.54	0.00	0.46

Source: Moody's/KMV for Moody's ratings and defaults and Credit Monitor EDFs

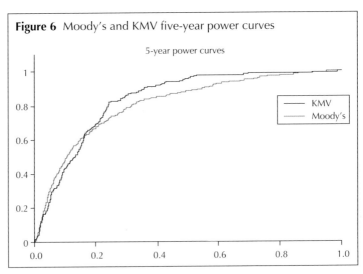

Figure 5 Moody's and KMV one-year power curves

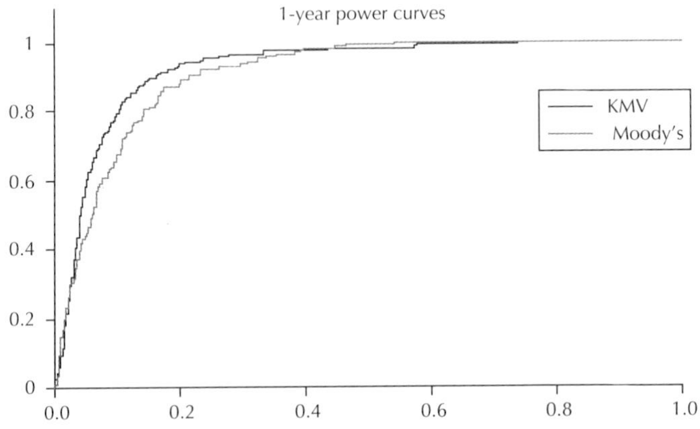

1-year power curves

Figure 6 Moody's and KMV five-year power curves

5-year power curves

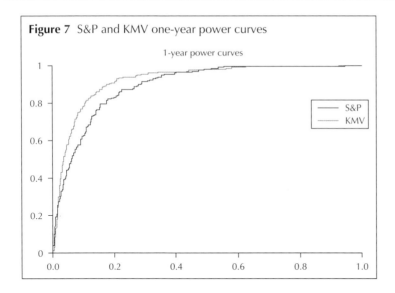

Figure 7 S&P and KMV one-year power curves

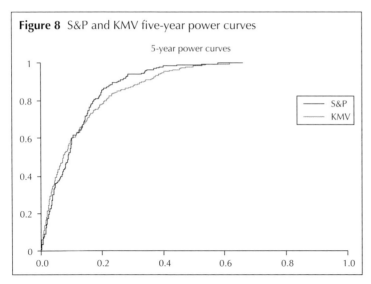

Figure 8 S&P and KMV five-year power curves

mapped Moody's rating, and 0% to the statically mapped agency rating. Conducting the same analysis with KMV and S&P data, we get close to the same relative weighting.

On a standalone basis, we also see that the KMV EDFs best explain the observed sample (likelihood value of –1,007 compared with –1,100 for dynamically mapped Moody's and –1,120 for statically mapped Moody's, and based on a more limited sample we see similar results comparing KMV with S&P). Even if we eliminate the greater resolution of KMV EDFs by placing them in bins that parallel the Moody's or S&P ratings grades and assigning to each the average PD of the bin, we find that the KMV indicators predict better at one year. By examining the power curves, we see that KMV's rank-ordering performance at one year exceeds that of Moody's and S&P. The KMV one-year power curve lies mostly above those of Moody's and S&P.

At a five-year horizon, the Moody's and S&P ratings perform relatively better, supporting the view that they embody a multi-year analysis. On a standalone basis, the Moody's ratings mapped (statically) to unconditional five-year PDs perform best, with the dynamically mapped ratings second and KMV's five-year EDF last. We get similar results in comparing KMV with S&P over a five-year horizon. In the regression analysis, we find that the best composite indicator places approximately equal weight on the KMV five-year EDF and the statically mapped Moody's rating. Combining KMV and S&P data, we also find that the best blended indicator puts about equal weights on the KMV five-year EDF and the statically mapped S&P ratings.

These preliminary results offer evidence that credit analysis for short- and longer-term exposures need to differ. Thus, banks may need to look ahead to developing separate short- and long-term ratings, with KMV EDFs when available playing a dominant role in the former, and agency ratings and other longer horizon indicators having a substantial role in the latter.

CONCLUDING COMMENTS

Accurate credit ratings stand out as central to Basel II and to most aspects of managing credit risk. In recent years analysts have introduced the concepts of PIT and TTC ratings, concepts that purportedly distinguish between some of the existing ratings systems and models.

To make these ideas operational, this chapter has defined a PIT rating as one that discriminates among borrowers based on the PD over a one-year horizon and a TTC rating as one that focuses on a longer horizon of five years or more. We observe that the PIT/TTC distinction matters if, as in interest rate modelling, one needs at least two factors to characterise the different term structures of credit risk associated with different borrowers.

This chapter introduced a method for translating agency ratings dynamically to one-year PDs. The approach applies the Credit-Metrics model to median EDFs for each agency grade in estimating latent factors that describe at a point in time whether one-year PDs are relatively high or low for each agency rating. The apparent TTC focus of agency ratings motivates this dynamic mapping approach.

We have also described statistical tests designed to evaluate the quality of different ratings systems as one-year (PIT) and five-year (TTC) default predictors. Initial results corroborate earlier findings that KMV EDFs outperform agency ratings at a one-year horizon. However, at five years the agency ratings perform as well as KMV five-year EDFs. This supports the agencies' contention that their ratings should be viewed as TTC indicators.

Much more analysis lies ahead before one can consider such results as well established. As they stand, however, they suggest that banks need to look ahead to developing separate ratings for short- and longer-term exposures.

---

1   PD, EAD and LGD are the standard Basel II definitions for: probability of default, exposure at default and loss given default, respectively.
2   Barclays utilises what is called the "Agency read-across matrix" as the master-scale in deter-mining one-year default probabilities by internal ratings grades. The matrix combines map-pings of agency ratings to Barclays business grades (BBG) and median one-year default probabilities to BBGs. Successful conversion of through-the-cycle agency ratings to one-year point-in-time representations of default rates as outlined in this chapter provides a means for comparing agency ratings with KMV EDFs to consistently derive BBGs within the matrix.
3   Also, see Treacy and Carey (1998) and Basel (2000) for a more detailed discussion of corpor-ate risk rating systems.
4   Keeping the discussion simple, risk-neutral spreads are required in pricing to incorporate risk premiums, which compensate for uncertainty around expected credit losses.
5   See Basel (2001), p. 12.
6   In writing this chapter we have undertaken an initial search of the literature to find the ori-gins of PIT/TTC and any related analysis. We have not, however, had the time to date to conduct a complete review of the literature, so the analysis is preliminary.
7   Moody's (1995), p. 7.
8   See Standard & Poor's (1996), p. 65. This is the first example of S&P use of through-the-cycle terminology.
9   See Treacy and Carey (1998).
10 See Treacy and Carey (1998), p. 899. In discussions with Mark Carey, to the best of his know-ledge, he believes that their 1998 article was the first to use the point-in-time terminology.
11 Results derived using Monte Carlo simulations of the z process and the CreditMetrics, single-factor, parametric representation of a conditional transition matrix, assuming a value of 0.1 for the obligor's correlation with general credit conditions. The unconditional matrix in the analysis contains estimated, KMV EDF-transitions across 17 EDF bins including default.

12 See Belkin, Suchower and Forest (1998a,b) for a discussion of one-factor credit models in the context of the CreditMetrics framework.

13 Barclays Capital is also developing new LGD models that incorporate the kind of cyclical credit factor described here, making these also point-in-time. Developing more complex LGD models with these types of cyclical credit factors, however, implies a more complex PD model as well – because there are partially offsetting impacts between LGD and PD due to variable default points in the PIT LGD model.

14 For example, see Crosbie and Bohn (2002).

15 "Out of sample" denotes an observation not used in the model estimation. "Out of time" indicates that an out-of-sample observation occurred within a time period not covered by the observations used in estimation.

16 Basel II's term for accepted agency ratings is "external credit assessment institution" (ECAI). The criteria for acceptance include objectivity, independence, international access/transparency, disclosure, resources and credibility.

BIBLIOGRAPHY

Aguais, S. D., and D. Rosen, 2001, *Enterprise Credit Risk Using Mark-to-Future*. Algorithmics Publications, September. pp. 3–15.

Altman, E., 1968, "Financial Ratios, Discriminant Analysis, and the Prediction of Corporate Bankruptcy". *Journal of Finance* **23**.

Basel Committee on Banking Supervision, 1999, "Principles for the Management of Credit Risk". Consultative Document, July.

Basel Committee on Banking Supervision, 2000, "Range of Practice in Banks' Internal Ratings Systems". Discussion Paper, January.

Basel Committee on Banking Supervision, 2001, "The New Basel Capital Accord, Consultative Document, the Internal Ratings-Based Approach", January.

Belkin, B., S. Suchower, and L. Forest, 1998, "The Effect of Systematic Credit Risk on Loan Portfolios and Loan Pricing". *Credit-Metrics Monitor*, April, pp. 17–28.

Belkin, B., S. Suchower, and L. Forest, 1998. "A One Parameter Representation of Credit Risk and Transition Matrices". *Credit-Metrics Monitor*, October, pp. 45–56.

Crosbie, P., and J. Bohn, 2002. "Modeling Default Risk". Working Paper, Moody's/KMV, January.

Friedman, C., and S. Sandow, 2003. "Model Performance Measures for Expected Utility Maximising Investors". Working Paper, Standard & Poor's Risk Solutions Group, January.

Kurbat, M., and I. Korablev, 2002, "Methodology for Testing the Level of the EDF Credit Measure". Working Paper, Moody's/KMV, August.

Moody's Investors Service, 1995, "Copper Perspective. Special Comment". Global Credit Research, November.

Moody's Investors Service, 2003, "Default and Recovery Rates of Corporate Bond Issuers – a Statistical Review of Moody's Ratings Performance", 1920–2002. Special comment, February.

Ranson, B., 2003., *Credit Risk Management*. Thomson – Sheshunoff.

Standard & Poor's, 1996. "Corporate Ratings Criteria". Standard & Poor's Rating Services.

Standard & Poor's, 2003, "Ratings Performance 2002, Default, Transition, Recovery and Spreads", February.

Stein, R., 2003, "Are the Probabilities Right?" Technical Report 030124 (revised), Moody's/KMV, May.

Treacy, W., and M. Carey, 1998, "Credit Risk Rating at Large U.S. Banks". *Federal Reserve Bulletin* xx(cc), November pp. 897–921.

Van Deventer, D., and J. Outram, 2002, "The New Capital Accord and Internal Bank Ratings". Monograph, Kamakura Corporation, May.

9

Basel II in the Light of Moody's KMV Evidence

Martti Purhonen*

Sampo Plc

Using Moody's KMV's expected default frequencies (EDFs), this chapter seeks to ask the questions:

❏ What is the relationship between the internal ratings-based (IRB) approach and the standardised approach in different continents?
❏ How volatile could the IRB capital requirements be?

A global study covering more than 19,000 public non-financial companies with total liabilities of €14,700 billion provides some answers.

To find out the potential capital requirements under IRB in different continents, a common measure of borrower default risk needs to be applied. In this study, San Francisco-based Moody's KMV's (MKMV) expected default frequencies (EDFs) were used since these probability-of-default (PD) estimates are consistently assigned for almost all public companies worldwide.[1] In addition to EDFs and Standard and Poor's (S&P) ratings, MKMV's public corporate database provides companies' total liabilities – not just bond issues, but also bank loans and other liability types.[2]

*The author would like to thank Moody's KMV, Esa Jokivuolle of the Bank of Finland's research department and Petri Viertiö of Sampo Bank's risk management. The views expressed in this chapter are those of the author and do not necessarily represent the views of Sampo Bank.

The database therefore enables the calculation of debt-weighted average risk weights under both IRB and standard approaches.

Rating agencies typically claim to utilise a "through-the-cycle" process, unlike MKMV with its "point-in-time" EDF credit measure (see Banking Committee on Banking Supervision, 2002). Higher volatility of MKMV's forward-looking EDF is demonstrated more precisely in transition matrices (see KMV Corporation, 1998).

According to the Basel Committee on Banking Supervision's survey on banks' internal rating practices, bank-rating systems generally evaluate the risk of a borrower or facility on a point-in-time basis, although considerable variability among banks does occur.[3] Therefore, MKMV's point-in-time EDF should be a good proxy of banks' true internal ratings under IRB approach.

PORTFOLIO SET-UP

Out of the three possible approaches for credit risk, this chapter covers the standardised approach and foundation IRB. The third approach for credit risk, advanced IRB, is not covered in this study. The foundation IRB approach is calculated with the April 2003 risk-weight formula published as part of the Basel II documents. Companies' total liabilities,[4] exported from MKMV's public corporate database, were used as a measure of aggregate debt. Liabilities include – in addition to bank loans, commercial paper and bonds – a certain amount of accounts payable and other liability types. This study assumes that banks would hold all these total liabilities.[5] The portfolios are presented in Table 1.

Undrawn commitments and credit-risk mitigation were ignored to simplify the process. Credit-loss issues and their effects on

Table 1 Portfolios for IRB and standard approaches (as of August 2003)

	Aggregate debt (euro billion)	S&P-rated debt (euro billion)	S&P-rated of total (%)
United States	5,611	5,027	90
European Union	4,452	2,848	64
Asia-Pacific	4,303	1,847	43
Latin America	301	98	32

capital ratios were also ignored. Only risk weight fluctuations of non-bankrupt companies were studied.

Distressed companies that still have their equity publicly traded – ie, defaulted companies – are included as long as their equity is traded.[6] Companies that are delisted, acquired or have filed for bankruptcies during the observation period are also included as long as liabilities and EDFs are incorporated prior to bankruptcy (or delisting, etc.) – but not afterwards. A reverse treatment applies for newly listed companies – each month's debt-weighted average risk weight is independently calculated, and some changes in portfolios' size and contents do occur.

IRB CALCULATIONS
IRB calculations were performed on a company-by-company basis. Risk weights were derived by taking one-year EDFs into Basel's risk-weight formula as a measure of the senior debt's default probability.[7] The nearly continuous two-decimal EDF scale runs from 0.03%[8] to 20.00%.[9] Risk-weight formulae were separately applied for each individual EDF value. The resulting risk-weight value was then multiplied to the corresponding liability value. In order to get the portfolio's weighted-average risk weight, indi-vidual risk-weighted assets were summed and divided by the corresponding sum of nominal liabilities. This calculation was then repeated monthly for each portfolio.

STANDARDISED APPROACH
Exactly the same portfolios were used for both IRB and standard approach calculations. Therefore, companies that are not S&P-rated were also included, with appropriate risk weighting of 100%. Other risk weights were 20% for S&P AAA and AA-rated, 50% for A, 100% for BBB and BB, and 150% for B and below. As with the IRB approach, nearly a seven-year history of debt-weighted average risk weights under the standard approach were constructed for each portfolio by repeating the calculation monthly using the company-by-company-based methodology.

THE RESULTS FOR THE IRB APPROACH
In 1998, the Russian currency crises and the Long-Term Capital Management debacle caused a sharp increase in aggregate risk

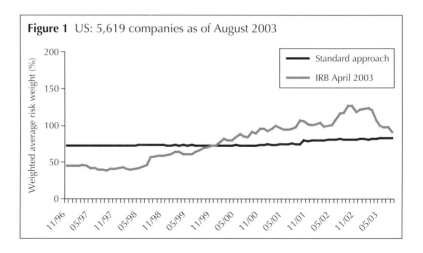

Figure 1 US: 5,619 companies as of August 2003

weight for the representative US portfolio (see Figure 1): capital requirement rose by 33% in three months – from May's risk weight of 42% to August's 56%. This was followed by a period of steady rises in capital requirements. Even 1999, which was the year of the peak bull market, did not provide any improvement in terms of risk weights: asset-value increases in equity-market-driven MKMV models were more than offset by the increase in leverage within the companies. On top of this, the bear market of the three consecutive years from 2000 to 2002 caused additional rise in capital requirements – aggregate risk weight peaked in September 2002 into 127%, along with the highest levels of both asset volatility and market leverage within the MKMV model. If measured with high-to-low ratio, the US portfolio had the highest variability within the IRB figures. The ratio of highest and lowest risk weight – 127% of September 2002 and 39% of September 1997 – was 3.27 with April 2003 formula.

The representative EU portfolio (see Figure 2) was also strongly affected by the events of 1998, although credit-quality deterioration occurred at a slower pace than in the US. The IRB risk weight was still below that of the standardised approach until the beginning of 2001. However, the rapid slowdown of the world economy substantially changed the situation by taking the EU portfolio's IRB weight into its 82-month high of 100% in September 2002. The EU portfolio had the highest variability in terms of annualised

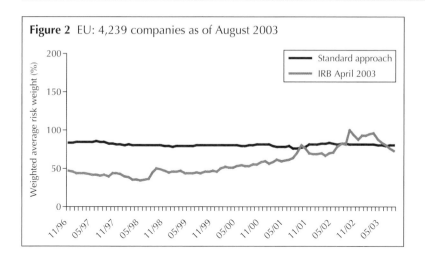

Figure 2 EU: 4,239 companies as of August 2003

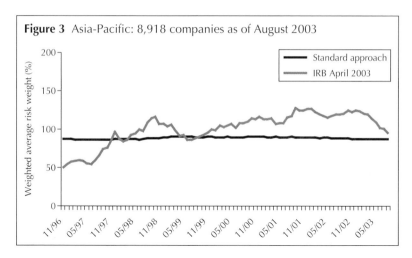

Figure 3 Asia-Pacific: 8,918 companies as of August 2003

volatility, 20%. This means that, if the risk weight is currently 73% (at August 2003), there is a 16% probability that the EU's risk weight exceeds 88% within a one-year horizon, assuming that risk weights are normally distributed.

The representative Asia-Pacific portfolio (see Figure 3) was already stressed by late 1996. Since then, the IRB curve has continued to rise as Japan's economy worsened. As the world's second largest economy, Japan contributes heavily to the aggregate risk weight. Within the Asia-Pacific portfolio, Japan represented 36% of the names and 69% of the debt as of August 2003.

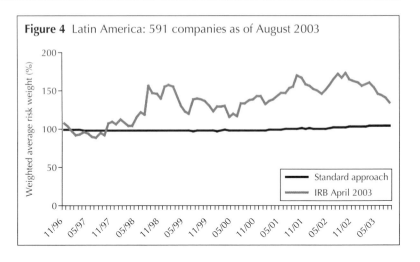

Figure 4 Latin America: 591 companies as of August 2003

Latin American companies (see Figure 4) had either very good or very bad credit quality. The number of companies with a maximum 20% EDF was 117.[10] This number represents 20% of the total number of the representative portfolio's corporate names. The number of obligors with an EDF of 1% or lower was 194, which represents 33% of all corporate names in the portfolio. The Basel II IRB formula published in April 2003 produced an 82-month average risk weight of 134%.

Figure 5 presents EU's IRB risk weight together with the EU's annualised percentage change of real GDP.[11] The MKMV model seemed to have some forecasting power in respect of GDP changes during the observation period. For example, the GDP declines of Q4/2001 and Q2/2003 were both signalled beforehand by MKMV-based IRB capital requirements.

THE RESULTS FOR THE STANDARDISED APPROACH

Out of the representative US portfolio's aggregate debt, only 10% is not S&P-rated and, therefore, attracted a constant, non-fluctuating risk weight of 100%. Given this high percentage of S&P-rated exposures, the risk weighting under the standardised approach is surprisingly low in volatility.

As of August 2003, the 10 largest US companies had total liabilities of €1,484 billion, representing 30% of the portfolio's S&P-rated exposures. An uneven distribution such as this has its downsides – when

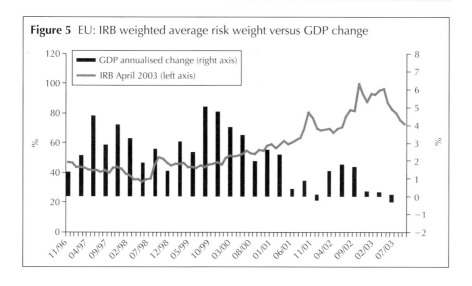

Figure 5 EU: IRB weighted average risk weight versus GDP change

Table 2 Risk weight comparison under standard approach

	82-month average (%)	Annualised volatility (%)	High (%)	Low (%)	High-to-low ratio
United States	75	3	83	72	1.15
European Union	81	4	86	76	1.13
Asia-Pacific	88	1	90	86	1.05
Latin America	99	1	104	97	1.07

Table 3 Risk weight comparison under IRB April 2003

	82-month average (%)	Annualised volatility (%)	High (%)	Low (%)	High-to-low ratio
United States	78	16	127	39	3.27
European Union	57	20	100	34	2.93
Asia-Pacific	100	17	127	50	2.57
Latin America	134	22	172	88	1.97

a few big obligors migrate, the whole portfolio migrates. For example, a sharp five-percentage-point increase in debt-weighted average risk weight between September and October 2001 was caused mainly by the simultaneous downgrade of General Motors and Ford Motor Company – the portfolio's second and third largest obligors, with combined liabilities of €622 billion, which represents 12% of the portfolio's S&P-rated debt.[12] However, judging by the 82-month average risk weight, the US portfolio had the lowest capital requirement under standardised approach, with its 75% risk-weighting.

Other portfolios had much less S&P-rated debt than the US portfolio. Due to this, the Asia-Pacific region[13] and Latin America[14] had especially low-volatility risk-weight curves with the 82-month averages close to 100% – the former with 88% and the latter with 99% risk weighting. Surprisingly, the EU portfolio[15] experienced a slight decrease in risk weight: from 83% in November 1996 to 80% in August 2003. There are two reasons for this: (i) some large companies had significant increases in their liabilities and were still having their S&P ratings listed at A− or better. These companies include telecoms[16] companies, but also some other large firms[17] in the EU portfolio; and (ii) a significant number of large, high-credit-quality obligors, such as Deutsche Post and British Petroleum, obtained an S&P rating in the middle of the observation period.

CONCLUSIONS

Judging from the 82-month average risk weights, the US portfolio had the lowest capital requirement under the standardised approach; and the EU portfolio, under the IRB approach. However, too many conclusions should not be drawn. For example, the Basel Committee's 2001 and 2002 quantitative impact studies provide more reliable results, because they incorporate true exposure data with appropriate credit risk mitigation treatments.

The IRB risk-weight curve flattening – ie, switching from the January 2001 IRB curve to the April 2003 curve – has been an efficient way to reduce regulatory capital volatility (see also Purhonen, 2002). However, high-to-low ratios remained at a fairly high level with the IRB April 2003 formula. For instance, US had a ratio equal to 3.27. This means that a bank using a pure point-in-time rating process would have needed a massive capital buffer in 1997, assuming that asset sales, capital raising or pro-cyclical (see Wilde and Erwin, 2001) "stop lending" decisions would not have been necessary in the late 2002. However, it should be noted that these MKMV-based IRB risk weights – without any point-in-time versus over-the-cycle adaptation – represent the upper ceiling of IRB volatility. The true banking system level IRB volatility would probably lie somewhere in between the standardised and IRB approach presented here.

Basel II emphasises the importance of diversification beyond credit-loss issues. Even though the granularity adjustment is now withdrawn from the Basel II proposals, diversification still has its indirect effect on capital requirement as a device for minimising regulatory capital volatility (see also Jokivuolle and Peura, 2001).

1   For more information on MKMV's EDFs, see Peter Crosbie and Jeffrey Bohn, 2002, "Modeling Default Risk", MKMV, January.

2   S&P senior implied debt ratings are embedded in MKMV's public corporate database.

3   Basel Committee on Banking Supervision, 2000, "Range of Practice in Banks' Internal Rating systems", January. Banks were asked to characterise their orientation as "point-in-time" or "through-the-cycle".

4   Total adjusted liabilities (book liabilities): sum of all short- and long-term liabilities, excluding deferred taxes and minority interest.

5   This should not create any major bias since what is primarily calculated here is debt-weighted average risk weight, not risk-weighted assets. In other words, all corporates are assumed to have some constant accounts payable percentage of total liabilities, regardless of issuer rating.

6   Sorting out the corporates that fulfil the regulatory definition of default would be impossible: in Standard Approach, S&P D-rated corporates are assigned an appropriate risk weight of 150%, but unrated defaulters with publicly traded equity are assigned a risk weight of performing unrated corporate, 100%. In IRB all corporates, also defaulted but not bankrupted, receive risk weights derived from their MKMV EDFs without any special treatment (although defaulters usually have an EDF of 20%, leading to a 352% risk weight).

7   All liabilities are assumed to be senior unsecured debt with loss-given default (LGD) equal to 45%.

8   According to the April 2003 Basel II consultative document, the floor on corporate PD estimate is 0.03%.

9   MKMV's EDFs are capped at 20%. EDF credit measures are bounded at both the low and high ends for essentially empirical reasons.

10 Number of corporates as of August 2003.

11 GDP change compared to previous quarter.

12 Both corporates were downgraded from A to BBB+ in October 2001; risk weight from 50% to 100%. In excess of these, only one risk weight effective downgrade occurred for the group of largest 10 obligors between November 1996 and October 2001: AT&T in November 2000 from AA− to A. This was partly offset by the group's only risk weight effective upgrade, SBS Communications in March 1997, from A+ to AA−.

13 Australia, China, Hong Kong, India, Indonesia, Japan, Korea, Malaysia, New Zealand, Pakistan, Philippines, Singapore, Sri Lanka, Taiwan, Thailand.

14 Argentina, Brazil, Chile, Colombia, Mexico, Peru, Venezuela.

15 Great Britain, Germany, France, Finland, Sweden, Denmark, Italy, Netherlands, Belgium, Luxembourg, Spain, Portugal, Greece, Ireland, Austria.

16 For example, BT and Telefonica. Out of largest ones, France Telecom was downgraded from A− to BBB+ in September 2001, and Deutsche Telekom from A− to BBB+ in April 2002.

17 For example E.ON, Volkswagen, and Unilever. The EU's second-largest obligor, DaimlerChrysler, was downgraded in October 2001 from A− to BBB+.

BIBLIOGRAPHY

Basel Committee on Banking Supervision, 2000, "Credit Ratings and Complementary Sources of Credit Quality Information", No 3, August.

Basel Committee on Banking Supervision, 2001, "The New Basel Capital Accord", Bank for International Settlements, January.

Basel Committee on Banking Supervision, 2003, "The New Basel Capital Accord", Bank for International Settlements, April.

Basel Committee on Banking Supervision, 2000, "Range of Practice in Banks' Internal Rating Systems", January.

Erwin W., and T. Wilde, 2001, "Pro-cyclicality in the New Basel Accord", *Risk*, *Credit Risk*, October, pp. S28–S32.

Jokivuolle, E., and S. Peura, 2001, "Regulatory Capital Volatility", *Risk*, May, pp. 95–8.

KMV Corporation, 1998, "Uses and Abuses of Bond Default Rates", March.

Purhonen, M., 2002, "New Evidence on IRB Volatility", *Risk*, *Credit Risk*, March, pp. S21–S25.

Section 3

Securitisations and Retail Portfolios

10

Basel II Capital Adequacy Rules for Securitisations and for Retail Exposures

Ashish Dev

KeyCorp

This chapter addresses two issues: (i) namely the Basel II Capital Adequacy Rules for Securitisations and (ii) the Basel II Capital Adequacy Rules for Retail Credit Exposures. They are addressed in two separate self-contained parts. Securitisations obviously cover tranches created out of an underlying pool of not only retail exposures but also commercial loans. The granular pool assumption, which is the starting point of underlying models for credit risk in securitisation tranches, is generally true only in the case of a pool of retail exposures.

BASEL II CAPITAL ADEQUACY RULES FOR SECURITISATIONS
Introduction

One of the motivations for Basel II is the fact that the lack of risk sensitivity in the capital adequacy rules under the current Basel I regime has prompted many banks to engage in "regulatory arbitrage" mainly through securitisations. "Regulatory arbitrage" is the avoidance of minimum capital charge through sale or securitisation of a bank's (high-quality or highly diversified) assets for which the true risk and the capital requirement imposed by the financial markets is much less than the regulatory capital requirement. From this perspective, developing the right capital rules under Basel II for securitisation tranches becomes all the more important. At the same time, securitisations can be relatively complex structures and a simple formulation of capital rules covering all aspects and all drivers of risk of securitisation is practically impossible.

At the very beginning of the Basel II process, the first consultative paper issued in 1999 did not refer to securitisation, except in the context of "regulatory arbitrage". The consultative paper issued in January 2001 (Basel (2001), also known as CP2) set forth certain broad principles for capital adequacy for securitisations. But there was no detailed formulation for calculating regulatory capital. A working paper issued in October 2001 introduced the *standardised* and *internal ratings-based* (IRB) approaches. Within the IRB approach, an ABS scaling factor approach and a supervisory formula approach were introduced. Neither of the approaches seems to have been based on a fundamental model of credit risk in securitisation tranches. With the publication of several models – Pykhtin and Dev (2002), Pykhtin and Dev (2003), Gordy and Jones (2003) – for credit risk in securitisation tranches over a short period since October 2001, there has been a realisation that rating alone does not capture the true credit risk of a securitisation. It has also led to a better understanding of the relative risks between senior and junior tranches (particularly thin tranches) and of the effect of granularity in the underlying pool of assets. All these have led to significant changes in the initial formulations.

The consultative paper issued in March 2003 – Basel (2003), also known as CP3 – incorporates these changes. In particular, the supervisory formula approach (one of the two IRB approaches) is primarily model-based with certain supervisory overrides. The ABS scaling factor approach (the other IRB approach) is referred to as the (external) ratings-based approach. In scope, the predominant approach is the ratings-based approach.

Scope of coverage

Banks must apply the securitisation framework for determining regulatory capital requirements on exposures arising from any traditional or synthetic securitisation or similar structure that contains features common to both.

A *traditional securitisation* is a structure where the cashflow from an underlying pool of exposures is used to service at least two different stratified risk positions or tranches reflecting different degrees of credit risk. Payments to the investors depend upon the performance of the specified underlying exposures, as opposed to being derived from an obligation of the entity originating those exposures. The stratified or tranched structures that characterise securitisations differ from ordinary senior/subordinated debt instruments in that junior securitisation tranches can absorb losses without interrupting contractual payments to more senior tranches, whereas subordination in a senior/subordinated debt structure is a matter of priority of rights to the proceeds of a liquidation.

A *synthetic securitisation* is a structure with at least two different stratified risk positions or tranches that reflect different degrees of credit risk. The credit risk of an underlying pool of exposures is transferred, in whole or in part, through the use of funded (eg, credit-linked notes) or unfunded (eg, credit default swaps) credit derivatives or guarantees that serve to hedge the credit risk of the portfolio. Accordingly, the investor's potential risk is dependent upon the performance of the underlying pool.

Examples of securitisation exposures include but are not restricted to: asset-backed securities, mortgage-backed securities, credit enhancements, liquidity facilities and credit derivatives.

Underlying instruments in the pool being securitised can include: loans, commitments, asset-backed and mortgage-backed securities, corporate bonds, equity securities and private equity investments. The underlying pool may include one or more exposures.

With respect to a given securitisation transaction, a bank can take the role of originator or investor. For risk-based capital purposes, a bank is considered to be an *originator* if it either (a) originates directly or indirectly the exposures included in the securitisation or (b) serves as a sponsor of an asset-backed commercial paper (ABCP) conduit or similar programme. An *investing bank* is an institution, other than the originator, sponsor or servicer that assumes the economic risk of a securitisation exposure. Capital may be assigned to a bank in either role depending on the economic substance of the transaction.

Banks are required to hold regulatory capital against all of their securitisation exposures, including those arising from the provision of credit risk mitigants to a securitisation transaction, investments in asset-backed securities, retention of a subordinated tranche, and extension of a liquidity facility or credit enhancement.[1] Repurchased securitisation exposures are treated as retained securitisation exposures.

When a banking organisation provides implicit support to a securitisation, it will be required, at a minimum, to hold capital against all of the exposures associated with the securitisation transaction as if they had not been securitised.

In order to exclude securitised exposures from the calculation of risk-weighted assets, an originating bank must ensure that the securitisation satisfies certain operational requirements. (Banks meeting these conditions must still hold regulatory capital against any securitisation exposures they retain.) Operational requirements differ for traditional and synthetic securitisations, but the essence of these requirements is that significant credit risk associated with the securitised exposures be transferred to third parties.

Clean-up calls – options that permit an originating bank or a servicing bank to call the securitisation exposures before all of the underlying exposures have been repaid – may result in a regulatory capital charge. A clean-up call is typically triggered when the pool balance has fallen below some specified level. In the case of traditional securitisations, this is accomplished by repurchasing the remaining securitisation exposures, while in the case of a synthetic securitisation the clean-up call may take the form of a clause that extinguishes the credit protection.

No capital is required if a clean-up call satisfies all of the following conditions:

❏ Its exercise must not be mandatory for the originating bank.
❏ It must not be structured to provide credit enhancement.
❏ It must only be exercisable when 10% or less of the original underlying pool remains.

When these conditions are not satisfied, capital is charged as if the exposures in the underlying pool were not securitised.

Standardised and IRB approaches

Basel II permits banks a choice between two broad methods for calculating their capital requirements for credit risk. One alternative, known as the *standardised approach*, will measure credit risk in a standardised manner, supported by external credit assessments. The alternative method, which is subject to the explicit approval of the bank supervisor, would allow banks to use their internal rating systems. This method is known as the *internal ratings-based* (IRB) approach.

Banks that apply the standardised approach to credit risk for the type of underlying exposures securitised must also use the standardised approach under the securitisation framework.

Banks that have received approval to use the IRB approach for the type of underlying exposures securitised (eg, for their corporate, retail or SL portfolio) must use the IRB approach for securitisations. Under the IRB approach for securitisations, separate methods for calculating capital apply for originators and investors. Investors are generally required to use a ratings-based approach (RBA). Investors are to use the alternative supervisory formula (SF) for certain exposures with the approval of their national supervisors. Originating banks must use either the SF or the RBA as discussed below. Conversely, banks may not use the SF or RBA unless they receive approval to use the IRB approach for the underlying exposures from their national supervisors.

Where there is no specific IRB treatment for the underlying asset type, originating banks that have received approval to use the IRB approach must calculate capital on their securitisation exposures using the standardised approach in the securitisation framework, and investing banks with approval to use the IRB approach must apply the RBA. Except for specific circumstances and for servicer cash advances, securitisation exposures are to be treated using either the SF or RBA as appropriate.

Capital requirements
Minimum capital requirements are calculated as the product of three factors: notional, capital factor and credit conversion factor (CCF). The calculated capital is given by

Capital = notional * capital factor * credit conversion factor

or, equivalently,

Capital = notional * risk weight * 8% * credit conversion factor

In this chapter, I will henceforth deal with capital factors rather than risk weights, as they have a one-to-one relationship.

In most cases, the appropriate notional is simply the notional of the securitisation exposure and CCF equals 100%. Special cases where this is not so include off-balance-sheet exposures, securitisations with early amortisation provision, and credit risk mitigation. They are discussed in Panels 1 and 2.

PANEL 1 STANDARDISED APPROACH FOR SECURITISATIONS

General treatment

Banks that apply the standardised approach to credit risk for the type of underlying exposures securitised (eg, for their corporate, retail or SL portfolio) must use the standardised approach for securitisations. Under the standardised approach, capital factors for rated securitisation exposures are given by Table 1 (long-term ratings) and Table 2 (short-term ratings).

Table 1 Capital factors for long-term ratings in the standardised approach

Rating	AAA to AA− (%)	A+ to A− (%)	BBB+ to BBB− (%)	BB+ to BB− (%)	B+ and below (%)
Investing bank	1.6	4.0	8.0	28.0	100.0
Originating bank	1.6	4.0	8.0	100.0	100.0

Table 2 Capital factors for short-term ratings in the standardised approach

Rating	A-1/P-1	A-2/P-2	A-3/P-3	All other ratings
All banks	1.6%	4.0%	8.0%	100.0%

For all unrated securitisation exposures, with a possible exception of (i) the most senior tranche and (ii) exposures above first loss position in asset-backed commercial paper (ABCP) programmes, the capital factor is 100%.

If the most senior tranche is unrated and the composition of the underlying pool is known at all times, the capital factor for the most senior tranche may be set equal to the capital factor for the underlying pool, subject to supervisory review.

Unrated securitisation exposures provided by sponsoring banks to ABCP programmes that satisfy the following requirements attract the greater of 8% and the highest percentage capital charge assigned to any of the underlying individual exposures:

❏ The exposure is economically above the first loss position, which must provide significant credit protection to the second loss position.
❏ The associated credit risk must be of investment grade.
❏ The institution holding the exposure must not retain or provide the first loss position.

Eligible liquidity facilities

An off-balance-sheet securitisation exposure may receive CCF less than 100% if it satisfies the following criteria determining *eligible liquidity facility*:

❏ The facility documentation must clearly identify and limit the circumstances under which it may be drawn. In particular, the facility must not be used to provide credit support at the time it may be drawn by covering losses already sustained (eg, acquire assets at above fair value) or be structured such that draw down is certain.
❏ The facility must be subject to an asset quality test that precludes it from being drawn to cover credit risk exposures that are in default.
❏ The facility cannot be drawn after all applicable credit enhancements from which the liquidity facility would benefit have been exhausted.
❏ Draws on the facility must not be subordinated or subject to deferral or waiver.
❏ The facility must result in a reduction in the amount that can be drawn or early termination of the facility in the event of default, as defined in the IRB approach, if the underlying pool or the quality of the pool falls below investment grade.

Eligible liquidity facilities with original maturity of one year or less receive a CCF of 20%, while the ones with the original maturity of more than one year receive a CCF of 50%. Banks may apply a 0% CCF to eligible liquidity facilities that are available only in the event of a general market disruption (ie, where a capital market instrument cannot be issued at any price).

Additionally, certain servicer cash advances may be eligible for 0% CCF. These cash advances must be cancellable without prior notice, and the servicer must be entitled to full reimbursement. This reimbursement right must be senior to other claims on cashflows from the underlying pool of exposures. Table 3 summarises the designation of CCFs for eligible liquidity facilities.

Table 3 CCFs for eligible liquidity facilities

Cancelable servicer cash advances	Available only in event of market disruption	Original maturity 1 year or less	Original maturity more than 1 year
0%	0%	20%	50%

Liquidity facilities that are not eligible receive 100% CCF.

Early amortisation provisions

Early amortisation provisions are mechanisms that, once triggered, allow investors to be paid out prior to the originally stated maturity of the securities issued. Generally, an originating bank is required to keep capital against retained or repurchased tranches of a securitisation. However, if a securitisation structure contains an early amortisation feature and the underlying pool contains exposures of a revolving nature (ie, exposures where the borrower is permitted to vary the drawn amount and repayments), the originating bank is also required to hold capital against the investors' interest in the securitisation. This capital charge is calculated as the product of the notional of the revolving part of the investors' interest, a capital factor and an appropriate CCF. The capital factor in this case is defined as the capital requirement per unit of notional that would apply had the exposures not been securitised. The CCF is determined as described below.

The CCF depends on whether an early amortisation feature is controlled or non-controlled. A *controlled* early amortisation provision must satisfy the following conditions:

❏ The bank must have an appropriate capital/liquidity plan in place to ensure that it has sufficient capital and liquidity available in the event of an early amortisation.
❏ Throughout the duration of the transaction, including the amortisation period, there is a *pro rata* sharing of interest, principal, expenses, losses and recoveries based on the balances of receivables outstanding at the beginning of each month.

❏ The bank must set a period for amortisation that would be sufficient for 90% of the total debt outstanding at the beginning of the early amortisation period to have been repaid or recognised as in default.

❏ The pace of repayment should not be any more rapid than would be allowed by straight-line amortisation over the period set out in the preceding criterion.

The CCF also depends on whether revolving exposures in the underlying pool are uncommitted retail credit lines (eg, credit card receivables). The uncommitted lines must be unconditionally cancellable without prior notice.

All committed retail and non-retail exposures in securitisations with early amortisation features receive 90% CCF if these features are controlled and 100% CCF if they are non-controlled.

The determination of the CCF for uncommitted exposures is based on the value of the three-month average excess spread. The banks must compare this excess spread with the following two reference levels:

❏ the level of excess spread at which an early amortisation is triggered; and

❏ the point at which the bank is required to trap excess spread (in cases when trapping of excess spread is not required, this reference point should be set 4.5% above the triggering level).

The bank must divide the distance between these two points into four equal segments. The CCF is determined by the segment where the excess spread falls into. For example, if an early amortisation is triggered at 0% and the trapping point is 4.5%, the interval between the two points is divided into four segments of 112.5 bp each. Table 4 shows the CCFs using this example.

Table 4 Credit conversion factors for early amortisation provisions

Three-month average excess spread	CCF	
	Controlled (%)	Non-controlled (%)
450 bp or more	0	0
337.5–450 bp	1	5
225–337.5 bp	2	10
112.5–225 bp	20	50
less than 112.5 bp	40	100

PANEL 2 INTERNAL RATINGS-BASED APPROACH FOR SECURITISATIONS

Banks that have received approval to use the IRB approach for the type of underlying exposures securitised must use the IRB approach for securitisations. Two approaches available within the IRB approach are: *ratings-based approach* (RBA) and *supervisory formula approach* (SFA).

Ratings-based approach

Capital factors in the RBA are determined by a tranche's credit rating and, to some extent, by the thickness of the tranche and granularity of the underlying pool. RBA capital factors for external long-term credit ratings and inferred ratings-based on long-term credit ratings are given in Table 5.

Table 5 Capital factors for long-term ratings in the IRB approach

Ratings	Capital		
	Thick tranches granular pools (%)	Base (%)	Non-granular pools (%)
AAA	0.56	0.96	1.60
AA	0.80	1.20	2.00
A	1.60	1.60	2.80
BBB+	4.00	4.00	4.00
BBB	6.00	6.00	6.00
BBB−	8.00	8.00	8.00
BB+	20.00	20.00	20.00
BB	36.00	36.00	36.00
BB−	52.00	52.00	52.00

RBA capital factors for external short-term credit ratings and inferred ratings-based on short-term credit ratings are given in Table 6.

Table 6 Capital factors for short-term ratings in the IRB approach

Ratings	Capital		
	Thick tranches granular pools (%)	Base (%)	Non-granular pools (%)
A-1/P-1	0.56	0.96	1.60
A-2/P-2	1.60	1.60	2.80
A-3/P-3	6.00	6.00	6.00

The banks must choose an appropriate column from Tables 5 and 6 according to the following rules:

❑ The left column is chosen if the effective number of the underlying exposures N (defined in the Appendix) is 100 or more and the seniority of the position relative to the size of the pool Q is greater than or equal to $0.1 + 25/N \cdot Q$ is defined as the total size (as a percentage of the size of the pool) of all positions rated at least AA− that are not more senior than the tranche of interest.

❑ The right column is chosen when the effective number of the underlying exposures N is less than 6.

❑ In all other cases, middle column is chosen.

Supervisory formula approach

For a tranche characterised by credit enhancement level L and thickness T, the SFA capital factor is calculated as the greater of $[S(L + T) − S(L)]/T$ and 0.56%, the latter being the floor for the capital factor for any tranche. The difference $S(L + T) − S(L)$ has a straightforward interpretation as the area under the curve representing marginal capital (the capital factor for infinitesimally thin tranche) and lying inside the tranche bounds, as shown in Figure 1.

Marginal capital is set to be 100% below K_{IRB} and declines to zero above K_{IRB}. One can divide any tranche into a large set of very thin

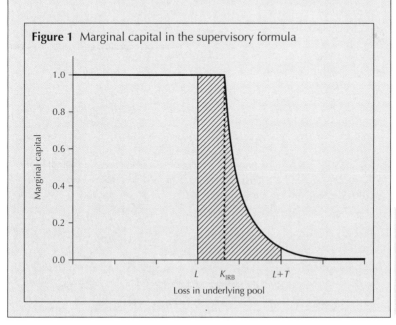

Figure 1 Marginal capital in the supervisory formula

tranches and calculate capital charge for that tranche as the sum of capital charges of the thin tranches. In the limit of infinitesimally thin tranches, this sum is given by the area under the curve. Detailed description of the supervisory formula is given in Panel 3.

IRB approach for originating banks

Originating banks must calculate the capital factor (ie, the capital charge expressed as a percentage of notional) for the underlying pool, denoted as K_{IRB}. For rated tranches with the upper bound (ie, $L + T$) below K_{IRB}, the capital charge is 100%. For rated tranches with credit enhancement level L above K_{IRB}, originating banks must use the RBA capital factors from Table 5 or 6. If the originating bank holds a rated tranche that straddles the K_{IRB} border (ie, $L < K_{IRB}$ and $L + T > K_{IRB}$), it must treat the exposure as two separate positions. The portion of the tranche that is below K_{IRB} attracts 100% capital. The capital factor for the portion of the tranche that is above K_{IRB} is determined by the RBA. For unrated tranches, originating banks must use the SFA. As we have seen in Figure 1, the supervisory formula is constructed in such a way that the portion of the tranche that is below K_{IRB} always attracts 100% capital. If the total capital requirement (as a percentage of notional) for securitisation exposures determined by RBA/SFA approaches exceeds K_{IRB}, the capital requirement may be reduced to K_{IRB}.

IRB approach for investing banks

For tranches rated BBB− or above, investing banks must use the RBA capital factors from Table 5 or 6. For tranches with ratings BB+ or below, as well as for unrated tranches, the capital factor is 100%. With the supervisory approval, the bank may calculate K_{IRB} and use the SFA for unrated tranches. In this case, the bank may choose to apply K_{IRB} as the capital factor for the securitised exposures.

Eligible liquidity facilities

Liquidity facilities meeting the definition given in the standardised approach are treated as any other securitisation exposure with a CCF of 100%. If the facility is externally rated, the bank may rely on the external rating under the RBA. If the facility is not rated, the bank must apply the SFA. An eligible liquidity facility that can be drawn only in the event of a general market disruption is assigned a 20% CCF under the SFA. If the eligible facility is externally rated, the bank may rely on the external rating under the RBA provided it assigns a 100% CCF rather than a 20% CCF to the facility.

Additionally, similarly to the standardised approach, certain servicer cash advances may be eligible for 0% CCF. These cash advances must be cancellable without prior notice, and the servicer must be entitled to full reimbursement. This reimbursement right must be senior to other claims on cash flows from the underlying pool of exposures.

Early amortisation provisions

An originating bank must use the methodology and treatment described in the standardised approach for determining whether any capital must be held against the investors' interest. For IRB purposes, the capital charge attributed to the investors' interest is determined by the product of the notional amount of the investors' interest, the appropriate CCF, and K_{IRB}. Banks must also hold capital against any retained exposures arising from the securitisation involving the assets comprising the investors' interest.

Discussion of issues

The Basel II capital adequacy rules for securitisation are a vast improvement over the current regulatory capital rules. They capture most of the drivers of credit risk in securitisation tranches. Equally important is the fact that in the process of their development over a period of about two years there has been a significant improvement in the understanding of credit risk in securitisation. Securitisations can be relatively complex structures and there are several important drivers of credit risk in securitisation tranches. A simple formulation of capital rules covering all aspects and all drivers of risk of securitisation is practically impossible. By necessity, therefore, capital rules for securitisation have to be somewhat complex if the significant risks are to be captured. At the same time, an effort to capture everything makes the formulation unmanageably complex. The balancing of complexity and of capturing significant risks is an art and it is often a question of interpretation as to whether the rules are too complex or not. As soon as there is more understanding of what drives the loss distribution and economic capital for a securitisation tranche, it may become clearer that a very reasonable balance has been struck in the Basel II formulation.

In the remaining sections we look at issues at a conceptual level, some of which can be addressed without making the Basel II formulations any more elaborate. The discussions are positive at times and critical at other times. But they do not detract from the overall quality inherent in the formulation and the very positive role it has played in bringing about a better understanding of credit risk in securitisation tranches.

Treatment of tranche versus treatment of bond

The formulation of the ratings-based approach and the supervisory formula approach brought to the forefront the fact that credit risk in corporate bonds and credit risk in securitisation tranches have to be modelled and understood in distinct ways. The loss distributions resulting from credit risk in a corporate bond and a similarly rated securitisation tranche can be widely different. There are significant differences in the risk drivers of the two. Recent analytical models – Pykhtin and Dev (2002, 2003), Gordy and Jones (2003) – provide a complete understanding of the risk drivers, and these models have been developed only while the Basel II capital adequacy rules for securitisation were being formulated. Just as important as quantifying the effects of significant risk drivers, the models underscore the difference in risk between a securitisation tranche and a corporate bond with the same public rating. One of the stark results of this difference is the fact that, in terms of economic capital and loss distribution, a highly rated (AAA or AA) tranche is much less risky than a similarly rated bond and a poorly rated (BBB or BB or B) tranche is much more risky than a similarly rated bond.

Total capital for originating bank and investors together

The RBA is an approximation to the true risk, and capital is specified in a few discrete buckets. Therefore, even though the total risk in the underlying portfolio is known to be K_{IRB}, the total capital for all the securitised tranches taken together cannot be expected to sum up to K_{IRB} exactly. In many situations it will be larger and in some situations it will be smaller. It is a matter of concern only if the total capital is widely different from K_{IRB}. In what follows are a few examples to show that this is not the case.

In Table 7, we can see three examples of securitisations. All securitisations are defined on a homogeneous, granular pool of consumer loans. All loans in the pool are characterised by 1% probability of default and 50% expected LGD, resulting in

Table 7 Comparison of total capital (regulatory and model-based) with K_{IRB}

Tranche description	Tranche definition (%)	Notional (%)	Expected loss (%)	Implied Moody's rating	Model capital		Regulatory capital (%)
					Pykhtin/ Dev (%)	Gordy/ Jones (%)	
Originator	0–4.70	4.70	10.61	NR	91.65	94.33	100.00
Investor	4.70–100	95.30	0.0010	Aa2	0.20	0.28	1.20
Total		100.00	0.500		4.50	4.70	5.85
Originator	0–4.70	4.70	10.61	NR	91.65	94.33	100.00
Investor	4.70–6.70	2.00	0.0425	Baa1	9.35	13.29	4.00
Investor	6.70–100	93.30	0.0002	Aa1	0.0007	0.0010	1.20
Total		100.00	0.500		4.50	4.70	5.90
Originator	0–3.00	3.00	16.46	NR	99.96	99.99	100.00
Investor	3.00–6.00	3.00	0.1935	Baa3	49.71	56.41	8.00
Investor	6.00–100	94.00	0.0003	Aa1	0.0076	0.0112	1.20
Total		100.00	0.500		4.50	4.70	4.37

an expected loss of 0.5%. Assuming an asset correlation formula suggested by Basel II for other retail exposures (it produces asset correlation of 12.6% at PD of 1%), we use the Basel formula for capital requirement to arrive at K_{IRB} equal to 4.70%.

In each example, we define a securitisation on this pool and assume that the originating bank keeps the first loss piece and sells all the tranches above it to investors. We calculate one-year expected loss (as a percentage of the tranche size) for each investor tranche, and use a Moody's table that relates tranche expected losses and rating (see Moody's, 2000, Table 2) to arrive at Moody's implied rating for the tranche.[2] This implied rating is only an indication of what the true Moody's rating might be. Then, we use the implied rating to find the capital factor for the tranche in question according to RBA (the middle column of Table 5). The total capital is calculated as the sum of capital requirements for all tranches (the capital requirement is the product of the tranche notional and the capital factor). For comparison, we also calculate capital from the Gordy–Jones (for which the SFA is based upon) and Pykhtin–Dev models. The Gordy–Jones expression for the capital factor for a tranche with credit enhancement level L and thickness T is $[K(L + T) - K(L)]/T$, where function $K(\cdot)$ is part of the supervisory formula defined in Panel 3. This expression is very similar to the supervisory formula, which adds the constraint of dollar-for-dollar capital below K_{IRB} by replacing function $K(\cdot)$ by $S(\cdot)$. In the Gordy–Jones framework, the total capital always sums up to K_{IRB}. In the Pykhtin–Dev model, the total capital is less than K_{IRB} because it assumes non-perfect correlation between the systematic factors driving losses in the underlying pool and the rest of the investor's portfolio.

The originator typically unloads some of the risk, so we assume that the first loss piece would not exceed K_{IRB}. In our first two examples, the first loss piece is from 0% to K_{IRB}. Since the originator is required to keep dollar-for-dollar capital up to K_{IRB}, the capital for the originator here will equal K_{IRB}. The total capital kept by the originator and the investors will necessarily be above K_{IRB}. Since the investors must use RBA, this capital will depend on how the securitisation is structured above K_{IRB}.

In our first example, there is only one tranche above the first loss piece. Moody's implied rating for this tranche is Aa2, resulting in the RBA capital factor of 1.2%. Multiplying this by the tranche notional (95.3%), we arrive at 1.15% as the capital charge for the investors. Adding this capital charge to K_{IRB}, we obtain the total capital of 5.85%, which is approximately 24% above K_{IRB}.

In the RBA, different structuring of securitisation above K_{IRB} may result in different capital. In our second example, we assume that the originator sold two tranches to the investors: a 2% thick mezzanine tranche right above K_{IRB} and the senior tranche. Implied Moody's ratings are Baa1 for the mezzanine tranche and Aa1 for the senior tranche, resulting in capital factors of 4% and 1.2%, respectively. The total regulatory capital in this case is 5.90%. The reason why it is so close to the capital factor in the first example is that RBA does not make a distinction between Aa1 and Aa2 ratings – the senior tranche received the same capital charge in both examples.

Surprisingly, cases where total regulatory capital is below K_{IRB} are feasible. In our third example, the first loss piece held by the originator is 3% thick, resulting in the capital charge of 3% for the originator. The two tranches kept by investors are a 3% thick mezzanine tranche and the senior tranche. Even though part of the mezzanine tranche is below K_{IRB}, it receives "investment-grade"

Baa3 rating, so that the investors will have to keep only 8% regulatory capital. The senior tranche has Aa1 implied rating as before, and the total capital in this case is 4.37%.

Application of supervisory formula approach to originating banks

Both investing banks and originating banks are required to use RBA whenever external ratings of a tranche are available. Only when no external rating is available are originating banks allowed to use SFA. However, RBA is necessarily inferior to SFA in terms of describing the risk underlying a securitisation tranche, and, therefore, SFA should be given priority over RBA whenever possible.

SFA is based on the Gordy–Jones model, which provides accurate description of the risk underlying a given tranche. This risk depends on the tranche's credit enhancement level and thickness, as well as on the underlying pool's granularity, credit quality and asset correlations. Therefore, capital cannot be determined by rating alone, and RBA cannot adequately describe the underlying risk regardless of its calibration. While RBA is useful for investors, who typically do not have complete information on the underlying pool, the superior SFA should always be used by originators, who do have this information.

Effect of granularity

In Tables 8 and 9, we see how capital factors computed with both the Gordy–Jones model and the Dev–Pykhtin model vary with the level of granularity by varying the number of loans in the underlying homogeneous pool. We compare capital for infinitesimally thin tranches (ITT) of "investment-grade" ratings computed according to these models with the RBA capital.[3]

As before, we use a Moody's table that relates ratings to expected losses. However, this time we start with a rating, find the one-year expected loss from the table, and then find the credit enhancement level of an ITT corresponding to this expected loss. We show only the capital factors from the middle column (base capital factors) of Table 5 because the left column is applicable only to thick tranches and the right column is applicable to extremely non-granular pools with effective number of exposures of fewer than six. Tables 8 and 9 differ by the probability of default of the borrowers in the pool.

Table 8 RBA capital versus model capital for infinitesimally thin tranches at different levels of granularity; PD = 0.15%

Moody's ratings	RBA capital (%)	Gordy/Jones capital (%)				Pykhtin/Dev capital (%)			
		N = ∞	N = 200	N = 50	N = 20	N = ∞	N = 200	N = 50	N = 20
Aa	1.2	0.000	0.004	0.121	0.172	0.000	0.001	0.038	0.102
A	1.6	0.002	0.532	1.470	1.243	0.009	0.269	0.931	0.945
Baa1	4.0	13.6	14.7	9.9	6.3	10.4	12.4	8.9	5.5
Baa2	6.0	43.1	28.0	15.6	9.5	33.0	24.9	14.6	8.5
Baa3	8.0	88.0	53.6	26.7	15.0	78.9	49.5	25.8	13.7

Table 9 RBA capital versus model capital for infinitesimally thin tranches at different levels of granularity; PD = 6.0%

Moody's ratings	RBA capital (%)	Gordy/Jones capital (%)				Pykhtin/Dev capital (%)			
		N = ∞	N = 200	N = 50	N = 20	N = ∞	N = 200	N = 50	N = 20
Aa	1.2	0.000	0.008	0.188	0.328	0.000	0.003	0.075	0.124
A	1.6	0.007	0.603	1.715	1.636	0.009	0.364	1.068	0.958
Baa1	4.0	14.4	16.2	11.8	7.3	10.4	12.7	9.8	5.9
Baa2	6.0	45.0	32.0	19.1	11.1	33.0	26.4	16.7	9.6
Baa3	8.0	90.5	62.9	34.8	19.2	78.9	55.2	31.9	17.9

Granularity has opposite effects on tranches of high and low ratings. Lack of granularity (smaller number of exposures) dramatically increases the riskiness of highly rated tranches. At the same time, tranches with lower ratings become less risky. The dependence of capital upon the credit quality of the underlying pool is surprisingly weak for lower ratings, but getting stronger for higher ratings.

As one can see from Tables 8 and 9, granularity has much stronger effect on capital than is reflected in the RBA, particularly for highly rated tranches.

Effect of thickness of tranche

Apart from its dependence upon rating, pool granularity and credit quality, capital for mezzanine tranches also depends on tranche thickness. Given an underlying pool, one can define infinitely many mezzanine tranches, all having the same expected loss (and

Table 10 RBA capital versus model capital for mezzanine tranches of different thickness defined on granular pool; PD = 0.15%

Moody's ratings	RBA capital (%)	Gordy/Jones capital (%)				Pykhtin/Dev capital (%)			
		T = 0	T = 1	T = 2	T = 3	T = 0	T = 1	T = 2	T = 3
Aa	1.2	0.000	0.000	0.000	0.000	0.000	0.000	0.000	0.000
A	1.6	0.002	0.006	0.022	0.065	0.009	0.016	0.038	0.084
Baa1	4.0	13.6	14.9	16.7	17.3	10.4	11.5	13.2	11.5
Baa2	6.0	43.1	39.6	33.8	29.1	33.0	31.6	28.6	25.4
Baa3	8.0	88.0	76.6	56.6	43.3	78.9	66.6	51.0	39.6

Table 11 RBA capital versus model capital for mezzanine tranches of different thickness defined on granular pool; PD = 6.0%

Moody's ratings	RBA capital (%)	Gordy/Jones capital (%)				Pykhtin/Dev capital (%)			
		T = 0	T = 1	T = 2	T = 3	T = 0	T = 1	T = 2	T = 3
Aa	1.2	0.000	0.000	0.000	0.000	0.000	0.000	0.000	0.000
A	1.6	0.007	0.010	0.018	0.035	0.009	0.012	0.020	0.036
Baa1	4.0	14.4	14.8	15.6	16.7	10.4	10.7	11.3	12.2
Baa2	6.0	45.0	44.3	42.6	40.4	33.0	31.8	32.1	31.2
Baa3	8.0	90.5	89.1	85.2	79.0	78.9	77.6	73.9	68.6

therefore Moody's rating) but different thickness. Both the Gordy–Jones model and the Dev–Pykhtin models were used to compute capital for a few of such tranches with for "investment-grade" ratings. In Tables 10 and 11, there is a comparison of these capital factors with the RBA capital factors (the middle column of Table 5). As before, the two tables differ by assumed probability of default in the underlying pool.

From these tables, we see that the dependence of capital upon thickness of a mezzanine tranche has opposite signs for tranches with high and low ratings. By comparing the tables, we can see that this dependence is stronger for underlying pools of higher credit quality.

The above results are applicable only to mezzanine tranches. For senior tranches, there is a one-to-one relation between their thickness and expected loss (and, therefore, rating).

Reasonableness of the floor

Basel II capital for any securitisation tranche has a floor of 56 basis points. In other words, even the best-rated tranche in the best of circumstances (granular pool of underlying assets) will attract 56 bps of capital. This floor is too high – the risk of a AAA tranche or even a AA tranche is such that the capital should be much less than 56 bps. It is evident from Tables 10 and 11 that a complete model would suggest minimal capital for AA-rated tranches (not to speak of AAA-rated tranches) when the underlying pool consists of a large number of assets. Even when the underlying pool is non-granular, the capital for an AA-rated tranche should be below 56 bps, as shown in Tables 8 and 9. The capital for an AAA-rated tranche, curved out of a non-granular pool of assets, should be much smaller than 56 bps.

The capital imposed by the floor may be a small fraction of the total capital for all the tranches taken together, but, for the investor holding only portfolios of AAA or AA tranches, the capital can be many times the true economic capital. Some banks hold large investment portfolios consisting of AAA-rated tranches. The existence of the unreasonably high floor will put these banks at a comparative disadvantage.

Conclusion

Basel II capital adequacy rules for securitisation attain a special significance, as one of the motivations of Basel II has been the fact that the lack of risk sensitivity in the capital adequacy rules under Basel I has prompted many banks to use securitisation as a means of "regulatory arbitrage". Securitisations have grown into a huge market over the last two decades in the US and are rapidly gaining ground in Europe. The capital adequacy rules for securitisation, therefore, cover credit risk of financial institutions, which are by no means insignificant.

Securitisation tranches are held by issuer banks and by financial institutions as investors, both of which are covered under the Basel II capital adequacy rules for securitisation. The rules apply to both traditional and synthetic securitisations, in particular asset-backed securities, collateralised debt obligations, mortgage-backed securities, credit enhancements, liquidity facilities and credit derivatives.

As with other parts of Basel II, there is a standardised approach and a more advanced internal ratings-based approach. Within the IRB approach, there is a ratings-based approach and a supervisory formula approach.

It is a rare occasion that the process of development of a regulatory rule leads to a better understanding of the risk or other characteristics of a financial instrument by the financial community as a whole. Typically, as in the case of most of Basel II, the regulatory rules or formulations incorporate methodologies already in use by enlightened practitioners in the industry. Basel II capital for securitisation is one of those rare instances. During the process of formulation of the supervisory formula approach and the ratings-based approach, the true drivers of credit risk in securitisation tranches have come to be explicitly recognised and the relative magnitudes of the effects of those drivers modelled and discussed. In addition, the fact that credit risk in corporate bonds and loans and that in securitisation tranches have to be modelled and understood in distinct ways has been emphasised, even though they may have the same rating. Both the supervisory formula approach and the ratings-based approach are based on (though modified) analytical results from new models of credit risk in securitisation tranches developed over the period between CP2 and CP3.

On the other hand, the realisation of the magnitude of the effects of the different drivers of credit risk in securitisation tranches makes it a hard task. The important risk drivers are the underlying pool's granularity, credit quality and asset correlations, as well as tranche thickness and of course the rating of the tranche. It is difficult to incorporate so many risk drivers and characteristics in a simple regulatory formulation or two. By necessity, therefore, capital rules for securitisation have to be somewhat complex if the significant risks are to be captured. At the same time, an effort to capture everything makes the formulation unmanageably complex. The balancing of complexity and of capturing significant risks is an art, which has been compounded by the fact that many of the effects of risk drivers have not been well known until the development of recent models. The lack of understanding of risk drivers biases the reader in concluding that the balance has been struck at too complex a level.

A better understanding of the risks will, in course of time, shift that bias in the opposite direction.

However, without adding any more complexity to the formulation of the ratings-based approach and the supervisory formula approach, some issues can be addressed to align capital closer to the true risk in securitisation tranches. The floor of 0.56% capital is too high – the risk of an AAA tranche or even an AA tranche is such that the capital should be much less than 0.56%. This is particularly true of securitisation with granular pools of underlying collaterals. The capital imposed by the floor may be a small fraction of the total capital for all the tranches taken together, but, for the investor holding only portfolios of AAA or AA tranches, the capital is many times the true economic capital. The effect of granularity reflected in the ratings-based approach is much less than the true effect. The capital required for tranches below BBB− is much less than the economic capital implied by the true risk of such mezzanine tranches. The difference between a non-investment-grade bond and a mezzanine tranche of identical rating is stark. The latter is many times riskier than the former. The ratings-based approach incorporates this difference directionally but not adequately in magnitude. The capital for AAA and AA tranches is too high, especially for a granular pool of underlying collaterals. The capital for BBB and BB tranches is too low.

A simplified formulation will necessarily lead to more capital under some circumstances and less under others, than warranted by a formulation that is more complex. The overall capital for securitisation under most circumstances, however, is not unreasonable and by no stretch of imagination can it be said that capital requirements will severely affect the securitisation market. The recognition of relative risks of senior tranches and mezzanine tranches may have a major effect on pricing but not on the overall demand and supply in the securitisation market.

The Basel II capital adequacy rules for securitisation are a vast improvement over the current regulatory capital rules. Not only do they capture most of the drivers of credit risk in securitisation tranches, but also in the process of their development over a period of about two years a more complete understanding of credit risk in securitisation has been achieved.

PANEL 3 TECHNICAL DETAILS OF THE SUPERVISORY FORMULA

Definitions

Credit enhancement level L is the ratio of the notional amount of all securitisation exposures subordinate to the tranche in question to the notional amount of all exposures in the pool.

Thickness T is the ratio of the nominal size of the tranche of interest to the notional amount of all exposures in the pool.

Effective number of exposures is calculated as

$$N = \frac{\left(\sum_i \text{EAD}_i \right)^2}{\sum_i \left(\text{EAD}_i \right)^2}$$

where EAD_i is the exposure at default for the *i*th borrower in the underlying pool and the summations are taken over all individual borrowers. Multiple exposures to the same borrower must be consolidated (treated as a single instrument). In the case of resecuritisation (ie, securitisation of securitisations), the formula applies to the number of securitisation exposures in the pool and not to the number of underlying exposures in the original pools.

Exposure-weighted average LGD is defined as

$$\text{LGD} = \frac{\sum_i \text{EAD}_i \text{LGD}_i}{\sum_i \text{EAD}_i}$$

where LGD_i represents the average LGD associated with all exposures to the *i*th borrower. In the case of resecuritisation, an LGD of 100% must be assumed for the underlying securitised exposures.

Supervisory formula

For a tranche characterised by credit enhancement level *L* and thickness *T*, the SFA capital charge is calculated as the greater of $[S(L + T) - S(L)]/T$ and 0.56%, where function $S(L)$ is given by

$$S(L) = \begin{cases} L & \text{if } L < K_{\text{IRB}} \\ K_{\text{IRB}} + K(L) - K(K_{\text{IRB}}) + (dK_{\text{IRB}}/\omega)(1 - e^{-\omega(L-K_{\text{IRB}})/K_{\text{IRB}}}) & \text{otherwise} \end{cases}$$

and

$$K(L) = (1-h) \cdot \left([1 - \beta(L; a, b)] L + \beta(L; a+1, b) c \right)$$

245

$$h = (1 - K_{IRB}/LGD)^N$$

$$c = K_{IRB}/(1-h)$$

$$v = \frac{(LGD - K_{IRB})K_{IRB} + 0.25(1-LGD)K_{IRB}}{N}$$

$$f = \left(\frac{v + K_{IRB}^2}{1-h} - c^2\right) + \frac{(1-K_{IRB})K_{IRB} - v}{(1-h)\tau}$$

$$g = \frac{(1-c)c}{f} - 1$$

$$a = g \cdot c$$

$$b = g \cdot (1 - c)$$

$$d = 1 - (1 - h) \cdot (1 - \beta(K_{IRB}; a,b))$$

In these expressions, $\beta(L; a,b)$ refers to the cumulative beta distribution with parameters a and b evaluated at L.

The supervisory-determined parameters in the above expressions are $\tau = 1,000$ and $\omega = 20$.

For securitisations involving retail exposures, subject to supervisory review, the supervisory formula may be implemented using simplifications: $h = 0$ and $v = 0$.

In the second section of this chapter, we look at the Basel II capital adequacy rules for the retail portfolio.

BASEL II CAPITAL ADEQUACY RULES FOR RETAIL

Introduction

The overall loan portfolio of most financial institutions consists of loans to individual consumers as well as to businesses. The former is generally referred to as "retail" and the latter as "corporate". In the US, the relative sizes of retail and corporate portfolios of financial institutions are of the same order of magnitude. While all best-practice banks manage the risk in their retail portfolios by product category and by customer score and other segmentation for many years, the present capital adequacy rules under Basel I distinguish only between mortgages and all other retail product categories.

The first consultative paper issued in 1999 at the very beginning of the Basel II process did not have an explicit methodology for capital adequacy for retail portfolios that was different from existing rules. The consultative paper issued in January 2001 – Basel (2001), which is known as CP2 – set forth capital adequacy formulation for retail portfolios. But many details were missing. A working paper issued in October 2001 provided details of the standardised and IRB (internal ratings-based) approaches. The risk weight curve was the same for all retail products. Another working paper issued in October 2002 introduced different risk weight curves (essentially different portfolio correlations) for three different product categories within retail. It also introduced correlation as a decreasing function of credit quality. The consultative paper issued in March 2003 – Basel (2003), which is known as CP3 – incorporates these changes.

Standardised and IRB approaches

Basel II permits banks a choice between two broad methods for calculating their capital requirements for credit risk in retail portfolios. One alternative, known as the *standardised approach*, will measure credit risk in a set manner. The alternative method, which is subject to the explicit approval of the bank supervisor, would allow banks to use their internal rating systems. This method is known as the *internal ratings-based* (IRB) approach.

Capital requirements

Minimum capital requirements are calculated as the product of three factors: exposure at default, capital factor, and credit conversion factor (CCF). The capital is calculated as

Capital = capital factor * EAD * credit conversion factor

or, equivalently,

Capital = risk weight * 8% * EAD * credit conversion factor

In this section, we will henceforth deal with capital factors rather than risk weights, as they have a one-to-one relationship.

In case of balance sheet loan amounts, the appropriate EAD is simply the nominal outstanding balance of the loan and CCF equals 100%. In case of off-balance-sheet retail exposures, appropriate credit conversion factor (of less than 100%) is to be used. For retail exposures with uncertain future drawdown (eg, credit cards), expectation of additional drawings prior to default can be reflected either in EAD or in LGD. This is to incorporate the different ways different banks have maintained their historical records.

In calculating EAD, on-balance-sheet netting of loans and deposits of a bank to or from a retail customer is permitted. When only drawn balances of retail facilities have been securitised, banks will have to hold required capital against the portion of credit lines that are un-drawn, in addition to capital (if any) required under Basel II securitisation rules.

PANEL 4 STANDARDISED APPROACH FOR RETAIL PORTFOLIO

The capital adequacy formula for retail exposures under the standardised approach is very simple. It can be summarised in the following way:

❏ Residential mortgage exposures receive capital factor is 2.8%.
❏ For all other retail exposures, capital factor is 6.0%.

It is pertinent to note that for all other (than residential mortgages) retail, even though there is no risk sensitivity, just as in Basel I, the minimum capital requirement is lower than under Basel I. This is perhaps the result of a growing recognition of the extent of diversification that exists in any retail portfolio.

To place the capital numbers in perspective and to contrast retail with corporate, the capital factors for corporate exposures, under the standardised approach, are shown in Table 12.

Table 12 Capital factors for corporate exposures under the standardised approach

Rating	AAA to AA−	A+ to A−	BBB+ to BB−	Below BB−	Unrated
Capital	1.6%	4.0%	8.0%	12.0%	8.0%

PANEL 5 INTERNAL RATINGS-BASED APPROACH FOR RETAIL PORTFOLIO

Under the IRB approach in Basel II, the three fundamental determinants of regulatory capital factor are: probability of default (PD), loss-given default (LGD) and correlation (asset correlation). Of these, PD and LGD are to be determined by the banks themselves based on internal estimates. Correlation is specified by the Basel II formulation itself. Since explicit incorporation of correlation and its functional form are somewhat new to the way risk management of retail portfolios is undertaken, we will discuss it at length in a separate subsection.

Probability of default (PD) is the likelihood that a given borrower will default within one year. PD is also the fraction of borrowers defaulting in a very large portfolio of similar borrowers. It is common in risk management of retail portfolios to segment the portfolio by score bands (FICO score, bureau scores and so on). Each score band has an associated good:bad odds ratio. There is a clear relationship between *probability of default* and *good:bad odds ratio*, given as follows:

$$\text{Odds ratio} = (1 - PD)/PD$$

Loss-given default (LGD) is a measure of the severity of loss once a loan has defaulted. It is simply equal to (1 − recovery rate). Recovery rate is the fraction of outstanding principal recovered, in present value terms, by the bank from a defaulted loan. Conceptually, LGD is similar to net to gross charge-off.

The expected loss (EL) of a portfolio of retail loans is simply the product of PD and LGD. However, the formula for capital is not so simple. The capital factor for retail in the IRB approach is given by the expression (see Panel 5 for more technical details):

$$K = \text{LGD} * N\left[\frac{N^{-1}(PD) + \sqrt{R}\,N^{-1}(99.9\%)}{\sqrt{1-R}}\right] - A * EL$$

where $N(\cdot)$ is the cumulative standard normal distribution function, R is the asset correlation (which in turn is a function of PD), and $A = 0.75$ for credit cards and 0 for everything else.

Table 13 Illustrative capital factors for retail exposures under the IRB approach

FICO score	PD (%)	Asset correlation (%)			Basel capital (%)			
		HE and mortgage	Other retail	Credit cards	Mortgage	HE	Other retail	Credit cards
>800	0.10	15.0	16.5	10.6	0.20	0.60	1.11	1.17
780–799	0.15	15.0	16.2	10.3	0.27	0.82	1.50	1.57
760–779	0.20	15.0	16.0	10.1	0.34	1.02	1.83	1.92
740–759	0.35	15.0	15.3	9.6	0.52	1.56	2.65	2.78
720–739	0.75	15.0	13.5	8.2	0.90	2.71	4.10	4.28
700–719	1.21	15.0	11.8	6.9	1.26	3.77	5.11	5.26
680–699	1.77	15.0	10.1	5.7	1.62	4.87	5.90	5.99
660–679	2.43	15.0	8.4	4.7	2.00	6.01	6.52	6.53
640–659	3.56	15.0	6.3	3.5	2.55	7.66	7.21	7.16
620–639	4.50	15.0	5.1	2.9	2.94	8.83	7.65	7.63
600–619	5.03	15.0	4.6	2.7	3.14	9.43	7.88	7.91
580–599	5.61	15.0	4.1	2.5	3.35	10.06	8.14	8.23
560–579	7.05	15.0	3.3	2.3	3.83	11.48	8.83	9.12
540–559	8.68	15.0	2.7	2.1	4.29	12.88	9.70	10.21
520–539	9.50	15.0	2.5	2.1	4.51	13.53	10.18	10.78
500–519	11.29	15.0	2.3	2.0	4.94	14.81	11.29	12.00
<500	17.36	15.0	2.0	2.0	6.10	18.29	15.35	15.80

In Table 13, illustrative capital factors have been calculated for retail exposures within different FICO score bands. For each FICO score band, the implied odds ratio has been converted to PD. The LGD assumptions (for illustrative purposes) are: LGD = 10% for mortgages, LGD = 30% for HE, LGD = 50% for other retail and LGD = 90% for credit cards.

Correlation as an important factor in the retail IRB approach

The two important determinants of the minimum capital requirement for retail exposures are PD and LGD, as already introduced. A *third* fundamental and very important determinant of regulatory capital is *correlation*.

Default events are correlated. The wellbeing of all obligors is affected by macroeconomic factors as well as by individual circumstances. Default correlations can be estimated from historical default rates. Correlations between default events are responsible for the heavy tail of portfolio loss distribution. Capital, as a tail percentile of the loss distribution, is very sensitive to the level of correlations.

Two types of correlation can be thought of: *default correlation* and *asset correlation*. *Default correlation* is a measure of the extent to which default of one obligor goes hand in hand with the default of another obligor. In the Basel framework (and other Merton-type models), an obligor defaults whenever its asset value falls below a certain threshold.

Asset correlation is the correlation between returns on assets of two obligors. Asset returns have two components: *systematic* (related to the state of the economy and it is the same for all obligors) and *idiosyncratic* (reflecting the individual circumstances of each obligor). Asset correlation is a measure of relative weight of the systematic component in asset returns. For a given asset correlation, default correlation increases as PD increases. For a given default correlation, asset correlation decreases as PD increases.

Empirical evidence for decreasing asset correlation

There are considerable industry data available on publicly rated bond defaults. Therefore, this is the first place to look for estimation of correlations and how the correlations vary with credit quality. Table 14 shows the results of estimation of default correlations and asset correlations from Moody's historical default rates. The asset correlation decreases significantly as credit quality deteriorates. Given the amount of data, the results in Table 14 are directionally indicative but each of the calculated correlation numbers has a wide confidence band.

It is not a big leap of faith to then assume that a similar pattern holds for a portfolio of loans. At any rate, there is some, admittedly weak, evidence for deceasing asset correlation as credit rating

Table 14 Parameter estimates from Moody's default rates from 1970 to 2001

	Moody's ratings			
	A (%)	Baa (%)	Ba (%)	B (%)
Mean default rate	0.01	0.15	1.21	6.53
St dev of default rate	0.06	0.28	1.33	4.66
rho_D	0.22	0.52	1.48	3.55
rho_A	22.8	15.9	13.0	11.8

worsens than for constant (or for that matter increasing) asset correlation as credit quality worsens.[4]

The bond market credit spread information provides more empirical evidence that suggests that asset correlation may be decreasing as credit quality deteriorates. Information is available publicly on credit spreads (average credit spreads for each rating over any long period of history) and default rate (average default rates for each rating over the same period of history).

As we go down the credit spectrum, the rate of increase in credit spreads is much smaller than the rate of increase in default rate. Assuming that the recovery rate does not depend on credit quality (it may depend on collateral or structure), the credit spread does not increase in proportion to expected loss. One possible conclusion is that the market must be ascribing higher portfolio diversification benefits to poorer-rated bond portfolios. In other words, the market implies decreasing correlation as PD increases in its pricing behaviour.

Conceptual arguments for decreasing asset correlation

In the Basel formulation, asset correlation decreases as PD increases. There are strong conceptual arguments justifying this relationship.[5] These arguments go like this:

❑ Default correlation is just as good a parameter as asset correlation. In fact some internal economic capital models have, implicitly, a constant default correlation. A constant default correlation implies a decreasing (with PD) asset correlation in the Merton framework as well as more generally.

❑ Consider a poorly rated (very high-PD) consumer earning hourly wages in an unskilled job and a highly rated (very low-PD) consumer with a professional white-collar job. The former may get drunk and not show up for work for more than a day; he or she may get fired and be unable to find another job easily; he or she may end up defaulting on a loan. This is idiosyncratic behavior and another poorly rated consumer is *not* likely to do the same thing at the same time. A similar idiosyncratic behavior on the part of a highly rated customer is not likely to result in a loss of livelihood and default. He or she is more likely to default due to a sector or the economy doing badly.

In other words, the proportion of idiosyncratic component in total credit risk is lower for highly rated consumers than for poorly rated consumer – this is the equivalent of saying that asset correlation is lower for poorly rated consumers.

The argument in the paragraph above is not to imply that either the total credit risk or the systematic component of it is lower for poorly rated consumers. They will be higher for poorly rated consumers than for highly rated consumers. That is a PD effect. The observation that many more poorly rated consumers default (seemingly together) when the economy sours than do highly rated consumers is a result of this effect. The asset correlation effect is different. It is the relative *proportion* of the systematic part to the idiosyncratic part, which is lower for poorly rated consumers and higher for highly rated consumers.

Need for more risk weight functions within retail

A regulatory capital adequacy framework has to limit, out of necessity, the number of product categories and the number of fundamentally different formulae. Therefore, it is unreasonable to expect a separate risk weight curve for every niche product, of which there are many in the retail world. On the other hand, creating a separate risk weight curve for all products of significant size, which differentiate themselves significantly in fundamental risk characteristic, is in line with the very first objective of Basel II vis-à-vis its risk-sensitive capital adequacy rules.

Home equity is one such product category. At least in the US., home equity loan is one of the fastest-growing segments of the consumer credit market. In the US, home equity products are already large and, if the growth rate continues, it will become one of the largest segments of the retail world. In CP3, home equity loans and credit lines are treated under the residential mortgages category. There are at least two conceptual arguments in favour of a separate risk weight curve for home equity products.

One of the reasons why asset correlation for residential mortgages is set at such a high level is to take into account the long-term nature of mortgage loans. The Basel retail framework does not have the maturity adjustment factor, and the effect of longer maturity on capital is incorporated into the framework through higher asset correlation. Since a typical maturity for home equity loans is significantly shorter than one for purchased-money first mortgages, the effective asset correlation R for home equity loans should be lower than the one for first mortgages.

The majority of residential mortgages in the United States are conforming mortgages, ie, mortgages insured by the US government and not kept by banks in their books. The mortgages banks keep in their books are those that do not qualify for the government insurance (issued to either consumers with poor credit quality or consumers who buy expensive houses). Home equity loans and lines of credit are based on all kinds of mortgages and thus have a much more diverse customer base than nonconforming first mortgages. Therefore, the asset correlation R used in the advanced IRB formulation for home equity products should be lower than the one used in the advanced IRB formulation for first mortgages.

IRB formulation for retail and alternative empirical methods

The Basel framework has an intrinsic advantage over any data-based empirical model. Regulatory capital should be calculated at the 99.9% confidence level with a one-year horizon. It means that the framework should be able to estimate an annual portfolio loss that happens on average once in one thousand years. Very few banks have enough data to build an empirical model capable of describing such rare events. However, a conceptual model based on sound fundamental principals needs only a moderate number of data to calibrate its parameters. After calibration it is capable of estimating losses at *any* confidence level. The Basel framework generally satisfies this criterion. Speaking from the perspective of statistical robustness, it is one thing to estimate the PD of a consumer based on several (say five to ten) years of default data, but a very different thing to estimate a high percentile from observation of annual losses over several (say five to ten) years. The former is statistically valid; the latter is not.

An empirical methodology based on observed data can be implemented in three possible ways, all of which have disadvantages at least conceptually. First, using the historical loss data to create an empirical loss distribution and reading off the appropriate percentile of the historical distribution. This requires so much data that it is highly unlikely that a typical bank (or for that matter any bank) will have so much historical data. Using cohorts and monthly or quarterly loss data can bootstrap the number of observations to a large number, but, to get to an empirical distribution of annual (because the horizon is one year, after all) losses, an assumption about an underlying random process has to be made implicitly or explicitly. Such a process is based on much less fundamental concepts than the Merton type Basel model.

Second, fitting a closed-form distribution (eg, beta or lognormal or Weibull) to the loss observations to estimate the parameters of the distribution. The appropriate percentile can be then calculated from the loss distribution with the specific estimated parameters. There is no prior reason why the fitted distribution should be the distribution of losses. Conceptually, this is far less defensible than the Basel framework based on economic fundamentals.

Third, estimating volatility (standard deviation) of the loss observations and computing capital as a fixed multiple of the standard deviation. This methodology is conceptually flawed. The main problem with this approach is that, fundamentally, portfolio loss volatility and capital (using a high confidence level) have different additivity properties. Different additivity properties for portfolio loss volatility and capital mean that the ratio of capital to volatility will change whenever portfolio composition is changed. Even for homogeneous portfolios, the capital-to-volatility ratio must depend on PD and the level of correlations (apart from its expected dependence on the confidence level). Therefore, a *fixed* multiple of portfolio loss volatility cannot adequately approximate capital. The following table shows how much the multiple can change as credit quality and intra-portfolio correlation change.

Conclusion

Basel II capital adequacy rules for retail exposures have evolved significantly over the last two years since CP2. The capital adequacy rules for retail cover credit risk of financial institutions, which are as significant as any other risk type. The retail portfolios have been separated into three broad product categories: residential mortgages, revolving (credit cards) and all other retail.

As with other parts of Basel II, there is a standardised approach and a more advanced internal ratings-based approach. Within the

Table 15 Ratio K/σ_L at $q = 99.9\%$ as function of PD and asset correlation

PD (%)	Capital-to-volatility ratio at $q = 99.9\%$			
	$\rho = 20\%$	$\rho = 10\%$	$\rho = 5\%$	$\rho = 2\%$
0.01	12.06	10.19	8.00	5.95
0.02	11.95	9.84	7.71	5.79
0.05	11.59	9.30	7.30	5.55
0.10	11.16	8.83	6.97	5.36
0.20	10.59	8.33	6.62	5.17
0.50	9.63	7.61	6.14	4.90
1.00	8.77	7.01	6.76	4.69
2.00	7.80	6.38	5.35	4.46
5.00	6.38	5.48	4.78	4.14
10.00	5.24	4.75	4.30	3.87

IRB approach, there is no foundation IRB approach (which is available for corporate exposures) but only the advanced IRB approach. In terms of risk sensitivity under the internal ratings-based approach, retail formulations are at the same level as the formulations for corporate exposures. The risk sensitivity for retail under the standardised approach, however, is much less than that for corporates.

The IRB approach for retail under Basel II incorporates concepts that are somewhat controversial and relatively new to the risk management of retail portfolios. One is decreasing asset correlation as credit quality goes down and the other is the (partial) recognition of future margin income as capital. Conceptually decreasing asset correlation can be justified, although the exact parameters perhaps need to improve as more data become available. The recognition of future margin income is limited to revolving credits only. In principle, it should be applicable to all retail products.

It is consistent with the objective of creating risk-sensitive capital adequacy rules under Basel II to have as many risk weight functions as there are products of significant size, which differentiate themselves significantly in fundamental risk characteristic, while keeping the number of distinct risk weight functions to a manageable level. Home equity is one product category that deserves a separate risk weight function.

APPENDIX: TECHNICAL DETAILS

Default correlation and asset correlation

For two obligors with probabilities of default PD_1 and PD_2, probability of both defaulting is:

$$PD_{12} = PD_1 * PD_2, \text{ if defaults are independent}$$

$$PD_{12} > PD_1 * PD_2, \text{ if defaults are dependent}$$

Default correlation ρ_D is a measure of the deviation of PD_{12} from $PD_1 * PD_2$.

Asset correlation ρ_A is the correlation between returns on assets of two obligors. Asset returns have two components: *systematic* (related to the state of the economy; same for all obligors) and *idiosyncratic* (reflecting individual circumstances of each obligor). Asset correlation is a measure of relative weight of the systematic component in asset returns.

For a given asset correlation ρ_A, default correlation ρ_D increases as PD increases. For a given default ρ_D, asset correlation ρ_A *decreases as PD increases.*

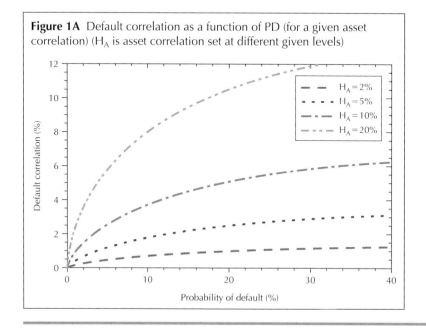

Figure 1A Default correlation as a function of PD (for a given asset correlation) (H_A is asset correlation set at different given levels)

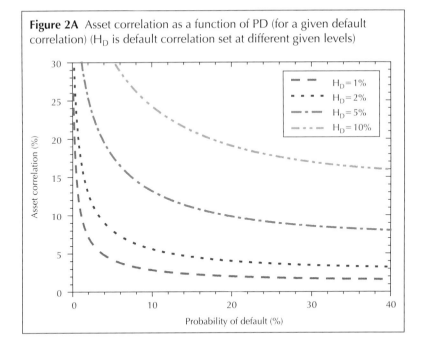

Figure 2A Asset correlation as a function of PD (for a given default correlation) (H_D is default correlation set at different given levels)

Advanced IRB formula

Capital is computed according to

$$K = LGD * N\left[\frac{N^{-1}(PD) + \sqrt{R}\, N^{-1}(99.9\%)}{\sqrt{1-R}}\right] - A * PD * LGD$$

where $N(\cdot)$ is the cumulative standard normal distribution function, R is the asset correlation (which in turn is a function of PD), and $A = 0.75$ for credit cards and 0 for everything else.

Asset correlation is a function of PD:

The formula in CP3 is

$$R = R_{min}\left(\frac{1-e^{-ap}}{1-e^{-a}}\right) + R_{max}\left(1 - \frac{1-e^{-ap}}{1-e^{-a}}\right)$$

where p denotes PD, R_{min} is the minimum value of correlation (at $p = 1$), R_{max} is the maximum value of correlation (at $p = 0$), and a is the steepness parameter.

The formula in ANPR is

$$R = R_{\min}\left(1 - e^{-ap}\right) + R_{\max}e^{-ap}$$

This formula is obtained by neglecting e^{-a} in the denominators of the CP3 formula (this is reasonable since $a = 35$ for "other retail" and $a = 50$ in all other cases).

Values of the parameters in R:

	$R_{\max}$ (%)	$R_{\min}$ (%)	a (%)
Revolving exposures	11	2	50
Residential mortgages	15	15	n/a
Other retail	17	2	35

1 Requirements for treatment as an eligible liquidity facility are enumerated in section 538 of the New Basel Capital Accord. Essentially the facility documentation must clearly identify and limit the circumstances under which it may be drawn. In particular, it cannot be used to provide credit support.

2 See Pykhtin and Dev (2002) for details of this calculation.

3 I excluded Aaa rating because Gordy–Jones capital factors for this rating are negligible even at N = 20.

4 However, the evidence of constant (with respect to credit quality) asset correlation is even weaker.

5 The IRB retail formulation in the January 2001 consultative paper implied a constant asset correlation. KeyCorp suggested a decreasing asset correlation function (as PD increases) to US regulators active in the Models Task Force of Basel as early as June 2001, based primarily on these conceptual reasoning and secondarily on some industry data.

BIBLIOGRAPHY

Basel Committee on Banking Supervision, 2001, *The New Basel Capital Accord,* Consultative Document, January.

Basel Committee on Banking Supervision, 2003, *The New Basel Capital Accord,* Consultative Document, April.

Gordy, M., and D. Jones, 2003, "Random Tranches" *Risk,* pp. 78–83, March.

Moody's Investors Service, 2000, "The Lognormal Method Applied to ABS Analysis" Special Report, *International Structured Finance,* July.

Pykhtin, M., and A. Dev, 2002, "Credit Risk in Asset Securitisations: an Analytical Model", *Risk,* pp. S16–S20, May.

Pykhtin, M., and A. Dev, 2003, "Coarse-grained CDOs" *Risk,* pp. 113–16, January.

11

IRB-Compliant Models in Retail Banking

Richard Norgate

KPMG

INTRODUCTION

This chapter describes the challenge that retail banking units are facing in order to satisfy the requirements of an IRB approach within Basel II. It must not be forgotten that the IRB approach is not the only way to satisfy future regulation but merely an option. However, a large number of organisations that have chosen to aim for an IRB approach are also building more than is required from a regulatory perspective and treating the work as being more about improving the risk management capability of the organisation than complying with regulations. And this makes sense: only time will tell how many non-IRB-compliant organisations remain, but some early predictions suggest that those that choose the standardised approach could be competitively disadvantaged or, at worst, likely candidates for takeover.

This chapter focuses on providing a pragmatic account of how to develop the models required to satisfy the IRB requirements for a retail banking organisation. The chapter frequently refers to a "bank", but obviously all the content of this chapter is equally valid for other retail lending organisations, in particular building societies and other mutual organisations.

BACKGROUND

This section provides some background for the rest of the chapter, including a summary of the historic evolution of credit risk measurement in retail banking and the evolution towards Basel II.

The evolution of risk regulation

Three key groups are involved in the development of the prudential regulations that will become a reality in the UK, namely:

❏ the Basel Committee on Banking Supervision at the Bank for International Settlements;
❏ the European Union (EU); and
❏ the Financial Services Authority (FSA).

Ultimately, it is only the requirements of the FSA that will need to be followed for a UK bank, but since these have not been fully determined yet, the best idea of what future regulations will look like has been defined by the Basel committee and the EU.

The process in other countries will be similar, though countries outside Europe may only have Basel and local regulators to follow, without the extra levels of complexity that the EU adds.

The Basel Committee on Banking Supervision at the Bank for International Settlements

The Bank for International Settlements (BIS) is the world's oldest international financial institution. It was established in 1930 in the post-World War I environment, and was the earliest organisation to move to foster cooperation among central banks. Over time its role has shifted towards focusing on monetary and financial stability, which is how it has become responsible for the new rafts of banking regulations.

One of the committees within BIS is the Basel Committee on Banking Supervision (otherwise, especially in the current environment, known simply as the Basel Committee). The Basel Committee was responsible for the development of the initial Basel capital accord of 1988, which has since been renamed Basel I.

Basel I was timely and was implemented in an environment that had seen a number of major bank failures as a result of under-capitalisation, and it was very successful in bringing more stability to the banking community by setting standard minimum capital requirements. Other than an adjustment for the way in which market risk is handled, Basel I remains in place, as originally defined, today. Over time it has been acknowledged that the capital banks hold should not be a simple function of the assets of that bank but should also vary according to the risk within the bank's portfolios, and it is this assumption that has led to the development of Basel II.

The European Union

Prior to the 1980s, UK banks and securities houses were treated quite separately from a regulatory perspective, with banks being regulated by the Bank of England, and a less formal regulatory environment existing for the securities markets. Over the intervening period, work has been done to help ensure that all organisations are treated similarly within the UK. It was also acknowledged that there were levels of disparity across Europe, and work started on moving towards a common market.

Over the late 1980s and the early 1990s, a large amount of work was done, culminating in the 1993 Capital Adequacy Directive (CAD, subsequently referred to as CAD1), which established a consistent set of capital requirements across all banks, building societies, and some investment firms.

CAD1 was followed a few years later by CAD2, which changed the way in which banks were allowed to measure their market risk, and there have been a number of consultative papers issued within the EU describing what will be in CAD3.

Essentially CAD3 will become the European law and, hence, this is arguably a more important document than the Basel Accord. Just to make things more interesting, there are differences between the two documents (though these are, on the whole, minor, especially for retail banks).

The Financial Services Authority

In the UK, of course, the most important issue will be the way in which the Financial Services Authority (FSA) implements the Basel Accord.

The FSA has recently published a consultative paper, CP189 (FSA, 2003), which describes the way in which Basel II will be implemented within UK financial institutions. While CP189 does not provide the full picture (in fact, it is far from this and was never designed to do this), it does give an insight into the way the FSA is thinking about Basel II. In particular, CP189 provides some details on a few key areas that organisations will need to consider, including: the type of data accuracy tests that will be used; the data that will be required for model calibration; and the information required for scorecard validation.

A note on the classification of retail banking products
Before we get into the detail of the models required, it is worth explaining the differentiation between banking products defined by Basel II. Full details of this are provided in paragraph 199 of CP3, but a quick summary is provided here. There are three distinct types of exposure within retail banking, and they are as follows:

❑ *Residential mortgage exposures* Residential mortgages are treated separately from all other products, and there are separate assumptions about the behaviour of portfolios of mortgages compared to other products.
❑ *Qualifying revolving retail exposures* A "qualifying revolving retail exposure" is simply a revolving portfolio. For example, a standard credit card portfolio would qualify as a Basel revolving retail portfolio, as would a portfolio of agreed overdrafts.
❑ *Other retail exposures* All other products (primarily personal loans) fall into this category.

Treatment of small business exposures as "retail"
All small business exposures (where the customer's total facilities are less than €1 million) can be treated as retail portfolios if the bank "treats such exposures in its internal risk management systems consistently over time and in the same manner as other retail exposures".

The evolution of retail credit risk measurement
The accurate measurement of credit risk in retail banking is a relatively new concept, and it is only in the last 50 years that

mathematical methods for measuring credit risk have been introduced. Prior to this period, credit risk was not measured *per se*, but the credit risk of an individual customer or account was assumed to be the same as that of the rest of the portfolio (unless something dramatic occurred, such as missing a number of payments of an instalment loan). In this way, if the historic loss on a mortgage portfolio was 5 basis points (bps), then the ongoing expected loss was assumed to be 5 bps. This approach falls apart as soon as there is a change in the economic climate. For example, as the 5 bps portfolio loss rate starts to increase, and as new (potentially higher-risk) customers continue to come onto the portfolio, there is a danger that losses can escalate out of control. It is certain that the risk in the portfolio is not understood well, let alone being actively managed.

Credit application scoring is a concept that was first introduced in the 1950s with the aim of providing a quantitative measure of credit risk (actually the methods used were methods for calculating a measure similar to probability of default (PD), though nobody used the term at that time). This has developed over the past few decades into an advanced tool for measuring the credit risk of an applicant at the point of application. Retail banking organisations currently use application scores to decide whether to approve facilities, as well as using the application score as an input into the limit-setting and pricing processes. As well as application scorecards, the intervening period has also seen the emergence and development of behavioural scorecards. A behavioural risk scorecard is a scorecard that calculates a measure of credit risk according to the way the customer behaves (ie, the way in which they use their banking accounts).

The development of both types of model was primarily driven by a need to understand the risk inherent in the portfolio, but a natural by-product of having such systems in place is that there is much less need for human intervention in the application and ongoing account management processes. And, in latter years, the drive to develop these scorecards has been driven as much by the need to achieve automation as much as by the need to achieve accurate risk measurement.

Regardless of motivation, this means that most retail financial institutions now have a good basis on which to develop their Basel models, as we discuss in Panel 1.

PANEL 1 REQUIRED RISK COMPONENTS

The IRB approach is fairly prescriptive in terms of what must be measured, and the components that must be measured are shown in Figure 1. As can be seen in the figure, the key components that need to be calculated are:

❑ *Probability of default (PD)* The probability of default measures the likelihood of a customer defaulting in a certain time period (but the PD says nothing about how much is lost if that default does occur). Credit cards have relatively high PDs, whereas mortgages have relatively low PDs.

❑ *Loss given default (LGD)* The loss given default measures how much is lost if a default occurs. For example, a mortgage will have a low LGD (assuming that the security covers the value of the loan), whereas unsecured products have very high LGDs.

❑ *Exposure at default (EAD)* The exposure at default measures how much the customer will owe if a default does occur. For a mortgage or personal loan, the exposure at default is likely to be close to the current balance (assuming that the default happens within a reasonable time frame), whereas for a credit card or line of credit the EAD will be close to the limit of the facility (this is a rather pessimistic view, but is generally the case since most people who default on their credit cards take them right up to (and beyond) the limit before defaulting).

These three components are collectively known as the Basel II model outputs since the main part of the Basel modelling is in calculating these factors. Once these three factors have been calculated, it is

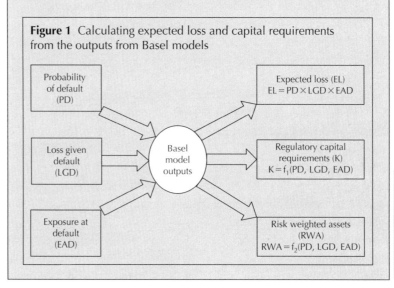

Figure 1 Calculating expected loss and capital requirements from the outputs from Basel models

Probability of default (PD)

Loss given default (LGD)

Exposure at default (EAD)

Basel model outputs

Expected loss (EL)
$EL = PD \times LGD \times EAD$

Regulatory capital requirements (K)
$K = f_1(PD, LGD, EAD)$

Risk weighted assets (RWA)
$RWA = f_2(PD, LGD, EAD)$

> relatively simple (in fact, it is only arithmetic with a set of rules) to determine the expected loss (EL), the regulatory capital requirements (K), and the risk-weighted assets (RWA).

MODEL DEVELOPMENT

We shall describe here the key steps in any model development, acknowledging that the process remains the same for developing models of any type (including PD, LGD and EAD), even though the content of the models may vary dramatically.

The key steps in model development are described in more detail in the sections below.

Data extraction

Data extraction can be very difficult, with data often being stored on a number of disparate legacy systems. One of the major impacts from Basel II has been the development of single data warehouses within retail banking organisations, which will aid the data extraction process for future model development. The types of data needed include application data (for application scorecards); transaction and statement data (for behavioural scorecards); end-of-month summary data (for all scorecards); loss data (for LGD models); and recovery data (again, for LGD models). In 2003, it is very rare for an organisation to have all of these data available for the appropriate time frames (bearing in mind that a typical scorecard development will need between two and four years' worth of historic data). Bad practice is rife in data extraction, and some of the worst examples of data extraction processes not going quite according to plan include:

❑ ignorance leading to unknown contravention of local data protection laws where data were transferred into another country for model development;

❑ IT staff being coerced into staying behind to help extract data from systems as they were unable to extract the data during the day due to other commitments; and

❑ model development staff being unsure of the meaning of data fields and guessing as to their meaning (only to find months later that the data fields used were completely inappropriate).

Data cleansing

Once the data have been extracted into a safe model development environment, the first task is to cleanse the data. This will involve removing all data that are irrelevant to model development, and adjusting data where they are known to be wrong. Examples of data cleansing include:

❏ *Removing "exclusions"* Accounts or applications will almost always be included within the raw data that should not be included within model development. These cases are known as "exclusions", and they will need to be excluded from model development samples. These will typically include areas such as: test accounts that have been stored on the system; applications were not correctly captured but the product is automatically approved); accounts that have been incorrectly marked (eg, accounts incorrectly marked as bankrupt).

❏ *Merging data from disparate systems* Once the exclusions have been removed, data from the different systems will need to be merged together. This is typically another area that is fraught with problems. A number of banking systems do not record account numbers of application systems, so it is not always easy to link application data to the data relating to the correct account. If one scorecard is being built for two different application systems (as happens quite frequently after a merger, where two systems continue side by side but using the same application scorecard, for example), then it is almost certain that the fields stored within the two systems will be different. This sounds straightforward, but it is always difficult in practice. One example of fields that are notoriously difficult to match is occupation codes, where one system will use one set and a second system will use a completely different – and not translatable – set.

❏ *Calculating variables* Once the data have been merged and data issues overcome, a number of additional variables will generally need to be calculated. One of the key variables that will need to be calculated for each application is the outcome variable. For PD modelling, this is simply a flag that records whether the account defaulted within a certain time period – which, once again, is something that is simple to define but can be fiendishly difficult to code. It is quite possible that the required fields do not exist, and so shortcuts or workarounds have to be coded.

Segmentation

Segmentation is the process through which the original dataset is split up into the most appropriate segments for model development. (Segmentation in this context should not be confused with the Basel-specific segmentation: this segmentation is unrelated to Basel and refers to a step in the model development process.) For application scorecards, different scorecards may be developed for applicants of different age, different residential status, different wealth, or any other number of factors. Behavioural scorecards are generally segmented depending on the customers' current delinquency status (eg, one scorecard for customers who are one to 29 days past due, another scorecard for customers who are 30 to 59 days past due, etc). LGD scorecards may be segmented depending on product type, security type or any of the application fields. The mathematical process used to choose segments can vary according to the complexity of the software available. At its simplest, segmentation involves looking at a number of key characteristics across a number of user-defined segments; at its most complex, segmentation involves cluster analysis to define what the segments should be. At all times, the segments identified need to be checked to ensure that they make business sense, as segmentation based purely on statistical reasoning with no business input is only likely to lead to false results.

Indeterminants

When developing a model, the definition of "bad" is usually clear-cut, but there are often groups of "nearly bad" customers within the population. For example, when the definition of bad is 90 days past due, there may be a number of accounts that are 60 days past due. Such accounts are too bad to be marked as good even though they have not yet achieved the level of "bad" defined.

The way in which these accounts is handled is to mark them as "indeterminants" and to remove them from model development. Models built in this way will demonstrate stronger predictive power as they will be able to identify more clearly between goods and bads.

Although indeterminants are removed for model development purposes, it is essential that they are brought back in to the dataset for model calibration purposes (otherwise the PDs quoted will not be accurate).

Sampling

The segmentation process will split the full set of data into separate files for each of the areas that require a model to be developed. Before full model development can be initiated, however, the dataset provided will have to go through a sampling process to provide a smaller set of data that will be useful for modelling purposes.

A typical portfolio will contain thousands (if not tens of thousands) of accounts, and it is likely that there will be too many accounts for a statistical package to be able to perform sensible analysis on such a large file. As such, some form of sampling may be required. Care must be taken when sampling to ensure that the sample is representative of the full dataset.

If the original dataset contains only a few bads (among a high number of goods), it is very useful (if not essential) that all of the bads are taken forward into model development. Such a method (where different sample rates are taken for different groups) is known as stratified sampling. When stratified sampling is performed, it is essential to ensure that the weights are correctly recorded against each observation in the sample. For example, if all bads were taken forward into the sample, they would each be given a weight of 1. If 1 in 10 accounts that were 60 days past due were taken forward, then each such account would be given a weight of 10, and so on, with every account being given a weight which shows how many cases from the full population that case represents in the sample. As a check, the total of the weights across the entire sample should equal the total number of observations within the original dataset.

Once the sampling process has been performed, it is useful to take a portion of this and keep it to one side for use within the model validation process. Such a sample is known as a hold-out sample. Hold-out samples are generally taken to be between 10% and 30% of the original sample, depending on the total number of cases available.

Model development

The mathematics used in the model development process may vary widely. Models that are developed with a binary outcome variable (eg, application and behavioural scorecards, where an applicant either defaults or does not default) are generally developed using logistic regression, and this can be shown to be the most effective form of regression. However, on occasions such models can be built using linear regression (this is generally done where certain parts of a model may need to be redeveloped more frequently – eg, where a new credit bureau has been launched and the bureau data will be of poorer quality at first but improve over time). On occasions, where data are limited (for example, on sub-portfolios where no accurate loss data are available at all), the modelling may be no more sophisticated than taking an average across that sub-portfolio.

Model validation

Once a model has been developed, a rigorous process of validation must be performed. This is one area where the FSA has already stated that a strict process must be followed. In fact, the FSA also requires the validation to be reviewed by a group independent from the model developers. In a major organisation, the team who validate the models could be part of a group risk-type function, and for smaller organisations this team could even be external to the organisation itself. The model validation must not only consider the statistical validation of the model but, more importantly, it must also consider the business validation of the scorecard, ensuring that all aspects of the model are intuitive and can be explained clearly and coherently from a business perspective.

Model calibration

The final step before a model is implemented is to calibrate the model. This involves taking the model outputs and converting them to a useful measure. For a number of models this is obvious, but for a model developed using regression techniques it needs to be done accurately to ensure that the output from the model is well understood.

Model documentation

It is vital that the model documentation is of a suitably high quality. The FSA has laid down guidelines in CP189 relating to model documentation, and these will need to be clearly followed. The validation process, described above, will not be possible if the scorecard documentation is not of a suitably high standard, and this is one area where banks will need to focus more than they have in the past.

MEASURING PD

PD is probably the most widely understood component of risk within retail banking. Most of the application and behavioural scorecards that exist within retail banking have been developed to measure PD.

If an organisation does not have application and behavioural scorecards, a significant amount of work will be required to develop these. The model development process is similar for both of these areas (as described in the model development section above), though each type of scorecard development has its own anomalies.

PD is the most important component of risk modelling for unsecured products, and it is a significant driver in the risk calculations for all lending products.

Application scorecard development

The kind of data used within application scorecards varies widely, but the general rule is that anything on the application form can be included in an application scorecard, not withstanding any local data protection or anti-discriminatory laws. Some typical fields that are used in application scorecard development are listed below:

❑ age;
❑ sex;
❑ educational qualifications;
❑ marital status;
❑ residential status (eg, homeowner, living with parents, etc);
❑ length of time at current address;
❑ industry in which the applicant works;
❑ job position (eg, director, manager, team leader, team worker, etc);
❑ length of time in current job;
❑ current banking product holdings; and
❑ length of time bank account held.

Each of these fields is known as a "characteristic" in model development.

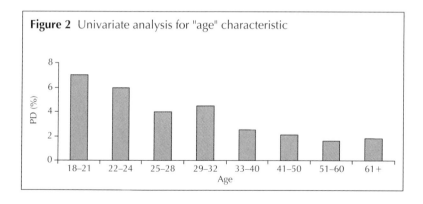

Figure 2 Univariate analysis for "age" characteristic

Univariate analysis

Initial analysis would look at each of these characteristics in isolation (ie, in a univariate way) to determine which was adding any useful information from a credit risk perspective. For each characteristic a univariate analysis would show the performance of certain attributes within the characteristic. For example, Figure 2 shows a typical univariate analysis for the "age" characteristic.

At this stage a number of the characteristics would be removed from the analysis, and a short-list of 8–15 characteristics (which represent the most predictive of the portfolio) would be taken forward into the next stage of model development.

These characteristics would then be taken into a regression algorithm to find the most suitable scorecard.

Reject inference

Application scorecards need to incorporate a process known as reject inference. What this process attempts to achieve is to take into account the fact that certain segments of applicants will have been rejected (and probably they will have been rejected on the basis of their application score on the previous generation of application scorecard). This means that those accounts on the portfolio will not be a random sample of applications but will exhibit certain biases. The whole area around reject inference is riddled with "art", and the amount of reject inference performed will vary widely according to the scorecard developers and the environment in which they operate. As with all stages of model development, the methods used are only valid if they can be substantiated by sensible business reasoning.

An extreme example of reject inference would be one where an existing scorecard penalises one segment of applicants very strongly. For example, it is generally acknowledged that tenants are a higher credit risk than home-owners, and let us assume that an existing scorecard strongly penalised tenants. This would mean that only those tenants who satisfied all the other positive criteria on the scorecard – ie, the low credit risk tenants – would be accepted onto the portfolio. Analysis at a later stage would then show that these tenants performed remarkably well. In fact, this analysis could show that tenants perform better than home-owners (since all home-owners were accepted, even the higher-risk ones). Without reject inference, a new scorecard would be developed that would actually penalise home-owners (since this is what the portfolio statistics show), and this would allow tenants to score well on the scorecard. And when that new scorecard was implemented, this would result in large numbers of tenants being accepted. It would only be after all of these tenants had been on the portfolio for a number of months that the true credit risk of these customers would be known, by which stage it would be too late.

Given the nature of scorecards, information on rejected applicants is not available, but reject inference is a way of inferring the performance of the rejected applicants so that this kind of problem can be avoided. At its simplest, reject inference involves building an "accept:reject" scorecard, which predicts how likely an applicant was to have been accepted, as well as an initial "good:bad" scorecard. Once both of these have been built, the performance of the rejects is inferred (based on their score through the good:bad scorecard), and these applicants are merged into the accepted population to provide a more complete picture. Obviously, as with any subjective process such as this, there are inevitably adjustments made to the outputs from reject inference, but if it can be shown to agree with business knowledge, then reject inference can be a very useful tool to allow relatively unbiased application scorecards to be developed.

Producing the final scorecard
Initial regression runs will almost certainly produce meaningless scorecards. It is only by observing the interaction between

Figure 3 An example application scorecard

Weight	Variable description
250	
−13	Accommodation type = "Rented"
57	Accommodation type = "Home owner"
−27	Age <23 years
−7	Age = 23–42 years
55	Education level = MBA
41	Education level = Masters/doctorate
18	Education level = Degree
−81	Occupation = High risk
−37	Occupation = Medium risk
26	Sex = Female
−42	Years in current job <3 years
−60	Time at current address <4 years
52	Time at current address >7 years

different variables, and by removing those variables which are not useful, or regrouping data together (eg, in the above example, there may be no reason why the 29–32 year olds are a higher risk than the 25–28 year olds – if not, then these groups would need to be combined) that a meaningful and intuitive scorecard can be developed.

A disguised example of an application scorecard is shown in Figure 3. As can be seen, all of the attributes of this scorecard are intuitively sensible. The way in which the scorecard has been developed ensures that these are also statistically robust.

Behavioural scorecard development
The process for developing behavioural scorecards is similar to that for application scorecards, with the exception that there is no reject inference to perform.

The characteristics that can be used within a behavioural score-card are much wider than those within an application scorecard, and are typically bounded only by the developers' imagination. It is sensible on these occasions to try to keep the list of characteristics as short as possible to allow the model development to be performed quickly, yet keep the list as long as possible to ensure that as many different variables are given the chance to come into the model.

Figure 4 Some typical characteristics used in behavioural scorecards

Ref No.	Characteristic
C14	Average balance to total value of debits ratio
C14a	Average balance to total number of debits ratio
C15	Minimum balance to total value of debits ratio
C15a	Minimum balance to total number of debits ratio
C16	Average credit balance to total value of debits ratio
C17	Average debit balance to total value of debits ratio
C18	Maximum balance to total value of credits ratio
C18a	Maximum balance to total number of credits ratio
C19	Average balance to total value of credits ratio
C19a	Average balance to total number of credits ratio
C20	Minimum balance to total value of credits ratio
C20a	Minimum balance to total number of credits ratio
C21	Average credit balance to total value of credits ratio
C22	Average debit balance to total value of credits ratio

Data that can be included within behavioural scorecards can include any of the following:

❑ balance data;
❑ credit limit information (generally only including agreed limit, as the other limits are beyond the customer's control);
❑ utilisation information;
❑ transactions (including use of ATMs, cards as a payment mechanism, cheques, standing orders and direct debits, etc);
❑ fees (broken down into the different types: late payment fees, over-limit fees, etc); and
❑ payments (cash payments into the account, cheque payments, automated payments).

For each of these fields, raw monthly data can be used, but the real power from behavioural scorecards comes from calculating averages and trends of these fields over a number of months. For example, seeing that a customer has increased their three-month average utilisation from 50% to 70% over the past six months is a good early warning that all is not well with that account.

The extract presented in Figure 4 is an example from an actual model development, showing the kind of detail that can be created.

As with the application scorecard, each of these should be considered in a univariate manner before moving forward to the full

Figure 5 An example behavioural scorecard

Description	Range	Weight
Intercept	(N/A)	231
Lowest monthly balance	x ≤ 5	12
(latest month)	5 < x ≤ 25	23
	25 < x ≤ 100	28
	100 < x ≤ 500	35
	500 < x ≤ 1,500	42
	1,500 < x	50
Total number of credits	x < 0	0
this months	x = 0	10
	x = 1	42
	x > 1	48
Excess amount (latest month) [3]	x = 0	42
	x < 0	0
(1,6) Trend in average balance [4]	x ≤ 25%	0
	25% < x ≤ 80%	10
	80% < x ≤ 150%	13
	x > 150%	0
Maximum days in continuous	x = 0	31
excess (latest month)	0 < x ≤ 5	12
	5 < x	0
Value of debits: Value of credits	x ≤ 0.735	23
ratio (latest month)	0.735 < x	0
	Divide by zero	0
3 month average total days in	x = 0	72
continuous arrears	0 < x ≤ 1	58
	1 < x ≤ 5	42
	5 < x ≤ 20	19
	x > 20	9
Total value of credits (latest month)	x ≤ 0	0
	0 < x ≤ 100	27
	100 < x ≤ 500	51
	x ≥ 500	81
Total number of dishonours	x = 0	91
last month	X > 0	0

regression analysis that will develop the scorecard. The sheer number of characteristics available will mean that the regression process will need to be managed carefully, and as before, simply passing all characteristics into a regression algorithm will not work on its own. The model development will need to involve business input at each stage to ensure that the scorecards being developed are intuitively correct.

An example of a behavioural scorecard is shown in Figure 5.

PANEL 2 CALIBRATING SCORECARDS TO PD

Having developed the appropriate application and behavioural score-cards, these need to be calibrated to a Basel PD measure. Up until this stage, it is not necessary to choose a Basel-aligned definition of default. The FSA's definition of default is reasonably harsh (six months in arrears), and there may be good reasons why an organisation may choose not to use this definition for the initial modelling work. In a num-ber of portfolios, especially mortgage portfolios, there simply will not be enough "bads" to develop a model if this definition is used, and so it is perfectly acceptable to use a less severe definition of default. However, the models will need to be used to predict a Basel-compliant measure of PD, and hence the calibration of the scorecards will need to measure the outputs from the scorecards in terms of a Basel PD. Generally, this calibration is not a difficult exercise (since a probability of "bad" can be easily mapped onto a probability of "Basel default").

The complexity in calibrating the scorecards is in ensuring that the application and behavioural scores are combined in such a way to give the most predictive PD measure. Obviously an account that is new to the portfolio will not have any prior behaviour, and so its PD must be calculated from the application score. Similarly, the application data for an account that is a number of years old will no longer be rele-vant, and its PD should be calculated mostly (if not wholly) from the behavioural score. There is a large grey period in between, during which time a certain percentage of the PD prediction will need to come from the application and the remainder from the behavioural score.

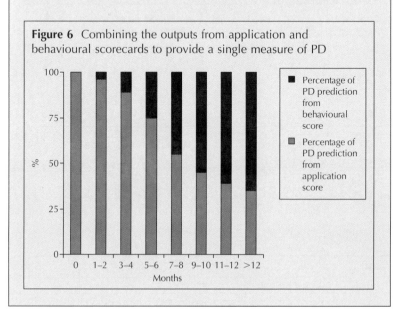

Figure 6 Combining the outputs from application and behavioural scorecards to provide a single measure of PD

> The simplest way to calculate what percentages of which score to use is to perform a regression analysis, with the two scores as the inputs, and observe the "scores" given to the two scores in this "calibration scorecard". Generally, accounts are split into a number of discrete age groups. This grouping can be reasonably arbitrary (with input from appropriate policy rules, where they exist), and a typical grouping would look like this: 1 month old; 2–3 months old; 4–6 months old; 7–9 months old; 10–12 months old; and >12 months old. The "score" for each scorecard for each of these segments is then calculated, which will demonstrate how much predictive power should come from the application score, with the remainder coming from the behavioural score.
>
> A typical output of this process is shown in Figure 6.

LGD

The second component of risk is the loss given default (LGD).

LGD measures the amount of the loan that would be lost if that account defaulted. For example, if a credit card defaulted owing £1,000, the loss associated with that account would be likely to be close to 100%, whereas a mortgage that defaulted owing £120,000 would be likely to turn into an actual loss of only a small percentage of that figure (assuming that the security was of appropriate value and that the bank had call over the security).

One of the main issues with LGD modelling is that it is difficult to obtain account-level loss data for use in model development. In particular, amounts written off are often not allocated back to an original account, and recovery (either pre- or post-write-off) data can be particularly hard to find.

As well as finding out what money was recovered from the customer, it is useful for these data to include the time at which the monies were recovered. This is especially the case where there are long time frames between the time at which the default occurs and the time by which the recovery was made.

LGD is often not a sensible thing for a bank to measure, especially when classified as "default". In this instance, it has to relate to the official Basel definition of default. What this means is that a number of the accounts that reached "default" for Basel purposes were never treated as defaulters by the bank, and they rejoined the main portfolio shortly afterwards.

The sensible way to overcome all of the issues around this is to split LGD into two sub-components: the probability of write-off and the loss given write-off. (The terminology gets slightly confusing, but bear with it – it is a worthwhile split).

We are, however, only calculating this function for those accounts that have reached the (Basel) definition of default, and hence the probability of write-off is actually the probability of write-off for those accounts that have already reached the Basel definition of default. Statistically speaking, this is the "Probability of write-off given default", denoted by $P(W|D)$. The "Loss given write-off" is much easier to describe, and is generally denoted as LGW.

Probability of write-off given default

Modelling of $P(W|D)$ is, in theory, a very similar exercise to modelling PD. The numbers of accounts involved are much lower and hence, the sampling process is much more straightforward. Having developed the samples, characteristics similar to those used for PD modelling can be used in $P(W|D)$ modelling.

There is one key variable for use in $P(W|D)$ modelling that is not available for PD modelling. This variable is the PD. In fact, there are a number of variables, including the application score, the behavioural score and time on books, as well as all of the more standard application and behavioural characteristics.

Probability of repossession given default

For secured products, it is often simpler to calculate the probability of repossession given default, since repossession is a much more obvious process than write-off. Obviously this split is intuitive from a business perspective, as those accounts that are repossessed are fundamentally different to those accounts that are not (whereas there may not be such an obvious distinction for those accounts that are written off). Obviously the precise definition that is used will depend on the bank's processes, and there is no simple one-size-fits-all solution to this part of the modelling.

Loss given write-off (or loss given repossession) can be split further, but it is arguable how much benefit there is from performing this split. Modelling at this stage can be so far removed from reality that the models are of no significant use.

If additional splitting is required, the obvious way to do this is to calculate a probability of shortfall given write-off (or repossession, since it is usually for mortgage products where this level of modelling is required within the overall LGD framework), and to multiply this by the expected shortfall (given write-off or repossession).

As you can imagine, the nomenclature starts to get silly as variables denoted as $E(S|W)$ and $E(S|R)$ start to appear, and it is the author's opinion that taking the modelling down to this level does not provide anything other than a bit of mathematical excitement for the modelling team.

Loss given write-off

Having calculated the probability of some event (be it shortfall, write-off, repossession or something similar), the remaining part of modelling is to calculate the "loss given event". For the rest of this section, we shall refer to this as loss given write-off, but the same concept could be used to model loss given any of the events described above.

The loss given write-off can be treated just the same as any other modelling in this area. There are a number of accounts that are being considered for modelling (ie, all those accounts that have reached write-off), and there are a number of factors associated with these accounts (including various scores, various application factors, behavioural factors, and other factors, such as loan-to-value ratio, original loan amount, time on books, etc).

Hence, at its most complex, the modelling in this area would involve developing some link between the characteristics and the response variables (ie, loss). However, at this stage, the quality of the data is usually sufficiently poor that this kind of full approach is not possible.

A common approach at this stage is just to take some of these input factors (typically including loan-to-value ratio and region) and produce a look-up table across each of the input factors.

This does not provide the most sophisticated model, but it does provide a model that is generally intuitive and works well.

The author has yet to see an organisation that is able to provide a full loss given write-off model combining a larger number of factors into a scorecard-type approach, though it is almost certain that some of the larger players in the UK will be getting close to this within the next 12–18 months.

Direct EL modelling

Rather than calculating PD and LGD as separate components, an alternative approach, which has started to gather momentum more recently, is to produce PD and EL models and to use these in parallel to calculate the LGD. PD and EL models can be produced using the methods above, and then an LGD can be calculated individually as LGD = PD/EL. (Actually, it is not quite this simple, as the EAD factor needs to be included, but the concept described here is correct.) If such an approach is followed, it can, on occasions, be shown to predict accurate EL data, but there are issues over calibrating back to LGD, as dividing outputs from different models is a notoriously difficult process to perform accurately. As well as the modelling difficulties, there are likely to be a number of areas in which such a direct modelling approach would be difficult to satisfy Basel requirements.

EAD

The final risk component that needs to be measured is the exposure at default (EAD). This is simply a prediction of how much money the customer will owe at the time they default (and, again, this is the Basel definition of default).

For example, a credit card customer with a (hard) credit limit of £1,000 will almost always owe a figure close to £1,000 when they default, and a mortgage customer whose balance today is £120,000 may owe less than £120,000 if there is a significant amount of time before the default happens, or they may owe more than £120,000 if they make no more payments after today (due to accrued interest).

Revolving unsecured products

For unsecured products, it is almost always the case that the bank will lose as much as they are prepared to lend, and so the simplest models state that LGD is simply equal to the maximum limit on that account. Given the way most revolving unsecured systems work, there are likely to be a number of limits on these accounts, including the agreed limit (ie, the limit agreed with the customer), the shadow limit (ie, the limit which the customer may go up to without payments being stopped), and the absolute limit (which is exactly that – the top limit to which the customer may borrow).

One key area for consideration within these EAD calculations is how to handle inactive accounts. Generally, inactive accounts are treated completely separately, but it is often difficult to predict what the exposure at default will be for inactive accounts. Obviously a conservative approach would take EAD to be equal to whatever the EAD would be for an active account, but there is benefit from performing further analysis to identify what the key drivers of accounts becoming active are, so that accounts that are likely to stay inactive can be identified and given the appropriately lower EAD figure.

Although EAD modelling can be done, the obvious answer is that the EAD for all revolving unsecured products is simply set to the customer's absolute limit. However, given that a defaulted account must have missed six payments, it is more prudent to set the EAD equal to the credit limit of the facility plus an extra six months worth of interest payments.

Unsecured repayments products

The EAD of an unsecured repayment product depends on the time it takes the customer to default. For example, a customer who stops paying now and defaults later will have a much higher exposure at default than a customer who pays consistently over the next six months before missing payments.

However, Basel II has a small trick up its sleeve to avoid the need for any complex calculations, and the EAD may not be less than current balance.

Analysis needs to be performed for individual portfolios (and sub-portfolios), but it is almost always the case that the EAD can simply be taken to be the current balance. As above, given that an account has to miss six payments before being classed as a default, prudence suggests that the EAD should be set to the current balance plus six months interest.

Secured products

Secured products are mostly secured, and, hence, a similar approach to that described in the section above can be followed.

Revolving secured products

One area that is not particularly well understood is the area of "cheque-book mortgages" (ie, the facility where the current account and mortgage all sit within the same credit limit). Where these products offer a re-drawdown facility, the EAD has the potential to be very high. In fact, the same philosophy as described above in an earlier section would suggest that the EAD figure should be set to the total limit of the facility plus an extra amount representing additional interest payments.

An implication of EAD calculations

One rather obvious implication of EAD calculations is that organisations will need to hold capital against the credit limit of all of their revolving facilities (including mortgage products). It is likely that this will lead to a situation where banks will find these capital requirements too high, and the banks will seek to actively reduce credit limits, especially on the more sensitive mortgage portfolios. It will be interesting to see (in a few years time, when Basel II has settled down) whether credit departments win the upcoming battle or whether marketing departments manage to hold on to what they will see as another victory and retain the current philosophy of unnecessarily high credit limits.

STRESS-TESTING AND ECONOMIC CYCLE ISSUES

The work described in the preceding four sections describes how to build the PD, LGD and EAD models required. Each of these models will have been developed from data covering a number of years. Typically the time scales will vary for each of the model types, and some typical examples are shown in the table in Figure 7.

The table in Figure 7 demonstrates that almost all of the risk component models are developed on data covering a time period of between one and three years (possibly with the exception of loss data, where the models are generally developed on whatever loss data are available, which may cover a longer time period). The positive message to come out of this is that data covering the past two to three years should be readily available (if not now, then at least once the appropriate Basel data storage solutions have been developed). The downside to using such short time scales is that the data only cover a small portion of an economic cycle and, as such, the outputs from the models will be likely to vary over an economic cycle.

One of the key requirements of Basel II is that the total regulatory capital requirements should not be particularly volatile, and the model outputs as calculated above are likely to vary considerably over an economic cycle, which will not result in a stable

Figure 7 Typical time-lines of data requirements for model development

Model	Typical data time-lines
Time of model development	January 2004
Application scorecard	Application data for 12 months from January to December 2002 Performance data: 12 months for each application (so in total, the 24* month period from January 2002 to December 2003)
Behavioural scorecard	Behavioural data: 6 months from July 2002 to December 2002 Performance data: 12 months from January to December 2003
Probability of write-off given default scorecard	Defaulted accounts from January to December 2002, including appropriate historic information (such as application data, behavioural data, etc) Write-off data for 12 months (or longer, dependent on the speed of the write-off processes) for each defaulted account
Exposure at default models	Exposure at default data for defaulted accounts over 12 months: January to December 2003 Exposure pre-default for the same accounts over the preceding 12 months (so in total 24* months from January 2002 to December 2003)
Loss given write-off model	Loss data for all written-off accounts over whatever time period is available

*Although it is only genuinely 23 months data that is required, it is often useful and sensible to extract data covering the entire 24 months.

capital requirement. The way that the revised accord attempts to ensure that capital requirements remain stable is that the outputs from the risk models must represent long-run average figures, rather than the point-in-time outputs that are produced in the methodologies described above, and hence some form of adjustment is required for each component.

Economic cycle adjustments

Account-level data are not available to make adjustments for economic cycle changes, and so some form of portfolio-level approach must be followed. At its simplest, this approach considers the linkages between "economic cycle" and each of the components, and provides an adjustment for this.

There are two dangers with these ideas: the idea of an "economic cycle" is more academic than practical, and different factors have different lengths, so it is not easily possible to define the length of an economic cycle, let alone the variation within a cycle. Second, this whole argument is in danger of being a self-fulfilling prophecy, since one of the drivers (or measures) or an economic cycle is the country-wide default rate.

Leaving these issues to one side, a sensible approach to making the required adjustments would be to take the bank's portfolio PD and LGD rates and to map these against some measure of the economic cycle to produce a model. The outputs from this model could then be mapped against long-run expectations of the economic cycle to produce the requisite long-run average PD and LGD figures.

Long-run average PD calculations

For example, let us consider a simple model that assumes that the economic cycle is made up of three factors: unemployment, interest rates, and house price affordability

Historic data on each of these factors are readily available from a number of sources. Taking these data, a simple linear regression can be performed to show the linkages between each of these factors and the PD rate. As an example, Figure 8 shows some disguised data that could be used as an input to this process.

Once the model has been developed, economic forecasts for each of the input parameters (in this case unemployment, interest rates, and house price affordability) could be obtained to generate forecasts of PD rates. These data could then be used to adjust the

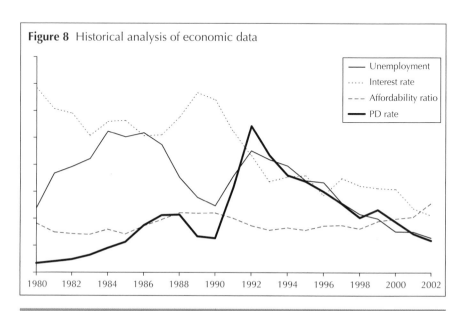

Figure 8 Historical analysis of economic data

PDs coming out of each of the models to give something close to a long-run average PD.

A note on how to make and apply the PD adjustments

It is generally acknowledged that if the PD rate of a portfolio increases, the increase in PD across each account can be calculated. This relationship in PD is not strictly linear, but it is generally assumed that the shift in the "log-odds" is linear. The "log-odds" is a term often used during model development, which relates to the log of the "odds ratio", which is in turn defined as the number of goods divided by the number of bads.

Hence, if the portfolio calculated PD is 5%, and the long-run average is 7%, the following calculations can be performed:

❑ Expected point-in-time PD = 5% implies that 5% of the portfolio defaults, so there are five bads for every 95 goods and, hence, the odds ratio = 95/5 = 19, resulting in a log-odds figure of 2.944.

❑ Expected long-run PD = 7% implies that 7% of the portfolio defaults, so there are seven bads for every 93 goods, and hence the odds ratio = 93/7 = 13.3, resulting in a log-odds figure of 2.587.

❑ Hence, there is an overall shift in log-odds from 2.944 to 2.587, that is, a shift of −0.357.

❑ This same shift can then be applied to the individual PD of each account within the portfolio to provide a long-run PD for each account.

❑ Therefore, an account with a score of 350 might map to a PD of 2.5%, which in turn maps to a log-odds of 3.664, which then follows the same adjustment of −0.357 to become 3.307, which then maps back to a PD of 3.53%.

The approach described here is much more advanced than a standard straight-line method, but there are a number of problems that mean that applying a portfolio change across individual accounts will never be straightforward.

Long-run average LGD calculations

The long-run average LGD is an important factor in calculating regulatory capital requirements, but it is a factor that is difficult to calculate. The amount and quality of data generally available for calculating a point-in-time LGD are low, and, as can be imagined, the amount and quality of data available for validating a long-run average are even worse.

Typical methods for LGD adjustment consider changes in house price through the cycle and provide an adjusted LGD based on the original method with adjustments to some of the input parameters.

While these methods are not the most sophisticated, they do provide some additional levels of information regarding likely recovery levels at different stages of an economic cycle.

Long-run average EAD calculations

Most organisations do not make any adjustments to the point-in-time EAD to calculate a long-run EAD, since the exposure at default is unlikely to change greatly when economic conditions change. The over-riding conservative expectation is that the customer will always take as much as possible, regardless of economic environment.

Other factors to be considered in long-run averages

If the capital requirements of an organisation are required to remain consistent over time, then there is also a requirement that a number of internal factors remain static over time as well. Changes to the organisation's policies can have huge knock-on impacts on loss rates, and hence capital requirements. For example, the loosening of credit policies could lead to a high number of customers of a particular segment coming into the portfolio that have previously not been on the portfolio (as an example, self-employed customers have a very different risk profile to employed customers, and changes to credit policy regarding self-employed customers would have such an effect). Similarly, a change to marketing strategy could lead to high numbers of different types of customers applying for facilities, and potentially a large number of these customers could be given facilities, which would again change the portfolio composition.

Any of these changes to the portfolio could potentially have a large impact on both the expected and unexpected losses within the portfolio, and this would lead to a change in regulatory capital requirements.

Stress-testing

Stress-testing is not something that has been traditionally done well in retail banking, and current efforts to move stress-testing methodologies forward are almost entirely a result of regulatory pressure.

However, the processes described above for developing long-run average forecasts actually tie in well with the concepts of stress-testing, and one of the best ways to stress the outputs from the model is to define a set of economic downturns, which through the models already developed can provide stressed PDs, LGDs, and EADs (if any change in EAD is expected through an economic downturn).

Stress testing is then simply a case of defining a set of downturn scenarios and performing the analysis for each scenario.

PULLING IT ALL TOGETHER

Once all the components have been calculated, as described in the sections above, it is relatively simple to pull everything together into a total regulatory capital number. Panel 3 and the sections to follow describe how the risk components can be combined to calculate a number of factors, including the expected loss, regulatory capital requirements, and an economic capital figure.

PANEL 3 EXPECTED LOSS CALCULATIONS

Once the PD, LGD and EAD factors have all been calculated, the calculation of the expected loss (EL) figure is just straightforward arithmetic.
To demonstrate the mathematics, let us consider two examples:

Example 1: Expected loss for a well-performing credit card
As an example, let us assume that the credit card has been on the book for 12 months, and so most of the information will come from the behavioural score. Let us assume that the account scores as follows:

❑ the application score alone gives a PD of 3.7%;
❑ the behavioural score alone gives a PD of 1.2%;
❑ the overall PD model generates a PD of 1.9% (and, hence, this is the most accurate PD figure available);
❑ in terms of LGD, the account has been calculated to have a P(W|D) of 40% and a LGW of 85%;
❑ the EAD is assumed to be 110% of the current credit limit; and
❑ the current credit limit is £1,500.

All of this information would give us:

$$
\begin{aligned}
\text{Expected loss} &= \text{PD} \times \text{LGD} \times \text{EAD} \\
&= 1.9\% \times 40\% \times 85\% \times 110\% \times £1{,}500 \\
&= £10.66
\end{aligned}
$$

Example 2: Expected loss for a poorly-performing mortgage
As an example, let us assume that the mortgage has been on the book for seven years, and so most of the information will come from the behavioural score. Let us assume that the account scores as follows:

❑ the application score originally gave a PD of 0.3%;
❑ the behavioural score alone gives a PD of 3.7%;
❑ the overall PD model generates a PD of 3.5% (and hence this is the most accurate PD figure available);
❑ in terms of LGD, the account has been calculated to have a P(W|D) of 75% and a LGW of 35%;
❑ the EAD is assumed to be 105% of the current exposure; and
❑ the current exposure is £125,000.

All of this information would give us:

$$\begin{aligned} \text{Expected loss} &= \text{PD} \times \text{LGD} \times \text{EAD} \\ &= 3.5\% \times 75\% \times 35\% \times 105\% \times £125,000 \\ &= £1,205.86 \end{aligned}$$

Regulatory capital

The regulatory capital requirement represents the unexpected loss within the portfolio, and once each of the risk components (PD, LGD and EAD) has been calculated, the calculation of regulatory capital is just a matter of plugging the risk components into the appropriate arithmetic model.

Before capital is calculated, there are a number of "floor" conditions that are applied to the components. These conditions include:

❑ PD must not be less than 3 bps;
❑ LGD must not be less than 10% (for mortgage products);
❑ EAD must not be less than 100% of current balance.

Once each of these conditions has been checked (and the appropriate adjustments made to the components), then the capital calculation can be made.

The precise rules for capital are defined in the latest version of the Basel accord but will not be spelt out here for reasons of brevity.

Using Basel inputs to calculate economic capital

Having put all the effort into calculating regulatory capital, it is a simple adjustment to remove the Basel floor conditions and use each of the risk components as an input into a standard economic capital framework.

At its most simple, this may involve simply feeding the risk components (without floors) into the standard regulatory capital calculator, or at its most complex, this work may involve feeding the inputs into a proprietary capital engine. Either way, there is a large benefit to be had from making use of the risk components.

USING THE MODELS

Developing models is only the start of the process, and there are regulatory requirements, as well as substantial benefits to be had from implementing and using the models in the existing businesses as quickly as possible.

Satisfying the FSA "use test"

The following sections are the key areas that have been identified by the FSA as "core credit" areas – that is, areas where the models will need to be used in order to qualify as an IRB-compliant organisation.

❑ *Credit approval* Obviously, the application scorecards should be one of the key inputs to the credit approval process. Once an account is on the book, its behavioural score should also be an input into further approval processes.

❑ *Individual limit setting* The application score should be one of the inputs into the overall limit-setting process at the time of application. For revolving facilities, the behavioural score should be a key input into the review process for the ongoing credit limit of the facility.

❑ *Portfolio limit setting* With the risk components in place, and economic and regulatory capital calculations being performed on a regular basis, the capital numbers will need to become key inputs into the growth strategies and, hence, the portfolio limits for all portfolios.

❑ *Reporting of credit risk information* Obviously, generating the risk components and using these components to make decisions is of little use if reporting continues in its old format. Considerable changes will be needed to ensure that reports are updated to include the new format of information. These reports will cover all areas, from scorecard monitoring and portfolio monitoring up to senior management reporting and board reporting.

❑ *Provisioning* Although the final details are still being drawn out (and, in particular, the interaction between Basel and International Financial Reporting Standards (IFRS) will need to be agreed), it is obvious that one of the key inputs to the provisioning process should be the expected loss figure calculated from the Basel models.

Using the models to generate business benefits

As well as the areas outlined by the FSA, there are a number of other areas where significant business benefits could be generated from using the outputs from the Basel models.

It is the author's view that, as at early 2004, most retail banking organisations will be focusing solely on the development and systems implementation of new risk models, rather than on the business implementation of the new models, and on integrating the new models into existing risk management process to make better decisions. It is likely that there will be significant benefits from doing so, and, in particular, those organisations that are able to implement the models into risk management processes in 2004 and 2005 are likely to be able to generate significant first-mover benefits.

❑ *Customer profitability calculations* Customer profitability is not something that is widely calculated in retail banking. The outputs from the Basel model calculate exactly what the expected loss is on each customer, as well as what level of capital is required to be held for each customer. If these outputs can be combined with models that calculate the costs associated with each customer and the revenue generated by each customer, then all of the models can be linked together to generate risk-adjusted profitability measures for all customers. The benefits from such calculations are potentially huge.

❑ *Strategy development* If customer profitability can be accurately calculated, sets of strategies can be developed to maximise the benefits from each segment of customers. For example, customers whose risk-adjusted profitability is below certain thresholds could be managed off the portfolio, and incentives offered to customers in the top band of risk-adjusted profitability.

❏ *Compensation* Once the metrics of customer profitability are in place, it is possible to start to reward staff based on the risk-adjusted profit generated by their customers. And once moves are made in this direction, there is likely to be a shift in culture throughout the industry to one of value creation.

❏ *Pricing* Again, with risk-adjusted profitability in place, risk-adjusted pricing could be reconsidered. This entire area is delicate, but a number of the potential obstacles can be overcome through judicious use of the outputs of the models to reduce the interest rates offered to certain segments of customers.

In summary, the use of the Basel models is almost limitless, and there are likely to be a number of major retail banking organisations that will make some significant gains through early implementation of the new models in their business processes.

BIBLIOGRAPHY

Basel Committee on Banking Supervision, Bank for International Settlements, 2003, *CP3: The New Basel Capital Accord, Consultative Document*, April.

Financial Services Authority, 2003, *CP189: The Report and First Consultation on the Implementation of the new Basel and EU Capital Adequacy Standards*, July.

Section 4

Regulatory Expectations and Disclosure Issues

12

Regulatory Priorities and Expectations in the Implementation of the IRB Approach

Ed Duncan

ISDA

This chapter attempts to reveal the regulatory priorities and expectations in the implementation of the Internal Ratings Based (IRB) approach. The IRB approach lies at the heart of new capital adequacy rules currently being developed, known as Basel II.

This chapter does not explore other important areas to be addressed by regulators in the implementation of Basel II, such as the proposed operational risk charge; supervisory reviews under Pillar Two; or the extensive disclosure requirements to be set out in Pillar Three. Instead, we focus entirely on the minimum standards for internal ratings, the cornerstone of the new credit risk capital charge. We do this by considering the Basel II literature on internal ratings. We look at the practicalities involved in implementation and outline what have up to now been the priorities of regulators in considering internal ratings systems, and then we conclude with a summary of the possible range of regulatory expectations for firms choosing to implement the IRB approach.

THE IRB APPROACH

Basel II gives a choice of methodology in the calculation of capital requirements for credit risk. One can either use a standardised approach (reliant upon external assessments of credit) or an IRB approach. Firms following an IRB approach are presented with an additional choice between either a foundation IRB approach (FIRB) or an advanced IRB approach (AIRB).

FIRB sits somewhere between the standardised and the advanced approach by allowing some use of internal estimates with some reliance also on external assessments. In a recent study on the "Current views on Basel II" by the consultants Ernst and Young, 45% of respondents were targeting the AIRB approach, while 30% were considering the FIRB approach. The percentage of prospective AIRB firms increases with the size and type of the firm, eg, 60% of large banks (assets over US$100 billion) are targeting AIRB.

Firms that qualify for an IRB approach will have to demonstrate that they meet certain minimum requirements. They will then be allowed to use their own internal estimates of the risk components to determine the capital requirements for their credit risk.

In general, internal rating systems are designed to quantify credit risk so that it can be ranked on a scale of the least risky to the riskiest. Ratings systems can take many forms, but generally will consist of an assessment of the risk of the borrower defaulting and an estimate of the amount that would likely be collected in the event of such a default. The ultimate objective of any rating system is, therefore, the meaningful differentiation of the risks associated with borrowers and the risks inherent in individual transactions. They are increasingly used for many different purposes across business lines, including, credit approval and limit setting, economic capital allocation, performance measurement, provisioning and pricing, credit portfolio monitoring, profitability analysis and management reporting. It is, therefore, in the firm's own interests to have good-quality internal ratings that are both accurate and consistent.

The Basel II documents describe the chief components of an internal rating system as the measures for probability of default (PD), loss given default (LGD), exposure at default (EAD) and effective maturity (M). The rating system itself is described more broadly as comprising all "the methods, processes, controls, and data collection and IT systems that support the assessment of credit risk, the assignment of internal risk ratings, and the quantification of default and loss estimates" (from the latest consultation paper on the Accord (European Commission, 2003a, referred to below as "CP3"), p. 356).

IRB systems vary across asset class and model type. They are continually evolving and the pace of development and level of sophistication differ widely across the industry. The extent to which they differ can be seen through the varied use of the components and inputs of internal ratings systems, including the use of master scales, the number of rating grades, the different time horizons involved (both in estimating PDs and assigning ratings), and the definition of default (some retail models merely seek to support an "accept/reject" decision function rather than determine PD). This makes it very difficult to generalise about current market practice. What the Basel Committee attempts to do with the IRB approach is to reflect the evolution of practice at the larger, more sophisticated firms. It does this by setting relatively high minimum standards for firms choosing to adopt the IRB approach, effectively "raising the bar" for the majority of other firms and, as a consequence, the minimum standards have become the target objective for most risk managers.

IMPLEMENTATION

Putting the theory behind Basel II into practice represents a big challenge for even the most sophisticated of firms in the industry. The challenge is made all the more difficult when considering the timetable in which firms and regulators have to implement Basel II.

Although finalisation of the Accord was temporarily delayed (Basel Committee meeting, Madrid, October 11, 2003), implementation is still scheduled to take effect on December 31, 2006. Due to many of the "minimum" standards for an IRB approach set out in CP3, including the strict data requirements, a "use" test, and senior management's understanding, much of the work and ongoing risk management needs to be put into place several years ahead of the implementation date. Basel II projects in most prospective IRB firms are therefore well under way.

Meanwhile, on the regulatory side resources dedicated to Basel II are under review. The emphasis on firms' own estimates of the components of risk and the quantitative and qualitative nature of evaluation ensures that the approval of IRB systems will be a labour-intensive exercise. In almost all Basel II countries, regulators will need to substantially increase the number and technical proficiency of their supervisory staff to implement the new capital framework adequately. The approach taken by many regulators to implementation will ultimately depend on the number of firms within their jurisdiction seeking IRB approval and the regulatory resources they have at their disposal. This will be discussed in more detail later in relation to implementation efforts made public by the US and UK regulators.

The starting point for all Basel II regulators is the detail contained in the New Accord as represented by the third consultative paper, CP3. Part III of this document looks at credit risk and the IRB approach, and Section H of part III (paras 349–500) outlines the minimum requirements for an IRB approach. Although this goes into considerable detail, many key decisions are left to the discretion of the respective national regulators. Areas for national discretion include exemptions for immaterial exposures, explicit or implicit maturity adjustments, determining the definition of default, the treatment of equity holdings, and the transitional arrangements for equity investments. International firms operating across borders, reporting to more than one regulatory authority, will need to be aware of any national or regional differences in how the discretionary items are applied.

For those based in the European Union, where the Basel Accord is converted into law and, additionally, applied to credit institutions and investment firms (not just banks as intended by Basel II), focus is required on the details contained in the proposed Risk Based Capital Directive (RBCD), which is represented by a consultation paper published by the European Commission in July 2003. The RBCD aims to update the EU capital adequacy frame-work in a manner consistent with Basel II, but "appropriately differentiated where necessary to take account of the specificities of the EU context" (European Commission, 2002).

The key areas for divergence in approach, at the time of writing, relate to the wider scope for implementation, the flexibility required for ongoing modernisation, the treatment of small- and medium-sized enterprises (SMEs), and the treatment of large exposure. The document also addresses many of the areas for national discretion set out during the Basel II consultation period, taking away some of the choices that EU member states would otherwise have had to have make and adding others. Of particular interest to this chapter is the inclusion of a EU proposal for a permanent opt-out from the IRB approach for bank and sovereign exposures (European Commission, Review of capital requirements for banks and investment firms, Working document, Article 50,

July 2003). Due to the complexity of the RBCD and its greater emphasis on qualitative standards, consistency of application will be hard to achieve. Different national jurisdictions need to interpret the new and complex framework in the context of their own history, experience and circumstances.

The difficulty faced by regulators is further compounded by the lack of finality in the Accord and that neither the contents of Basel II nor the RBCD have been agreed. This uncertainty is perhaps reflected in hesitancy among the majority of regulators to develop and share their thinking on implementation. The UK's implementation proposals (known as CP189 and published by the Financial Services Authority in July 2003) are based only on the work at the Basel level, and not on the EU's draft proposals, despite the fact that the UK will have to implement the RBCD and not Basel II. This is because the draft proposals for the RBCD had not been published at the time. In the US, the ANPR (Advanced notice of proposed rulemaking, published jointly by the Federal Reserve Board, the Office of the Comptroller of the Currency, the Federal Deposit Insurance Corporation, and the Office of Thrift Supervision in July 2003) represents a continuing dialogue between the various US regulators and domestic firms, the results of which will form an overall US position on whether or not the Accord gets US backing. It is, therefore, difficult for regulators to be precise in answering questions on technical issues regarding implementation and IRB approval.

REGULATORY PRIORITIES AND EXPECTATIONS

This section identifies the key regulatory priorities in implementing an IRB approach: the collection and use of credit data, the initial and subsequent validation process, and the use of external models. A number of other implementation issues are also highlighted that are increasingly gaining regulatory attention. These include the "use test", the "experience test", procyclicality, and home versus host issues. These are all explained in relation to the challenges that they represent to the industry and the likely expectations of the supervisory authorities. The priorities identified are a reflection of the implementation work conducted by both firms and regulators to date and as indicated by the emphasis placed on them in CP189 and the ANPR.

DATA

There is a recurring theme of data accuracy and integrity throughout the revised Accord. The industry identified the upgrading of the quality of credit information as the single largest challenge they faced in implementation. However, neither the revised Accord nor RBCD go into detail on the standards required for credit information. Without much to go on, the regulators responsible for implementation responded by prioritising data and data requirements as areas needing more work and further guidance. Data accuracy is fundamental to a regulators' approval of an IRB approach. Time and money spent on the progressive approaches of Basel II will be to no avail if the underlying data capture processes and supporting infrastructure are insufficient. Firms and regulators will have to have absolute confidence that all risks are correctly identified, measured and reported, internally and externally.

Basel II states that a bank must collect and store data on key borrower and facility characteristics to enable compliance with all other requirements and serve as a basis for supervisory reporting (CP3, p. 391). It requires a process for vetting data inputs into a statistical default or loss prediction model which includes an assessment of the accuracy, completeness and appropriateness of the data specific to the assignment of an approved rating (CP3, p. 379). This implies comprehensive documentation of the risk assessment that is followed and that proves compliance with internal policy in a quantitative way. Basel II also requires a review of governance arrangements, including separation of duties across the firm, between risk and finance, and appropriate senior management accountability. It also stipulates a direct link to a firm's performance management approaches and quantifiable evidence that supports approval of an IRB approach.

It is clear that different levels of sophistication in data capture and maintenance exist today. This ranges from those firms which have yet to invest in the necessary IT projects to improve the data in their internal ratings systems to those firms which envisage no problems with data requirements, boasting good information about borrowers dating back over 10 years. However, the implementation of data standards under Basel II will have a far-reaching impact on all firms seeking IRB approval.

In the UK, the data requirements are likely to be implemented via numerous quantifiable tests for data accuracy, with self-assessment scorecards that include a mix of regulator- and firm-specified targets that can be assessed through quantifiable tests, and "core targets that will apply to all firms" (CP189, 3.66). An overall "pass mark" will depend on the mandatory and supplementary targets agreed with each firm. They envisage a "rising hurdle" for firms seeking IRB approval covering any aspects that need improving. Although this clearly recognises that there will be differences in the data requirements between firms, the focus on mandatory targets and data accuracy scorecards implies a "one size fits all" approach to IRB approval. To the extent that the scorecards and mandatory targets reflect the practice in the more sophisticated, larger firms, this may result in other prospective IRB firms struggling to jump the hurdles.

The US on the other hand appears to have been more flexible. They recognise in the ANPR that data elements will vary by institution and even among business lines within an institution, and thus allow for "latitude" in firms managing their data. They do, however, go on to outline quite stringent supervisory standards (denoted by an "S" in the ANPR) that will be a challenge for all firms seeking IRB approval. These include data collection of sufficient depth, scope and reliability to validate IRB system processes, validate parameters, refine the IRB system, develop internal parameter estimates, apply improvements historically, calculate capital ratios, produce internal and public reports, and support risk management. The "hurdle" in this list that stands out is the requirement to be able to apply improvements to your rating systems historically. This implies that where new drivers of risk come to light, IRB firms will need to be able to retroactively reallocate grades accordingly. This can only be achieved if the new data have been collected for borrowers or facilities in the past and firms have somehow anticipated what data might be considered useful in the future.

From the industry's perspective, there is still a lot of work to be done in order to meet these minimum data requirements for maintaining internal estimates. On the corporate side, the challenge relates to the lack of default data, automation of the data processes (where data are still being captured and stored on paper within a credit/relationship file), and granularity. Corporate exposures can be further subdivided into investment-grade and non-investment-grade borrowers. Acute problems lie in investment-grade portfolios where few or no default data are available. This is most apparent in the data required for LGD and EAD estimates. IT systems in a number of areas will need to be extended, and interfaces must be established to meet standards at the onset of the implementation of the Accord. These IT projects are both costly and time-consuming. This is why many firms look to external default data to supplement their own internal collections.

There is a wide range of practice when it comes to the use of external data, whether supplied by a vendor or through a pooling exercise. Firms can use it to enhance internal ratings systems in a number of ways: the data can be used in the model development process, in the ratings themselves, or as part of a validation or benchmarking process. A considerable amount of judgement is involved in the use of external data – review and approval of the data, statistical analysis reviewed by oversight bodies (eg, parameter review boards), adjustments made where definitions differ, etc. In general, however, firms' use of external data enhances their internal ratings process.

The main regulatory concern about using external data in calculating estimates is whether it is applicable to the firm's business (are the default criteria of an external rating in line with internal or regulatory requirements?). The quality of the data is also a concern – with a lot of external data being confidential and not publicly available, the quality of the rating could, by association, be unknown. Firms in the UK are encouraged to use external data under CP189 (3.129) in the context of satisfying the Basel II requirement that "all relevant and available information" be considered (CP3, p. 410). However firms must show that data are relevant to the portfolio to which they are being applied.

Data challenges on the retail side are distinct to those on the corporate side. Regulators will be looking for volume, granularity and consistency in default data. Problems of consistency could be due to potential differences in the definitions of key characteristics within bank groups and across banks' internal rating. Maintaining consistent retail data has been made more difficult by the frequency with which definitions have changed and also the extent to which national discretion plays a part.

PANEL 1 VALIDATION OF INTERNAL RATINGS SYSTEMS

The validation of internal ratings systems lies at the heart of the IRB approval process. In order for regulators to be comfortable with the use of IRB firm's internal estimates, they need to be confident that the firms have in place a robust system of validating those estimates. Regulators have recognised the importance of validation in the process of approving IRB approaches, and a fair amount of work has been done at the international level through the Basel Committee's Research Task Force and, at a country level, through consultation with industry and cooperation with industry surveys, such as the "Internal ratings validation study" conducted by ISDA, the BBA and the RMA (and published jointly by the associations in June 2003).

The industry currently uses a wide variety of methods for ratings validation. The methods, issues and approaches to validation vary depending on the type of models used, the availability of default data and additional information such as the existence of external ratings. In general, institutions that have been using ratings for a longer period of time and have built up internal data histories tend to utilise more quantitative/statistical techniques – where the data permit this approach. The history of the rating system and the quantity of data vary with each asset class. In general, retail exposures use different scorecard-type models that can rely on a rich source of data. Ratings are less volatile and expected loss is easier to estimate. Corporate exposures generally consist of relatively few obligors and just a few years of data. Here, large systematic factors or drivers of credit quality can cause volatile annual default rates. With estimates based solely on just a few years worth of internal data, these models may be poor indicators of long-run default rates. Among bank and sovereign exposures, default rates are scarce or non-existent. Firms tend to rely more on external ratings for assessing credit quality, assigning PDs, and/or validation.

As a starting point, Basel II states that "Banks must have a robust system in place to validate the accuracy and consistency of rating systems, processes, and the estimation of all relevant risk components" (CP3, p. 463). Although CP3 does not provide much guidance on implementation beyond this, there are further paragraphs that mandate, for IRB-qualifying firms, specific statistical tests for validation across all exposures and model types. These include the requirement to regularly compare realised default rates with estimated PDs and to demonstrate that realised default rates fall within an expected range (CP3, p. 464). The proposed standard also mandates the use of other quantitative validation tools and comparisons with relevant external data sources (CP3, p. 465). No further detail on the specific statistical tests or the other quantitative validation tools is provided.

In the UK, as a result of CP3 and in line with the philosophy of "self-assessment", the Financial Services Authority (FSA) has developed an IRB validation scorecard for each firm to fill out. The scorecard contains information on materiality, type of data, mapping to external sources, length of observation period, impact of differences in definitions (from Basel II definitions), and information on stress-testing and macroeconomic conditions. The validation document must cover all portfolios for which IRB recognition is sought. However, expectations are that more depth will be required on all significant corporate and retail portfolios, although it is not quite clear whether a different scorecard for "significant" portfolios will be provided. In the retail segment, a far greater number of rating tools are used compared to corporate portfolios. In the internal ratings validation study mentioned earlier (ISDA, BBA, RMA (2003)), two firms admitted to having over 50 statistical models for their retail asset class. Under the UK proposal for IRB validation, it is not made clear how many of these retail models would require an IRB validation scorecard. In reality there may be a limited need to validate each model individually since the development and validation techniques, as well as the scorecard methodologies involved, are likely to be similar (if not identical) across the range of models used, even when these have been developed for different portfolios.

In the US, the ANPR defines validation as the set of activities designed to give the greatest possible assurances of ratings system accuracy. The US expects a greater level of validation work than is currently being undertaken and divides the implementation requirements into four stages: evaluation of developmental evidence, process verification, benchmarking, and back-testing. The US interpretation of Basel II again seems to be more flexible than the approach proposed by the UK. In the UK the proposals have a strong quantitative bias where they expect firms "to strive for models with the highest statistical measure" (CP189, 3.105). In the US they recognise that for certain exposures a qualitative validation process will assume greater importance. They also suggest that validation in its early stages will depend on "bank management's exercising informed judgement about the likelihood of the rating system working and not simply on empirical tests" (ANPR).

It is clear that firms' internal ratings systems rely heavily on expert judgement, no more so than in the area of large corporate exposures. A large proportion of banks' exposures is – and will be for the foreseeable future – covered by expert judgement-type rating systems. If the rating process includes elements of qualitative judgement, any statistical validation work covering performance of the whole system should include tests of the performance of the qualitative judgements. The ANPR recognises that as the dependence on judgment rises, ratings reviews will have to be undertaken increasingly by experts.

The US is arguably more explicit in its proposed requirements for the benchmarking and back-testing of internal ratings. The ANPR states that banks must benchmark their internal ratings against internal market and other third-party ratings. They also expect IRB firms to statistically back-test systems, establishing tolerance limits for differences between expected and actual outcomes. Finally, firms will be expected to have a well-documented policy defining what should happen if tolerance limits are broken. In Europe the RBCD also mandates the comparison of outcome to prediction (back-testing), but is more vague about the use of benchmarking techniques, requiring that at a minimum firms undertake annual comparisons between their own default experience and default experiences available elsewhere. The use of benchmarking against external ratings as a form of validation raises issues with regard to the unknown quality of external ratings. IRB firms will have to become familiar with the methodology and definitions employed by the external vendors and convince themselves that they are relevant to the portfolios being validated.

The requirement to back-test models has met with considerable resistance from the industry and represents one of the biggest validation challenges for a prospective IRB firm. It has been suggested that credit risk parameters, such as PDs, LGDs and EADs, require longer periods over which to assess their validity than implied by the type of back-testing being proposed. Firms have suggested that differences between estimates of PD and actual defaults in a given year do not represent errors requiring specific explanation and corrective action but require a longer-term validation technique.

INDEPENDENCE IN VALIDATION WORK

Under both sets of proposals, a fair degree of independence is required in validation work. The integrity of the rating and estimation processes and the extent of independent oversight and assessment will have a major part to play in the integrity of the resulting estimates, whatever the quantitative validation results. CP189 specifies that the validation work should be performed with the participation of independent staff. The work will also need to be signed off by an "appropriately senior committee". The US defines an independent rating process as "one in which the parties responsible for the approving of ratings and transactions are separate from the sales and marketing and in which persons approving ratings are principally compensated on risk-rating accuracy" (ANPR). Unlike in CP189, the ANPR specifies that the full board or a committee of the board must approve key elements of the IRB system.

EXTERNAL MODELS

As indicated in both the section on data and in Panel 1 on the validation of internal ratings systems, a dominant feature of ratings systems, particularly for corporate exposures, is the use of external models and data. Basel II does not provide a detailed approach for regulators to follow in its approach to the use of external models and data in "internal" ratings systems, but the problem exists for all regulators attempting to implement Basel II. In many cases the same models and data providers are in question.

There is a difference between how banks use external vendor models in the internal rating process. The internal ratings validation survey by ISDA, BBA and RMA (2003) showed that in North America, for corporate and middle-market portfolios, rating methodologies based on equity market information (like Moody's KMV Credit Monitor) or company financial information (like Moody's RiskCalc) represent an integral part of the rating assignment process and are often used in a hybrid approach in conjunction with expert judgement. In Europe, such external vendor models are more often used as a benchmark or validation of the rating derived by the internal rating model. Market-based methodologies do not generally lend themselves as primary sources for rating assignments outside of North America as fewer companies use the equity markets to raise funds.

In the UK, two broad aspects are identified for validating external models: whether the model does what it sets out to do; and whether it is an appropriate model for the portfolio it is being applied to. The UK regulator does not plan to undertake model accreditation because of the potential legal, behavioural and competitive consequences of such an approach. Instead, to achieve their aims, they have suggested a dual effort in validation between the vendors and the firms themselves. This is likely to involve the two parties filling out an "external vendor grid" to cover a full range of issues, such as model design and purpose, explicit calibration adjustments made, quantitative tests that can demonstrate the appropriateness of model use, any known model or data limitations, and vendor responsibilities and accountabilities.

The US approach is slightly different. The ANPR takes each Basel II component separately, PD, LGD and EAD, and investigates the different "mapping" techniques involved. Mapping is defined as the process of establishing a correspondence between the bank's current obligors and the reference obligor data used in the default model. This encompasses the process by which a firm may map an obligor to a particular external rating grade and assign the long-run default rate for that rating to the internal grade. The ANPR outlines mapping scenarios for the estimation of each component that will either "pass" for IRB approval or "fail". The mapping process is a key part of any internal rating system, even when reference data are drawn from internal default experience. As such, the US expects mapping policies and procedures to be well developed and well documented, with any exceptions to policy reviewed and justified.

OTHER REGULATORY PRIORITIES
The "use test" (CP3, p. 406)
An IRB approach will need to be embedded within the risk management culture of the firm. The Basel II and RBCD requirement that IRB systems play an essential role in the credit approval, risk management, internal capital allocation and corporate governance functions is known as the "use test". IRB systems should not simply be "bolted on" to satisfy the regulator but should be fully integrated into the business and risk management culture of the firm.

In the UK, a further scorecard for documentary evidence to demonstrate compliance with the use test has been proposed. Similarly, in the US documentation will be required to show full incorporation within the credit risk management, internal capital allocation and corporate governance functions of IRB banks. Any divergences, where internal ratings are not being used, will need to be fully explained.

The experience test (CP3, p. 407)
In addition to the use test, it is a Basel II and RBCD requirement that a firm must have been using an internal rating system broadly in line with the minimum requirements for at least three years before use of an IRB approach for regulatory capital purposes. There are some transitional arrangements left for national discretion and which the UK plans to employ. The UK plans to relax some of the minimum requirements for IRB approval for the first three years from implementation, most notably the data observation periods for retail exposures.

Procyclicality

The provisions of Basel II and the RBCD provide two mitigants against procyclicality. First, as part of Pillar one, by requiring firms to consider longer time horizons in estimating parameters (CP3, pp. 376–8). Second, by requiring firms to conduct stress tests that consider the effects of an economic downturn with the aim of taking action in advance to anticipate an increase in capital requirements.

In the US, firms are expected to adopt a "rating philosophy" with respect to assessment horizons in IRB systems. The US identifies a "through-the-cycle" rating system as one that considers a richer assessment of the possibilities and considers the implications of hypothetical stressed circumstances. A "point-in-time" rating does not. In the UK, a "through-the-cycle" rating system aims to leave a borrower's rating unchanged over the course of the credit/business cycle but expects default levels for each grade to vary with the cycle. The UK, if allowed by the RBCD (at least for a transitional period), does not plan to be prescriptive on the use of assessment horizons. However, it does expect to penalise so called "point-in-time" techniques with additional Pillar two capital requirements.

In reality, assessment horizons and historical data pools vary across ratings, and appropriate controls, documentation and senior management oversight ensure that firms take account of all the relevant inputs. Generally, firms use qualitative factors that are "point-in-time" (eg, a share price might be considered "point-in-time", as the only share price that matters is the share price now) combined with expectations for the future and therefore neither "point-in-time" or "through-the-cycle". There is still considerable scope for additional clarity on the implementation requirements for assessment horizons. It will be a significant challenge for the larger, more sophisticated US firms to adopt a single "rating philosophy" based on theoretical terms that are difficult to define and may become outdated with further advances in risk management techniques in the future.

The application of specific appropriate stress scenarios is likely to be a mechanism for banks seeking compliance under an IRB approach. Currently, stress-testing tends to be conducted at a group level, stressing the portfolio as a whole against macroeconomic shocks. Such tests do not involve feeding different economic variables into the rating models to generate alternative stressed rating outputs. This could well be required under the New Accord. In the UK it is suggested in CP189 that firms include in their Pillar one capital calculation the potential for capital requirements to increase with the cycle resulting from the expected downgrading of borrowers and/or a higher long-run estimate of default for borrowers in a grade.

In the US, a bank's capital management policy must be consistent with its ratings philosophy in order to avoid capital shortfalls in times of systematic economic stress. Also, the functions performed by risk management are expected to include the performance of portfolio stress tests.

Home host issues

The regulation of internationally active groups and concerns over the separation of responsibilities between home and host regulators have recently moved up the list of regulatory priorities. As this chapter has hopefully illustrated, the IRB approach requires complex validation and ongoing supervision covering many parameters and processes. The industry is concerned that different IRB approaches or data requirements emerge for each individual jurisdiction. This would result in the costly development of parallel systems, with all the testing, implementation and maintenance that implies. Basel II recognised the need for increased cooperation between regulators and set up the Accord Implementation Group (AIG) in early 2002. The AIG has developed principles to facilitate cooperation and exchange of information. This work is ongoing, but the UK in CP189 support a "lead regulator" model, a model that is currently in place for Basel capital reviews.

CONCLUSION

The third quantitative impact study (Bank for International Settlements, Basel Committee on Banking Supervision (2003), "QIS3") conducted by the Basel Committee over year-end 2002/03 clearly showed the benefits in terms of lower capital requirements for the majority of exposures of adopting an IRB approach. However, given the complexity of implementing Basel II, the existence of national discretions and inevitable national and regional variants of

Basel II, international firms will have to conduct detailed cost–benefit analysis before willingly committing to an IRB approach.

The Basel Committee goals remain clear: to ensure that the aggregate amount of capital required in the banking system as a whole does not materially increase as a result of implementing the new framework and to ensure that the new framework is risk-sensitive. Plans for implementation at a national level will undoubtedly reflect the existing style and culture of regulation already in place in each country. This is confirmed by reviewing the proposed implementation plans of the US and UK regulators, and also by cross-referencing them with Basel II and the RBCD. The perceived scope of implementation will also determine how regulatory efforts will have to change going forward. In the US, the IRB approach will initially be made mandatory for just over 10 firms, which will enable the current framework of regulation to prevail. In Germany, with over 30 banks seeking IRB approval for corporate, bank and sovereign exposures alone, they are building up a staff of examination officers (in total, 600 people for Bundesbank and BaFin) for a move away from off-site-oriented supervision to a more US-style on-site regime.

There is still much work for the industry and the regulators to do before implementing and approving IRB approaches. In a recent study by Norton Rose, 30 prominent institutions were asked whether the different approaches to implementation between the US and Europe were a cause for concern. 96% of respondents were deeply concerned about the inconsistencies, with 46% of these stating that it was a major concern that urgently needed to be addressed.

Key differences in the implementation of the Accord could result in confusion in relation to the adequacy of a bank's IRB methodology. Different approaches to models, parameterisation and data validation in different jurisdictions complicate the issues of home versus host supervision, with tensions arising from slightly different and incompatible standards being applied to the same processes by different supervisors.

The publication of proposed implementation guidance by the US and UK regulators represents a positive step in the convergence of international capital standards. The industry is in the process of commenting on both CP189 and the ANPR, and both the US and the UK have committed to further consultation. This will hopefully encourage other G10 regulators to be more open and transparent in their thinking and that global efforts by both firms and regulators alike will contribute to a uniform application of Basel II and a level playing field in minimum capital requirements.

BIBLIOGRAPHY

Bank for International Settlements, 2002, "Internal Ratings, the Business Cycle and Capital Requirements: Some Evidence from an Emerging Market Economy" BIS Working paper 117, by Segoviano M. A. and P. L. Monetary and Economic Department, September. Available from www.bis.org/publ/work117.pdf.

Bank for International Settlements, Basel Committee on Banking Supervision, 2003, Quantitative Impact Study 3 – Overview of Global Results (QIS3), May. Available from www.bis.org/bcbs/qis/qis3results.pdf.

Bluhm, C., and L. Overbeck, 2001, Irreconcilable differences. *Risk,* October. Available from www.risk.net.

Corcóstegui, González-Mosquera, Marcelo and Trucharte, 2003, "Analysis of Procyclical Effects on Capital Requirements derived from a Rating System" Paper presented at Basel Committee/Banca d'Italia workshop, 20–21 March.

Ernst and Young, 2003, "Current Views on Basel II" Risk Survey by Philippe d'Ornano and Simon Penny.

European Commission, 2002, Working Document of the Commission Services on Capital Requirements for Credit Institutions and Investment Firms – Cover Document, November.

European Commission, 2003a, "Review of Capital Requirements for Banks and Investment Firms" Commission Services Third Consultation Paper (CP3). July.

European Commission, 2003b, "Review of the Capital Requirement for Credit Institutions and Investments Firms – Third Quantitative Impact Study," EU results. July.

Federal Reserve Board, Office of the Comptroller of the Currency, Federal Deposit Insurance Corporation, and Office of Thrift Supervision, 2003, Advanced notice of Proposed Rulemaking (ANPR): Risk Based Capital Guidelines; Implementation of New Capital Accord; Internal Ratings Based Systems for Corporate Credit and Operational Risk Advanced Measurement Approaches for Regulatory Capital, July.

Financial Services Authority (FSA), 2003, "Report and First Consultation on the Implementation of the New Basel and EU Capital Adequacy Standards" Consultation Paper 189 (CP189), July.

Heid, F., 2003, "Is Regulatory Capital Pro-cyclical? A Macroeconomic Assessment of Basel II" Paper presented at Basel Committee/Banca d'Italia workshop, 20–21 March.

ISDA, 2003, Discussion Points with AIG Members on Data Issues, April. Available from www.isda.org.

ISDA, BBA, RMA, 2003, The Internal Ratings Validation Survey, June. Available from www.isda.org.

Moody's Investors Service, 2003, Default & Recovery of Corporate Bond Issuers – a Statistical Review of Moody's Ratings Performance, 1920–2002. Moody's Special Comment, Exhibit 37, February.

Norton, R., 2003, Banks feel the bite. Survey on the New Basel Capital Accord, *The Banker* Special Supplement, October.

Ong, M. K., 2002, *Credit Ratings, Methodologies, Rationale and Default Risk.* London, Risk Books.

Rowe, D., 2003, No cure through the cycle. *Risk*, March, 50. Available from www.risk.net, http://db.riskwaters.com/data/risk/articles/0303/riskanalysis.pdf.

13

Market Discipline and Appropriate Disclosure in Basel II*

Lawrence J. White

Stern School of Business, New York University

INTRODUCTION

This is an excellent time to be addressing issues of financial disclosure for financial conglomerates. After decades of debating an end to the Glass-Steagall and Bank Holding Company Acts' limitations on banks' participation in other parts of the financial services universe, the US Congress finally passed the Gramm-Leach-Bliley Act in 1999. Less than three years later, two large financial conglomerates – Citigroup and JPMorgan Chase – received stunning public rebukes for their roles in the accounting and corporate governance manipulations of some of their clients.

Simultaneously, the Bank for International Settlements' (BIS) Basel Committee on Banking Supervision has proposed a revision (henceforth, Basel II) to its 1988 capital standards, in which "market discipline" – driven by public disclosure – is one of the three "pillars" for strengthening the safety and soundness of banks (see BIS, 1998b, 2000a, 2001b–d, f, h).

This chapter will address the disclosure issues for financial conglomerates principally from the same perspective as that of the

*An earlier version of this chapter was presented as a paper at the Joint US–Netherlands Roundtable on Financial Services Conglomerates, 24–5 October 2002. The author would like to thank Mark Carey, Richard Herring, Anjela Kniazeva, Diana Kniazeva, Robert Litan, James Moser and the participants at the Roundtable for valuable comments on an earlier draft.

Basel Committee: that disclosure is important for the safety and soundness of banks. We will, however, reach substantially different conclusions with respect to three important disclosure issues: the role of market value accounting; the frequency of disclosures; and the role of subordinated debt.[1]

We will start by asking why any special disclosure might be required for financial conglomerates. This question leads directly to a discussion of what is special about financial conglomerates. We will also address the question of "disclosure to whom?". There are at least two potential audiences for information disclosures: financial regulators; and the public investors, creditors and customers of a financial conglomerate. Issues of the appropriate structure for a financial conglomerate, and the information revelation that should accompany that structure, will also be raised. Finally, we will return to our main theme: what constitutes appropriate disclosure for a financial conglomerate?

Much of the discussion will reference the financial and regulatory institutions of the US and their experiences. The insights and lessons to be drawn from the discussion, however, have wider applications.

WHY SHOULD THERE BE ANY SPECIAL DISCLOSURE FOR FINANCIAL CONGLOMERATES?

We start with fundamentals: why should there be any special disclosure for financial conglomerates? This line of inquiry leads immediately to an even more basic question: what is special about financial conglomerates that would warrant special disclosure?

The specialness of a financial conglomerate must rest with the presence of a depository and/or an insurance company embedded within it. We will start with a depository – specifically a bank.[2] Panel 1 explains what makes a bank special.

PANEL 1 WHY BANKS ARE SPECIAL

The specialness of banks is generally attributed to their generic combination of assets and liabilities: relatively illiquid assets (usually loans) and highly liquid liabilities (deposits). This combination makes them potentially vulnerable to depositor withdrawal "runs" (see, for example, Diamond and Dybvig, 1983; Postlewaite and Vives, 1987;

Chen, 1999). In addition, banks are at the centre of the payments system, so they have constant creditor– borrower relationships among themselves, leaving them exposed to potential losses (and pre-emptive runs) at each other's hands.

This specialness of a bank is best illustrated by a stylised balance sheet, presented in Figure 1. The bank's assets are primarily the loans that it makes. Its liabilities are primarily the deposits that it has gathered (and uses to fund its assets). The difference between the value of its assets and the value of its liabilities is its net worth or owners' equity. In the financial world, this is frequently described as "capital". The bank of Figure 1 is solvent and would be considered adequately capitalised by the standards established by the Basel Committee in 1988.

It is important to note that the bank's capital is simply the arithmetic difference between the bank's assets and its liabilities. The bank's capital has no separate existence or measurement, except as represented by this arithmetic difference.

Let us now examine a second stylised balance sheet in Figure 2, where the bank has suffered a substantial reduction in the value of its assets. Instead of the positive capital of $8 of Figure 1, the value of the bank's deposit liabilities in Figure 2 exceeds the value of its assets by $12; its capital is now −$12. It is badly insolvent.

Figure 1 Stylised balance sheet of the ABC bank (solvent), as of December 31, 200X

Assets	Liabilities
$100 (loans)	$92 (deposits)
	$8 (net worth, owners' equity, capital)

Figure 2 Stylised balance sheet of the ABC bank (insolvent), as of December 31, 200Y

Assets	Liabilities
$80 (loans)	$92 (deposits)
	−$12 (net worth, owners' equity, capital)

Typically, the depositors do not have recourse against the owner of the bank to cover the shortfall – either because of a legal structure of limited liability for the owners of a corporation (in this case, the bank), or a legal structure of personal bankruptcy that limits liability for the bank's owner, or both. Consequently, the depositors will have to absorb and distribute the loss somehow among themselves.

Though the absorption of loss by liability holders (ie, creditors or lenders) is a general problem where limited liability is present, liability holders generally try to protect themselves (eg, through covenants and lending restrictions) against the risk-taking and other behaviours by corporate owners that could cause losses for the lenders. Limited liability is, however, a special problem with respect to banks, for at least three reasons. First, some bank depositors may be relatively unsophisticated and poorly informed, and in a poor position to protect themselves against the losses from a bank's insolvency (ie, they are unlikely to develop covenants and lending agreements); also, banks are more opaque (and thus more difficult to be informed about) than are other enterprises (see Morgan, 2002).

Second, and related to the first, banks are especially vulnerable to withdrawal runs by imperfectly informed depositors, who may be uncertain about the financial condition of their bank and who fear that they may have to absorb some losses. Because the bank's loan assets are generally less liquid (it typically keeps only a small amount of cash on hand) than are its deposit liabilities, even a solvent bank cannot immediately satisfy all of its depositors' demands for withdrawals – or even the withdrawal demands of more than a small fraction of depositors. If forced to meet the demands of more than that small fraction, the bank must (a) borrow from somewhere;[3] (b) call in its loans and/or liquidate its illiquid assets at short notice and likely at less value than would occur from a more orderly and leisurely sale; or (c) shut its doors and delay paying its depositors until its loans are repaid or assets can be sold in an orderly way, thereby reneging on its liquidity commitment to its depositors.

Accordingly, a "prisoners' dilemma" problem may well arise: Though a bank may be solvent and informed depositors know that it is solvent, they may fear that other depositors are worried about the condition of the bank and that the latter's withdrawals would strain the bank's resources. In that case, even the knowledgeable depositors would want to race to the bank to withdraw their funds first. But such a general race to the bank will put strains on even solvent banks, thus making everyone worse off.

Third, there may be a "contagion" effect, where depositors of one bank, seeing a run on another bank, may fear for the solvency of their bank – or may just fear that other depositors of their bank will become worried and begin to withdraw, etc. Alternatively, because banks are at the centre of the payments system and are frequently in the position of being a short-term lender or borrower *vis-à-vis* other banks, the insolvency of one bank may cause a cascade of insolvencies of other creditor banks (or may cause a contagion of runs by banks-as-creditors who have imperfect information and fear insolvency, etc).

Some version of the above scenarios (plus the perceived position of banks as special lenders) has caused the American polity, since the early 19th century, to consider banks to be special and to develop special prudential ("safety and soundness") regulatory regimes to deal with their specialness. At the centre of such regimes have been efforts to maintain their solvency – to keep them "safe and sound". Since 1933, federal deposit insurance has provided an additional layer of assurance to depositors (and, thus, an additional damper on potential depositor runs), by protecting them against regulatory failure; in an important sense, with deposit insurance in place, prudential regulation becomes the rules that protect the deposit insurer (as well as protecting uninsured depositors and other creditors).

There are four major components to prudential regulation: (a) minimum capital requirements; (b) activities limitations;[4] (c) management competency requirements; and (d) in-the-field examiners and supervisors to enforce the rules. The minimum capital requirements are the direct effort to maintain a bank's solvency. This was the primary focus of the 1988 Basel Accord and remains as the first of the three pillars of Basel II. The activities limitations should be seen primarily as efforts to limit risk (although limitations on banks' activities have also taken on a heavy political overtone in the US, as industries that have feared banks' competition have lobbied heavily to prevent banks from entering their areas). There are some important structural issues related to activities limitations and information revelation, to which we will return below. Management competence is related to "operational risk", which is a component of the capital requirement that is the first pillar of Basel II. And the enforcement of the rules requires in-the-field examiners and supervisors, with effective supervision serving as the second pillar of Basel II.

Activities limitations, and the appropriate structure for a bank

Let us proceed on the assumptions made in Panel 1 that banks are special, and that safety-and-soundness regulation is an appropriate means of dealing with their specialness. Activities limitation has been a traditional tool of safety-and-soundness regulation. The logic for limitations can be seen from a re-examination of Figures 1 and 2: if the bank is to remain solvent (ie, its capital is to remain positive) despite the uncertainties of future outcomes, then minimum capital requirements must be specified for all of the activities that could negatively affect the bank's balance sheet.

There is an immediate implication: the only activities that are appropriate for a bank are those that are "examinable and supervis-able" and, thus, can be regulated in a manner that is consistent with the safe-and-sound operation of a bank.[5] In practice, this would mean an activity for which regulators are capable of setting suitable capital requirements and making judgements about the competence of the bank's management in managing the activity. This examinable-and-supervisable decision ought to be a regulatory judgement; but the political appointees at the leadership of the regu-latory agency should be held accountable for those judgements.

Any activity that is not appropriate for a bank (because regulators are not able to set capital requirements and/or judge managerial competence in the activity) should nevertheless be permitted for the owners of a bank, for a bank holding company, for an affiliate or subsidiary of the holding company, or for a bank subsidiary – so long as the bank cannot count the net worth of the subsidiary as an asset of the bank. This last qualification is frequently described as the subsidiary's being "separately capitalised". By contrast, if the bank could count the net worth of the subsidiary as an asset, then this arrangement would be the financial equivalent of allowing the bank to undertake the activity directly. But, by assumption, the activity is not permitted in the bank because it is not "examinable and supervisable". With the subsidiary's net worth not counting as an asset of the bank, the financial failure of the subsidiary would not directly affect the bank; but the bank could still take advantage of whatever organisational or legal advantages that might apply to having the activity in the subsidiary. Figure 3 provides a highly stylised and condensed picture of the consequent structure of the locations of appropriate and inappropriate activities for a bank.

As a practical matter, it is clear that loans and loan-like products are highly likely to be deemed appropriate for a bank: regulators are familiar with them and believe that they can set appropriate capital requirements and judge managerial competence. What about the two financial services that were at the centre of two decades of contention in the US about their appropriateness for banks – securities activities and insurance activities? The logic of the "examinable and supervisable" approach is that their placement

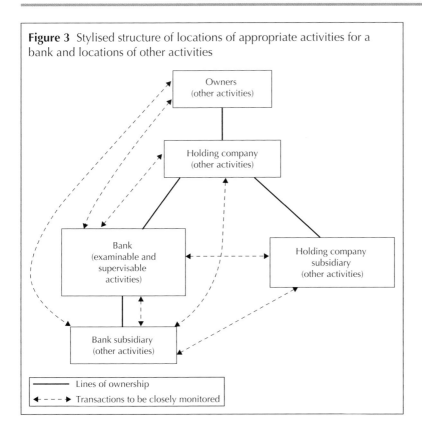

Figure 3 Stylised structure of locations of appropriate activities for a bank and locations of other activities

within a bank, or alternatively somewhere in a related entity, ought to be the result of a judgement by bank regulators about their ability to set capital requirements and judge managerial competency.

And what if a bank decides that it wants to operate a fast-food restaurant? Though bank regulators might be able to hire restaurant consultants who could provide advice as to appropriate capital levels and ways of judging managerial competence, it seems likely that bank regulators would decide that this activity was not an area of their expertise and ought not to be permitted for a bank – but should be permitted for a bank's owners or for a bank's subsidiary.

Finally, even with activities sorted by examinable and supervisable criteria, the transactions (eg, loans, or asset sales or purchases) between the bank and its owners, affiliates and subsidiaries must be closely monitored, because they provide a ready means for resources to be siphoned from the bank. The bank may overpay for some services that it buys or undercharge for some services that its sells and thereby cause its insolvency. The bank subsidiary has an advantage over the bank holding company as a place for such activities. If the bank overpays for some services from its subsidiary (or undercharges for some services sold to the subsidiary), any dividends from the subsidiary to the bank's "parent" holding company would have to pass through the bank and thus can be "trapped" there by regulators to offset the inappropriate transaction. However, to the extent that the subsidiary is less than 100% owned by the bank, it becomes more like a part of the holding company and thus more susceptible to straight siphoning (Edwards, 1979). Also, even with a subsidiary that is 100% owned by the bank, if that subsidiary transacts directly or indirectly with the owner, then the subsidiary can overpay or undercharge and still be a conduit for siphoning.

There are also indirect ways that a bank can be weakened to the benefit of its owners. The bank may misprice transactions to friends of the owners, who in turn provide payment or favours to the owners. Or, in the context of a financial conglomerate, a bank may provide loans to a company whose equity shares are being underwritten by the conglomerate's securities affiliate. Though such loans may have a sound basis in the special information that the securities affiliate possesses and forwards to the bank, the loans may instead be a way that the bank provides risky support for the client company so that the securities affiliate reaps benefits from the company through investment banking fees.[6]

Consequently, such direct and indirect transactions between the bank and its owners and affiliates must be on arm's-length terms and monitored closely, and penalties for violations must be severe.

The similarities with insurance companies and defined-benefit (final-salary) pension funds

Part of the logic that supports prudential regulation extends to at least two other financial institutions: insurance companies, and defined-benefit (final-salary) pension funds.[7] Figures 1 and 2 can readily be adapted to portray stylised versions of each. For either, the assets can be loans or other investments. Instead of deposit liabilities for banks, the insurance company would have the likely claims of its insureds as its liabilities, and the pension fund would have its pensioners' likely claims. An insolvency for either, along the lines of Figure 2, would mean that the assets of the institution were inadequate to cover the claims.

Though neither type of institution is subject to the "runs" problems of banks, their claimants are likely to be poorly informed and/or in a poor position to protect themselves against actions that could put their claims at risk. Accordingly, it is not surprising that every state in the US has a prudential regulatory regime that applies to insurance companies and that all states currently have mutual guarantee funds that serve as a financial backup for a claimant whose insurance company has become insolvent. Similarly, since 1974, the claimants of defined-benefit pension funds have had recourse to guaranty coverage provided by the federal Pension Benefit Guaranty Corporation (PBGC), and the PBGC and the Department of Labor's Pension and Welfare Benefits Administration have prudential regulatory powers (albeit weak) *vis-à-vis* defined-benefit pension plans and their corporate parents.

APPROPRIATE DISCLOSURE (1): TO REGULATORS

The prudential regulatory regimes that surround banks need information about their regulated institutions. Since the maintenance of solvency is the primary goal of the regulation, we will first focus on the representation of solvency as depicted in the balance sheet of Figure 1; though our focus here is primarily on the balance sheet, the profit-and-loss statement is inexorably linked to it, so our discussion will implicitly cover that as well. We will also discuss the riskiness of the balance sheet (and thus activities limitations are implicitly covered) and the special concern about transactions with affiliated parties.

A. Financial statements
1. A market value accounting approach[8]
Capital serves two important functions. First, it is the direct indicator of solvency – the direct buffer that protects depositors (or the deposit insurer) against a decline in the value of the assets. Second, because capital is essentially the owners' equity in the bank, greater

capital is a disincentive to risk taking, since the owners' relative stake in the bank (which would be at risk) is larger.

The logic of these functions points strongly toward regulators' receiving balance-sheet information that best represents this buffer and the incentives/disincentives. This logic points to the use of market-value accounting (MVA), where market values are used wherever possible for asset and liability values.[9]

Unfortunately, that is not the accounting system that is the standard for financial statement presentation – whether intended for regulators or for the public. Instead, the standard accounting system in the US – "generally accepted accounting principles" (GAAP) – is a backward-looking, historical cost-based system for assigning values to assets and liabilities. Though GAAP does have some elements that reflect current market values, it is primarily historical cost-based in its orientation, and that is the perspective that pervades standard accounting.[10]

The drawback to GAAP for the purposes of safety-and-soundness regulation is straightforward: a bank's solvency defin-itionally diminishes as the value of its assets declines (or the value of its liabilities increases). And it is just at the time of diminished solvency that the owners' incentives to take greater risks increase (since the owners have less to lose); but the "downside" of that risk taking will mean even greater losses and possible insolvency. Accordingly, bank regulators should want to know about declines in asset values as rapidly as possible, so as to limit the risk-taking behaviour that might exacerbate those declines.[11] But GAAP, with its historical orientation, is slow to recognise asset value changes, down or up, and thus does not serve regulators well.

Though this slowness to recognise asset value changes looks even-handed, it is not. First, regulators' concerns are asymmetric. They care much more about insolvency than about overly high levels of capital. Second, banks have a ready but dangerous strategy to circumvent GAAP's slowness to recognise asset gains: sell the assets that have embedded gains.[12] But banks can continue to hold assets that have declined in value and continue to account for them at acquisition cost. In essence, GAAP provides banks with a valuable option.

This strategy of selling "winners" to recognise gains (which can be sent, via dividends, to owners), while holding "losers" at historical cost, can logically lead to a balance sheet with only overvalued assets, whose current (market) values are below their nominal values that are listed on the balance sheet. This is not a recipe for the maintenance of the true solvency of a bank.[13]

It might appear that the numbers on the balance sheet would not matter, so long as regulators know the "true" (ie, market values) of assets and liabilities. And, since the mid-1990s GAAP in the US has required a footnote statement of the market values of financial assets. But regulators are largely driven by what is represented on the balance sheet, not what is in footnotes. The regulatory rules are largely written in terms of capital as reported on the balance sheet. The ability of regulators to restrict a bank's behaviour is driven by the balance sheet's report of capital, as is the regulator's ability to appoint a receiver and thus wrest control from the owners. For example, during the period of the 1980s and early 1990s, when almost 1,500 commercial banks in the US became insolvent and required regulatory action, bank regulators complained that they knew that some of these banks were in financial difficulties but that their apparently healthy (GAAP) balance sheets forestalled earlier preemptive action (see FDIC, 1998).

There are two main objections to a system of MVA (see, for example, Engelke, 1990; Fisher, 1992). First, opponents claim that it would introduce more volatility into banks' income statements. Support for this claim is sometimes provided by a "backcasting" of historical bank experiences and showing how their reported incomes would have been more volatile if a MVA framework had been in place. But this argument fails to acknowledge that volatility as measured by market values is what regulators should care about. Even more important, the backcasting exercise fails to recognise that banks would change their behaviour if they knew that the MVA framework would be the standard for future reporting.[14] To the extent that they care about reported volatility, banks would hedge and otherwise modify their behaviour in ways that would reduce volatility as reported in the MVA framework. This additional hedging and other behaviour modifications might be costly; but, if market value reporting is what is important, this is the right framework within which the trade-offs between the smoothing of income flows and the costs of doing so should be considered.[15]

A second objection is that some assets and liabilities may have no ready markets for valuation purposes, and thus estimates would be required – opening the door to potential error and manipulation. This argument has become progressively weaker, as larger portions of banks' assets have become securitised or otherwise sellable. Further, significant parts of a bank's balance sheet already require estimates and judgements: eg, asset lives and depreciation, the timing of when the value of an asset should be considered impaired and written down and the extent of the write-down, the liability costs of future retirees' benefits.

Still, even where there are no perfect substitutes that have market valuations, there may be close substitutes that, through modelling, can be related to the balance-sheet assets in question. The modelling, of course, must be validated, first by the bank's auditor and ultimately by the regulator.[16] But even imperfect modelling, if done and monitored responsibly, is likely to be an improvement over the backward-looking focus of historical cost accounting. Only where market analogues and reliable modelling are not available ought historical costs to be the standard.

The same general principles should apply to the valuation of liabilities as well.

2. The frequency of reporting

The current standard of frequency of reporting of financial statements is once a quarter, though regulators can require more frequent reports from banks that are of concern. This is far too infrequent. Banks do not slide into difficulties only at the end of a calendar quarter.

In an age when every bank is or should be wholly electronic in its financial accounts (and thus the marginal costs of frequent reporting ought to be quite small), more frequent reporting is both desirable and feasible. Weekly reporting should be the immediate goal, and daily reporting ought to be a near-term goal. Daily reporting is the standard for securities firms and investment banks. It should also be the standard for commercial banks and other depositories.

3. The Basel Committee's approach

Unfortunately, the Basel Committee is hostile to MVA,[17] embracing the historical cost orientation of GAAP. Though the committee acknowledges the "sell winners, hold losers" problem, it is worried about increased volatility and imperfect estimates. The committee shows little recognition of regulators' needs to know up-to-date market information about a bank's assets and liabilities and thus its capital. The committee has consequently greatly weakened the effectiveness of its capital standards.

The Basel Committee's approach to frequency of reporting is one of silence as to specificity (see BIS, 2001e). Again, this weakens the effectiveness of its capital standards.

B. Riskiness
The necessary information
The primary regulatory approaches to riskiness should be an insistence on adequate capital (for activities that are examinable and supervisable) and the exclusion of activities that are not examinable and supervisable. Essential to the determination of adequate capital levels is a measure of the risk characteristics of the assets and liabilities, including any covariance effects. And essential to that determination are forward-looking stress tests that indicate how well the institution's capital (ie, the net arithmetic outcome of assets less liabilities) survives a variety of unfavourable macro-economic scenarios. Further, of course, all such outcomes must be calculated in MVA terms.

Consequently, regulators need detailed information about the types, amounts, characteristics and histories – including covariances – of all assets and liabilities of a bank. And they need a standardised stress test that is sufficiently comprehensive and detailed so as to be able to use all of the information to forecast outcomes.

Further, because transactions with owners and affiliates are potential vehicles for siphoning resources out of the bank, detailed information about such transactions is essential. In addition, information about indirect transactional advantages provided to owners or their affiliates is necessary.

Finally, a requirement that banks issue a tranche of tradable long-term subordinated debt as part of their required capital – say, equal to 2% of their assets – would provide regulators with an additional source of information, from the capital markets.[18] The presence of subordinated debt would bring to the bank a group of stakeholders whose interests would be similar (though not identical) to those of the regulator, since the holders would not gain from the "upside" of risk taking and would be the first parties affected by the "downside" after the owners' equity was erased. If it were issued as long-term debt with layered maturities, its holders could not all run on the bank simultaneously. The pricing of the debt would itself be an important source of information. And the layered maturities would mean that the bank would be rolling over and reissuing the debt at frequent intervals, providing an additional important source of information.

The Basel Committee's approach

The Basel Committee's Basel II proposals have three different approaches to risk. First, and simplest, is the committee's "standardised approach" to credit risk (see BIS, 2001g). Similar to its 1988 capital standards, the standardised approach has a number of risk categories ("buckets"), with a capital requirement (risk weight) for each category. The standardised approach expands the number of buckets (as compared to the 1988 standards) and includes as additional relevant information the bond ratings of any borrower that has rated debt.[19] But the standardised approach has serious shortcomings: it does not encompass an explicit forward-looking stress test (to the extent that companies' bond ratings are part of the process, however, forward-looking stress tests are indirectly present, since stress tests are a component of bond ratings); it does not acknowledge covariances (except for explicit hedges and other explicit offsets); and it relies on GAAP rather than MVA for measurements of capital.

Second is the committee's "foundation internal ratings-based approach", whereby a bank can provide its own estimates of default probabilities (see BIS, 2001a). The Basel II document provides the other risk components, including loss-given-default, exposure at default and allowances for offsets. Forward-looking stress tests are expected to be part of the bank's estimation procedure. But the stress tests need not be conducted any more frequently than once every six months. Again, covariances are not explicitly acknowledged. And, again, all capital measurements rely on GAAP rather than MVA.

The third method is the committee's "advanced internal ratings-based approach", whereby a sufficiently sophisticated bank can provide its own estimates of the other risk components, but is otherwise similar to the "foundation" approach.

Further, the committee takes no specific stand on what activities are or are not appropriate for a bank, although it is suspicious of "significant" equity holdings in commercial enterprises,[20] and it recognises the risks of transactions with affiliates.

The committee's concerns about special disclosure with respect to financial conglomerates appear to be focused largely on the risks of multi-stage financial leveraging or gearing (see BIS, 1998a, 1999a). This issue is readily demonstrated in a modification of Figure 1, as shown in Figure 4. Instead of all US $100 of the top-tier bank's assets being devoted to loans, US $8 has been devoted to an equity investment in a subsidiary second-tier bank. With that US $8 of equity, the subsidiary bank can attract US $92 in deposits and make US $100 in loans – or even itself set aside US $8 for an equity investment in a third-tier bank, etc. Thus, in principle, the multi-tiering means that the original $8 of equity in the top-tier bank has achieved substantially greater leverage (and reduced protection for deposits) than the 12.5-to-1 capital-to-assets of the simple bank of Figure 1. The committee also points out that this multi-tiering could occur with an insurance company or a securities firm as the parent or the subsidiary.

The committee's approach to the multi-stage leveraging problem is to insist on consolidation at the parent level for the purposes of determining adequate capital, ie, ensuring adequate capital at the parent bank level so as to take into account the full leverage of the overall conglomerate. However, the committee fails to acknowledge explicitly that this multi-stage leveraging is a general problem that applies to any equity positions taken by the bank.

Finally, the committee fails to endorse a requirement for the issuance of subordinated debt, a mechanism that (as was argued above) would yield additional valuable information for regulators.

To summarise, the Basel Committee's approach falls substantially short of appropriate disclosure to regulators – in terms of the accounting framework employed, the frequency of reporting and the specifics of addressing risk.

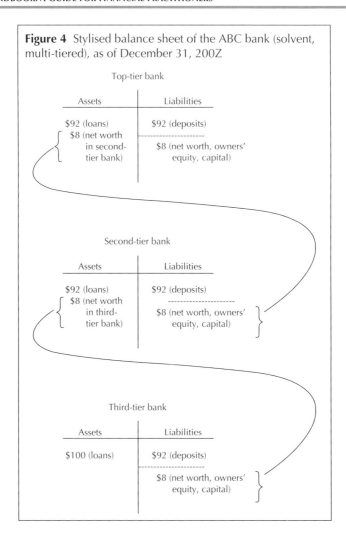

Figure 4 Stylised balance sheet of the ABC bank (solvent, multi-tiered), as of December 31, 200Z

Top-tier bank

Assets	Liabilities
$92 (loans)	$92 (deposits)
$8 (net worth in second-tier bank)	$8 (net worth, owners' equity, capital)

Second-tier bank

Assets	Liabilities
$92 (loans)	$92 (deposits)
$8 (net worth in third-tier bank)	$8 (net worth, owners' equity, capital)

Third-tier bank

Assets	Liabilities
$100 (loans)	$92 (deposits)
	$8 (net worth, owners' equity, capital)

APPROPRIATE DISCLOSURE (2): TO THE PUBLIC

Appropriate public disclosure by publicly traded companies is a broad topic that extends considerably beyond the issues surrounding financial conglomerates. The Basel Committee's interests in disclosure do not extend broadly, however. They are solely concerned with disclosure as the third pillar to support the safe-and-sound operation of banks. Nevertheless, the broader context is worth considering before focusing on the committee's concerns. We discuss these issues in Panel 2.

PANEL 2 TWO BROAD VIEWS OF THE APPROPRIATE DISCLOSURE REQUIREMENT

Generally, the extent to which regulatory involvement in public disclosure is required depends on one's view of investors. I will offer two broad views, in order to highlight the contrasts.[21]

1. The asymmetric information-awareness model

This approach starts by assuming that potential lenders and investors are aware of the asymmetric information problems that pervade finance. They realise that potential borrowers have more information about themselves and about their prospects for repayment than do the lenders and that actual borrowers may know more about their actions and the effects on repayment than do the lenders.[22] Lenders therefore recognise that they need to acquire information about prospective borrowers, so as better to assess the riskiness of the prospective borrowers and to decide to whom to make loans (and to whom to say no) and on what terms; and to monitor borrowers' actions after advancing a loan, so as to be able intervene if circumstances warrant.

Let us describe the lenders/investors in this paradigm a bit more. They are *aware* of their informational limitations. Loosely, we might describe them as "*knowing* that they don't know what they don't know". They may occasionally be fooled by deliberately misleading information; but they will learn from this experience and move on. They will rarely be fooled by vague or inadequate information. Because they are *risk-averse* as well as *aware*, the presence of less (or inadequate) information about a prospective borrower will cause the lenders to fear the worst about that borrower and to add a large risk premium in their consideration of whether to lend and on what terms.

In this context, financial statements provide an important source of information about enterprises that want to borrow, which will help the *aware* lenders to pierce the fog of asymmetric information in assessing prospective enterprise borrowers beforehand and in subsequently monitoring enterprise borrowers. Equivalently, financial statements allow an enterprise to emerge from the fog of asymmetric information and better show its true prospects.

However, financial statements are not free: resources are required to gather, process, certify, and disseminate an enterprise's financial statements. Greater details and specificity of disclosure – though providing greater assurance to lenders – are generally more costly. Also, enterprises are reluctant to reveal proprietary information that they fear may be used by competitors to the latter's advantage and the former's disadvantage. Further, with respect to an enterprise's managers *vis-à-vis* its investor-shareholder-owners, the managers would generally prefer to reveal less to the shareholders, since less information revelation gives the managers greater flexibility of actions. But revelation of more (useful) information helps dispel the asymmetric information fog *vis-à-vis* investors and reduces the costs of equity capital to the enterprise.

Consequently, the enterprise will try to find the cost-minimising point in the trade-off between the higher direct costs of greater information disclosure and the lower costs of capital from greater revelation. This cost-minimising point should yield the most efficient financial statement disclosures for that enterprise.

With a multiplicity of enterprises in an economy, this quest for efficient disclosure would appear to yield a multiplicity of formats and accounting systems – perhaps one for each enterprise. But the transactions costs for lenders and investors of "translating" the various firms' financial statements – in essence, the "network" aspects of financial reporting and the role of accounting – indicate that such a multitude of systems would itself be costly for enterprises and their lenders/investors, because of the "incompatibility" (comparison) costs. Accordingly, enterprises face a further set of disclosure trade-offs – between the lower transactions costs of adhering to a more widely used accounting system, versus adhering to a less widely used system that is better at portraying a specific enterprise's information.

In this context, the role of government regulation with respect to disclosure is relatively modest. It consists primarily of policing disclosure fraud and helping the "system" of firms and their investors/lenders deal with the "network" aspects of disclosure. The latter would involve helping the system decide on whether one or a few accounting systems will be the basis for disclosures (as a "template" – see Dye and Sunder, 2001; Sunder, 2002) by the enterprises that will be subject to the comparisons of the capital markets of an economy.

2. The "investor protection" model

As compared with the "awareness" paradigm that was just described, an "investor protection" model entails more than just protecting investors from deliberately misleading information (ie, fraud) and helping them navigate the "network" issues. Instead, the lenders/ investors in this model are not fully aware of their informational limitations. They can be fooled by vague or inadequate information; they don't realise that they need to pierce the asymmetric information fog (or impose a large risk premium for remaining in the fog).

These lenders/investors need not be complete dupes: instead, they just can't deal appropriately with vagueness.[23] Consequently, opportunistic corporate managers will take advantage of this gullibility by remaining vague; some lenders/investors will experience losses as a consequence; and, rather than learning from their experience and moving on, the lenders/investors instead will subsequently stay away from the securities markets (and tell their friends to do likewise), thereby reducing the liquidity and depth of the markets and raising the costs of capital.

This model appears to drive the policies of the SEC and of the Congress, as is indicated by (for example) Sutton (1997) and Levitt (1998). This approach calls for a much more active role for government regulation of disclosure, beyond policing fraud and dealing with network issues. Disclosure must be mandated, with extensive detail required.

From the two broad views highlighted in Panel 2, we can now address the question of appropriate disclosure of financial conglomerates to the public. As a first approximation, requiring the same general framework of financial disclosure from financial conglomerates as from other publicly traded companies in the economy seems about right. After all, from the perspective of shareholders or of creditors (other than insured depositors), financial conglomerates are just another set of firms embedded in the asymmetric information fog with which they must deal.

There are, though, two qualifications to this position that should be made. First, as was argued above, banks (including, but not limited to, those that are part of a larger conglomerate structure) ought to be required to issue subordinated debt. The holders of this subordinated debt may well demand additional financial disclosures from banks. This is all to the good.

Second, because securities firms are at the centre of the operations of the securities markets, their errant actions are more likely to yield negative externalities for the overall markets. Consequently, they should bear a higher responsibility with respect to their disclosures concerning their activities – for example, to the disclosures that relate a securities analyst's recommendations to other aspects of the analyst and the securities firm. These disclosures could include the personal portfolio of the analyst, the past performance of the analyst, the past movement of the analyst's portfolio prior and subsequent to a recommendation, and the securities firm's other relationships with the enterprise that is being recommended. Accordingly, when a securities firm is an affiliate of the bank, the customers of the securities firm should receive disclosures about any connections between the securities affiliate's underwriting activities and analysts' recommendations and the bank's lending.

The Basel Committee's approach

As was noted above, the Basel Committee's approach to public disclosure for financial conglomerates is not rooted in general disclosure concerns. Instead, the committee envisions information disclosure as bolstering "market discipline", which serves as the third pillar for safety and soundness in banking.

The committee's arguments in support of disclosure are surprisingly brief, consisting of about a page and a half in a supporting document (see BIS, 1998b). In essence, the committee argues that the transactors with a bank can be a constraint on risk taking by the bank if they are aware of the bank's actions and positions. With information revelation, the bank's creditors, counterparties, customers, suppliers and so on can find out about risk taking earlier and can protect themselves earlier by ceasing their relationships with the banks or insisting on improved terms for a continuation of the relationship. These reactions, in turn, will deter the bank's management from embarking on the course of risk taking in the first place.

Consequently, the committee mandates an extensive menu of public disclosure for a bank. Indeed, it is difficult to distinguish between the committee's expectations for information disclosure for regulators and its expectations for disclosure to the public. The former disclosures, of course, can be expected to remain as confidential information; the latter most certainly are not. In that connection, the committee does not address the trade-offs between the short- and long-run efficiency consequences of the public disclosure of proprietary information and the potential benefits to transactors and ultimately for safety and soundness.

Further, the committee does not address how effective market discipline can be if the transactors with banks believe that governments will intervene and "bail out" the bank and its transactors (beyond the explicitly insured depositors). If the belief in bail-outs is pervasive, then the disclosure will be largely irrelevant, and market discipline will be largely absent. In addition, the transactors are likely to be sophisticated parties (and would have to be, in order to be able to absorb and use the elaborate menu of information disclosures recommended by the committee). Why would they not be able to protect themselves by making their own information demands (or declining to transact)? Also, why might not the ratings provided by bond rating firms provide the information that transactors need? Finally, by not endorsing the mandatory issuance of subordinated debt, the committee has forgone an important potential source of market discipline and of market pressures for information disclosure (see Calomiris and Litan, 2000).

In sum, though "market discipline" has a resounding ring, the committee's arguments for public information disclosures generally and for its specific disclosures are weak indeed. And the committee has undermined its best opportunity for achieving market discipline by failing to endorse mandatory subordinated debt.

CONCLUSION

The issues involving the appropriate information disclosures for financial conglomerates have been and will continue to be an important area for policy concern. As this chapter has argued, there are at least two audiences for information disclosures: bank regulators, and the general public. They should be distinguished, and appropriate policies should be developed for each audience.

There is little doubt that the goals of Basel II – to improve the safety and soundness of banks – are worthy. The specific measures chosen, however, are more open to question. By eschewing the three most important steps that could be taken to improve information disclosure – market value accounting (MVA) for banks' reports to regulators, daily electronic submission of those reports, and the issuance of subordinated debt – the Basel Committee has fundamentally undermined the achievement of those goals.

1 This chapter draws heavily on White (2003).
2 Throughout this chapter I will refer to "banks" broadly as covering all depositories: financial institutions that hold financial assets as their primary assets and fund themselves with "deposits" that are highly liquid (ie, withdrawable largely on demand at fixed nominal values).

3   A lender of last resort – the central bank – can provide loans to a bank and thus help it deal with depositor withdrawals. But then the central bank is effectively a creditor to the bank and must concern itself with the bank's solvency.

4   By "activities" I mean broadly any kinds of assets, liabilities, or ongoing business operations.

5   This discussion draws heavily on White (1996a) and Shull and White (1998).

6   There is also a converse possibility: that the securities affiliate touts and underwrites the equity shares of a weak company so that the commercial bank can have its loans repaid. Though this arrangement strengthens safety and soundness, it raises larger issues of investor deception that will be addressed below.

7   A defined-benefit (final-salary) pension fund is one in which an employer has promised retirees a specified level of retirement benefit payments. By contrast, a defined-payment (money-purchase) pension fund is one in which a retiree's receipts are linked to what the retiree (while employed) previously paid into the fund (along with any payments from the employer) and the subsequent investment performance of those paid-in funds.

8   This discussion draws heavily on White (1991a; 1991b); see also Kaufman *et al* (2000).

9   In the accounting literature, this is frequently described as "fair value" accounting.

10   This backward-looking, cost-based orientation is a general feature of accounting systems outside the US as well; consequently, we will refer to this orientation and its problems with references to "GAAP" considered broadly and not just applying to the US.

11   The incentives for risk-taking behaviour are likely to be driven by owners' knowledge of the market-value-based measurement of their net worth rather than by any GAAP-based measure.

12   Under some circumstances, financial institutions may not even have to sell the assets but may be able simply to reclassify them within their portfolios, from a "hold-to-maturity account" to a "held-for-sale account"; see Barta (2002).

13   Also, GAAP's slowness to recognise gains can lead companies generally to engage in uneconomic behaviour, such as a sale and the leaseback of a facility, just so the company can recognise the gain on its balance sheet.

14   The Basel Committee's backcasting exercise (BIS 2003) to examine the capital consequences of its proposed (Basel II) capital standards suffers from the same drawback.

15   The "higher-volatility" criticism of proposals that would place only some parts of the balance sheet on an MVA basis is similarly misplaced. To the extent that banks care about reported volatility, they will modify their behaviour. It is the trade-off of the increased costs of that behaviour, against the gains from the improved balance-sheet information, that should be weighed and argued.

16   This should rule out the wild overoptimism that apparently governed some of Enron's "mark-to-market" modelling and valuations.

17   This hostility can be found in BIS (1998c, 1999b, 2000b).

18   This argument is advanced forcefully by Calomiris and Litan (2000) and Kaufman *et al* (2000). See also Board of Governors and US Treasury (2000).

19   For a critique of that inclusion, see White (2002b, 2002c).

20   The committee mandates that equity holdings that are in aggregate in excess of 60% of the level of the bank's capital should not be counted as an asset for the bank. See BIS (2001b).

21   This discussion draws heavily on White (2002a); see also Easterbrook and Fischel (1984), Diamond (1985), Fishman and Haggerty (1989), Diamond and Verrecchia (1991), Elliott and Jacobson (1994) and Ball (2001).

22   In the interests of brevity, I will describe the problem in terms of lenders and borrowers; but the same issues arise with equal force with respect to investors and seekers of equity finance.

23   "We [the SEC] pursue this mandate [to protect investors] not through merit regulation – allowing only 'healthy' companies to trade their securities – but by market regulation. ... The goals of this approach are to prevent misleading *or incomplete* financial reporting and to facilitate informed decisions by investors" Levitt (1998, p. 79; emphasis added).

BIBLIOGRAPHY

Ball, R., 2001, "Infrastructure Requirements for an Economically Efficient System of Public Financial Reporting and Disclosure", in R. E. Litan and R. Herring (eds), *Brookings-Wharton Papers on Financial Services 2001* (Washington, DC: Brookings Institution), pp. 127–82.

Bank for International Settlements, 1998a, Basel Committee on Banking Supervision, "Supervision of Financial Conglomerates", February.

Bank for International Settlements, 1998b, Basel Committee on Banking Supervision, "Enhancing Bank Transparency", September.

Bank for International Settlements, 1998c, Basel Committee on Banking Supervision, "Sound Practices for Loan Accounting, Credit Risk Disclosure and Related Matters", October.

Bank for International Settlements, 1999a, Basel Committee on Banking Supervision, "Supervision of Financial Conglomerates", February.

Bank for International Settlements, 1999b, Basel Committee on Banking Supervision, "Sound Practices for Loan Accounting and Disclosure", July.

Bank for International Settlements, 2000a, Basel Committee on Banking Supervision, "A New Capital Adequacy Framework: Pillar 3", January.

Bank for International Settlements, 2000b, Basel Committee on Banking Supervision, "Report to G7 Finance Ministers and Central Bank Governors on International Accounting Standards", April.

Bank for International Settlements, 2001a, Basel Committee on Banking Supervision, "The Internal Ratings-Based Approach", January.

Bank for International Settlements, 2001b, Basel Committee on Banking Supervision, "The New Basel Capital Accord", January.

Bank for International Settlements, 2001c, Basel Committee on Banking Supervision, "The New Basel Capital Accord: An Explanatory Note", January.

Bank for International Settlements, 2001d, Basel Committee on Banking Supervision, "Overview of the New Basel Capital Accord", January.

Bank for International Settlements, 2001e, Basel Committee on Banking Supervision, "Pillar 2 (Supervisory Review Process)", January.

Bank for International Settlements, 2001f, Basel Committee on Banking Supervision, "Pillar 3 (Market Discipline)", January.

Bank for International Settlements, 2001g, Basel Committee on Banking Supervision, "The Standardized Approach to Credit Risk", January.

Bank for International Settlements, 2001h, Basel Committee on Banking Supervision, "Working Paper on Pillar 3 – Market Discipline", September.

Bank for International Settlements, 2003, "Quantitative Impact Study 3 – Overview of Global Results", May.

Barta, P., 2002, "Fannie Mae Critics Pounce on Boost in Holder Equity", *Wall Street Journal*, p. A2, 25 October.

Board of Governors of the Federal Reserve System and the US Department of the Treasury, 2000, *The Feasibility and Desirability of Mandatory Subordinated Debt* (Washington, DC), December.

337

Calomiris, C. W., and R. E. Litan, 2000, "Financial Regulation in a Global Marketplace", in R. E. Litan and A. M. Santomero (eds), *Brookings-Wharton Papers on Financial Services 2000* (Washington, DC: Brookings Institution), pp. 283–339.

Chen, Y., 1999, "Banking Panics: The Role of the First-Come, First-Served Rule and Information Externalities", *Journal of Political Economy*, **107**, October, pp. 946–68.

Diamond, D. W., 1985, "Optimal Release of Information by Firms", *Journal of Finance*, **40**, September, pp. 1071–94.

Diamond, D. W., and P. H. Dybvig, 1983, "Bank Runs, Deposit Insurance, and Liquidity", *Journal of Political Economy*, **91**, June, pp. 401–19.

Diamond, D. W., and R. E. Verrecchia, 1991, "Disclosure, Liquidity, and the Cost of Capital", *Journal of Finance*, **46**, September, pp. 1325–59.

Dye, R. A., and S. Sunder, 2001, "Why Not Allow FASB and IASB Standards to Compete in the US?" *Accounting Horizons*, **15**, September, pp. 257–71.

Easterbrook, F. H., and D. R. Fischel, 1984, "Mandatory Disclosure and the Protection of Investors", *Virginia Law Review*, **70**, pp. 669–715.

Edwards, F. R., 1979, "Banks and Securities Activities: Legal and Economic Perspectives on the Glass-Steagall Act", in L. G. Goldberg and L. J. White (eds), *The Deregulation of the Banking and Securities Industries* (Lexington, MA: Heath), pp. 273–94.

Elliott, R. K., and P. D. Jacobson, 1994, "Costs and Benefits of Business Information Disclosure", *Accounting Horizons*, **8**, December, pp. 80–96.

Engelke, G., Jr, 1990, "Mark-to-Market Accounting: What *Is* Real Value?" *Financial Managers' Statement*, **12**, January/February, pp. 33–4.

Federal Deposit Insurance Corporation, 1998, *Managing the Crisis: The FDIC and the RTC Experience, 1980–1994* (Washington, DC).

Fisher, D. J., 1992, "*Con:* Market Value Accounting Boils Down to 'Trust Me' Values", *Journal of Corporate Accounting & Finance*, **3**, Spring, pp. 327–32.

Fishman, M. J., and K. M. Haggerty, 1989, "Disclosure Decisions by Firms and the Competition for Price Efficiency", *Journal of Finance*, **44**, July, pp. 633–46.

Kaufman, G. B., *et al,* 2000, *Reforming Bank Capital Regulation: A Proposal by the US Shadow Financial Regulatory Committee* (Washington, DC: American Enterprise Institute).

Levitt, A., 1998, "The Importance of High Quality Accounting Standards", *Accounting Horizons*, **12**, March, pp. 79–82.

Morgan, D. P., 2002, "Rating Banks: Risk and Uncertainty in an Opaque Industry", *American Economic Review*, **92**, September, pp. 874–88.

Postlewaite, A., and X. Vives, 1987, "Bank Runs as an Equilibrium Phenomenon", *Journal of Political Economy*, **95**, June, pp. 485–91.

Shull, B., and L. J. White, 1998, "The Right Corporate Structure for Expanded Bank Activities", *Banking Law Journal*, **115**, May, pp. 446–76.

Sunder, S., 2002, "Regulatory Competition among Accounting Standards within and across International Boundaries", *Journal of Accounting and Public Policy*, **21**, pp. 219–34, Autumn. New Haven, CT.

Sutton, M. H., 1997, "Financial Reporting in US Capital Markets: International Dimensions", *Accounting Horizons*, **11**, June, pp. 96–102.

White, L. J., 1991a, *The S&L Debacle: Public Policy Lessons for Bank and Thrift Regulation* (New York: Oxford University Press).

White, L. J., 1991b, "The Value of Market Value Accounting for the Deposit Insurance System", *Journal of Accounting, Auditing, and Finance*, **6**, April, pp. 284–301.

White, L. J., 1996a, "The Proper Structure of Universal Banking: "Examinability and Supervisability", in A. Saunders and I. Walter (eds), *Universal Banking: Financial System Design Reconsidered* (Chicago, IL: Irwin), pp. 682–95.

White, L. J., 1996b, "Competition versus Harmonization: An Overview of International Regulation of Financial Services", in C. Barfield (ed.), *International Trade in Financial Services* (Washington, DC: American Enterprise Institute), pp. 5–48.

White, L. J., 2002a, "Globalized Securities Markets and Accounting: How Many Standards?" presented at the American Enterprise Institute Conference, "Is GAAP Worth Fighting For?", 13 March.

White, L. J., 2002b, "The Credit Rating Industry: An Industrial Organization Analysis", in R. M. Levich, G. Majnoni and C. Reinhart (eds), *Ratings, Rating Agencies and the Global Financial System* (Boston, MA: Kluwer), pp. 41–63.

White, L. J., 2002c, "An Industrial Organization Analysis of the Credit Rating Industry", in M. K. Ong (ed.), Credit Ratings: *Methodologies, Rationale and Default Risk* (London: Risk Books), pp. 85–102.

White, L. J., 2003, "What Constitutes Appropriate Disclosure for a Financial Conglomerate?" in Robert W. Litan and Richard Herring (eds), *Brookings-Wharton Papers on Financial Services 2003* (Washington, DC: Brookings), pp. 245–72.

Section 5

Implementing the Advanced Measurement Approach for Operational Risk

14

Implementing a Basel II Scenario-Based AMA for Operational Risk

Ulrich Anders and Gerrit Jan van den Brink

Dresdner Bank

BASEL II REQUIREMENTS FOR OPERATIONAL RISK

Simply speaking, operational risks are the risks originating from the firm's operational processes. Operational risk is the risk of suffering losses in processes caused by inadequacies or failures or insufficient quality in the organisation, technology, knowledge, staff, infrastructure, control function or other resources. The higher a possible loss will occur, the higher the operational risk.

With Basel II, operational risk is now subject to regulatory review: (a) the management of operational risk needs to fulfil qualitative requirements; (b) there will be a capital charge for operational risk similar to capital charges of both credit risk and market risk. With these, Basel II seems to pursue the following goals: (a) operational risk in banks should be adequately managed and (b) banks must be able to cover large operational risk losses through equity capital.

According to the current regulatory requirements, banks should:

❏ assess their operational risks;
❏ collect their losses caused by operational risks;
❏ implement operational risk indicators; and
❏ calculate and set aside risk capital.

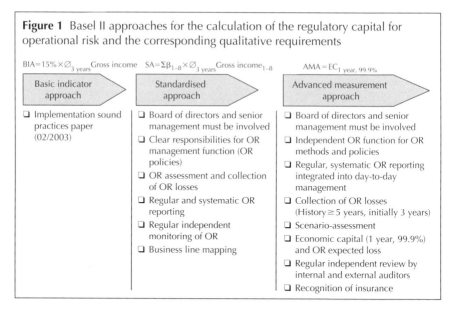

Figure 1 Basel II approaches for the calculation of the regulatory capital for operational risk and the corresponding qualitative requirements

$BIA = 15\% \times \varnothing_{3\ years}$ Gross income $SA = \Sigma\beta_{1-8} \times \varnothing_{3\ years}$ Gross income$_{1-8}$ $AMA = EC_{1\ year,\ 99.9\%}$

Basic indicator approach	Standardised approach	Advanced measurement approach
❏ Implementation sound practices paper (02/2003)	❏ Board of directors and senior management must be involved ❏ Clear responsibilities for OR management function (OR policies) ❏ OR assessment and collection of OR losses ❏ Regular and systematic OR reporting ❏ Regular independent monitoring of OR ❏ Business line mapping	❏ Board of directors and senior management must be involved ❏ Independent OR function for OR methods and policies ❏ Regular, systematic OR reporting integrated into day-to-day management ❏ Collection of OR losses (History ≥ 5 years, initially 3 years) ❏ Scenario-assessment ❏ Economic capital (1 year, 99.9%) and OR expected loss ❏ Regular independent review by internal and external auditors ❏ Recognition of insurance

Basel II has three proposed methods for the determination of the regulatory capital for operational risk:

❏ the *basic indicator approach* (BIA);
❏ the *standardised approach* (SA); and
❏ the *advanced measurement approach* (AMA).

The required capital for the basic indicator approach amounts to 15% of the average gross income of the bank over the last three years. Banks that use this approach do not need to comply with other qualitative requirements (although in some countries the sound practices for the management and supervision of operational risk will apply). Contrary to the BIA, banks applying the AMA are allowed to calculate the regulatory capital themselves by using their own internal models. These banks are subject to qualitative requirements and their implementation will be reviewed by the regulatory supervisors. The various approaches and the requirements are depicted in Figure 1.

The implementation of an AMA has the advantage that the regulatory capital based on AMA can be expected to be lower than the regulatory capital based on the BIA.

At first glance, the absolute cost for implementing the AMA seems high. However, the marginal cost is not. A considerable part of the qualitative requirements for the implementation of an AMA already have to be complied with, since either laws (such as the Sarbanes-Oxley Act) or other regulations (such as the ones regarding governance) require them or they are sensible from a risk–return management perspective anyway.

The standardised approach lies between the basic indicator approach and the AMA. The qualitative requirements of the standardised approach are – apart from the capital calculation – largely similar to those of the AMA. The implementation of the standardised approach, however, seems only reasonable for retail-oriented banks, since retail banking and retail brokerage activities will be charged with only 12% instead of the basic indicator approach's 15%.

WHAT IS A SCENARIO-BASED AMA

The Basel II proposals allow a range of alternatives within the AMA regime. They are classified as follows:[1]

❑ the *loss distribution approach* (LDA);
❑ the *scenario-based AMA* (sbAMA); and
❑ the *risk drivers and controls approach* (RDCA).[2]

Since all three types of approaches need to fulfil the qualitative information requirements – eg, to assess operational risks and to collect operational risk losses – they differ basically only in the emphasis on the information used to compute regulatory capital. The LDA puts its emphasis for the computation of regulatory capital on historical loss data, whereas the sbAMA puts its emphasis on the assessment of forward-looking "what-if" scenarios. Both approaches use Monte Carlo techniques for their capital calculation. The RDCA does likewise and then uses a series of weighted questions (some of which could be interpreted as scenarios) whose answers yield a score for the allocation of the overall capital number to individual business units. In order to better understand the rationale behind the sbAMA some basic definitions need to be given.

Risk is determined as a combination of severity and frequency of potential loss over a given time horizon. Risk can be expressed in the dimensions of potential loss severity and potential loss frequency measured in units of a given monetary unit and the number of times per year: for example, a potential loss of €10,000 three times a year, or a potential loss of €15,000 four times a year, or perhaps a potential loss of €500,000 once every hundred years. Risk is a reflection of vulnerability. The evaluation of risk should, therefore, focus on vulnerabilities. Risk can be reduced by transferring it or by improving the quality of the underlying risk factors.

The evaluation of risk is inextricably linked to scenario analysis. Scenario analysis is also applied to market risk and credit risk. In market risk the scenarios are typically based on changes in financial market prices – eg, a yield curve shift of 20 bp – and in credit risk, on changes in creditworthiness: eg, a default or downgrade of a certain customer.

Generally speaking, scenarios are potential future events. Their assessment involves answering two fundamental questions. First, what is the potential frequency of a particular scenario occurring? Second, what is its potential loss severity?

For the assessment of operational risks, the scenarios usually relate to the critical resources on which businesses depend. These resources are sometimes also called operational risk factors or drivers. Common operational risk factors are human expertise/knowledge, management, internal services/information, external services/suppliers, information technology, infrastructure (office communication, land, premises, etc.), controls against unauthorised activities or unintentional errors, controls against external criminal activities, preparation for external events (eg, catastrophes) and legal pre-requisites (eg, contracts).

The questions raised by the scenarios are:

❏ how likely can one or a combination of these resources fail for a critical period of time in a particular business context?
❏ what is the resulting negative impact?

If either the likelihood of failure over a critical time period or the impact is negligible, the bank apparently does not face any risks.

PANEL 1 SCENARIO-BASED AMA

A scenario-based AMA (sbAMA) is an approach that places the evaluation of scenarios at the centre of both capital calculation and operational risk management. A sbAMA has the following characteristics:

❏ It is focused on a forward-looking assessment of the key operational risks in an organisation, taking into account both the internal control environment and external threats.

❏ It is an approach that employs the technique of individual scenario projection in a fashion similar to market and credit risk.

❏ It is based on all available information such as expert experience, internal or external losses, key risk indicators (KRIs) and quality of control environment.

❏ It eventually leads to a sound economic capital number that helps to incentivise prudent and proactive operational risk management.

❏ It creates a forward-looking risk-management function that provides a direct link to specific business management actions and is, therefore, responsive to both changes in internal and external environment.

An sbAMA will only feed information to a capital computation model if the information is relevant to the operational risk profile of the bank. Thus, an sbAMA needs answers to the "what-if" questions in the scenario assessment.

The sbAMA comprises six main steps, which are illustrated in Figure 2 and will be individually described in the main text of the chapter.

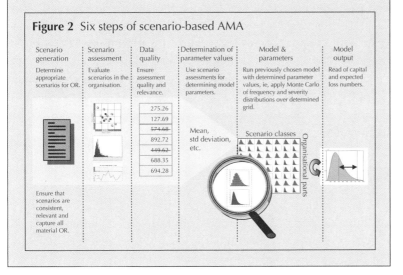

Figure 2 Six steps of scenario-based AMA

Scenario generation	Scenario assessment	Data quality	Determination of parameter values	Model & parameters	Model output
Determine appropriate scenarios for OR.	Evaluate scenarios in the organisation.	Ensure assessment quality and relevance.	Use scenario assessments for determining model parameters.	Run previously chosen model with determined parameter values, ie, apply Monte Carlo of frequency and severity distributions over determined grid.	Read of capital and expected loss numbers.

275.26
127.69
574.68
892.72
449.62
688.35
694.28

Mean, std deviation, etc.

Scenario classes

Organisational parts

Ensure that scenarios are consistent, relevant and capture all material OR.

The six steps of the scenario-based AMA presented in Panel 1 are now described in detail.

Step 1: Scenario generation

Scenario generation represents the first step of the sbAMA. The aim is to determine scenarios that capture all material operational risks. These scenarios can be applied consistently across the bank if they are relevant to specific organisational units of the bank. This is achieved by following a clearly documented procedure involving a sequence of steps.

First, all risk factors reflecting the operational risk profile (ie, vulnerabilities of the organisation) are identified from the experience of experts using all available information such as historical loss data. These risk factors can be categorised into scenario classes.

Second, this common set of scenario classes is applied to different organisational units thereby ensuring consistency across the whole organisation, even though the individual scenarios per class will differ due to the different vulnerabilities per organisational unit (eg, different IT systems).

Third, on the basis of the scenario classes, business experts determine the individual scenarios that are relevant for the organisational unit that is assessing its operational risk (eg, if an organisational unit is not vulnerable to IT failure, it does not make sense to evaluate the risk of the breakdown of IT-systems). Business experts do this based on their business knowledge, experience and expectations, while referring to relevant loss data and the full range of loss types to ensure that the scenarios identified are comprehensive as well as relevant. Here again, techniques such as guided discussions in workshops are used to steer the scenario identification in the right direction. For assessment purposes, these scenarios should be documented. An example is visualised in Figure 3.

Step 2: Scenario assessment

The second step of the sbAMA involves the assessment of the generated scenarios. This is achieved through managerial expertise based on a blend of information such as historical losses, key risk indicators, insurance coverage, the quality of relevant risk factors and the control environment, as well as relevant industry experience. The balance of the individual elements in the blend depends on the number and quality of historical data available and their relevance to the current scenario assessment, given the extent of internal and external change facing the business.

Figure 4 illustrates the result of a scenario assessment of 10 individual scenarios in a particular organisational unit. On the right-hand side, risks caused by the failure of risk factors are represented as a risk matrix, dependent on their potential loss

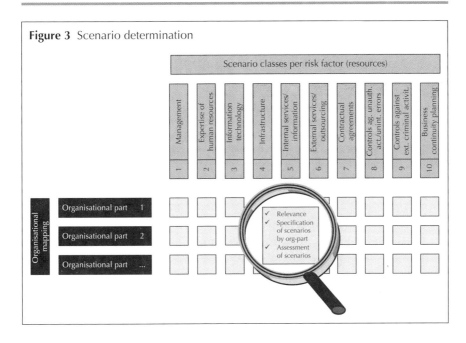

Figure 3 Scenario determination

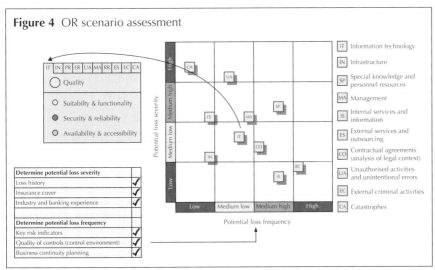

Figure 4 OR scenario assessment

frequency and severity. On the left-hand side, the quality of each risk factor is scored by way of assessing the quality dimensions of the risk factor, since the better the quality, the lower the risk becomes. The assessment of the scenario can incorporate loss history, insurance coverage, industry and banking experience, key risk indicators, quality of the control environment and the existence of business continuity planning.

It is important to note that the "what-if" question in the scenario drives which data should be used. For instance, the use of historical data may be preferred for evaluating the potential frequency and severity of a particular scenario, where good quality data are available and the level of change is minimal.

Where insufficient historical data are available, experts must estimate the potential loss frequency and severity for a specific scenario, given their experience and business knowledge. Similar to the process for scenario generation, the assessment is performed in the form of guided discussions or formalised questionnaires to ensure comprehensiveness and consistency.

Frequency and severity estimates should reflect typical and upper bound values. In order to achieve credible results, scenario assessment requires clear definitions and guidelines enshrined in a standardised process, appropriate training and independent challenge of the experts' estimates. Furthermore, it is key that the assessment be based on a clear view of the business area activities or processes and that corresponding data sources be available.

A scenario assessment needs a defined workflow to ensure that the desired quality is achieved and that the results are consistent. The central operational risk oversight function should set up the questionnaire. It will also set up coordinators for the organisational units where this is necessary.

The coordinators will then determine the business experts who will fill in the questionnaires (so called *assessors*) for a particular part of an organisational unit and who will approve the questionnaires (so called *approvers*). In addition, the coordinators will also assign reading rights to certain authorised persons, including themselves. These activities are supported by the central operational risk oversight function of the organisation.

In order to implement the workflow described, a technical platform is required that, ideally, is intranet-based so that the scenario assessment questionnaire can easily be distributed in a secure environment across the bank. The intranet tool must also provide for an administration tool that allows questionnaires, users and their roles

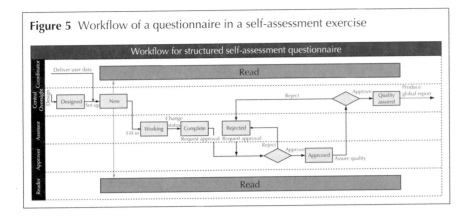

Figure 5 Workflow of a questionnaire in a self-assessment exercise

to be set up. It is also important that the experts who participate in the self-assessment immediately obtain the scenario assessment report that is produced with the help of their input. This makes the assessment process transparent, and helps the experts to understand the connection between their input and the output in the form of the risk matrix. Furthermore, every mathematical computation within the self-assessment process, in particular for the aggregation of risk matrices, must be well documented and easy to understand, otherwise it is unlikely to be accepted within the organisation.

Step 3: Data quality
Once the scenario assessment has been completed, the validity of the results must be ensured. Therefore, the third step of the sbAMA ensures that the resulting data from the scenario assessment (which will subsequently be used for risk capital modelling) reflect the operational risk profile and are of good quality. In other words any under- or overevaluation of frequency or severity needs to be corrected in the data quality-assurance process.

The validation of the scenario assessments can be based on (a) organisational information, (b) financial information, such as losses, (c) key risk indicators, and (d) psychometric analysis of reliability and validity of the completed questionnaires themselves. More specifically,

(a) The organisational validation works in three independent stages. First, in order to ensure quality of input, each expert's evaluation needs to be approved by a different person. Second, the internal audit function reviews the expert's evaluation as part of their internal audit. Wherever they perform an audit of processes, they review whether the scenario assessment reveals a good reflection of risk and quality. Third, the independent oversight function has the task of ensuring consistency across different questionnaires as well as the quality of the answers. This is achieved by accompanying the completion of the questionnaires (in person or by means of a call centre), by comparing similar processes that have been evaluated by different experts, and by examining questionnaires in detail.

(b) The scenario assessment provides estimates of potential loss severity and potential loss frequency for operational risk categories. The product of the two estimates is called *operational risk cost*. Operational risk costs are used for provisioning against individual operational losses. Operational risk costs are usually applied to products or business lines, and are booked into a standard risk cost account. They are called *cost* because they add to the costs of doing business. If they are used in the company, they are explicitly reported in the internal management accounts. Individual actual operational losses are then covered from the operational risk cost account. The way to validate the scenario assessments is to compare the sum of the actual losses against the total standard risk costs. Over a sequence of years, the operational risk costs should be sufficient to provide cover for all sorts of expected operational losses.

(c) Key risk indicators are used to indicate operational risks or a change in the operational risk profile. They need to be set up specifically for individual activities if they are to be meaningful, since different activities may require different indicators, and even the same indicator may need a different interpretation in different situations, such as different warning levels. An analysis of a particular set of key risk indicators for a particular activity will reveal whether their past development is consistent with the scenario assessments for this activity.

(d) The science of psychometrics provides a number of well-proven statistical methodologies for the purpose of evaluating completed questionnaires. Such methodologies are principal component analysis, dependency analysis, correlation test

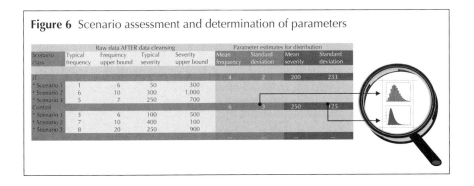

Figure 6 Scenario assessment and determination of parameters

| Scenario class | Raw data AFTER data cleansing | | | | Parameter estimates for distribution | | | |
	Typical frequency	Frequency upper bound	Typical severity	Severity upper bound	Mean frequency	Standard deviation	Mean severity	Standard deviation
IT					4	2	200	233
• Scenario 1	1	6	50	300				
• Scenario 2	6	10	300	1,000				
• Scenario 3	5	7	250	700				
Control					6	3	250	125
• Scenario 1	3	6	100	500				
• Scenario 2	7	10	400	100				
• Scenario 3	8	20	250	900				
	...				...		...	...

and consistency statistics. They help to derive considerable knowledge about both individual questionnaires and the set of questionnaires as a whole. The methodologies also allow for filtering out deviating questionnaires for a more detailed analysis and subsequent quality assurance.

If all these validation techniques are applied prudently, the overall result of the questionnaire exercise will be of a very high quality and its data can serve as a valid basis for further capital calculations.

Step 4: Determination of parameter values
In the fourth step, any required parameter values for the distributions employed in the model are determined from the scenario assessment data, once their quality is assured.

For instance, if the model employs an individual frequency and severity distribution for each cell of the matrix that combines scenario classes and organisational units, each frequency and severity distribution must be provided with the estimates of its individual parameter values, ie, usually at least mean and standard deviation. The parameter values for each individual distribution can be determined by utilising the usual statistical techniques for parameter estimation on the basis of the data that results from the scenario assessments, which fall into the same cell. This is illustrated in Figure 6.

The process of determining reliable parameter estimates usually is a manual one and needs to be performed by a trained expert. The process cannot be automated; however, it can be supported by standard off-the-shelf statistical software packages.

Step 5: Model and parameters

The fifth step deals with the application of the model, which means that at this point in time the model must already exist. This is important because the risk model also reflects the scenario classes and determines the necessary parameter values. The way to build a good risk model has been described in Anders (2003).

In this step the determined parameters are entered into the risk model. The usual models use Monte Carlo simulation techniques to aggregate all individual distributions per scenario class and organisational unit into an overall aggregated potential loss distribution.

Basically, a Monte Carlo simulation is a big dice-rolling exercise where the dice are shaped such that their different sides fall with different frequencies (given by the corresponding distributions). One set of dice is for the frequency distributions, the other set for the severity distributions. Each iteration starts with a roll of one of the frequency dice. The number that falls determines how often the corresponding severity die has to be rolled. Say, for instance, the frequency die shows 3. This means that we roll the corresponding severity die 3 times. The severities are all added up to make the potential loss for this iteration. This procedure is repeated many times, resulting in the corresponding number of potential losses. The histogram of these potential losses makes up the overall aggregated loss distribution. The overall procedure and the resulting aggregated potential loss distribution are illustrated in Figure 7.

Step 6: Model output

The sixth step of the sbAMA is the output of the risk capital model. Risk capital is the amount of capital to protect the company with a certain probability against insolvency due to high severity losses. Risk capital therefore expresses the overall potential loss severity for a given potential loss probability. Risk capital is the output from a risk model. Risk capital must be justifiable in size and based on a consistent risk model that is applied across and within organisations. Regulatory capital is risk capital for which the regulators set the probability against insolvency. Economic capital is risk capital for which the probability is determined by the internal economic reasoning of the bank through the use of some internal model. The computation of economic capital and regulatory capital should

Figure 7 Compounding distributions with parameter values $P_1 \ldots P_k$ by help of Monte Carlo, where the parameter values are estimated on the basis of risk profiles or historic loss data corresponding to defined scenarios

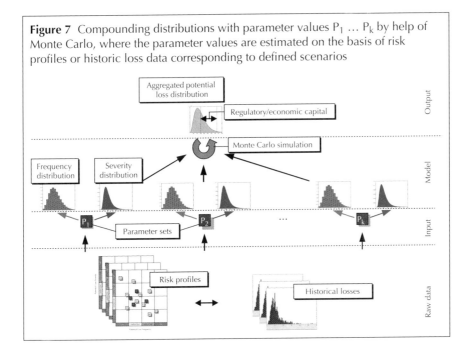

ideally result from the same model. However, the model parameters and assumptions may differ due to a differing rationale or restriction set by the regulators.

From the overall loss distribution, values for economic or regulatory capital can be derived by identifying the quantile we are interested in. The quantile is the absolute value that corresponds to a given percentile. For example, the 99-percentile of the histogram of these potential losses is reflected by the amount that is greater than 99% and smaller than 1% of all potential losses. The difference between the quantile corresponding to the percentile in the tail (say 99%) and the mean of the distribution is the economic capital for the chosen percentile. The mean is sometimes called *expected* (potential) loss and the difference between the quantile and the expected loss is usually called *unexpected* (potential) loss.

Further, valuable management information can be derived from the calculations. It can easily be demonstrated how much a difference in scenario assessments affects the overall model outputs in terms of economic or regulatory capital. This not only provides a basis for sensitivity analysis on the model but also produces the right incentive, since managers can, *ex ante*, see the effect on risk capital that can be achieved by improving their operational risk profile.

THE IMPACT OF ECONOMIC CAPITAL
The aim of economic capital calculation

The quantification of operational risks cannot be regarded as a goal in itself. The higher-level goal is an improvement in the management of operational risks. At the same time, this objective imposes the general conditions for quantification issues. The methodological issues concerning the models used (based on different distributions) and the interpretations of the parameters should also be checked against this higher-level goal.

The objectives derived from this higher-level goal for the quantification of operational risks can be divided into two categories: (i) supervisory objectives and (ii) management objectives within the bank.

The supervisory objectives can be summarised as follows. The optimisation of risk management is implemented through risk-sensitive capital adequacy in order to achieve a robust overall financial system. As soon as the regulatory capital requirements exceed the existing regulatory capital, the bank is not allowed to take the risk. In this case, it must first remove other existing risks before it can take new risks. The supervisory objectives therefore limit the risks to which a bank can be exposed to. By limiting the operational risk through capital adequacy requirements, the quality of the risk management becomes a competitive advantage. The bank with the best risk-management system in place will be allowed to have the least capital requirement for operational risks. The released capital can then be used for other risk types and to generate other sources of income.

The management objectives within the bank are as follows:

❑ improvement of risk awareness within the bank;
❑ optimisation of risk–return relationship;
❑ adequate pricing of banking products; and
❑ improvement of organisational procedures.

It is perhaps not directly apparent that the quantification of operational risks can improve risk awareness within the bank. It is often asserted that a quality-based approach is sufficient to raise the level of risk awareness. Various risk-assessment methods are used to evaluate the amount of the loss – or even the losses arising from operational risk events – from the qualitative aspect by subdividing them into various classes (such as "high", "medium", "low"). Such a scale of evaluation is not unusual – particularly among so-called "self-assessments". Dresdner Bank also had a qualitative perspective in its first self-assessment some years back. In the following self-assessments, however, experts were asked to estimate the frequency and amount of the loss in absolute terms, ie, number of times per year and EURO amounts. The result was that the experts arrived at different evaluations, which, in turn, also affected particularly the implementation of risk-mitigating actions. A loss potential in real monetary terms brings the reality and extent of a potential loss into sharper focus than the mere designation of, say "high" risk.

The second objective is the improvement of the risk–return relationship of the bank. In order to illustrate the relationship between risk and return in terms of figures, quantification of the risk is imperative. Bank management attempts to use the shareholders' equity to achieve the maximum profit while taking into account the risk taken.

The third objective refers to the pricing of banking products. It is meaningful only if the risks are adequately taken into account. That is not to say that all costs can be passed on directly to the customer. The bank should, however, have as complete an overview as possible of the costs for each product. This becomes all the more important when the production chain of the financial institutions is broken down into separate units. Particular consideration should be given, in this respect, to any plans to outsource production process activities. If a payment transaction service provider does not include the operational risk costs and equity rate for the risk capital for operational risks in the calculation of product costs, then there is a great danger that the underlying business model will not be profitable.

The final objective of quantification of operational risks is the improvement of organisational procedures. If, following quantification, the bank notices capital concentrations on a number of processes, then that is a good starting point for further analysis. Similarly, redundancies and inefficiencies in the organisational procedures can be revealed, which would lead to unnecessary tie-ups of risk capital. The causes of the capital tie-up should be established in order to draw up suitable alternative solutions. Particular consideration may be given to the implementation of appropriate control measures and the transfer of risk to insurances.

Impact of economic capital on business decisions

If specification of risk capital were an end in itself the above mentioned objectives are unlikely to be achieved. The calculated risk capital must now be used in such a way that incentives are created for improved management of operational risks. For this purpose one can make use of the performance measures that are already defined for the computation of risk-return-relationships in practice.

In addition to the *return on risk-adjusted capital* (RoRAC), which is calculated as follows,

$$\text{RoRAC} = \frac{\text{Net income} - \text{Standard risk cost}}{\text{Risk capital}}$$

the *economic value-added* (EVA) is also used. EVA is determined as follows:

$$\text{EVA} = \text{Net income} - \text{Standard risk costs} \\ - \text{Rate of capital} \times \text{Risk capital}$$

If such performance measures are incorporated in the incentive system, then the managers responsible will also be incentivised to take care of the operational risk. An incentive system works, however, only if the following principles are adhered to:

❑ Remuneration for good operational risk management should be up-to-date.
❑ Remuneration should be in a comprehensible relationship to the actions implemented.
❑ Remuneration should be given only if implementation of the actions can be established objectively.

Specifications of incentives should be independent of the decision-making competence of the assessing manager. Mixtures of "compensations" with other remuneration components should be avoided.

Determination of risk capital has another advantage. It resolves the difficulty of representing the benefit of risk-reducing actions.

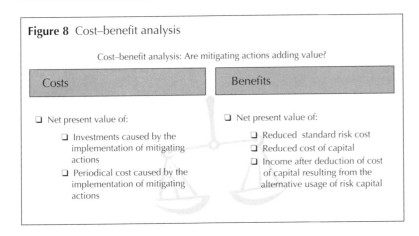

Figure 8 Cost–benefit analysis

Cost–benefit analysis: Are mitigating actions adding value?

Costs	Benefits

❏ Net present value of:

    ❏ Investments caused by the implementation of mitigating actions

    ❏ Periodical cost caused by the implementation of mitigating actions

❏ Net present value of:

    ❏ Reduced standard risk cost
    ❏ Reduced cost of capital
    ❏ Income after deduction of cost of capital resulting from the alternative usage of risk capital

Such actions cost money, and therefore must be justified particularly in times when banks have a strong focus on cost savings. Figure 8 will help to explain the cost-benefit-analysis of possible risk-mitigating actions.

The following procedure describes the individual steps that are needed in order to identify possible risk-mitigating actions:

1. *analysis* of the risk drivers that contribute most to the calculated risk capital;
2. *determination* of risk-mitigating actions that help to reduce capital contributions of risk drivers;
3. *estimation* of the associated initial and periodic costs of possible actions;
4. *expert assessment* of the effect of the actions taken on the level of operational risk costs and risk capital;
5. *calculation* of the capital, taking into account the actions; and
6. *calculation* of the present value of the costs and benefits (reduced cost of capital and reduced operational risk cost).

It is possible to go one step further in the analysis. If capital is sparse the freed-up capital might be used for credit or market risk in order to generate extra income. This component can also be considered in the cost-benefit analysis as an "opportunity profit".

If the calculated present value is positive, then it is worthwhile to perform the evaluated risk-reducing action.

PANEL 2 IMPLEMENTATION IN PRACTICE – THE DRESDNER BANK CASE

In contrast to market and credit risk, operational risk deals with the whole area of the bank's business activity. That means that the topic is not restricted to a relatively small number of specialists, but must reach, instead, to a large number of business managers. Consequently, two indispensable preconditions must be created: (a) clear organisational structure and (b) clear, comprehensible and basic definitions so that everybody knows what is being talked about and what language is used in order to maintain clarity. As a rule, both are recognised as self-evident, but are portrayed as extremely time-consuming in terms of organisational implementation of the Basel II Operational Risk requirements.

The next step should be taken only when this has been achieved. This step consists of defining reporting templates on the elements of operational risk. Reporting templates then produces the information requirements to draw up the reports. If these requirements are known, then it is necessary to specify the work processes of how the information should be collected. In the final stage, the process is automated, where necessary, by means of an IT system.

The following sections describe the IT system ORTOS (see Figure 9) used by Dresdner Bank, not to present the IT system itself, but rather to explain in specific terms the following points in connection with the system: the benefit of individual procedures, the mechanism used to collect data, the aim of data collection in the form of reports, and the form of the organisational implementation.

Product flows with STORM

Product flow mapping is the systematic recording of business processes. In order to be able to record such processes in full, it is best

---

Figure 9 ORTOS – Operational risk tool suite

STORM II ❏ Product flows by help of an *Organisational mapping*

GOLD II ❏ Weaknesses by help of an *Operational risk loss collection and analysis*

TESSA III ❏ Risks by help of a *Structured self-assessment*

KORIS ❏ Day-to-day monitoring by help of *Key risk indicators*

OPEC II ❏ Regulatory/economic capital by help of a *Statistical model*

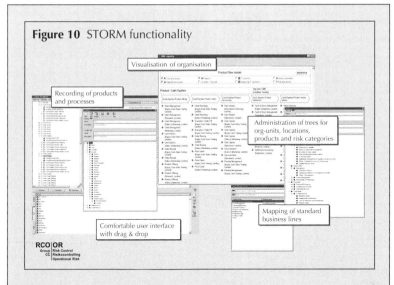

Figure 10 STORM functionality

to follow the product flows of the organisation. In doing so, it is necessary to ask which business processes exist in order to offer, sell, deliver, calculate or administer a product to an external customer. Recording the processes is a prerequisite for being able to allocate to them assessments, losses or indicators for operational risks (see also Anders and Sandstedt, 2003a).

STORM (Support Tool for Operational Risk Mapping) is a central IT application for bank-wide recording of processes using a company's product flows and staff tasks as a starting point.

The product flow is the path taken by a bank product in several stages through the processes of the organisation. It begins with the tender, and continues through the sale, production and fulfilment of the product, and ends with its administration. Staff tasks are tasks that an organisation must fulfil due to strategic, legal and regulatory requirements (eg, preparation of a balance sheet, internal audit). The recording of processes with STORM is used as a basis for controlling operational risks, as operational risks arise in the bank's processes as a result of errors or shortcomings. Risk-controlling maintains the data centrally in STORM in conjunction with the organisational units. The organisational units monitor the accuracy of entries using visual reports. Data maintenance is ongoing. In order to keep maintenance effort and costs to a minimum, the organisational units are included at not so granular a level. Products and locations change comparatively rarely, and are therefore recorded in more detail.

STORM represents a basis for data interchange between the ORTOS systems and structured risk analysis by organisational unit, location of product. For this purpose, STORM administers all of the hierarchies for the categories for their risk data by cause, event and effect, and enables them to be changed. Products can be brought together in hierarchical product groups. STORM supplies this data to TESSA, GOLD and KORIS, ie, the users of these systems see the STORM data as a categorisation of their relevant loss, risk and indicator data. The STORM data are available to the OR coordinators of the corporate divisions, corporate centre units and subsidiaries. The information recorded in STORM can be called up in the form of analyses and reports.

Loss data collection with GOLD

Collection and analysis of *loss data* is necessary to understand the occurrence of current losses from operational risks in business processes (see also Anders and Platz, 2003). Losses that occur on a regular basis as a result of the same causes can be avoided by making changes to the underlying processes. For this reason, loss data from operational risks is allocated to the business processes and classified by risk cause category, event type and effect type. The risk cause categories must be identical to those used in the self-assessment so that a comparison is possible between the assessment and materialisation of operational risks. The losses from operational risks are also used to validate both evaluations from the self-assessment and the level of the calculated risk capital.

GOLD (Global Operational Risk Loss Database) is a software application that enables the collection, analysis, reporting and archiving of losses from operational risks. The software is an intranet-based application that can be used throughout the group.

Losses from operational risks arise from weaknesses or errors in processes. The financial impact of the losses can be found in the profit-and-loss account, eg, payment of damages, goodwill payments or write-offs.

One of the tasks of operational risk-controlling units consists in analysing the causes of losses. The prerequisite for this is the consistent collection of losses that are recorded using the same pattern. GOLD supports this approach. Losses from operational risks are generally found on the bank's expense accounts – a systematic analysis or group-wide consistent analysis is not possible, however, on this basis. This weakness is remedied by the use of GOLD.

In principle, losses can occur in all processes. Therefore, all employees in the bank group have the facility to record a loss in GOLD. In order to ensure the quality of the data input, a work process has been implemented in GOLD. Reported losses must be accepted by the person with the responsibility for the budget of the process within the work process. This guarantees a justified allocation of a loss and an incentive to remedy an error. The processes are maintained in the STORM module, which is accessed by GOLD.

Figure 11 GOLD functionality

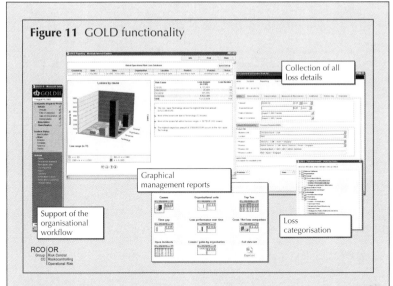

The GOLD workflow is supported by sending emails. It ensures that superiors are kept informed of losses and that they must confirm losses within their approval authority. All information that describes a loss with sufficient accuracy is recorded in GOLD. For an analysis to be meaningful, a minimum level of information is required, eg, the date of the discovery and its occurrence, and a description and the causes of a loss.

Self-assessment with TESSA

TESSA (Technical Structured Self-Assessment) is an intranet application for the systematic identification and assessment of operational risks using a structured self-assessment. The structured self-assessment is based on a rigidly structured questionnaire, which is used by experts in the organisational units to assess the processes of their relevant working area in respect of operational risks.

TESSA can record risk and quality assessments in a structured fashion and represent them clearly. The system makes risk assessments transparent by reporting the relevant risk causes by estimated amount of loss and loss frequency in the risk matrix presented. This report is supplemented by a quality evaluation of the risk factors in the processes. If the quality is not appropriate in relation to the risk, then there is a need for action on the part of management.

The risk assessments are processed in a report, either separately for each questionnaire, or in aggregated form over several questionnaires. Aggregation can be via the organisational unit, location or product. As a prerequisite, the questionnaires must be allocated to the processes recorded with STORM that are to be evaluated.

Figure 12 TESSA functionality

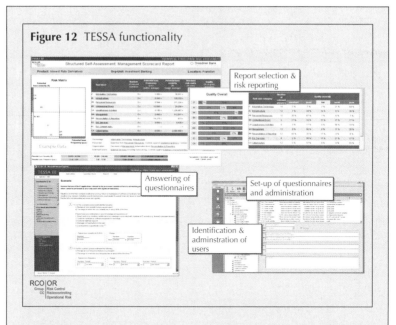

The TESSA questions on operational risks are based on defined scenarios, eg, "failure of an important (to be determined) IT system over a critical (to be specified) time period". For each scenario, an expert estimates both the probability with which it could occur and the severity of the potential loss.

The questions on quality in the relevant processes are arranged according to the criteria of functionality, security and availability. Furthermore, information on risk-reducing measures and other problem areas per risk cause are collected in the questionnaire. The answers to the questionnaires are input locally by those questioned via the intranet in TESSA.

The participants are nominated by the organisational units in such a way that they are able to assess the processes of their relevant unit competently in respect of risk and quality. The risk assessment of the experts is checked for conclusiveness by the risk control unit using the losses from operational risks that have actually occurred and that are registered in the central loss database (GOLD) and collected continuously by the organisational units. In addition, Audit, as part of its process-related test procedures, checks the quality of the risk process for operational risks in the organisational units.

Risk indicators with KORIS

KORIS (Key Operational Risk Indicator System) is an intranet application that supports the collection, analysis and reporting of

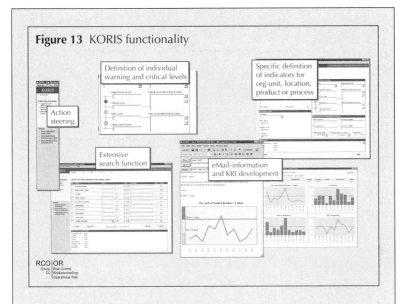

Figure 13 KORIS functionality

risk indicators for the early identification and monitoring of operational risks.

Risk indicators are values that are designed to deliver early-warning signals for changes in the operational risk profile of business processes or business areas. An early-warning signal is generated when an indicator exceeds an individually defined threshold value. The risk indicators must have a predictive capability in order to give management sufficient time to respond to indicated operational risks. For example, the risk indicator "utilisation of capacity of the processing IT system" is used to evaluate the risk-factor information technology in the securities handling process. If a threshold value of, for example, 85% utilisation is exceeded, then an early-warning signal is generated for the management responsible.

KORIS is used to support the management responsible for day-to-day monitoring. Analysis of the risk indicators provides management with up-to-date information about changes to the operational risk profile of the bank in order that impending losses from operational risks can be countered in good time by taking the appropriate measures.

Risk indicators can be defined individually; allocation to location, organisational unit, product, process, risk category and collection frequencies are possible. Each risk indicator is assigned to a person responsible (including deputies) who enters the required data in the system. Alternatively, the risk indicators can be read into KORIS automatically via a standard interface.

When defining a risk indicator, threshold values (for warning and critical values) are issued. If the values of an indicator exceed these

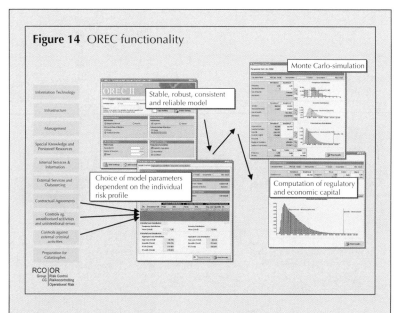

Figure 14 OREC functionality

threshold values, then persons stored in KORIS are automatically notified by email. This ensures up-to-date reporting, which guarantees the maximum time for a response.

In addition to the notification function, aggregated risk indicators can be shown based on the data recorded. These indicators display the processes of several risk indicators over a period of time together in graphical form. Furthermore, KORIS offers the opportunity to represent the values of a risk indicator graphically over time, thus enabling a trend analysis. Negative trends can therefore be identified and remedied at an early stage. KORIS can be used to create graphic reports automatically, eg, for regular management reporting.

Risk capital with OREC

In order to summarise the data collected in the organisation using self-assessment, loss data and risk indicators, the so-called risk capital for operational risks is calculated using a Monte Carlo method. Risk capital expresses an organisation's capital requirements with which unexpected losses from operational risks can be covered with a degree of certainty without the company's becoming insolvent. The risk capital must be broken down into organisational units, locations or business areas and product lines. It is used to compare the risk profiles within the organisation over a specific period of time, or between specific risk types, such as market risks, credit risks or operational risks (see also Anders, 2003; Brink, 2003b).

The OREC (Operational Risk Economic Capital) engine is an IT application for calculating the economic and regulatory risk capital for operational risks. OREC allows the simple, documented, quality-assured and user-driven application of a statistical model for calculating risk capital for operational risks.

To calculate risk capital, a statistical model is required that is robust, consistent and stable over time. This should rule out the possibility of changes to the risk capital being caused by changes to the statistical model. The model used in OREC for calculating the risk capital is a standard model whose origins lie in actuarial theory. It is based on distributions for the frequency and severity of potential losses that are brought together using Monte Carlo simulation to form an aggregated distribution of potential losses. The unexpected loss is calculated from the aggregated distribution of potential losses as the difference between a previously defined quantile (eg, 99%) and the expected loss. This measure is used to describe the risk profile, so that comparisons can be drawn over time and across various business areas.

Calculation of risk capital with OREC is divided into four stages:

1. *Specification of the model:* Any risk factors can be used. Various special distributions can be taken into account for the associated distribution assumptions of the amount of loss and the frequency of the loss. When calculating the aggregated potential loss distribution, it is possible to specify whether or not the risk categories are dependent on each other.
2. *Choice of parameters:* The model parameters that are specified based on the underlying data can either be imported into OREC automatically or entered manually.
3. *Calculation of results:* The calculated results are displayed on the screen. They can be printed out, exported or processed further.
4. *Documentation of results:* The calculation configurations, parameter groups and calculations carried out can be stored separately from each other. A clear summary of the results can be printed out.

1   http://www.newyorkfed.org/pihome/news/speeches/2003/con052903.html.
2   The risk drivers and controls approach (RDCA) was formerly called the scorecard approach.

BIBLIOGRAPHY

Anders, U., 2003, "The Path to Operational Risk Economic Capital", in Carol Alexander, *Operational Risk: Regulation, Analysis, Management, FT* (Prentice Hall), pp. 215–26.

Anders, U., and J. Platz, 2003, "Creating an Op Risk Loss Collection Framework", *Operational Risk*, September, pp. 24–7.

Anders, U., and M. Sandstedt, 2003a, "An Operational Risk Scorecard Approach", *Risk*, S 48–51, January.

Anders, U., and M. Sandstedt, 2003b, "Self-Assessments for Scorecards", *Risk*, S 39–42, February.

Brink, G. J. van den, 2002, *Operational Risk, the New Challenge for Banks* (Palgrave Publishers Ltd).

Brink, G. J. van den, 2003a, "From Data Entry to Process Control", in Brink, G. J. van den (Ed.), *Banking/ Trading – Operations Management* (Palgrave Publishers Ltd).

Brink, G. J. van den, 2003b, "Quantifizierung operationeller Risiken, Ein Weg zur Einbettung in den Management-Zyklus", in *Risk News*, **01**, pp. 26–36.

15

Loss Distribution Approach in Practice

Antoine Frachot; Olivier Moudoulaud; Thierry Roncalli*

Groupe de Recherche Opérationnelle;
Global Risk Management; Credit Agricole SA

INTRODUCTION

Intense research has been conducted over the past few years to address issues raised by the practical implementation of the advanced measurement approaches (AMA), in particular the loss distribution approach (LDA), presented in the Basel II proposals. Indeed, we believe that most of these issues are now sufficiently clarified to allow for a survey on operational risk quantitative techniques. This is the aim of this chapter.

The roots of quantitative LDA come from actuarial techniques that have been used by the insurance industry for a number of years. It is, of course, a very natural idea, apart from the fact that

*Antoine Frachot is the head of the Groupe de Recherche Opérationnelle (GRO) and Thierry Roncalli is the head of Risk Analytics at GRO. Olivier Moudoulaud is research assistant at GRO. Correspondence should be addressed to Groupe de Recherche Opérationnelle, Crédit Lyonnais, Le Centorial, 8, rue du Quatre Septembre, 75002 Paris, France (antoine.frachot@creditlyonnais.fr or thierry.roncalli@creditlyonnais.fr). We warmly thank Maxime Pennequin, global head of OpRisk management at Crédit Agricole/Crédit Lyonnais. We would like to give a special thank to John S Walter (Bank of America) for his valuable comments and many enlightening discussions. We are also grateful to Patrick de Fontnouvelle (Federal Reserve of Boston) and all ITWG members, in particular Andrea Colombo (Banca Intesa), Riccardo Cateni (Banca Intesa), Yimin Shih (Citigroup), Joseph Sabatini (JP Morgan), Georges Graziani (Bank of Montreal) and Tony Peccia (Bank of Montreal). Finally, we would like to thank David Kurtz (GRO, Crédit Lyonnais) for discussions on durations in Poisson processes.

actuarial techniques could not be imported directly without due regard for the specific needs of operational risks, most notably the reporting bias and the paucity of data. Quantitative people who have looked closely at empirical data will agree that these two features about OpRisk data have a dramatic impact on capital charge. However, these two facets about data cannot be neglected altogether even though they introduce greater complexities and more sophisticated computations than most practitioners prefer.

This chapter aims to describe how a full loss distribution approach can be implemented in practice and how both quantitative and qualitative points of view can be reconciled. We chose to be as pragmatic as possible and not more sophisticated than necessary. In particular, we chose to drop some interesting issues since they would require too much effort in return for too little benefit in terms of a more accurate capital charge calculation. We had benefited from our experience at Credit Lyonnais and discussions we had been involved in over the last couple of years. In some sense, we mimic the process that gave birth to the so-called internal ratings-based (IRB) formulae proposed by the Basel Committee for credit risk: quants first started from a highly sophisticated credit risk model and downgraded it until it turned out to be an acceptable, implementable and pragmatic proxy of the "correct" capital charge. As an example it is worth noting that, at some time in the downgrading process, it appeared that simplicity demands that credit risk is assumed to be driven by only one source of risk, which is furthermore assumed to be normally distributed. All credit risk specialists will agree on the point that both one-factor and normal distribution assumptions are very simplistic but unrealistic assumptions, so that the resulting capital charge is accurate enough to represent an acceptable measure of risk. We tried to follow the approach here.

The second contribution of this chapter is to give some numerical calculations of the accuracy of capital charge estimates. Since the severity and frequency estimations are processed with few available data, it is crucial to have a clear view of the inaccuracy of capital charge estimates. Furthermore, an estimate of the inaccuracy is an important tool for determining the number of losses (both external and internal) that are necessary to obtain a reliable estimate of the capital charge.

This chapter follows the practical steps below for implementing an LDA:

❑ Step 1: severity estimation;
❑ Step 2: frequency estimation;
❑ Step 3: capital charge computations;
❑ Step 4: confidence interval;
❑ Step 5: self-assessment and scenario analysis.

For each of these steps, we try to give illustrative examples. We also relegate all the demanding mathematics into panels. This hopefully allows for a more reader-friendly chapter.

SEVERITY ESTIMATION

This is probably the most difficult task. Because available loss data are plagued by various sources of bias, textbook techniques cannot be used directly. This is the unfortunate case where our require- ments – simplicity and accuracy – contradict each other. Treating data as if they were textbook, unbiased data for the sake of sim- plicity is unacceptable, since it may lead to highly inaccurate and entirely flawed capital charge (see Baud, Frachot and Roncalli, 2003; de Fontnouvelle *et al*, 2003). Therefore, we really have to accept some level of complexity. It is, however, possible to make simplying assumptions that deteriorate the accuracy of capital charge to an acceptable extent.

Scaling issues and reporting biases

Let us consider that the severity distribution has to be estimated from, say, m sets of loss data coming from m different "providers" (with "provider" meaning either a business unit within a bank or an external entity/consortium). Severity calibration is a matter of choice that depends on either of the following two cases:

Case 1
The m sources of loss data are assumed to be drawn from the same primary probability distribution but loss data are reported accord- ing to some (possible) different thresholds. In other words, when we pool the m sources of data together, we are not mixing data that would be different in nature. We are just mixing similar data but these data are "packaged" differently.

Case 2

The m sources of loss data come from different primary probability distributions and thus have to be rescaled. In addition, they may also be reported according to some different thresholds. In this case, it really means that we try to mix data that are fundamentally different in nature.

We argue that Case 2 is obviously the more general case and certainly the more realistic case. Who would contradict the fact that "external fraud" losses, for example, are structurally different from one country to another, from one large bank compared with a small one, etc? However, Case 2 is too complex to be addressed properly and the benefits would probably not be worth the effort. There are some reasons why we advocate this position.

First, even though some tentative work has been done to rescale severity distributions (see Shih, Samad-Khan and Medapa, 2000), such a task requires large sets of data and sets of data coming from different sources (ie, external and internal). It is unreasonable to assume that this is always feasible for all risk types. There is no doubt that the OpRisk community will investigate this point in the coming years when datasets will get larger and more robust. But for now it is unrealistic to consider that a reliable scaling function can be estimated.

Second, scaling formulae must be derived for each bank. Nothing ensures that scaling formulae can be imported from one bank to another bank. The scaling formula is a mechanical transformation that says how the "internal" severity distribution is to be compared with the "external" one. As a result, if we accept the logic of Case 2 above, we should acknowledge that each bank may have to estimate its own scaling formula.

Third, there may be more differences between two business units within a bank (for example, if they operate in rather different countries) than one between an internal business line and an external one. Hence, if we accept the logic of Case 2, we should also think of deriving a scaling formula for data coming from two different business lines within the bank. This is certainly hard work, which is beyond the resources dedicated to OpRisk in our banking institutions.

Last, but not least, some remarkable work done by de Fontnouvelle *et al*, 2003 shows that, empirically speaking, scaling issues are not so dramatic. The authors provided evidence that there are great similarities between different sources of loss data (eg, OpVantage, OpRisk Analytics), *once reporting biases have been properly corrected.*

Our suggestion is to abandon Case 2 and to consider that reporting bias is the most important issue, in the same spirit as in Fontnouvelle *et al*, 2003. Perhaps Case 2 and the scaling issue should be left for some future Basel III discussion. As a result, the task of calibrating severity distributions is made simpler as only reporting biases have to be considered.

How to adjust for reporting bias?

Since loss data are reported conditionally on being lower than some threshold, severity estimation is subsequently affected in the sense that the sample severity distribution (ie, the severity distribution of reported losses) is different from the unconditional one (ie, the severity distribution one would obtain if all losses were reported). Unfortunately, the unconditional distribution is the more relevant for calculating capital charge and also for being able to pool different sources of data in a proper way. As a consequence, linking the sample distribution to the unconditional one is a necessary task.

Accordingly, the sample distribution is in fact a conditional distribution, which must be recognised as such when writing the maximum likelihood (ML) program. This point is now widely acknowledged (see Baud, Frachot and Roncalli, 2002; Fontnouvelle *et al*, 2003) even though solving such a conditional ML program is not so easy. Furthermore, Baud, Frachot and Roncalli (2003) have proved that neglecting reporting bias implies very poor estimates of the severity distribution. In particular, in the absence of an appropriate adjustment, pooling data from different sources (with different data collection thresholds) results in strongly biased severity distribution, which appears much riskier than it actually is.

For practical calculations, it is probably not necessary to go as far as Baud, Frachot and Roncalli (2002) have suggested. In their paper, the authors propose a general treatment of threshold correction. They consider that, for external databases, there are as many data collections as contributors and therefore they propose to treat these thresholds as stochastic. This is certainly true and realistic but is complicated to tackle, as the corresponding likelihood is quite sophisticated. Here we rather suggest that each dataset have one threshold and that the stated threshold corresponds exactly to the one that is actually used in practice unless there exists strong counter arguments.

Mathematically, calibration is done by maximising the log-likelihood function. (See Panel 1.) For sake of simplicity, suppose that the severity distribution is lognormal with parameters μ and σ, then one has to solve:

$$\max_{(\mu,\sigma)} \ell_n(\mu,\sigma) = \sum_{i=1}^{n} \ell\left(\zeta_i, \mu, \sigma / H_i\right)$$

where n is the number of losses, $\ell(\zeta_i, \mu, \sigma / H_i)$ is the log-likelihood of the ith loss (reported subject to the threshold H_i).

PANEL 1 SEVERITY ESTIMATION

The expression of the log-likelihood function is now common knowledge. Let us consider a dataset whose threshold is H, the sample distribution is equal to:

$$f_{sample}(x; \mu, \sigma / H) := \mathbf{1}\{x \geq H\} \cdot \frac{f(x; \mu, \sigma)}{\int_{H}^{+\infty} f(y; \mu, \sigma) dy}$$

$$= \mathbf{1}\{x \geq H\} \cdot \frac{f(x; \mu, \sigma)}{1 - \mathbf{F}(H; \mu, \sigma)}$$

where $f(x; \mu, \sigma)$ is the true probability density function (which is assumed to be a lognormal distribution $LN(\mu,\sigma)$) and $\mathbf{F}$ is the corresponding cumulative distribution function. As a result, the log-likelihood function is:

$$\ell_n(\mu, \sigma) = \sum_{i=1}^{n} \ln f\left(\zeta_i; \mu, \sigma\right) - n \times \ln\left(1 - \mathbf{F}(H; \mu, \sigma)\right)$$

where ζ_i is the ith loss and n is the number of losses. This is the second term, which corrects for reporting bias. We see in particular that it vanishes when the threshold is equal to zero. As a consequence, if thresholds are low, then this last term is negligible but, on the contrary, has a huge impact when they are significant or if they differ significantly from one dataset to another. This bias correction is essential for ensuring that different sources of data are pooled together properly.

How to treat aggregate loss data?

In some instances, loss data are not reported on a single-loss basis but are aggregated instead. In this case, only the aggregate value is reported into the internal database. Assuming that we also know the underlying number of events corresponding to this aggregate loss, we may wonder whether this aggregate loss carries valuable information for the purpose of severity estimation. How to extract this information is not straightforward (see for example Frachot, Georges and Roncalli, 2001, for a discussion of the generalised method of moment (GMM)). GMM is not too complicated to implement, although it is more difficult to tackle both single-losses and aggregate losses simultaneously since maximum likelihood and GMM techniques are too different to be combined together easily.

There is also an issue related to the data collection threshold: data losses are assumed to be reported on a single basis provided they are higher than the threshold. As a consequence, as soon as a precise threshold will be set, aggregate losses will become less and less a cause of concern. Therefore, we do not address this item here.

FREQUENCY ESTIMATION

If we still try to stick to simplicity, it is a good idea to assume that the frequency distribution is a Poisson distribution. This distribution has many appealing features. First, it is widely used in the insurance industry for modelling problems similar to operational risks. Second, it needs only one parameter (called λ) for the distribution to be entirely described. Third, the ML value of this parameter is simply the empirical average number of events per year. However, some care is necessary when reporting biases exist. For obvious reasons, if one bank's reporting cut-off is set at a high level, then the average number of (reported) events will be low. It does not imply, in any sense, that the bank is allowed to put a lower amount of capital than another otherwise identical bank which uses a lower threshold. It simply means that the average number of events must be corrected for reporting bias as well.

It appears that the calibration of the frequency distribution comes as a second step (after calibration of the severity distribution) because the aforementioned correction needs an estimate of μ and σ for its calculation. This is rather straightforward: the difference (more precisely the ratio) between the number of reported events and the "true" number of events (which would be obtained if all losses were reported, ie, with a zero-threshold) corresponds exactly to the probability of one loss being higher than the threshold. This probability is a direct by-product of the severity distribution. Panel 2 gives the mathematical expression of this probability, which in turn provides a straightforward way to make the appropriate correction.

What about external data and scaling issues? Exactly as earlier we may have information on frequency of events experienced by competitors or by the whole banking industry. The extent to which they can be seen as valuable information remains unclear as long as the scaling function is unknown. Here, the scaling function gives the link between the number of events experienced by one bank and its business size (or any variable that may be considered as relevant for evaluating the expected number of events).

PANEL 2 FREQUENCY ESTIMATION

The expression of the unconditional frequency parameter is given by

$$\lambda = \frac{\lambda_{sample}}{Pr\{loss > H\}},$$

which is mathematically equal to

$$\lambda = \frac{\lambda_{sample}}{1 - F(H; \mu, \sigma)}.$$

In practical terms, one has to compute the average number of reported events by year (which is an estimate of λ_{sample}) and to use the previous estimates of μ and σ to uncover the true frequency distribution.

For example, previous literature in the past has suggested that a square-root pattern may be appropriate for modelling the scaling function (ie, the number of events of one bank is linked to the square root of its business size). Other works have proposed the use of credibility theory as a way to adjust internally estimated frequencies (Frachot and Roncalli, 2002). However, we should honestly acknowledge that these methods are hardly implementable because, again, few risk managers have enough data to test and calibrate such functional links. Before a Basel III round takes place, it may be preferable to take internal frequencies of events for granted, provided that they have been validated by the banks themselves (and preferably corrected by some expert-based adjustments when necessary). Quantitative adjustments using external frequencies require data that are not available today and, therefore, would create more confusion.

CAPITAL CHARGE COMPUTATION

Once the frequency and severity distributions have been calibrated, the computation of capital charge is quite simple, provided we agree on its precise definition. Capital charge processing is done thanks to Monte Carlo simulations, which are standard skills among quants. We shall not spend much time here to detail how to set up a Monte Carlo scheme since many papers have done this before. We prefer to give our understanding of some widely discussed issues related to capital charge calculations.

What is the definition of the capital charge?

There remain ambiguities surrounding the definition of the regulatory capital charge. We are aware of at least three distinct definitions:

❑ *Definition 1* (OpVAR): The capital charge is the 99.9th percentile of the total loss distribution.
❑ *Definition 2* (OpVAR unexpected loss only): This is the previous OpVAR from which expected losses are subtracted. The current Basel II proposal seems to accept this definition as long as the bank can demonstrate that it has adequately provided for expected losses through pricing, reserves and/or expensing practices.
❑ *Definition 3* (OpVAR above threshold): The capital charge is the 99.9th percentile of the total loss distribution where only above-the-threshold losses are considered.

PANEL 3 MATHEMATICAL DEFINITION OF CAPITAL CHARGE

If N is the random number of events, then the aggregate loss is $L = \sum_{i=0}^{N} \zeta_i$.

The three definitions mentioned in the chapter can then be expressed in mathematical terms as:

❑ **Definition 1**: $Pr\{L > OpVAR\} = 0.1\%$.
❑ **Definition 2**: $Pr\{L > OpVAR + EL\} = 0.1\%$ where EL is the expected total loss $E\left[\sum_{i=0}^{N} \zeta_i\right]$.

❑ **Definition 3**: $Pr\left\{\sum_{i=0}^{N} (\zeta_i \times 1\{\zeta_i \geq H\} > OpVAR)\right\} = 0.1\%$ where

$1\{\zeta_i \geq H\}$ equals 1 if the loss exceeds the threshold H and 0 otherwise.

The three definitions can be implemented through Monte Carlo simulations with roughly the same level of complexity, but they obviously give different figures.

How does reporting bias affect capital charge estimate?

The way capital charge is influenced by the level of the data collection threshold depends on the definition.

❑ *Definitions 1 and 2:* Since these definitions never mention any reference to the data-collection process, the two capital charges are independent of any threshold that may be used in practice. In both cases, capital charge represents the amount of capital a bank needs to set aside for operational risk. As such, it should not depend on the way loss data are reported. In particular, the fact that a bank's risk management policy does not have specific reporting threshold indicates that only loss data higher than the threshold will be captured in its risk management system, but this does not say anything about the intrinsic riskiness of the bank. As a consequence, setting a reporting threshold should not affect the capital charge. If previous steps have been carefully followed, that is, if appropriate correction has been taken to neutralise reporting bias, then the *numerically calculated* capital charge is also invariant with respect to the threshold.
❑ *Definition 3:* As the threshold value enters explicitly in the definition, then the capital charge does depend on the threshold.

Since in Definition 3 all losses below the threshold are excluded, the total aggregate loss is thus below the one that enters Definition 1. As a result, the capital charge in Definition 3 becomes lower as the threshold is set at a higher level.

More subtle is the fact that the threshold may affect the accuracy of the capital charge since frequency and severity parameters' accuracy does depend on the threshold. Intuitively, accuracy is likely to deteriorate when the threshold is set at a high level because the calibration of the severity distribution relies on too few data. In other words, the extrapolated part of the severity distribution becomes too important. Therefore, as far as Definitions 1 and 2 are concerned, the trade-off that results in an optimal threshold has more to do with the balance between the costs of collecting data and the accuracy of the capital charge than with the level of the capital charge itself.

How to aggregate capital charges for different loss types and business lines?

This issue remains to be addressed. From a theoretical point of view, one can admit that aggregate losses by risk type are not perfectly correlated and thus summing up all capital charges together is highly conservative. The first point to be discussed is to clarify which correlation we are talking about. As the capital charge results from two sources of randomness – frequency and severity – there are also two possible sources of correlation.

As an example, we may find that aggregate losses for, say, external fraud and internal fraud are correlated because either frequency of events or severity of events are correlated. In the former case, we should observe that historically the number of external fraud events is high (respectively low) when the number of internal fraud events is also high (respectively low). This is a sensible way to consider correlation between aggregate losses of two different event types. On the contrary, we feel much less comfortable with the other way, ie, severity correlation. In effect, a basic feature of actuarial models requires the assumption that individual losses are independent within one specific risk type. *It is, therefore, conceptually difficult to assume simultaneously severity independence within each class of risk and severity correlation between two classes.*

Subsequently, we would rather assume that correlation between aggregate losses by event type is fundamentally conveyed by the underlying correlation between frequencies. By analogy with credit risk models, we expect that, even with strong frequency correlation, aggregate losses may show low levels of correlation. Furthermore, one may also guess that it is particularly true for high-severity events since severity independence likely dominates frequency correlation. This point is confirmed by our calculations in Panel 4, which show that, even if two risk types occur with highly correlated frequencies, aggregate losses show low levels of correlation.

Since strong frequency correlation might not translate into strong correlation of aggregate losses, we conclude that diversification

---

PANEL 4 AGGREGATION OF LOSSES ACROSS RISK TYPES

Let us consider two aggregate losses $L_1 = \sum_{i=0}^{N_1} \zeta_i^1$ and $L_2 = \sum_{i=0}^{N_2} \zeta_i^2$. In order to obtain tractable formulae, we assume that the two frequency distributions have the same parameters, ie, $\lambda_1 = \lambda_2 = \lambda$. If N_1 and N_2 are perfectly correlated, then $N_1 = N_2 = N$, and we have,

$$\mathrm{cov}(L_1, L_2) = E\left[L_1 L_2\right] - E\left[L_1\right]E\left[L_2\right]$$

$$= E\left[\sum_{i=0}^{N} \zeta_i^1 \sum_{i=0}^{N} \zeta_i^2\right] - \lambda^2 E\left[\zeta^1\right]E\left[\zeta^2\right]$$

$$= E\left[N^2 E\left[\zeta^1\right]E\left[\zeta^2\right]\right] - \lambda^2 E\left[\zeta^1\right]E\left[\zeta^2\right]$$

$$= \left(\mathrm{VAR}\,(N) + E^2\,[N] - \lambda^2\right) \cdot E\left[\zeta^1\right]E\left[\zeta^2\right]$$

$$= \lambda \cdot E\left[\zeta^1\right]E\left[\zeta^2\right].$$

We deduce that an upper bound of the correlation between the two aggregate losses is:

$$\mathrm{cor}^+(L_1, L_2) = \frac{E\left[\zeta^1\right]E\left[\zeta^2\right]}{\sqrt{\left(\mathrm{VAR}\left(\zeta^1\right) + E^2\left[\zeta^1\right]\right) \times \left(\mathrm{VAR}\left(\zeta^2\right) + E^2\left[\zeta^2\right]\right)}}.$$

We remark that the correlation between the two aggregate losses does not depend on the Poisson parameter λ. When the severity distributions

---

are lognormal, we obtain after some computations the following results:

$$cor^+\left(L_1, L_2\right) = \exp\left(-\frac{1}{2}\sigma_1^2 - \frac{1}{2}\sigma_2^2\right).$$

The correlation is then a very simple formula which depends only on the values σ_1 and σ_2. Moreover, we remark that the function is decreasing with respect to these parameters. We report in Figure 1 the relationship between σ_1, σ_2 and $cor^+(L_1, L_2)$. For high severity loss types, $cor^+(L_1, L_2)$ is very small. For example, when $\sigma_1 = \sigma_2 = 2$ and $\sigma_1 = \sigma_2 = 2.2$, $cor^+(L_1, L_2)$ takes respectively the values 1.8% and 0.8%.

Figure 1 Upper bound of the correlation between two aggregate losses

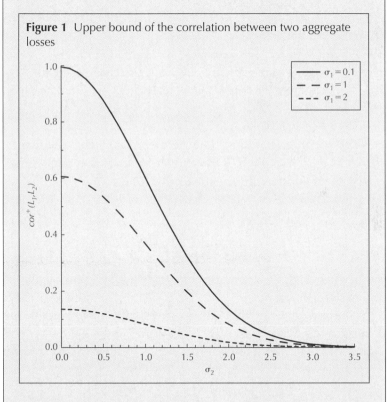

Remark: We point out that even for low-severity loss types, the correlation between the aggregate losses is very small. It cannot be bigger than 10%, which is certainly very conservative. This corresponds to the case where $\sigma_1 = \sigma_2 = 1.50$.

effects could be worth being taken into account as they may significantly reduce the total capital charge (compared with the full-correlation feature that is assumed when adding together capital charges of all event types and/or business units).

As a conclusion for this paragraph, according to the basic principle of actuarial science as represented by LDA models, correlations between aggregate losses are necessarily low. Our numerical computations suggest that the correlation is well below 10%. Finally, aggregation of capital charges can be performed by using the Normal approximation presented in Frachot, Georges and Roncalli, 2001, where the Normal approximation works as if aggregate losses were Gaussian.

CONFIDENCE INTERVAL

The previous procedure provides an estimation of the capital charge, which is uncertain by nature. One can guess that the regulators will expect a bank to demonstrate that its estimate is not too far from the fair value. This is a crucial point in operational risk modelling because of the paucity of data, which normally translates into poor accuracy. As will become clear later, confidence interval is the basic tool for justifying the computed capital charge as well as for addressing numerous issues.

The inaccuracy of the capital charge is directly linked to the inaccuracy of the estimators of the three underlying parameters λ, μ and σ. Therefore, building a confidence interval of the capital charge can proceed as follows:

❏ first, derive the (in some cases, approximate) distribution of the underlying estimators;
❏ draw from these distributions a sufficiently large number of simulations; and
❏ finally, for each path, compute the capital charge and then obtain its empirical distribution.

Parameters' accuracy

The most critical point is of course the methodology for building an approximate distribution of the estimators of the underlying parameters. For the frequency parameter λ, this task is straightforward because we know the exact distribution of the estimator (which is also a Poisson distribution). For the two remaining parameters, μ and σ, of the severity distribution, we can follow two different methodologies:

❑ Bootstrap methods; and
❑ Gaussian approximation (for example, because ML theory applies).

We are in favour of the second method because most people (in particular regulators) are much more familiar with Gaussian distribution than with Bootstrap methods. Furthermore, commercial packages can implement this methodology at almost no cost while Bootstrap methods may require some further developments. The last question that remains to be answered is to derive the precise Gaussian distribution satisfied by the estimators of the severity parameters. This is done in the Panel 5. It is worth saying that it can be derived as a by-product of Step 1 (severity calibration) and thus does not require significantly more effort.

Finally, we see that the accuracy of the frequency estimator improves when the number of recorded years T grows, and with an order of magnitude of $\sqrt{T}$. As an example, using a five-year historical length instead of a three-year length improves accuracy (as measured by the standard deviation) to an extent of 30% (ie, $\sqrt{5/3} = 1.29$). Similarly, the accuracy of the severity estimators follows the same pattern and behaves as $\sqrt{n}$, where n is the number of (both internal and external) losses.

PANEL 5 CONFIDENCE INTERVAL COMPUTATION

If the number of events is assumed to be Poisson, then the ML estimator of the annual number of events $\hat{\lambda}_T$ is the average number of events per year for the last T years (if T is the number of recorded years). The estimator is Poisson-distributed in the following sense:[1]

$$T \times \hat{\lambda}_T \sim P(T \times \lambda)$$

From ML theory, the estimators $\hat{\mu}$ and $\hat{\sigma}$ are approximately Gaussian with,

$$\begin{pmatrix} \hat{\mu}_n \\ \hat{\sigma}_n \end{pmatrix} \approx N\left(\begin{pmatrix} \mu \\ \sigma \end{pmatrix}, \Omega_n \right),$$

---

where Ω_n is the inverse of the so-called Fisher information matrix,

$$\Omega_n = -\begin{pmatrix} \partial^2 \ell_n / \partial \mu^2 & \partial^2 \ell_n / \partial \mu \partial \sigma \\ \partial^2 \ell_n / \partial \mu \partial \sigma & \partial^2 \ell_n / \partial \sigma^2 \end{pmatrix}^{-1}$$

ℓ_n is the log-likelihood function introduced in Step 1. Therefore, we just have to compute its second derivative with respect to the parameters. Since Step 1 requires maximising the log-likelihood, this second derivative is also computed in the course of the optimisation (if a standard Newton-Raphson algorithm is used). In this sense, it appears to be a by-product of Step 1.

Remark: We assume that the estimator $\hat{\lambda}$ is independent with respect to the estimators of the parameters of the severity distribution. This assumption seems natural. However, we cannot assume that $\hat{\mu}_n$ and $\hat{\sigma}_n$ are independent. From ML theory, $\hat{\mu}_n$ and $\hat{\sigma}_n$ are asymptotically independent only when the threshold H is zero (see Figure 2).

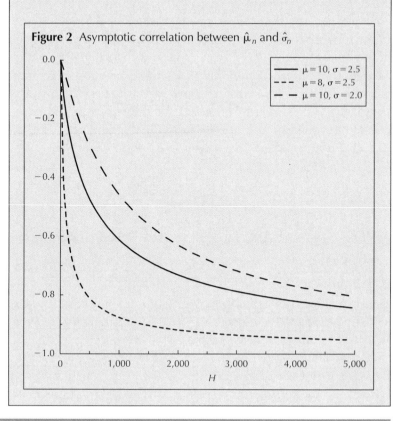

Figure 2 Asymptotic correlation between $\hat{\mu}_n$ and $\hat{\sigma}_n$

Capital charge accuracy

As capital charge is directly linked to the frequency and severity parameters, its accuracy is easily derived from the above results. Generally speaking, the probability distribution of any function of the underlying parameters can be computed provided we know the distribution of the underlying parameter estimators and we are able to calculate its first derivatives with respect to the parameters.

In practice, we simulate paths of frequency and severity parameters according to the approximate distribution derived in the previous subsection, then, for each path, we compute the capital charge and we eventually obtain its probability distribution. Consider the following numerical example. Suppose that $\lambda = 100$, $\mu = 9$ and $\sigma = 2$. The number of recorded years is $T = 5$ years and the number of losses is n = 1000. Since the average number of events per year is $\lambda = 100$ and the number of recorded years is 5, it is rather unlikely that all the 1,000 losses may come from internal databases. As a result, this example assumes that internal databases are supplemented with external losses. Finally, we also assume that the threshold is equal to 5,000 euros. In Figure 3, we report the following ratios:

$$R_{Freq} = \frac{OpVAR\left(\hat{\lambda}_T, \mu, \sigma\right)}{OpVAR\left(\lambda, \mu, \sigma\right)}$$

$$R_{Sev} = \frac{OpVAR\left(\lambda, \hat{\mu}_n, \hat{\sigma}_n\right)}{OpVAR\left(\lambda, \mu, \sigma\right)}$$

$$R_{Freq+Sev} = \frac{OpVAR\left(\hat{\lambda}_T, \hat{\mu}_n, \hat{\sigma}_n\right)}{OpVAR\left(\lambda, \mu, \sigma\right)}$$

R is then the ratio between the capital charge estimator (for various cases) and the true capital charge. R_{Freq} (and respectively R_{Sev}) corresponds to the case where the frequency parameter (respectively the severity parameters) is the only parameter assumed to be random. It allows us to assess which part of the total inaccuracy is attributable to each parameter. The real-life case where both the frequency and severity parameters are random is captured by

$R_{\text{Freq+Sev}}$. In order to give an idea of the accuracy of the capital charge estimate, we may estimate the value c defined as follows:

$$\Pr\left\{Op\hat{V}AR \geq (1-c)\times OpVAR\right\} = \alpha$$

where $Op\hat{V}AR$ is the capital charge estimate and $OpVAR$ its true value.[2] This criterion is well suited for regulatory purposes since regulators will probably focus on the risk of underestimating the capital charge.

Figure 3 Probability density function of $Op\hat{V}AR$

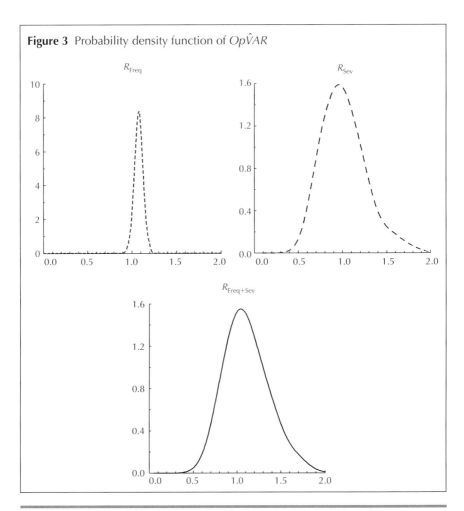

Using the previous numerical values for λ, μ and σ, and defining $Op\hat{V}AR$ as $OpVAR(\lambda, \hat{\mu}_n, \hat{\sigma}_n)$ – we treat here the frequency parameter as given and not random – we obtain the following results for c:

n/α	75%	90%	95%
100	42%	60%	68%
1,000	16%	26%	31%
10,000	5%	9%	12%

As an example, for $n = 10,000$ losses, the capital charge may be underestimated by less than 15% (if we consider a 95% level of confidence). We remark that the error increases with the confidence level α and decreases with the number of losses of the database. Now, if we consider that both the frequency parameter and the parameters of the severity loss distribution are random – $Op\hat{V}AR$ is now defined as $OpVAR(\lambda_T, \hat{\mu}_n, \hat{\sigma}_n)$ – the results become:

n/α	75%	90%	95%
100	26%	50%	58%
1,000	5%	18%	24%
10,000	−1%	5%	7%

Finally, if we suppose the severity as given and non-random ($\mu = 9$ and $\sigma = 2$), $Op\hat{V}AR = OpVAR(\hat{\lambda}_T, \mu, \sigma)$ is a function of the number of years T, and we may verify that the error c decreases with T.

As a conclusion, we must stress the fact that capital accuracy depends on the value of the frequency and severity parameters. In particular, capital accuracy is probably different whether it is computed for low-severity/high-frequency or high-severity/low-frequency events. In this sense, there is no one-size-fits-all rule for deriving capital charge accuracy. Therefore, we argue that capital charge amounts make sense only if the associated accuracy is given. Finally it is worth saying that our results confirm that external data may be necessary in some cases.

OTHER ISSUES

Previous sections have shown how to build a sound and pragmatic LDA that addresses the most important issues. We now turn to some remaining issues and questions.

Goodness-of-fit tests

It is probably interesting to search for the distribution that fits the best loss severity or to wonder if the Poisson distribution is well suited to modelling frequency. These questions should perhaps be left for future research, as they could provoke endless discussions. If the entire OpRisk community commits itself to use one definite set of distributions (say, Poisson × Lognormal), it would greatly simplify comparisons between banks' capital charges, and these benefits would largely encompass the (probably small) loss of accuracy due to the use of one-size-fits-all distributions.

Data sufficiency

This issue can now receive a rigorous attention due to our analysis of confidence intervals. Since capital charge accuracy depends directly on the number of observed losses, we just have to check whether the capital charge is calculated with an acceptable accuracy, where "acceptable" means that the confidence interval is not too wide.

Let us consider the problem of the previous section. We have computed the value c satisfying $Pr\{Op\hat{V}AR \geq (1 - c) \times OpVAR\} = \alpha$ for a given value of $\alpha - n$ and T are fixed. Now, c is set to an "acceptable" level and we want to find n^* such that $Pr\{Op\hat{V}AR \geq (1 - c) \times OpVAR\} = \alpha$ if $n \geq n^*$. It then answers the question of the number of external losses necessary to achieve an acceptable accuracy.

Example 1

Suppose that $\lambda = 100$. We assume that T is 5 years. Moreover, we assume that the threshold is equal to 5,000 euros. In Figure 4,

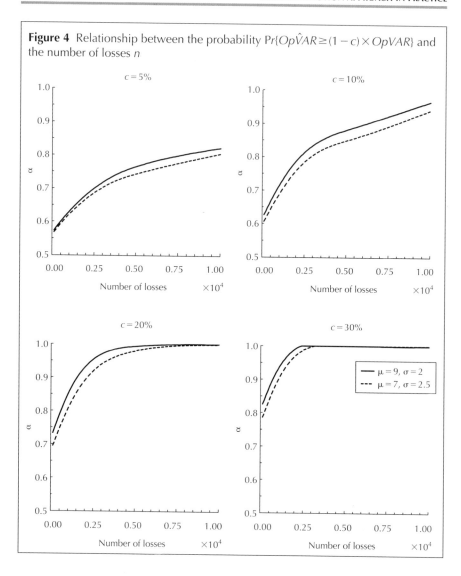

Figure 4 Relationship between the probability $Pr\{Op\hat{V}AR \geq (1-c) \times OpVAR\}$ and the number of losses n

we report the relationship between the probability $Pr\{Op\hat{V}AR \geq (1-c \times OpVAR\}$ and the number of losses n. It is now easy to find the minimum observation n^* for a given value of α. For example, if $c = 20\%$ and $\alpha = 80\%$, n^* is approximately equal to 580 for $\mu = 9$ and $\sigma = 2$; and 940, for $\mu = 7$ and $\sigma = 2.5$. If $c = 25\%$ and $\alpha = 80\%$, n^* takes the values 240 and 490, respectively.

PANEL 6 LINKING ESTIMATE ACCURACY AND THE NUMBER OF LOSS DATA

If we suppose the frequency as given and non-random, we may find an analytical expression of n^*. From ML theory, we recall that the estimators $\hat{\mu}$ and $\hat{\sigma}$ are approximately Gaussian with:

$$\sqrt{n}\left(\begin{pmatrix}\hat{\mu}_n \\ \hat{\sigma}_n\end{pmatrix}-\begin{pmatrix}\mu \\ \sigma\end{pmatrix}\right)\to N\left(0,\mathfrak{I}^{-1}\right)$$

where $\mathfrak{I}$ is the Fisher information matrix. Because we define $Op\hat{V}AR$ as $OpVAR(\lambda,\hat{\mu}_n,\hat{\sigma}_n)$, we have:

$$\sqrt{n}\left(OpVAR\left(\lambda,\hat{\mu}_n,\hat{\sigma}_n\right)-OpVAR\left(\lambda,\mu,\sigma\right)\right)\to N\left(0,\mathfrak{I}_h^{-1}\right)$$

with

$$\mathfrak{I}_h^{-1}=\left[\partial_\mu OpVAR\left(\lambda,\hat{\mu}_n,\hat{\sigma}_n\right)\quad \partial_\sigma OpVAR\left(\lambda,\hat{\mu}_n,\hat{\sigma}_n\right)\right]\times$$
$$\mathfrak{I}^{-1}\begin{bmatrix}\partial_\mu OpVAR\left(\lambda,\hat{\mu}_n,\hat{\sigma}_n\right) \\ \partial_\sigma OpVAR\left(\lambda,\hat{\mu}_n,\hat{\sigma}_n\right)\end{bmatrix}$$

If we solve the equation

$$\Pr\left\{Op\hat{V}AR\geq(1-c)\times OpVAR\right\}=\alpha$$

we find that

$$n^*=\left(\frac{\Phi^{-1}(\alpha)}{c\times OpVAR(\lambda,\mu,\sigma)}\right)^2\mathfrak{I}_h^{-1}$$

If we apply this formula to our previous example, we obtain the results given in Table 1.

Table 1 Required number of data

		α					α		
c	60%	70%	80%	90%	c	60%	70%	80%	90%
10%	240	1,040	2,700	6,260	10%	400	1,740	4,500	10,430
20%	60	260	670	1,560	20%	100	430	1,120	2,600
30%	20	110	300	690	30%	40	190	500	1,150
40%		60	160	390	40%	20	100	280	650
50%		40	100	250	50%	10	60	180	410

$\lambda = 100$, $\mu = 9$, $\sigma = 2$, $H = 0$. $\lambda = 100$, $\mu = 9$, $\sigma = 2$, $H = 5000$.

		α					α		
c	60%	70%	80%	90%	c	60%	70%	80%	90%
10%	410	1,760	4,540	10,530	10%	820	3,530	9,110	21,120
20%	100	440	1,130	2,630	20%	200	880	2,270	5,280
30%	40	190	500	1,170	30%	90	390	1010	2340
40%	20	110	280	650	40%	50	220	560	1320
50%	10	70	180	420	50%	30	140	360	840

$\lambda = 100$, $\mu = 7$, $\sigma = 2.5$, $H = 0$. $\lambda = 100$, $\mu = 7$, $\sigma = 2.5$, $H = 5000$.

SELF-ASSESSMENT AND SCENARIO ANALYSIS

The concept of scenario analysis should deserve further clarification. Roughly speaking, when we refer to scenario analysis, we want to express the idea that bank experts and experienced managers have some reliable intuitions on the riskiness of their own business and that these intuitions are not entirely reflected in the bank's historical, internal data. As a first requirement, we expect that these internal experts have the opportunity to give their approval to capital charge results. In a second step, one can imagine that the experts' intuitions are directly used in severity and frequency estimations.

Experts' intuition can be captured through scenario building. More precisely, a scenario is given by a potential loss amount and the corresponding probability of occurrence. As an example, an expert might assert that a loss of 1 million euros or higher is expected to occur once every five years. This is a valuable information in many cases, either when loss data are rare and do not allow for statistically sound results or when historical loss data are not sufficiently forward-looking. The issue that has to be addressed is how one can extract useful information from experts' scenarios and how it can be plugged into a conventional LDA framework.

It is quite easy if we notice that scenarios can be translated into restrictions on the parameters of frequency and severity distributions. Once these restrictions have been identified, a calibration strategy can be designed where parameters are calibrated by maximising some standard criterion (such as maximum likelihood) subject to these restrictions being satisfied (at least approximately). As a result, parameter estimators can be seen as a mixture of the estimator based on loss data and the scenario-based implied estimator. Panel 7 details how it can be done provided one is able to weigh scenario-based information relatively to loss-data-based information.

PANEL 7 SCENARIO ANALYSIS

Let us consider a scenario defined as: "a loss of x or higher occurs once every d years". Let us also assume that the frequency distribution is a Poisson distribution (with parameter λ) and that the severity distribution is a lognormal distribution (with parameters μ and σ). With these notations, λ is the average number of losses per year, $\lambda \times (1 - F(x; \mu, \sigma))$ is the average number of losses higher than x and finally $1/[\lambda \times (1 - F(x; \mu, \sigma))]$ is the average duration between two losses exceeding x.[3] Consequently, for a given scenario (x, d), parameters are restricted to satisfy:

$$d = \frac{1}{\lambda \times \left(1 - F\left(x; \mu, \sigma\right)\right)}$$

It is obvious that three different scenarios suffice to calibrate the three parameters λ, μ and σ. Suppose that we are confronted with different scenarios $\{(x_j, d_j), j = 1,\ldots,p\}$. We may estimate the implied parameters

---

underlying expert judgements by using a quadratic criterion:

$$\left(\hat{\mu}, \hat{\sigma}, \hat{\lambda}\right) = \arg\min \sum_{j=1}^{p} w_j \left(d_j - \frac{1}{\lambda \times \left(1 - \mathbf{F}\left(x_j; \mu, \sigma\right)\right)} \right)^2$$

where w_j is the weight associated to the jth scenario. Our experience shows that it works best with standard optimal weights (ie, proportional to the inverse of the variance of d_j).

Let us consider the following example:

x (in millions of euros)	1	2.5	5	7.5	10	20
d (in years)		1/4	1	3	6	10	40

Using the standard optimal weights, we obtain $\hat{\lambda} = 654$, $\hat{\mu} = 8.60$ and $\hat{\sigma} = 2.08$. We may compare directly these estimates to those calibrated using loss data. Moreover, if loss data are available, calibration can be achieved by maximising some criterion[4] obtained as a combination of maximum likelihood and the previous restrictions:

$$\max_{(\mu, \sigma)} \left(1 - \varpi\right) \ell_n \left(\mu, \sigma\right) - \varpi \sum_{j=1}^{p} w_j \left[d_j - \frac{1}{\lambda \times \left(1 - \mathbf{F}\left(x_j; \mu, \sigma\right)\right)} \right]^2$$

where ϖ is a weight reflecting the confidence one places on expert's judgements.

CONCLUSION

This chapter was aimed at providing a comprehensive survey of all technical issues raised in the course of implementing a loss distribution approach (LDA). Although quite technical, these issues are nevertheless important, as they have a major impact on capital charges if incorrectly tackled. Our experience has taught us that reporting bias is probably one of the most prominent issues, but fortunately can be overcome by choosing the appropriate maximum likelihood techniques. Secondly, we have shown that confidence intervals are very useful tools to address some issues such as data sufficiency. Furthermore, we have derived an approximate, but reliable, way to compute this confidence interval. Finally, further research will have to focus on scaling issues and the goodness of fit tests as databases become larger.

PANEL 8 THE METHOD OF MAXIMUM LIKELIHOOD

The method of maximum likelihood is a very popular estimation technique. We recall here some results that can be found in every handbook on statistical estimation (see for example Davidson and MacKinnon, 1993).

Let θ be the vector of parameters to be estimated and Θ the parameter space. The likelihood for the ith observation, that is the probability density of the observation i considered as a function of θ, is denoted $L_i(\theta)$.

Let $\ell_i(\theta) \equiv \ln L_i(\theta)$ be the log-likelihood of $L_i(\theta)$. Given n independent observations, the log-likelihood function is:

$$\ell_n\left(\hat{\theta}_n\right) = \sum_{i=1}^{n} \ell_i(\theta)$$

$\hat{\theta}_n$ is the maximum likelihood estimator if:

$$\ell_n\left(\hat{\theta}_n\right) \geq \ell_n(\theta) \quad \forall \theta \in \Theta$$

The main properties of the ML estimator are *consistency, asymptotic normality* and *asymptotic efficiency*. In particular we have,

$$\sqrt{n}\left(\hat{\theta}_n - \theta_0\right) \rightarrow N\left(0, \Im^{-1}(\theta_0)\right)$$

where $\Im(\theta_0)$ is the Fisher information matrix, and θ_0, the "true" value of the vector of parameters. Recall that,

$$\Im(\theta_0) = E_{\theta_0}\left[-\frac{\partial^2 \ell_i(\theta_0)}{\partial\theta\,\partial\theta^T}\right].$$

Let $h(\theta)$ be a real function of the vector of parameters θ. Then, $h(\hat{\theta}_n)$ converges almost surely to $h(\theta_0)$ and we have:

$$\sqrt{n}\left(h\left(\hat{\theta}_n\right) - h(\theta_0)\right) \rightarrow N\left[0, \frac{\partial h(\theta_0)}{\partial\theta^T}\Im^{-1}(\theta_0)\frac{\partial h(\theta_0)}{\partial\theta}\right]$$

PANEL 9 THE DISTRIBUTION OF THE DURATION BETWEEN TWO LOSSES EXCEEDING A GIVEN VALUE X

We assume that the number of losses is a Poisson process with intensity λ. We note T_i as the time when the ith loss occurs. It means that the durations $e_i = T_i - T_{i-1}$ between two consecutive losses are independent and exponential with parameter λ. We assume that the losses ζ_i are *iid* with distribution F. Denote d_j as the duration between two losses exceeding x. It is obvious that the durations are *iid*. It suffices now to characterise d_1. We have:[5]

$$\Pr\{d_1 > t\} = \sum_{i \geq 1} \Pr\{T_i > t; \zeta_1 < x, \cdots, \zeta_{i-1} < x; \zeta_i \leq x\}$$

$$= \sum_{i \geq 1} \Pr\{T_i > t\} \mathbf{F}(x)^{i-1} (1 - \mathbf{F}(x))$$

$$= \sum_{i \geq 1} (1 - \mathbf{F}(x)) \mathbf{F}(x)^{i-1} \sum_{k=0}^{i-1} e^{-\lambda t} \frac{(\lambda t)^k}{k!}$$

$$= (1 - \mathbf{F}(x)) \sum_{k=0}^{\infty} e^{-\lambda t} \frac{(\lambda t)^k}{k!} \sum_{i=k}^{\infty} \mathbf{F}(x)^i$$

$$= e^{-\lambda t} \sum_{k=0}^{\infty} \frac{(\lambda t)^k}{k!} \mathbf{F}(x)^k$$

$$= e^{-\lambda(1 - \mathbf{F}(x))t}$$

It shows that d_1 follows an exponential distribution with parameter $\lambda \times (1 - \mathbf{F}(x))$. The average duration between two losses exceeding x is also the mean of d_1 or

$$\frac{1}{\lambda \times (1 - \mathbf{F}(x))}.$$

1 We verify that plim $[P(T \times \lambda)]/T = \lambda$ where $P(T \times \lambda)$ is the Poisson distribution of parameter $T \times \lambda$.

2 Here OpVAR is defined according to Definition 1 of the previous section.

3 A rigorous proof of this result is given in Panel 9.

4 It corresponds to the penalised-maximum-likelihood method.

5 To establish this result, we use the fact that a finite sum of exponential times is an Erlang distribution.

BIBLIOGRAPHY

Basel Committee on Banking Supervision, 2001, "Operational Risk", Consultative Document, Supporting Document to the New Basel Capital Accord, January.

Basel Committee on Banking Supervision, 2001, Working Paper on the Regulatory Treatment of Operational Risk, September.

Basel Committee on Banking Supervision, 2002, Quantitative Impact Study 3, Technical Guidance, October.

Baud, N., A. Frachot, and T. Roncalli, 2002, "Internal Data, External Data and Consortium Data for Operational Risk Measurement: How to Pool Data Properly?", Working Paper, Crédit Lyonnais, Groupe de Recherche Opérationnelle.

Baud, N., A. Frachot, and T. Roncalli, 2003, "How to Avoid Over-estimating Capital Charge for Operational Risk?", *Operational Risk*, February.

Davidson, R., and J. MacKinnon, 1993, *Estimation and Inference in Econometrics* (Oxford University Press).

De Fontnouvelle, P., V. DeJesus-Rueff, J. Jordan, and E. Rosengren, 2003, "Using Loss Data to Quantify Operational Risk", Working Paper, Federal Reserve Bank of Boston, Department of Supervision and Regulation.

Frachot, A., P. Georges, and T. Roncalli, 2001, "Loss Distribution Approach for Operational Risk", Working Paper, Crédit Lyonnais, Groupe de Recherche Opérationnelle.

Frachot, A. and T. Roncalli, 2002, "Mixing Internal and External Data for Managing Operational Risk", Working Paper, Crédit Lyonnais, Groupe de Recherche Opérationnelle.

Shih, J., A. Samad-Khan, and P. Medapa, 2000, "Is the Size of Operational Loss Related to Firm Size?", *Operational Risk*, January.

16

An Operational Risk Ratings Model Approach to Better Measurement and Management of Operational Risk

Anthony Peccia

Bank of Montreal

MODELLING OPERATIONAL RISK: WHAT FOR?

Partly in response to regulatory initiatives coming out of the Basel II proposals (see Banking Committee on Banking Supervision, 2003) and partly in response to fear of being left behind by their competitors, many banks are devoting resources to measure operational risk. Like any measurement process, whether it be key performance measures, market risk or operational risk, the success and the usefulness of the measurement depends less on the sophistication of the measurement model and more on two important elements: (1) what the measure tells management that otherwise would not be known, and (2) how the results of the measure will be used to influence management practice. These two elements are the outcome of the measurement process.

There are many starting points in developing an operational risk measurement model. Not all will lead to the same endpoint. It is always best to have a clear picture of the outcome and then design the components to achieve that desired outcome. Figure 1 describes some of the most common outcomes that business management wants from a measurement model. Note that these outcomes address several connected, but distinct, components: awareness of the risks (the biggest operational risk), the P&L impact of those risks, the capital impact of those risks and benchmarking.

Figure 1 The outcomes of an operational risk measurement model

To manage Op risk effectively, business leaders need to be able to answer these questions

❑ What are my biggest operational risks?

❑ What hits can I expect my P&L to take from my biggest operational risk?

❑ How bad can those hits get?

❑ How bad can those hits really get in stress situations?

❑ How will changes to my business strategy or control environment affect those hits?

❑ How do my potential hits compare internally or externally?

The outcome list can be made richer by drilling down each component further. However, it is best to stop at this level, build the measurement model to yield answers to these questions test the model, work out the necessary and inevitable adjustments to ensure the model gives reasonable estimate answers and see how the measurement model works in practice.[1] Observing how the model influences management practices can test all of these steps. Only after the model has proved itself to be useful in practice should further enhancement work begin. However, these enhancements should be driven by business management's need to manage operational risk better and not by a desire by operational risk managers to clamour for more sophisticated models.

PANEL 1 MODELLING OPERATIONAL RISK: WHERE SHOULD WE START?

Once a clear picture of the outcome of the measurement model has been created, the model, regardless of its form, needs to be anchored within an integrated operational risk management framework. This ensures that, as the measurement model is being developed, the many assumptions, considerations and design decisions that must be made along the way are made in a consistent manner and that the measurement process is always aligned with the management process.

Once again, Basel II provides a useful starting point. The integrated framework for managing operational risk consists of five basic steps:

❑ Step 1: identification;

❑ Step 2: measurement;

❑ Step 3: monitoring;

❑ Step 4: capital requirements; and

❑ Step 5: control.

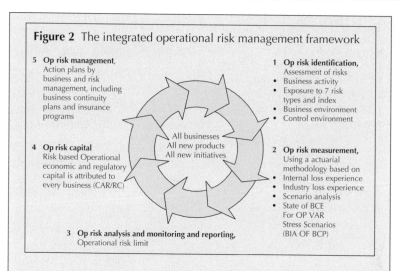

Figure 2 The integrated operational risk management framework

5 **Op risk management**, Action plans by business and risk management, including business continuity plans and insurance programs

4 **Op risk capital** Risk based Operational economic and regulatory capital is attributed to every business (CAR/RC)

All businesses
All new products
All new initiatives

1 **Op risk identification**, Assessment of risks
• Business activity
• Exposure to 7 risk types and index
• Business environment
• Control environment

2 **Op risk measurement**, Using a actuarial methodology based on
• Internal loss experience
• Industry loss experience
• Scenario analysis
• State of BCE
For OP VAR Stress Scenarios (BIA OF BCP)

3 **Op risk analysis and monitoring and reporting**, Operational risk limit

In this panel, I have made capital requirement explicit, which includes both economic and regulatory capital, where they differ, whereas it is implicit in Basel II, since the whole proposal revolves around meeting minimum regulatory capital requirements.

Figure 2 illustrates the framework, and it also illustrates three important features of the framework: (1) the framework applies to all businesses within the financial institution, whether those business are covered by Basel II or not; and (2) the framework applies to all new products and all new initiatives prior to their launch.

Figure 2 also illustrates the practice of continuous improvement as symbolised by the flowing circle. This is an important practice to implement. Without continuous improvement, it is easy to spiral into a perpetual cycle of trying to achieve perfection or continuously adding enhancements without ever getting around to delivering anything practical. This point cannot be emphasised enough. Seeking a measurement model that, at the onset, will take all major possible factors that influence the level of operational risk may seem desirable, but it usually ends up lengthening the model delivery cycle time unnecessarily. It may also complicate the model to a point where it becomes hard for senior management to understand. This, of course, significantly reduces the measurement model's effectiveness and stands a higher chance of losing support from senior management.

Using Panel 1 as a guide, let us start with the first component of the framework: risk identification.

MODELLING OPERATIONAL RISK: HOW TO IDENTIFY OPERATIONAL RISK

One of the main difficulties with modelling operational risk is that, although the industry and regulators have converged on a standard definition of operational risk, this definition remains too elastic to be useful for developing a useful measurement model. The standard definition, which states that operational risk is the potential for loss due to inadequate, or a failure in, people, processes, systems or external events, is, nevertheless, a giant step forward from the days when operational risk was loosely defined as any risk other than market or credit risk.

A useful measurement model needs more specificity. So let us look at what factors could influence the level of risk. First, casual observation shows that the type of business activity influences the level of operational risk. For example, retail banking activities generally require the development, delivery and processing of huge numbers of standardised products, processed through standardised processes, and they involve generally low-financial-value trans-actions. By contrast, derivatives-trading activities involve relatively few but higher-financial-value and non-standardised transactions. Intuitively we know that any process that has many small independent transactions will have small standard deviations around the mean because a few failed transactions will have only a minor impact on the total. However, in the case of a few large transactions, even one failure will have a large impact on the total and therefore is characterised by a high standard deviation. Retail banking is therefore less operationally risky than trading complex derivatives.[2]

Consequently, business activity is a factor that determines the level of operational risk. Basel II has provided eight standardised business activities. Although no bank is organised into these pure and distinct activities, the eight standardised business activities nevertheless represent a reasonable starting point for distinguishing different levels of operational risk within the various and many business activities carried out by large banking institutions.

Next, size obviously matters. All things being equal, a retail banking operation that is twice the size of another very similar retail banking operation will have more operational risk. Whether the risk is directly proportional to the size or whether it varies in a non-linear fashion with size remains to be seen. After all, that is what a good measurement model should tell us. At this point, it is sufficient to consider size as another key factor in determining the level of operational risk. Generally the size of the risk is referred to as the exposure adopting the Basel II nomenclature; we shall henceforth use the term *exposure index* to refer to the operational risk size factor.

Continuing with the example of retail banking, the level and type of operational risk is dependent on where and how the retail banking is conducted. A retail bank operating in the US is exposed to a different level of employment-practice operational risk than, say, a bank operating in the UK. A retail bank that delivers new services and products primarily through the Internet is growing rapidly and has a relatively weak control environment. It is clearly more prone to operational risk than a stable retail bank, which delivers traditional banking services primarily through a branch network and within a stronger control environment. These several factors, which at an intuitive level all experienced operational risk managers would agree determines the level of operational risk, can be categorised separately as the business (external and internal) and the control environments.

The examples I discussed above, such as the US retail banking versus the UK retail banking, Internet banking versus branch network, stable versus rapid growth and the traditional products versus new products, are some of the characteristics that distinguish different business environments. More will be said about a systematic way of identifying those factors within a business environment that influence the level of operational risk. For now it is sufficient to note that the business environment in which the banking operation is conducted is the key factor that influences the level of operational risk. The fact that the adequacy of the control environment influences the level of operational risk is self-evident. The elements of control environment that determine the adequacy and, therefore, the level of operational risk will be elaborated on later.

In summary, we have identified four operational risk factors that determine the level of operational risk. These are:

1. type of business activity;
2. the size of the activity otherwise called the exposure index;

3. the business environment; and
4. the control environment.

Any operational risk measurement model must take each of these factors explicitly into account if the measurement model is to be of practical use to business management. There is no point in developing an operational risk measurement model if the model does not provide management with insight into how the risk factors, some of which they have control over and some of which they do not, determine the level of operational risk.[3] This is an important point that cannot be emphasised enough. Most of the statistically based operational risk models that have been developed to date fail to incorporate these risk factors directly.[4] Take a familiar example. I visit a doctor, and, after examining me, he tells me that I have a high risk of a heart attack. It is an important and interesting statement, but at this point it is not very useful to me. I would like to know what I could do about it. In other words I would like to understand the risk factors that have led to my being rated a high risk factor. The doctor will then tell me that certain risk factors are genetically determined and some are lifestyle-determined. This is valuable information since, although there is nothing I can do about the genetic factors, there much that I can do about the lifestyle factors.

In medicine, the components of each of the risk factors are often referred to as *key risk indicators*. Similarly, the four operational risk factors described above, namely the business activity, the exposure index, and the business and control environments, constitute the key operational factors, and the subcompacts are the associated key risk indicators.

Two important conclusions can be derived at this point. First, we have clarified what key operational risk indicators are (sub-components of the key risk factors) and what they are used for (to determine the level of operational risk). Secondly, although these operational risk factors may in an indirect or minor way influence the level of expected loss, they are not by design used for that purpose. Instead, it is better to use key performance indicators for gaining insight into the level of expected loss and key risk indicators to understand that level of unexpected loss.[5]

Up to now we have been developing the concepts that form the foundation of the measurement model. Figure 3 illustrates these

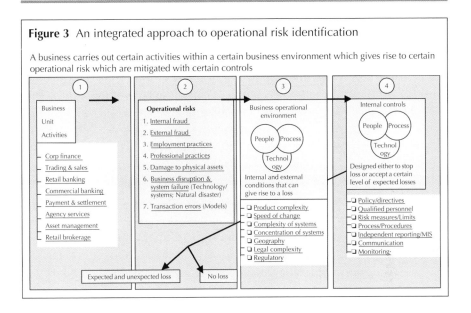

Figure 3 An integrated approach to operational risk identification

A business carries out certain activities within a certain business environment which gives rise to certain operational risk which are mitigated with certain controls

concepts in a pictorial form that is easy to remember and structure. Each of these will be treated separately later on, so the details are not important at this time. What is important is that these are the concepts that form the foundation of the operational risk model we will be building.

Any properly constructed measurement model must have well-defined, standardised elements, including inputs and outputs. As stated in Figure 3, a business caries out certain activities within a certain business environment, which gives rise to certain operational risk that can be mitigated by enforcing certain controls. The first thing to standardise is the operational risk categories. For this, the standard Basel II event categories are used. Although these are not ideal, in the sense that they are not perfectly mutually exclusive and capture all possible operational risks, they are nevertheless adequate at this point, given the level of current development in operational risk. Recall that Basel II provided for eight standardised business categories, which adequately describe the major banking business categories. What about activities that do not fit into the standardised eight? Financial institutions that carry out activities that are outside the scope of Basel – such as life insurance or property and casualty insurance – are advised to simply add to the list.

MODELLING OPERATIONAL RISK: HOW TO CONSTRUCT A LOSS-DISTRIBUTION MODEL?

Most operational risk measurement models are statistical or actuarial constructs that require that a frequency distribution for losses and a severity of loss-given occurrence distribution be developed form the historical loss experience. These individual distributions are then combined using Monte Carlo simulation to arrive at the aggregate loss distribution. The aggregate loss distribution gives the probability for the loss amount and is used to derive both the expected loss and unexpected loss, given some confidence interval. Beyond normal conditions, stress situations are generally treated outside these models and they require the creation of specific stress scenarios. There are several variations of this type of model and both regulators and practitioners in the industry commonly refer to these variations as the loss-distribution approach (LDA).

Figure 4 illustrates the process generally used for LDA. The LDA operational risk measurement models are a very sensible approach. The concepts rely heavily on actuarial (frequency/severity) loss-distribution models developed and used by the insurance industry. The LDA approach is one of the recognised approaches

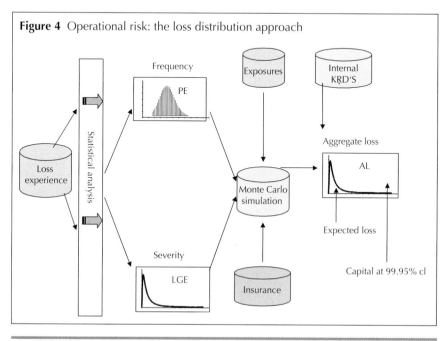

Figure 4 Operational risk: the loss distribution approach

under the Basel II Advanced Measurement Approaches (AMA) for calculating the minimum regulatory operational risk capital charge. Basel II set that capital requirement equal to the unexpected loss at the 99.9% confidence level.

The steps sound simple: obtain the internal loss history, use standard statistical techniques to fit the data to a standard frequency distribution (say the Poisson distribution), and then fit the processed historical data into a standard severity distribution (say the lognormal distribution) by performing a Monte Carlo simulation, incorporate the effects of key risk indicators to take into account the likelihood that potential future losses may be different from the actual historical loss experience, add the effects of insurance that may reduce the severity of losses once they occur, and finally derive the aggregate loss distribution from which the expected loss and unexpected loss capital levels are obtained.[6] What could be more straightforward? What could be more difficult? is a better question. The difficulty lies not in the processes mentioned above but in the lack of credible internal operational risk data.

MODELLING OPERATIONAL RISK: WHERE ARE THE DATA?

The LDA family of operational risk measurement models requires a vast amount of operational risk data (eg, loss and key risk indicators as noted above) for use in both calibration and validation. Just how much data are needed will be addressed shortly. For the moment, few, if any, banks have collected sufficient internal operational risk data necessary to fit the required distributions as outlined in the previous section.[7] There is an underlying assumption among many operational risk managers and regulators that the data problem will solve itself over time as banks collect and share operational risk data through consortium data pools. This then brings us back to the problem of how many data are actually sufficient.

As illustrated in Figure 5, demonstrated by the most commonly used Poisson distribution, 1,082 individual loss data points are required to obtain an estimate of the expected number of losses within a 5% error and with a 90% confidence level (see Cook).

This suggests that, with the exception of high-frequency and necessarily low severity events, there would not be sufficient internal loss history to fit a frequency distribution with any reasonable degree of confidence.[8]

Figure 5 How much is internal data sufficient?

Number of losses required: Poisson distribution

	Confidence		
Error	99%	95%	90%
2.5%	10,623	6,147	4,326
5%	2,656	1,537	1,082
7.5%	1,180	683	481
10%	664	384	271

The problem regarding the lack of sufficient data is compounded exponentially when one tries to fit a severity distribution, since this task requires reasonable estimates of both the expected severity and its variance. For example, a simple simulation of the lognormal distribution will show that over a million data points are required to reasonability fit the distribution to only a 90% degree of confidence. This simply means that there will never be sufficient data points to derive, with great confidence, any of the measures (expected loss and especially the unexpected losses) prescribed in the standard LDA.

How can one measure operational risks, then? Various practitioners have suggested three solutions to arrive at credible data sets. These are: lengthening the time horizon, pooling data to create industry data and supplementing data with synthetic scenario-based data. These solutions have also found their way into Basel II discussions at a conceptual level, although the Basel Committee is currently silent on exactly how these proposed solutions are to be implemented in practice. As I will describe in the following section, each of these solutions has severe limitations.

First of all, for low-frequency events (ie, loss events that happen once in every five years or less), the amount of time needed to achieve a reasonable estimate of the loss distribution would make most of the loss data stale and irrelevant. That is because banks are very dynamic entities, with rapidly changing control environments and ever-changing business environments. Incorporating stale and irrelevant data that are more than three or five years old will significantly distort the actual risk profile of the bank.

Using industry data to augment scarce internal data introduces other problems. Since the actual, as opposed to the measured, operational risk is dependent on the four risk factors, pooling data should be done only for banks that share the same four factors, namely, business activity, exposure index, business and control environments. This raises two issues. First, many of the data are not currently available, nor have any industry or regulatory data standards been developed. Secondly, even if the data were available, there are no generally accepted methods for dealing with exactly how these four risk factors are to be incorporated. This chapter will deal with some of the research regarding the use of industry data and will present a rating-based actuarial operational risk measurement model that has evolved from that research. But, before delving into that, let us deal with the two remaining proposed solutions to the problem of insufficient internal data.

Most banks, when attempting to measure operational risk for the first time, start with scenario-analysis-derived data. This approach may, however, significantly reduce the credibility of the data set. To see this, let us analyse how these synthetic data are arrived at. At its most simple form, management for a particular line of business, along with expert support functions such as legal, technology and others, are given a description of a particular loss event, say rogue trading. This event, along with varying degrees of specificity around the situation that gave rise to the loss event, is referred to as the scenario. Business management are then asked to first estimate the frequency of the loss event within their business and then estimate the severity of the loss given the occurrence of the event. The estimating process can take various levels of sophistication, ranging from point estimates of the expected and worst-case frequency and severity to range estimates for each. At first inspection, this method appears to be a very reasonable approach. After all, business management is closest to the business. Businesspeople are experts at running their own businesses, and are, therefore, in a better position to provide the required estimates. The problem is that business management normally has very little or no experience with the low-frequency events that we are asking them to estimate. By their very nature, low-frequency events happen very rarely and are, therefore, very difficult to assess. How are business management, or for that matter anyone else without the actual experience of such rare and infrequent events, to be able to derive the intuition and expertise to make reasonable estimates of the frequency of occurrence with any degree of accuracy or confidence? You might as well ask business management how likely it is that they will experience a heart attack in the next year. Not many would trust that estimate, not even the business manager. However, if business managers were asked how likely it is that they will eat within the next year, they will provide you with a very accurate estimate of the number of times. In both cases business managers are experts at running their bodies and yet, in the heart-attack example, there is no confidence in the frequency estimate, whereas in the eating example there is a high degree of confidence. The main point is that, whether it is operational risk events or other events, judgement can be relied on to provide only reasonable estimates of the frequency for high-frequency events. However, for high-frequency losses, judgement is not required, since sufficient data can easily be obtained. Scenarios simply cannot be relied upon to fill the gap for estimating frequency when there are insufficient loss data.

Generally, business expertise can be used to obtain, at the very least, a first approximation of the financial impact of the operational risk event. This estimate can be anchored in business facts and, therefore, can have a high degree of credibility if done correctly. For example, a head of trading may not be able to estimate how frequently a rogue trading event can happen, but – based on the average transaction size, the number of transactions processed in a day, the number of traders, the time it takes to detect a rogue trading event – an analysis of the control and trade capture systems, etc, could provide a reasonable estimate of the financial impact of the rogue trading event. The same process can be used to obtain a reasonable estimate of the financial impact of most other operational risk events. In fact, the same business manager could even accurately estimate the financial consequences of a heart attack, given some facts about recovery time and surgical costs. It is clear that scenario analysis can be very useful for estimating the severity distribution. And it can be used to overcome a major obstacle to data sufficiency.

MODELLING OPERATIONAL RISK: HOW TO MODEL RARE EVENTS?

In operational risk, unexpected losses happen very infrequently. Consequently, there will always be a lack of sufficient data to apply the standard statistical techniques that have been developed for, say, market risk. As we have seen in earlier discussions, there have been attempts to remedy the situation by incorporating industry data and scenario analysis data. However, these suggestions provide only inadequate patches to the current dilemma. In some instances, these ad hoc patches actually reduce the credibility of the resultant unexpected loss estimates, rather than increase it.

As with any modelling endeavour, when one path proves to be a dead end, try a different path. There are other risk areas that have faced the same lack of sufficient data situation, namely credit risk and casualty risk. Consider a typical casualty risk associated with the risk of driving a car. For a typical driver, the occurrence of car accident, especially a major car accident, is fortunately a rare event. Nevertheless, car accidents do happen with regularity and, at the general population level, there are sufficient data to develop frequency and severity distributions, which can then be used to develop loss distribution for the average driver.

Without further additional data, we could apply this average driver distribution to any given driver and determine the unexpected loss for that driver. Of course, we all know that some drivers are better drivers and drive safer cars on less accident-prone circuits (country road versus motorway, for instance) and, therefore, the average loss distribution overstates the better driver's risk profile, while understating the worse-than-average driver. To correct this, we first augment the loss dataset with associated risk factors/indicators. This allows us to parse the population dataset into sub-population datasets. These sub-population loss datasets have common risk factors/indicators and are generally referred to as a *risk class*. Actuarial techniques can now be applied to this class of drivers to determine the risk profile of the average driver within this class. This is a clear improvement over using only the entire population loss distribution to determine the risk profile for a particular driver. It does, however, still associate the particular driver with the average driver within a class of drivers that share similar risk characteristics, and the problem of either overstating or understating the actual risk profile of the particular driver, although reduced, remains. To get around this, additional risk factors/indicators can be collected with each loss and each risk class can be further sub-classified. There comes a point however, apart from the cost of gathering an increasing amount of information with each loss, when the resultant subclass no longer has sufficient loss data points to derive a credible loss distribution. At this point, the process of further subdividing the risk classes stops. In fact the parsing process, should stop when the resulting risk classes have just sufficient loss data points.

The process described above is standard practice in the insurance industry. A particular exposure index is chosen and, based on the loss distribution for each class, the expected and unexpected rates are determined, which, when applied to the exposure index of the particular driver, yields the expected loss and unexpected loss for that driver.

This process has a clear parallel with the Basel II approaches to quantifying operational risk.[9]

At the most basic level, all banks are grouped into one class. Based on the loss data and gross income as the exposure index, the unexpected rate at the 99.9% confidence level (α in Basel nomenclature) is derived. Applying α to the gross income of any particular bank will yield the unexpected loss for that bank and, therefore, its minimum regulatory capital for operational risk. Despite criticism levied against this approach as being overly simplistic, it is grounded in well-established approaches used in the insurance industry that insure similar risk as operational risks. The calibration of α remains an issue, however, but as banks put in place systematic operational loss collection systems, the issue should disappear. The working group of the Basel Committee has also been collecting the industry loss data and recalibrating α. The approach just described is called the Basic Indicator Approach in the Basel II documents.

Basel II next parsed this industry loss data into eight different operational risk classes by using standardised business activity as risk factor. Loss distributions were then derived for each of these eight operational risk classes and, once again, using gross income as the exposure index, individual unexpected loss rates (denoted by β) were determined for each of the classes. The unexpected loss at the 99.5% confidence level for any one of the eight operational risk classes is then simply determined as the product of β and the associated gross income for that operational risk class/business activity.

Since banks engage in several business activities and most large internationally active banks engage in all of them, the operational risk unexpected loss for a given bank can be derived by adding the unexpected losses for each of the standard business activities the bank conducts. This may overstate the risk since it assumes perfect correlation between risks in each of the class. It is the best that can be done at this stage since there are not sufficient data to determine the actual correlation, and from a regulatory point of view it is better to overstate than to understate, albeit within reason. This approach is called the standardised approach in Basel II.

Next, we describe the advanced measurement approach (AMA), which was introduced in Basel II in its realisation that the standardised approach did not recognise other risk factors such as differences in the business and control environments within each of the eight operational risk classes. However, rather than develop the logical extension to the basic indicator approach and the standardised approach, it took a detour and allowed for each bank to develop its own loss distributions based primarily on its own loss data, ignoring the fact that fortunately there will never be sufficient internal loss data to be able to accomplish this task.[10] In addition, *ad hoc* patches of external data and scenario analysis, as described earlier, were introduced. As we have seen in the example of the risk associated with driving a car, the logical extension to the first two approaches is to further subdivide each of the eight operational risk classes into different subclasses according to difference in business and control environments. This is the approach that will be presented in detail in the remaining sections of this chapter. It will be referred to as the *operational risk rating model*. Panel 1 describes the elements of the operational risk rating model. Panel 2 explains how it works.

PANEL 2 THE OPERATIONAL RISK RATING MODEL: WHAT IS IT?

As shown in Figure 6, the operational risk rating model picks up where the standardised approach ends. The model introduces two additional risk factors – the business and the control environments – to further refine the operational risk classes.

This model has intuitive appeal to business management. First, they can easily relate to the car analogy, and, therefore, the model makes

---

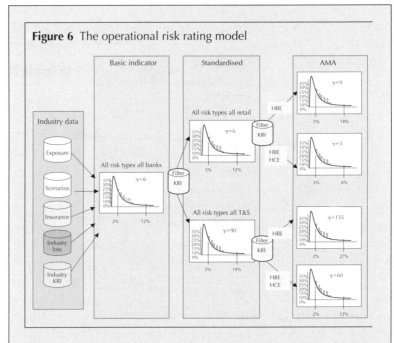

Figure 6 The operational risk rating model

logical sense to them. More importantly, by tying the measurement of their operational risk and thus their capital requirement to their business and control environments, they have been given a direct way to determine the trade-off between spending more by improving their business and control environment and reducing their operational risk capital requirement.

At a technical level, the operational risk rating model also integrates industry data, scenario analysis (for severity only) and the business and control environments directly into the model and not as ad hoc patches.

The operational risk rating model present in Panel 1 rests on a foundation of solid and proper risk identification, and integrates the identification process right into the measurement process. As described earlier, the exposure to operational risks is determined by the four operational risk factors:

❏ type of business activity;
❏ the exposure index;
❏ the state of the business operational environment in which the activity is carried out; and
❏ the state of the control environment.

The actual amount of operational risk present at any given point in time is determined by the specific elements of each of these operational risk factors at that time. These specific elements vary from time to time and from situation to situation, and, therefore, developing an exhaustive list of all the elements that affect operational risk is not meaningful. Instead, the identification component of the model specifies the methodology for identifying what the operational risks are and for identifying the specific elements of each of these risk factors that influence the level of the risk in any given specific situation.

The measurement component of the model specifies the relationship between the type of activity, the exposure index, the state of the business and control environments in which these activities are undertaken and the amount at risk.

Let us now examine the identification component in detail. The first step in the operational risk identification process is disaggregating the bank into its various standardised business activities using the eight Basel II categories, with the addition of other non-Basel categories as required.

The next step is to identify the specific operational risks that each of these standardised business activities is exposed to. Again, we will use the seven Basel II operational risks as a starting point (see Figure 7).[11] Since the specific risk within each of the seven operational risks varies with the business activity, it is important to drill down one more level. For example, both asset management and retail banking are exposed to professional practices risk. However, asset management is exposed to account churning under professional

---

Figure 7 The Basel operational risk types

Internal fraud
Losses due to acts of a type intended to defraud, misappropriate property or circumvent regulations, the law or company policy, excluding diversity/discrimination events, which involves at least one internal party.

External fraud
Losses due to acts of a type intended to defraud, misappropriate property or circumvent the law, by a third party.

Employment Practices and workplace safety
Losses arising from acts inconsistent with employment, health or safety laws or agreements, from payment of personal injury claims, or from diversity/discrimination events.

Professional practices
Losses arising from an unintentional or negligent failure to meet a professional obligation to specific clients (including fiduciary and suitability requirements), or from the nature or design of a product.

Loss or damage to assets
Losses arising from loss or damage to physical assets from natural disaster or other events.

Business disruption and system failures
Losses arising from disruption of business or system failures.

Transaction processing risk
Losses from failed transaction processing or process management, from relations with trade counterparties and vendors.

practices, while retail banking is not. Retail banking is exposed to lender liability under professional practices, while asset management is not.

Once the specific risks have been identified for each risk type and for each business activity, the specific elements of the business and control environment that have a direct effect on the level of operational risk need to identified. To do this in a systematic manner, standard elements of each have to be developed, just as Basel II did for the business activities and for the operational risk types. Fortunately, there are ready-made standards for the control environment. They have been developed previously by COSO and COBIT.[12]

The control environment shown in Figure 8 is an adaptation of the COSO/COBIT internal control framework. It presents the general elements of any control environment. What is important here,

Figure 8 The control environment

Control drivers	Characteristics
Policy/directives	Policies/directives current primitive. Policies/directives provide adequate guidance. Polices/directives are known/followed.
Qualified personnel	Turnover. Sufficient FTE to execute the control environment described for managing this risk. Personnel have the appropriate skill sets to execute and monitor the control environment.
Risk measures/limits	Risk measures or limits exist for this activity. Risk measures or limits at an appropriate threshold for this activity. Risk measures or limits are breached regularly.
Process/procedures	Sufficient process exist to manage this activity. Processes documented. Documented processes reflect current practices and processes. Established processes exist to manage this activity.
Independent reporting/MIS	Adequate information sources are available to understand what is occurring in your business activities. Information is not available when it is needed or is dated. Reporting is not clear and concise (ie, complete).
Communication	Communication channels exist for this business activity (ie, Do you know whom to contact when you have a question?) When communication channels are used, there is a timely response.
Monitoring	Adequate oversight exists for the activities described in the control environment. Monitoring activity is independent of the unit that performs the day to day work within the LoB.

until either Basel II or some industry group establishes the standards, is not that these specific elements are the ultimate standards, but, rather, that it is meant only to demonstrate how they or any other standard can be incorporated into the operational risk measurement model.

Let us now see how this works in practice. First, each of these elements is rated on a five-point scale, based on the extent of the gap. The five-point scale can range from, say, a major gap, through above-average gap, average gap and below-average gap to minor gap, relative to some best-practices standards. Each of these rating can be assigned a numerical value ranging from, say, 1 to 5. This will facilitate the aggregation of the individual ratings for each control element and for the determination of the composite rating for the entire control environment. The aggregation methods can be additive, giving equal weighting to each control element or weighted differently, if it is determined that, for a specific business activity and a specific operational risk type, certain control-element gaps have more of an effect on the level of risk than others. For simplicity of illustration, this chapter will use the simple additive approach.

A similar approach needs to be developed for the business environment, but unfortunately there is no equivalent to the COSO/COBIT framework from which the elements of the business environment can be developed. I present in this panel a specific approach to establishing the elements of the business environment. The goal is not to propose these as standards but to illustrate how they can be incorporated into the operational risk rating model. Figure 9 illustrates the specific elements of a business environment rating framework.

As with the elements of the control environment, each of these can be rated individually along a five-point scale, which then can be aggregated to obtain a composite rating for the business environment. The five-point scale rates the business environment in terms of complexity and stability, with higher complexity and lower stability increasing the operational riskiness of the business environment. This rating scheme is an illustration of a simple but important first step. The rating scheme can also be made more sophisticated as the business environment becomes progressively more complicated.

The rating of the control environment was presented first because it is easier to illustrate how it can work in practice due to the existence of ready-made industry standards, eg, COSO and COBIT. In practice, however, the business environment should be rated first and then the control environment should be rated relative to best practice appropriate to that environment. For example, a highly complex, unstable business environment requires a higher degree of controls to keep the risk within an acceptable level than does a simple stable environment.

Figure 9 The business environment

Environmental drivers	Characteristics
Product complexity	Familiar market; P/L complexity; Valuation complexity; Maturity/uniqueness
Process complexity	Number of processes
Systems complexity	Maturity of technology; Complexity of technology; Few things through a single system; Standalone, centralised/ multiple regional points; Many things through a single system.
Geography	Urban/rural presence; Exposure to natural disaster; Exposure to terrorism; Crime environment; Political stability
Legal complexity	Jurisdiction; Standardised document and affect on class suits; specialised documentation affect on suits; Fiduciary aspect to activity; Number of laws governing business activities; Court tested
Regulatory complexity	Multiple regulatory bodies; New regulatory bodies; New or existing regulatory bodies with evolving mandates; Multiple domestic, foreign, or multi-national jurisdictions; Complex or new regulation
Speed of change	Rapid expansion
Rapid downsizing

Once the business and control environments have been individually rated, the aggregate rating for each business activity and for each operational risk type can be obtained by combining the two, either through a simple additive process or a more sophisticated process depending on whether the bank is just starting out with the rating system or it has been in place for a while.

Figure 10 illustrates how the rating system, when applied to say the retail banking business activity and the internal fraud operational risk type, can be reported in a way that is easy to understand. This visualisation of the rating is, of course, supported by the report of the specific factors that gave rise to individual rating for each of the elements of the business and the control environments.

Once this process has been done for a specific operational risk type, it is repeated for each of the other six, until the operational risk profile for a specific business activity can be obtained.

Figure 11 illustrates how the operational risk profile for, say, retail banking can be represented in terms of what are sometimes called heat maps, where black indicates a high degree of risk while grey represents a low degree of risk. This is a simple three-point scale, but as before it is only a starting point and can be easily evolved into a more elaborate and granular scale, sufficient to meet the business needs.

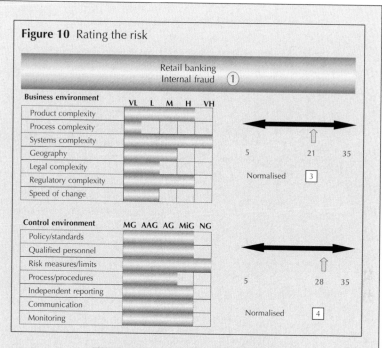

Figure 10 Rating the risk

Retail banking
Internal fraud ①

Business environment	VL	L	M	H	VH
Product complexity					
Process complexity					
Systems complexity					
Geography					
Legal complexity					
Regulatory complexity					
Speed of change					

5   21   35

Normalised ③

Control environment	MG	AAG	AG	MiG	NG
Policy/standards					
Qualified personnel					
Risk measures/limits					
Process/procedures					
Independent reporting					
Communication					
Monitoring					

5   28   35

Normalised ④

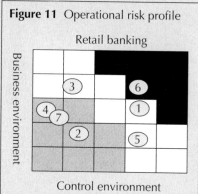

Figure 11 Operational risk profile

Retail banking

Business environment

Control environment

Each of the circled numbers represents a particular operational risk type. For example, the number 1 represents internal fraud and, in this example, it has a medium business environment rating combined with above-average control gaps, leaving the net risk white. In other words, even though the control gaps are above average, the residual risk remains average.[13] There are two important points to realise here. First, when control gaps are determined within the context of the actual business environment, control gaps are not seen as issues to be

> closed. Instead, control gaps are seen as issues to be managed in order to achieve the desired risk profile. Therefore, if the resultant rating for, say, business disruption and systems failure risk is black due to the combination of the business environment and the level of controls, business management now has the opportunity to either spend the money to reduce the control gaps or live with the control gaps along with the higher capital requirements. In order to be able to make this trade-off, the qualitative rating of the risk needs to be translated into a quantitative determination of the resultant expected and unexpected loss.[14] In addition, the rating scheme presented so far can yield the same qualitative risk profile for two very different business activities. And yet, intuitively, operational risk managers would agree that a high risk in say trading and sales has a higher loss profile than a high risk for retail banking. For these reasons, the qualitative operational ratings profile needs to be calibrated to an objective quantitative potential loss profile. This is the job of the operational risk rating model.

THE OPERATIONAL RISK RATING MODEL: CALIBRATING THE RISK

The process for arriving at the different loss profiles was described earlier in Panel 1. The process was illustrated in Figure 8. I reproduce Figure 6 in Figure 12 for ease of reading and to illustrate how the qualitative operational risk profile can be calibrated into an operational loss profile.

In summary, industry loss data, along with the associated business activity, the business and control environments are used to derive a loss profile for each class of risk. The loss profile is actually the loss rate profile, since the exposure index is used to normalise losses into loss rates.[15] Recall that the loss rate at the business activity level is called β, and we now introduce the loss rate Vega[16] to describe the loss rate for the different business and control environments within a business line and for each operational risk type. In other words, β is split into various Vegas – one for each combination of business and control environment. For example, retail banking has a β of 12%, which represents a retail bank with average business and control environments, ie, medium/white. Given that there are seven operational risks, the Vega for retail banking medium/white risk is 1.7% (12/7).

Where do the actual βs and Vegas come from? As illustrated in Figure 12, the βs are derived from splitting the industry loss profile

Figure 12 Calibrating the risk

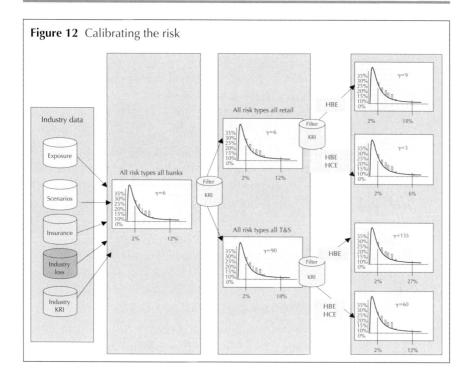

into the eight standardised business-activity profiles and for each resultant loss profile first determining the worst-case loss at some specified confidence level and then dividing that by the gross income (Column 2 in Figure 12). In a similar manner, Vegas are obtained. First each of the specific standardised business-activity loss profiles is spit into the seven risk categories and than for each of these risk categories each is split into the three levels of risk (high/black, medium/white and low/grey at its simplest level) of the operational risk profile. Once this is done for each operational risk class, the Vega is obtained by dividing the resultant worst-case loss at the same prespecified confidence level and then dividing the result by gross income. Repeating this for each risk type and for each business activity completes the calibration. Just a β of 12% for retail banking means that for ever every dollar of gross income the average retail bank puts 12 cents at risk due to operational risk. A Vega of, say, 1.8% for the high-risk fraud in retail banking means that for every dollar of gross income, a retail bank with high fraud risk would have to put at risk 1.8 cents of capital for fraud risk.

Now, the process for obtaining the capital, or for that matter any other aspect of the loss profile, for a specific bank can be broken down into a series of steps. First, break down the bank into the standardised business activity. Then for each activity, determine the operational risk profile using the process described earlier. After this, find the corresponding industry-derived Vegas for each operational risk type within each business activity. Aggregate the Vegas to obtain a composite Vega for the business activity.[17] Use the exposure index to convert the individual business activity's operational risk loss rate profile to the actual operational risk loss profile. Then aggregate the loss profile for each business activity into the bank loss profile, using correlations as appropriate and substantiated by data.

The following will illustrate how this can work in practice. Suppose that, by using the process described above, the following Vegas have been determined for retail banking, and trading and sales respectively: Low = 0.10%, Average = 0.17%, High = 0.26% and Low = 0.17%, Average = 0.26%, High = 0.45%.

With the risk profiles as illustrated in Figure 13, the composite Vega would be obtained as follows. For retail banking, there is one operational risk type rated high (illustrated in Figure 13 by the circled number 6 within the retail banking risk profile) and, therefore, associated with a Vega of 2.6, there are three risks (numbers 1, 3 and 5) that have been rated average and therefore have a corresponding Vega 1.7, and the remaining three risks have been

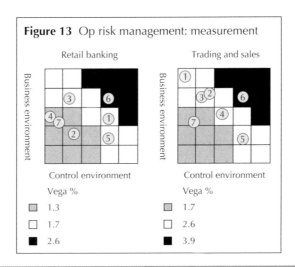

Figure 13 Op risk management: measurement

Retail banking

Trading and sales

Business environment

Business environment

Control environment

Control environment

Vega %

1.3

1.7

2.6

Vega %

1.7

2.6

3.9

rated low and therefore have a Vega of 1. Summing the individual weighted Vegas yields composite Vega of 11% for this retailing banking activity.[18] This is one percentage point lower than the beta for retailing banking. If the associated gross income with this particular retailing banking was, say, US$5,000 million, then the associated capital is US$550 million (11% of 5,000), rather than US$600 million (12% of 5,000) associated with an average-risk retailing banking.

Continuing this process for the trading and sales activity with the risk profile as illustrated in Figure 13 yields a composite Vega of 19%. This compares with a β of 18% for the average trading and sales activity as calibrated by Basel II, indicating the trading and sales activity represented in Figure 13 is more risky than the average trading and sales.

The capital requirement for the trading and sales activity represented in Figure 13 is obtained by multiplying its aggregate Vega by its gross income. Therefore, suppose that this trading and sales activity had a gross income of US$3,000 million then the capital requirement would be US$570 million (19% of 3,000) rather than US$540 million (18% of 3,000) associated with an average-risk trading and sales operation. If these were the only two activities the bank was conducting, the total capital would be US$1,120 million (550 plus 570) and this compares to a capital requirement of US$960 million based on an average bank as calibrated by Basel II.[19] The higher capital reflects that this bank has a higher proportion of trading and sales compared with the average bank and that the riskiness of its trading and sales activity, as represented by its Vega of 19% versus the β of 18%, is also higher than average.

The above discussion illustrates how the operational risk rating model works and how it relates both the qualitative drivers of the operational risk and the quantitative/financial impact of those drivers to the capital requirements. The calibration of the model shown here is for illustrative purposes and must await industry loss and key risk indicator information to derive the actual risk classes and their associated α, β, and Vegas. The model also shows how each component integrates into one coherent methodology and ensures consistency by requiring, through the calibration process, that α represents the (weighted) average of β, and that the β for each business activity represents the (weighted) average of the Vegas.

CONCLUSION

We started this chapter with the objective of developing an operational risk measurement model that would provide management not only with a measure of the expected and unexpected losses but also a deep understanding of the controllable and uncontrollable risk factors that have a major and direct influence on the level of operational risk. This requires that the model be based on a solid and coherent risk identification process, which first identifies the nature of the operational risk and second the relative level of the operational risk. The nature of the operational risk is determined through the identification of the business activity, and the specific operational risk types to which the activity is exposed to. The relative level of the operational risk is determined through identification of the exposure index, and the key risk indicators that reflect the business and control environments. These operational risk factors are used to assign an operational risk rating to each line of business. So far the process has yielded only a qualitative assessment of the risk. To obtain a measure of the risk, each of the ratings has to be assigned to a specific aggregated loss distribution. This is done by:

1. using the same risk factors to first partition the combined external loss and scenario analysis severity data set into subsets, with one subset for each risk rating; and
2. developing frequency and severity distributions for each rating.

Once these distributions are obtained, Monte Carlo simulation is used to arrive at the aggregate loss distribution for each rating. Obtaining the loss distributions (more specifically the expected and unexpected loss) for a particular line of business is then a matter of assigning a rating to the business and looking up the corresponding loss distribution assigned to that rating. In addition, since each loss distribution is matched with a set of risk factors, business management has an easy way of determining the effects of changing their risk factors by the type and level of their operational risk. No longer are the business and control environments *ad hoc* modifiers to an isolated measurement of the risk – they are built-in. The operational risk rating model also overcomes one of the central problems of operational risk modelling, which is the perpetually insufficient relevancy of loss data for rare operational risk events.

This operational risk rating measurement model gives business management the same level of transparency and understanding of the drivers of operational risk as they are accustomed to getting for their credit and market risk models. This provides an excellent first step in integrating operational risk management practices into business management practices. We say a first step, because the model can clearly be improved. However, once business management and risk management units have integrated the measurement model into their business and risk control practices, further levels of granularity and enhancements can be added to this model. Models should always only be improved through use. In other words, it is always possible to think of more and better features to add. Lack of imagination is usually *not* the issue, whereas having the greatest impact on practice for the least development cost *is* the issue. What best to do, can only be discovered by prudently, not blindly, using the model in running the business.

Shortly after becoming accustomed to operating the model, business management will often point out that their own loss experience would suggest that they are quite different from the operational risk rating to which they have been assigned, ie, a lower risk. If there is sufficient internal loss data to at least suggest that this may be the case, credibility theory may be used to incorporate the specific internal loss experience and thereby generate a more accurate and lower expected and unexpected loss for that line of business. Credibility theory has a large body of literature within actuarial sciences and a long history of practice within the insurance industry. However, this is not the topic here but for some future publication.[20]

---

1   It is important to realise that any model is only a partial reflection of the actual risk and therefore any measurement will only be an estimate of the actual risk.

2   The high-volume low value of each transaction makes the operational risk of each transaction relatively small. However, because these transactions are developed, delivered and processed through standardised process, they expose the bank to a concentration of operational risk that can exceed transactional level risk of the low-volume high value of complex derivatives trading. This happens when transactions are linked and therefore not independent. For example, a minor error in a program that calculates the foreign exchange rate for credit card transactions would cause each transaction be slightly off. However, given the very large volume of transactions processed by the program, the aggregate error would be very large.

3   In theory all factors are under the control of business management, since management can choose to relocate, switch, deliver change, change the products, etc, these change initiatives may take a long time to complete, and they in turn may introduce their own operational risk. As a result it is reasonable to assume that the business environment is significantly less under management control than the control environment.

4   This observation is based on operational risk models that have been offered by various vendors or presented by various operational risk managers at various conferences.

5   Key performance indicators are metrics generally associated with key performance factors such as cost efficiency, staff productivity and process efficiency and cycle time. There is a symmetrical relationship between key performance indicators and key operational risk indicators. If one envisions a risk continuum form zero potential loss to expected loss to unexpected losses, one can imagine a gradual transformation/replacement of key performance indictors with key operational risk indicators. And since management manages the entire risk continuum both are equally important.

6   Many banks have begun major efforts in systematically collecting, categorising, evaluating and reporting operational risk losses. Since most operational losses were buried in various and sundry general ledger accounts and not generally tracked, this work usually involves both major (depending on the level of granularity) costly system and process changes.

7   Basel has indicated that initially three years' worth of internal loss data will be sufficient and that subsequently there should be five years' worth of data.

8   High-frequency losses must by necessity be associated with low-severity losses, otherwise the bank would go bankrupt quickly, and therefore, from a measurement perspective, it is a non-issue.

9   The following will describe the Basel approach in the context of the insurance paradigm described in the above. Whether Basel actually followed this path, and it probably did not, is largely irrelevant, and describing the Basel approach through paradigm provides the foundation for the approaches and helps understand them better.

10 The exception being high-frequency, low-severity losses associated with fraud in retail credit card operational or routine errors in processing censers.

11 Some of the Basel names have been changed to shorten them and to make them more descriptive.

12 COSO is a voluntary private-sector organisation dedicated to improving the quality of financial reporting through business ethics, effective internal controls, and corporate governance. COSO was originally formed in 1985 to sponsor the National Commission on Fraudulent Financial Reporting, an independent private-sector initiative that studied the causal factors that can lead to fraudulent financial reporting and developed recommendations for public companies and their independent auditors, for the SEC and other regulators, and for educational institutions. COBIT has been developed as a generally applicable and accepted standard for good information technology (IT) security and control practices that provides a reference framework for management, users and IS audit, control and security practitioners.

13 This conclusion is not automatic: it would have to be supported by the individual ratings and the aggregation process. In a different situation with different individual ratings, the aggregation process could have resulted in rating the residual risk high, ie, black.

14 This is similar to the developments in credit risk where internal credit risk rating systems need to be calibrated to probability of default and loss given default metrics.

15 The loss rate profile is obtained by dividing the loss profile by the exposure index. So id the expected loss is US$100 and the exposure index is US$1,000 then the expected loss rate is 10%.

16 Gamma could have been used to describe this loss rate, but in operational risk gamma has been associated with the ratio of the unexpected loss to the expected loss.

17 Note that the aggregate Vega for a business activity with an average risk profile has to be calibrated to the beta for that business activity since the Beat by construction is the loss rate for the average risk of a particular business activity.

18 The actual aggregate Vega is 10.7% but has been rounded to 111% to avoid spurious accuracy.

19 The average bank has been calibrated by Basel II, under the Basic Indicator Approach, to have an operational risk capital requirement of 12% per unit of gross income. In this case the total gross income is $8,000 millions and therefore the capital requirement is $960 millions.

20 An Introduction to Credibility Theory; Longley-Cook, Laurence H.; *Proceedings of the Casualty Actuarial Society 1962 Vol: XLIX Page(s): 194–221;* Casualty Actuarial Society: Arlington, Virginia.

BIBLIOGRAPHY

Basel Committee on Banking Supervision, 2003, "The Third Consultative Paper on the New Basel Accord", April.

Cook, L., and H. Laurence, "An Introduction to Credibility Theory", *Proceedings of the Casualty Actuarial Society 1962, vol XLIX,* pp. 194–221 (Arlington, Virginia: Casualty Actuarial Society).

Section 6

Loss Database and Insurance

17

Constructing an Operational Event Database

Michael Haubenstock*

Capital One

INTRODUCTION

Capturing a history of operational events has become a standard practice for an operational risk management framework. An event history has demonstrated value for both the quantification and qualitative analysis of risk. This chapter deals with the practical aspects of internal data collection, from detection through reporting. Clear direction and guidance has been given by the Basel Committee and regulators on the necessity for event data.

Regulatory requirements embodied in the Basel II proposals for operational risk management tend to be oriented toward a capital charge for operational risk. Yet industry practice often extends beyond the regulatory guidelines. These minimum regulatory requirements will be discussed here, as well as key decisions to be made on how and where to extend the event database beyond regulatory requirements. In addition, in many places the regulatory guidance is not specific, stating only that organisations should develop consistent policy. Key areas where specific organisational decisions and policies are required will also be identified.

*The author would like to acknowledge Jeff Hause, manager for the event collection process at Capital One, for his contribution to and review of this chapter. The author would also like to acknowledge Eric Brule of Capital One, Ladd Muzzy, First Vice President, ABN-AMRO, and John Thirlwell, Executive Director, Operational Risk Research Forum for their thoughtful comments.

This chapter is organised into the following major sections:

❑ Basel II and regulatory requirements
❑ The benefits of collecting operational events
❑ Data collection standards
❑ The event collection process
❑ Roles and responsibilities
❑ Creating a supportive culture
❑ Reporting the results

BASEL AND REGULATORY REQUIREMENTS

The Basel II proposals refer to loss data in several different contexts. In the Sound Practices Paper, the Committee refers to collecting loss data as a component of both risk identification and monitoring.[1] In the third Consultative Paper (CP3), loss data is a tool to validate risk estimates, a component of risk reporting, and a key input to any Advanced Measurement Approach (AMA) model.[2] In addition, CP 3 sets the standard for seven standard categories of operational event risk.

At the time of this writing, the supervisory guidance on AMA from the US regulatory agencies provides more specific guidance on loss event data as one component of requirements to be eligible to qualify for AMA approaches.[3] In summary, it states:

> The institution must have at least five years of operational risk loss data, captured across all material business lines, events, product types and geographic locations. For early adopters, there is a caveat that as little as three years of data may be considered sufficient on a provisional basis. Data needs to be comprehensive and non-overlapping.
>
> The institution must be able to map operational risk losses to the seven loss-event type categories and standard business line categories.
>
> The institution must have a policy that defines when an operational risk event becomes a loss event and must be added to the loss event database. The policy must provide for consistent treatment across the institution.
>
> The institution must provide consistent operational risk data thresholds for event capture and reporting.
>
> Losses that have any characteristic of credit risk, including fraud-related credit losses, must be treated as credit risk for regulatory capital purposes. The institution must have a clear policy that allows for a consistent treatment of loss classifications (eg, credit, market, operational risk) across the organisation (also known as border issues).

PANEL 1 THE BENEFITS OF COLLECTING OPERATIONAL EVENTS

In addition to being a regulatory requirement, collecting operational events has a potential direct benefit to any institution. Overall, the event collection effort, as a component of an operational risk management framework, should help contribute to the goal of reduced actual incidents and amount of loss, as well as overall quality of service and products. More specifically, the primary benefits are:

❑ *Increasing awareness of operational risks* Tracking and reporting of actual events helps raise awareness that exposures can happen and are potentially harmful to the organisation.

❑ *Quantification of exposure* One element of awareness is how much operational risk is costing the organisation. Most times, after first completing an event collection exercise, institutions find the actual cost to be much higher than originally anticipated. This helps focus resources on mitigation efforts where they are needed. Benchmarking between business areas may also provide insight into opportunities for improvement.

❑ *Analysis of root causes* Each event has a root cause(s) and may identify opportunities to improve controls. Repeated occurrences and resulting trends may point out new areas for improvement. They may signal specific processes, functions or businesses that have deficient controls and pose a greater threat to the organisation. Taking preventive action is the actual decision-making that hopefully will result from the collection effort.

❑ *Check and balance over self-assessment processes* First, events provide an objective source to estimate frequency and severity in self-assessment processes. Second, actual events act as a quality check over self-assessments. If events occur without a corresponding risk, then the assessment should be updated. If risks are identified without any related experience, then the frequency can be reexamined to assure it is reasonable, and/or the quality of controls to detect events may be re-evaluated.

❑ *Quantification of capital* As highlighted in the regulatory guidance, loss events form a primary input for many approaches to quantify operational risk capital, whether using a top-down or bottom-up approach.

Event databases are most often used to track events with a quantifiable Profit and Loss (P&L) impact. They can also be used to track events that could have had a P&L impact, but fortunately did not. These are often called "near misses". Therefore, the more general terminology "event database" is used here instead of the more commonly used terminology of loss database.

DATA COLLECTION STANDARDS

This section discusses the various standards that must be set for any institution to establish a consistent event collection process. Standards include the definition of what constitutes an event, thresholds for collection, how to classify and quantify events, confidentiality guidelines, and required policies. Not only must standards be codified in policy, but they must be continually reinforced with training and practice.

What is an operational event?

An operational event can be defined as:

> An event due to failed or inadequate processes, people or systems, or exposure to external events that caused, or potentially could have caused, a material loss or adversely impacted stakeholders.

The definition refers to stakeholders with the intent of being inclusive of quality, reputation, regulatory, business interruption or other effects that might impact customers, vendors/partners, employees, shareholders or other constituencies. Moreover, this definition encompasses the Basel II definition of operational risk of failed or inadequate processes, people, or systems or exposure to external events. An event is an actual occurrence, not a potential one.

The range of operational events is very large. To illustrate this range, consider a few examples:

❑ The investment in development of a new software system is written off as a loss after it is determined the system will not meet requirements and the development effort is scrapped.

❑ A fraud ring penetrates security controls and through identity theft, manages to obtain credit that then has to be written off.

❑ A former employee accuses the company of discrimination, and a payment is made to settle the complaint.

❑ Procedures are found to be out of compliance with certain regulations, and a compliance fine is assessed by regulatory agencies.

❑ The company is found guilty of anti-trust practices, and a settlement is paid.

❑ Service quality is disputed, and a portion of monies due from a customer is waived.

❑ An error in an operational process results in mis-charging customers.

Basel II requires that only direct losses be captured in an event data collection process. Direct losses, often called effects, are defined as:

❑ Write-downs of assets
❑ Regulatory/compliance penalties
❑ Legal payments/settlements (including all litigation costs)
❑ Customer restitution
❑ Loss of recourse
❑ Loss of physical assets

The rationale behind these definitions is that the effects are objective and directly measurable on a consistent basis by all institutions. Basel II is oriented toward a capital charge for operational risk, and consequently the definition of operational risk and related events is purposefully narrow to keep measurement objective on an equal basis across institutions. Other types of effects, discussed later in this chapter, are more problematic to measure consistently across institutions and have been excluded from the Basel II requirements.

A key question all institutions must answer is if, and where, practices should extend beyond Basel II requirements? The answer is potentially where enhancements can help improve the operational risk management discipline.

It is important that every institution define its own data collection policy and related guidelines to establish its own rules. Some institutions may wish to establish practices that go beyond Basel practices. Even if collection is limited to Basel II guidelines, given that some of the guidelines are vague, the most important thing is to have rules and consistently apply them across products, geographies and risk categories. Some of the key issues related to defining exactly what an event is, and issues related to the scope of event collection, described below. Best practice would be to collect all these events:

❑ *Near misses* These are typically defined as events where some type of failure occurred, but no financial loss was incurred. Any significant event has potential lessons learned. While near misses do not cause any direct loss, in another set of circumstances there could have been a real loss. It is valuable to know about the frequency that operational risk events occur and whether a zero direct loss was a result of well-established controls or just luck. Institutions must determine if and where near misses should be collected.

❑ *Indirect losses (also known as associated costs)* Indirect losses may include effects such as business interruption, forgone income, reputation risks and poor quality. While outside the Basel II definition of operational risk, indirect losses are within the common industry definition. Although difficult to quantify, many institutions do make efforts to quantify some or all of these effects. Some may be directly measurable, others not. For example, estimating the exposure of a business interruption by using some form of standard cost by hour of downtime or per employee impacted. Another potential treatment is to simply identify that these indirect effects occurred for any particular event.

❑ *Profits* Some operations can result in accidental profits. Examples are common in trading floors where an incorrect operation and a favourable market movement results in a gain. Some firms do record these events as another source of causal analysis.

❑ *Credit losses* Guidance from Basel II has clearly delineated the treatment of credit and operational losses. However, there are many instances where credit and operational events coexist. Capture by the root cause (operational) can assist in the analysis of causes and related control improvement opportunities, just like other operational events. For example, there should be rules for each type of fraud. Frauds occurring in obtaining credit (eg, overstating collateral, or misrepresenting financial condition) will usually be considered credit losses. However external fraud is within the definition of operational risk and items such as credit card frauds are within the scope of event collection. Capturing all credit events with operational causes can enhance the value of the database. This implies that credit loss events need to be excluded from any operational risk capital calculations to avoid double counting.

❑ *Timing events* This is an item that is unclear in regulatory guidance. Timing events may result in a current period P&L change, but often not in a real loss of cash flow. Consequently the question is whether or not this is an operational loss and whether to record it in the database and use it in capital calculations. Examples include mark-to-market model errors, accounting or accrual errors and subsequent reversals/corrections, account reconciliation write-offs, and errors in intra-company books that might affect internal business areas/entities but not the external consolidated statements. Some of the large infamous rogue trading losses are a form of timing event since income was over recognised and then a loss taken subsequently. Since these cases involved a violation of policy and in some cases an intentional hiding of losses, these events are usually considered hard direct losses, rather than timing events.

❑ *Strategic events (also known as business risk)* A clear definition is necessary to differentiate operational versus strategic risk events. While Basel excludes strategic risks from the definition of operational risk, the boundaries are not clear. For example how would one classify the costs related to pulling out of a country, a failed product introduction, restructuring costs after a layoff, excess real-estate capacity due to mis-forecasting and changing business volumes, or increased supplier costs incurred to meet customer service standards?

What is the right loss threshold?

As a matter of simple cost versus benefits, each institution has to set its own threshold for event capture. This is the amount below which events do not need to be recorded. Most institutions use a threshold between zero and US$25,000, most often US$10,000. The policy may differ by risk or business area. Generally, capturing smaller events (eg, below US$10,000) requires a high level of automation and little description (eg, credit card frauds, small retail banking write-offs, and P&L adjustments that can be captured through the general ledger). Where events are recorded manually, there is obviously a cost and that is an important consideration in setting the threshold.

Some useful benchmarks are provided by the following industry consortium efforts to collect and share events:

❑ The Basel CP2 exercise asked institutions to submit events over US$10,000.
❑ The Operational Riskdata Exchange Association (ORX) consortium uses US$25,000.
❑ The American Bankers Association consortium uses US$10,000.
❑ The British Bankers Association consortium uses US$50,000.

When event collection is instituted internally, resistance from some business areas is common. The level of threshold is a common debate, with the argument that if the threshold is raised, the majority of the value of events will be captured at a much lower cost. While this is statistically true, not all the benefits of event capture would be obtained. Capturing lower value events has great value in that:

❑ Small events are necessary to perform any trend analysis. The larger events are rarer and differ in value, making any trend analysis much more difficult.

❑ Without capturing small events, many root causes of events can be missed. For every event, large and small, the underlying cause should be determined. The fundamental question is "Could this event happen again? And could it be larger the next time?"

❑ Small events could be larger ones in the making. They could be an early warning of one event that could grow (eg, an error in a system resulting in incorrect accounting) or an indication of repetitive small events that could add up to be something much more material over time.

❑ It may assist in determining what level of loss is considered expected. In many organisations, managers attribute some operational risk events as "the cost of doing business". Hence it may be implicitly or explicitly accounted for in the budgeting process or in the pricing of products. Only through the collection of small events can this distinction be made clear.

Where a threshold is set, there are many events that fall below this threshold. Institutions should be   high frequency events that could add up to material losses, find ways to capture them, and apply the appropriate level of risk mitigation tools to these events to optimise cost versus benefit.

Loss categorisation

Regulators have provided recommendations on seven categories of operational risk (See Panel 2). The seven categories are what are called "event-based". This means that the basis for categorisation is what actually occurred, not the cause or the weakness in controls that caused or permitted the event to occur.

This is important to understand in order to consistently classify events. For the risk categories, two levels of detail are provided, the

PANEL 2 RISK EVENT CATEGORIES

Primary	Secondary
Execution, delivery and process management: Losses from failed transaction processing or process management, from relations with trade counterparties and vendors	Transaction capture, execution and maintenance Monitoring and reporting Customer intake and documentation Vendors and suppliers
Clients, products and business practices: Losses arising from an unintentional or negligent failure to meet a professional obligation to specific clients, or from the nature of product design	Suitability, disclosure and fiduciary Improper business or market practices Product flaws
System failures: Losses arising form disruption or system failures	Systems Systems security
Internal fraud and illegal activity: Losses due to acts of a type intended to defraud, misappropriate property or circumvent regulations, the law or company policy, excluding diversity/discrimination events, which involves at least one internal party	Unauthorised activity Theft and fraud
External fraud and illegal activity: Losses due to acts of a type intended to defraud, misappropriate property or circumvent the law, by a third party. Excludes credit losses covered by the allowance for loan losses, but includes frauds committed by external parties attempting to obtain credit. Does not include vendor fraud	Illegal activity (non-product) Product fraud
Employment practices and workplace safety: Losses arising from acts inconsistent with employment, health or safety laws/agreements,from diversity/discrimination events	Employee relations Safe environment Diversity and discrimination
Damage to physical assets: Losses arising from loss of or damage to physical assets from natural disaster or other events	Disasters and other events

first being the seven primary categories, and the second being a set of sub-categories. The regulatory guidance provides a third level of example events. Some institutions use a third level of categorisation for further details. This is particularly valuable for categories like systems failures, where further breakdown of detail, such as between hardware, software and network issues, would be particularly valuable. If there is a high volume of events in any second level categories, additional breakdowns help in the analysis and associated preventive efforts.

There is an ongoing industry debate on which risk categories to actually use. Most would agree that the categories are fairly comprehensive but could use some refinement. Some institutions are proposing a revision to the standard regulatory risk categories. Examples of other categories include project risk and external mal-intent.

In reality, there is no one set of event categories that would be considered relevant to all institutions. What is important is that the institution should use or develop those event categories that are relevant to the organisation, its businesses, products, markets, and can be understood and applied broadly. Moreover it will provide direction to the organisation and assure a base level of consistency. The only regulatory requirement is to be able to map to the standard definitions. For the purposes of this chapter, the regulatory definitions are used.

Experience has shown that these categories are easy to apply in the majority of incidents, but additional guidance is needed for some events. Some of areas where the Basel definitions are vague are listed below, along with some potential rules that can provide clarifying guidance.

❑ *Systems versus input errors* If a wrong input has been made into a software program, resulting in a loss, is it an execution error or a systems failure? One potential rule is that if one would look to the IT department to manage this issue, it is then a systems failure; otherwise, it is an execution error.

❑ *Events occurring in PC software (eg, spreadsheets)* Although PC and other end user computing software can be considered a system, is "systems failure" the appropriate category for software applications controlled exclusively by business areas? A potential rule is that if the application is managed outside the IT area, it should not be classified a systems failure. This rule keeps all IT-related issues apart.

❏ *Errors in the credit decision process* An operational error in credit decision processes is a borderline issue between two categories: Clients/Products/Business Practices and Execution/Delivery/ Process Management. The guidance for neither category seems to cover this process. If credit models are used, we can classify in the model failure subcategory of Clients/Products/Business Practices. Other related errors could also be placed here for consistency. This is logical in that this category contains mostly risks that affect the customer base, eg, issues that occur prior to closing or booking a client transaction. The other alternative classification is that the credit decision process error is an execution error.

❏ *Inadvertent errors in terms, conditions or disclosures given to customers* This is also a borderline issue between two categories: Clients/ Products/Business Practices and Execution/Delivery/Process Management. Since this is an error, as opposed to a judgment about what to disclose, a potential rule is that it is an execution error.

❏ *Vendor issues resulting in increased costs* What happens if a vendor issue results in increased and unexpected costs? There is a subcategory for vendor and supplier failures. In an outsourcing situation, a vendor processing, vendor fraud, or IT error could be categorised in the same category as if it had occurred internally, presumably since processes should be similar and we can aggregate lessons learned from both internal and vendor sources. The alternative is to assign all issues caused by vendors to the vendor and supplier subcategory. The latter helps to aggregate issues of all types with any one vendor so problematic vendors can be readily identified.

❏ *Service decisions to incur increased direct costs* What happens if a product offering has a slight error or chance of error? There is a strategic decision to move ahead, and a loss results. Given the known chance of error, is the resulting loss an operational loss or a strategic loss? It is generally easier to say that all errors that result in a loss are operational in nature.

❏ *Project risk* Where a major project fails to deliver anticipated benefits, or is cancelled, is the cost an operational loss? Basel II is somewhat clear that failed systems projects be classified as systems failures. Projects without a large IT component are less clear, and some organisations have created a new risk category to include project risks. Obviously, a disciplined project management framework, including cost management, is required to detect and quantify any events. Strategic decisions to stop a project (eg, a reprioritisation of resources) would likely be a strategic risk and not an operational one.

❑ *Malicious damage and terrorism* These could be treated as fraud or physical damage. One argument would be to fall back on the cause which in this case is fraud. Another would be to treat it as physical damage since other accidental damages would have a similar loss distribution and this category would be better aligned with insurance coverage.

❑ *Non-compete settlements* A common settlement is when a business originator (eg, stock broker) leaves one firm and joins another with a client base. If there was a non-compete agreement, there is often a settlement paid by the new institution. Is this internal fraud, employment practices or a business risk? Since there was a legal breakdown, the technical answer might be internal fraud.

❑ *Compliance settlements* Illegal activity (eg, environmental penalties, privacy, money laundering, patent infringement) can be considered internal fraud, execution or business practices.

Loss effects and valuation

Valuing loss event means the quantification of financial loss. Industry practice commonly uses six effect categories. These categories provide a comprehensive list of relatively easy to measure direct expense types. The categories and some examples of each are listed in Panel 3. Many institutions, however, may wish to go beyond the regulatory definitions to capture other effects of an operational event. Other effect categories to consider capturing include the following:

❑ *Credit impacts* While excluded from the definition of operational risk for capital purposes, there are clearly many operational issues that impact credit risk. Some are immediate, where a loss was taken that could have been prevented or reduced by proper

PANEL 3 EFFECT CATEGORIES

Effect is the consequence that the event has to the company. The following intend to ensure the accurate and consistent classification and quantification of effects. Some events may produce a loss in one effect category while resulting in revenue in another effect category.

Effect Type	Definition	Includes	Excludes	Valuation methodologies
Basel effect categories: direct expense				
Legal liability	Judgments, settlements and other legal costs in the defense of the institution, related parties and the assets; both tangible and intangible	Payments to settle legal suits or threatened legal action Payments court costs and related items Payment of external counsel and expert witnesses Fees incurred due to Service Level Agreement (SLA) violations with external parties	Internal counsel costs	Actual amount of fine or settlement
Regulatory action	Fines or the direct payment of any other penalties, such as license revocations	Direct penalties and fines from regulatory agencies or trade groups Payments to external counsel and expert witnesses	Costs associated with regulatory exams	Actual amount of fine or settlement. If multiple-year payment, record the amount of the GAAP reserve established or total value of payments to be made in the next 12 months

441

Effect type	Definition	Includes	Excludes	Valuation methodologies
Restitution	Payments to third parties on account of operational losses for which the institution is legally responsible	Payments to customers or waiver of balances owed due to direct harm caused to the customer/vendor	Postage or materials costs incurred in communicating issue and/or resolution to customer (see *Cost to fix*) Reversal of fees and interest that were incorrectly recognised	Actual amount of payments/waivers. If multiple-year payment, record the amount of the GAAP reserve established, or total value of payments to be made in the next 12 months.
Loss of recourse	Losses experienced when a third party does not meet its obligations to the institution, and which are attributable to an operational mistake or event	Assets and revenue (fee and interest) recorded on the G/L but will not/cannot be collected	Revenue lost due to failure to establish terms with customer (see *Forgone revenue*) Reversal of fees and interest that was incorrectly recognised	Actual amount of principle, fees or interest expected and not collected over the next 12 months
Write-down	Direct reduction in the value of assets (including increased costs) due to theft, fraud, unauthorised activity, operational errors	Material misstatements or errors in accounting practices Significant project overruns or failed projects Reduction in value of systems due to reduced functionality or effectiveness	Credit losses	Record direct reduction in value of assets or unexpected increase in expenses Events with lagging settlements or recoveries can be valued with management

Loss or damage to assets	Direct reduction in value of depreciable physical assets due to some kind of accident	Incremental increases in fraud losses Direct reduction to intangible assets Direct reduction to the value of assets, or increases to liabilities costs incurred in production of defective product	Software applications Intangible assets Costs to temporarily resume operations Decreased productivity due to losses	Fraud events (rings or defense failures) are settled/valued 2 quarters after occurrence, to allow the majority of incoming frauds and recoveries to occur Actual GAAP book value (carrying value), or portion thereof, of asset replaced
		Gross damage to physical assets including buildings, contents, computer equipment and production machinery		
Cost to fix *Cost to fix*	Incremental direct costs incurred to bring business back to operational level	Incremental costs incurred in repair of defective product or system. For example, cost of letters sent to notify customers of error Cost to identify and correct immediate cause(s) of event. Includes overtime paid to recover from extended downtime in processing environments	Incremental cost of operations after cause has been corrected Cost to re-run operation Long-term mitigation plans to prevent re-occurrence of event or generally improve control structure	Actual amount of direct labour, equipment, and services utilised Increases in the incremental value of assets due to improvements should be excluded where practical.

443

Effect type	Definition	Includes	Excludes	Valuation methodologies
		Direct labour and material costs incurred in communicating issue and/or resolution to customer	Time exempt employees spend to resolve issue	
Credit losses				
Credit losses	Increases in charge-offs due to failures of people, process or systems	Incremental increase in charge-offs or default rates caused by operational events	Increases in fraud rates Decreases in credit losses	Present value of increased charge-offs
Impact to revenue/margin				
Forgone income	Lost income or opportunities for revenue Decrease in product profitability	Lost fee and interest opportunities/income that has not been recorded in the G/L due to pricing, modelling, communication or execution errors	Fees and interest waived that we have recorded in the G/L Reversal of fees and interest that was incorrectly recognised Positive revenue flows received due to increases in risk	Pre-tax reduction in estimated revenues from population Use the present value of revenue and fee cash flow at the standard discount rate Where applicable, re-run models to determine actual effects
Business interruption	Inability to process work for an extended period of time	Idle time of hourly employees	Overtime to recover from operational event (see *Cost to fix*)	Actual amount of lost utilisation

Recoveries

Recoveries – insurance	Recoveries of operational losses due to insurance relationships	Reimbursement by insurance companies for covered incidents (excluding co-payment) Reimbursement from third party maintenance contracts on equipment or computer hardware		Actual value of payments received from vendors
Recoveries – other	Recoveries of operational losses due to other means (vendor charge-backs, legal action, fraud recoveries, etc.)	Recoveries from law suits or judgments Recovery of fraud losses Payments from third parties to correct errors caused by third parties Service level fines received	Strategies implemented to limit losses associated with operational losses	Estimated/actual recoveries for the 12-month period following the last event
Recoveries – credit losses	Recoveries of credit losses	Strategies implemented to limit credit losses	Normal credit recoveries conducted by recovery groups	Incremental decrease in 5-year NACO from original expectations of population

operational practices at origination or thereafter. There also are instances where credit was granted that was inconsistent with the original intent, the problem is eventually discovered, and hence increased losses will be recognised in the future over the life of a portfolio. Valuation then implies estimating the present values of future losses.

❑ *Cost to fix* These are the internal and external costs incurred to recover from an operational event. Usually it is mostly labour related, but it could also involve materials and other direct costs as well. Valuation usually implies some element of standard costs for internal personnel time used to fix the problem.

❑ *Business interruption* Systems downtime, loss of access to facilities, power outages or other causes create missed deadlines, lost productivity and lost business opportunities or even delays in cash flow (say, from collections). Valuation also requires a standard cost per employee hour lost or system downtime.

❑ *Forgone income* This is lost income from an operational event. Examples include offers/commitments quoted at the wrong price and delays in offers/sales. This may also require present valuing future impacts.

There are additional areas where internal rules are needed for valuation of effects. There is no perfect answer to these problems, but internal guidance is necessary for consistency. Some of these areas are:

❑ *Recording losses that have occurred over time and multiple events* Sometimes one event has occurred over a period of time and has gone undetected, and a loss is subsequently recognised in the current time period, long after the event has occurred. These are typically not present nor future valued, but the total amount is recorded in the year the problem was discovered (this would theoretically match an accounting entry). Where a single cause has resulted in multiple occurrences of a similar error, these are typically counted as one event. Similarly, common plans of actions, like a fraud scheme, with multiple losses are usually counted as one event.

❑ *Offsets and gains* What happens when there is a loss, particularly a credit loss, and there is income generated (eg, interest or fees)? Do the income amounts offset the loss? The result could be zero or even positive, but in any case profitability is less than originally targeted, or there would not be a loss event. One potential rule is to ignore offsets so as to focus attention on the loss and not have to deal with the issue of whether the profit is positive but less than targeted.

❑ *Foreign currencies* Events requiring currency translation are frequently problematic. Is the conversion rate selected at the time of loss, or is it the current rate at time of reporting?

❑ *Non-finalised events* Some events are discovered and can be valued using estimates, but final figures are often not available after a very long time. Examples are credit recoveries, insurance settlements and legal settlements/litigation. It is usually preferable to record an estimate as soon as feasible so as to make the event visible. Estimates of legal litigation may not be recorded to avoid risk of discovery by the other party.

❑ *Recoveries* As mentioned above, some recoveries (credit, insurance, legal) may take time, but others happen quickly. A decision must to be made whether and how a recovery amount should be recognised. This not only has implications from a modeling perspective (ie, the impact of an event), but also has intrinsic value in evaluating ancillary programs as insurance premiums and coverage.

❑ *Internal reclassifications* Sometimes accounting errors are discovered, resulting in a reclassification of costs within the company. A business unit could therefore incur a loss while someone else has a gain. This is similar to timing issues described in the previous section. While there is a desire to capture errors, senior management is most concerned with items that have a real P&L impact, so most companies would not report this.

❑ *Exit from a product or market* An organisation's ability to adapt to changing market conditions necessarily dictates the exit from existing products and markets. If these are considered operational events, rules are needed on how treat events that have occurred in the past and how to quantify them.

Confidentiality of the event data

Event data is generally considered very sensitive information. There is no standard for disclosure and there is a general concern about the information becoming publicly available, particularly in litigious societies like the United States. Each institution must create its own confidentiality and security policy over the data, balancing the desire for risk transparency and the opportunity to learn from the information with the need to keep the data secure.

For example, many institutions limit access of business area representatives to data from that business area only. Some sensitive data such as human resourse issues and some legal events may be more restricted. Executive management would typically receive details for only the largest events. Obviously the central risk management function managing the database sees all the information, but this is a very limited number of people. Sharing profile information (eg, totals, percentage mix), including benchmarking, without all the supporting event details can fulfill the need to share information without widely sharing the details.

Operational event collection policy

As the various components of the event collection process are defined, the actual rules for any one institution should be formalised into an event collection policy, approved by the relevant authorities. A comprehensive policy would include:

❑ Definition of what constitutes an operational loss event.
❑ Statement that loss data will be captured.
❑ Minimum threshold(s) for what shall be reported individually and captured in the event database.
❑ Event and effect category descriptions.
❑ Responsibilities of business areas, risk management and other parties, as applicable.
❑ Criteria for timely data capture (eg, 48 hours from detection).
❑ Valuation guidelines, as applicable.

THE EVENT COLLECTION PROCESS

The event collection process can be described in three primary phases as depicted in Figure 1. The first phase, Process Infrastructure, is about the establishment and maintenance of the process. The second phase involves the execution of the process. The third phase, Monitoring and Control, is designed to ensure that event collection is timely, thorough and accurate. The second two phases are both continual activities. Each of these phases is discussed in the following sections.

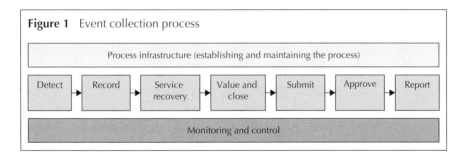

Figure 1 Event collection process

Process infrastructure
The goal of this phase is to create an environment to support the on-going detection and recording of operational events and incorporate the findings into the risk management process. The key components are establishing organisational responsibilities and ownership of data, the related tools and supporting technology.

The process begins with an initial assessment of the organisational environment to support event collection. Typically, the related parties include the central Operational Risk unit, business area risk managers, other business area staff and, in some cases, some business area "experts" who may manage and/or collect certain types of events. An initial inventory of the current state is a helpful starting point, resulting in an inventory of what types of events are captured through existing processes, the size/complexity/information capture for those events, the volume of events, and the resources dedicated to the collection process. This inventory can then be used to determine the gaps in information availability and where new processes should to be installed.

The key roles for business area personnel in the process are event detection, collection and control. There are four simplified models for the responsibilities of the related parties as they relate to event collection.

Generally, one of the decentralised options provides the strongest model for most organisations. The centralised model, while simple, creates a process distant from where events actually occur, resulting in difficulty ensuring that the process is complete. The centralised model also creates the least amount of buy-in from the business areas. This is a classic example of the tradeoff between corporate comparability and business line specifics.

Option	Responsibility		
	Detection	Collection	Control
Centralised	Business area risk manager	Business area risk manager	Business area risk manager
Decentralised – option 1	Business area	Business area risk manager	Business area risk manager
Decentralised – option 2	Business area	Business area experts	Business area risk manager
Decentralised – option 3	Business area	Business area	Business area risk manager

The first decentralised model puts the onus of detection on the business areas, but the data collection and control process is owned by the business area risk managers. This minimises training, yet keeps business areas involved. In the second alternative, business areas assign responsibility to one or more risk experts for data collection. This would typically be synergistic with other roles, such as event investigation or reporting. The third alternative asks business areas to not only identify but also to value and record all events. In all cases, the risk managers provide overall control over

---

Figure 2 Coverage matrix

				Associate responsible for	
Process	**Loss event**	**Detection/tracking method**	**Possible costs (1)**	**Detection**	**Reporting**
Phone sales (*Example*)	Forced to fulfill on incorrect terms presented to customer	Monthly profitability analysis on portfolio	Higher losses (S) Lower Income (S) Court costs to settle	B. Jones	Rob Manager
–	–	–	–	–	–
–	–	–	–	–	–

the process. Different business units may elect alternate approaches, or mature through experience, becoming more and more decentralised as the level of expertise increases.

A coverage matrix (see Figure 2) can be a good way to document event responsibilities. Identify for each process the potential events, how they are detected and tracked, and who is responsible. A comparison against the risk category definitions can help assure that there is responsibility assigned for all types of potential events, regardless of how rare.

Events are typically captured in two basic methods, from existing systems and through a manual data entry process. It is preferable to capture as much data as possible through existing systems to eliminate additional processes and errors. Common departments that have dedicated databases are:

Department	Event type
Legal	Litigation and settlements
Compliance	Compliance fines
Insurance	Property losses and insurance recoveries
Human resources	Workman's compensation claims, discrimination and employee settlements
IT	Systems outages
Various operational areas	Process errors
Treasury	Settlement failures
Accounting	Accounting corrections
Credit	Credit losses with operational causes
Security/Investigations	Internal, external frauds
Trading	Failed trades, settlement failures

Where existing systems are in place to detect/record events, there will have to be an assessment of the controls, information collected, and valuation guidelines to assure adequacy and consistency with the desired process. It would be rare to have all the needed information captured in current systems. Additional process or changes can be planned where necessary. Where events are not collected, detective controls and collection processes should be established.

A manual data entry process is required to record events not captured through existing systems. This process is outlined in the next section.

Responsibility for capturing some types of events may be assigned to a central group. For example, legal settlements, human resources issues, information technology failures, frauds and damage to physical assets could be available from the Legal, HR, IT, Security and Insurance departments, respectively. If there is no central system, these areas would follow the manual data entry process. Where a central group is not responsible, business areas should identify events in their areas, as appropriate.

Lastly, there is the technology used to record and report events. Leading practice is to have some sort of automated event database with the capability for business areas to record event data as events occur. Experience has shown that spreadsheets, paper and email will not provide lasting support. The database can accept data from other systems, where applicable. In fact, a central application may eventually replace some of the decentralised event collection systems and create more overall efficiencies. Typical contents for the loss database are included in Panel 4. Note that many of the data requirements identified herein go beyond regulatory requirements.

In any solution, it is important that the system can sum all quantifiable effects of any one event together. Two alternative solutions are commonly found. In the first one, there is one "record" for each event with the capability to record multiple effects and their related dates. An alternate approach is to record each effect separately with some common key to tie the data together for event reporting.

PANEL 4 CONSIDERATIONS FOR INFORMATION TO CAPTURE

Name	Name of person submitting event
Event identifier	Unique number for each event
Date of discovery	Date event was detected
Organisational unit	Identifier to organisational table
Start date	Date the event first started to occur
End date	Date the event occurred
Date of settlement/ valuation	Date the event was finalised and valued. Should be in the same month where the majority of accounting impact occurred.

Data source	Where event was found (eg, from what system it was captured, or by what manual process)
Short description	Short sentence identifying event. No names, places or dates should be included; also no reference to the institution name or company-specific products should be included (this is the description that might be sent to a consortium)
Description	Description of the event leading to the loss. Should list the cause(s), the event, the effects on the business, and the corrective action. Names of specific individuals should not be included
Record status	Select either "loss", "near-miss", "aggregate" or "open issue"
Primary event category	Classify each event by the appropriate Basel event category. Note: only used for operational risks, not credit risks
Secondary event category	Classify each event by the appropriate Basel secondary event category.
Currency	Identify currency of entry of costs in other data fields
Legal cost/settlement cost	Judgments, settlements and other legal costs in the defense of the corporation, related parties, and assets; both tangible and intangible
Regulatory compliance cost	Fines or the direct payment of any other penalties such as license revocations
Restitution cost	Payments to third parties on account of operational losses for which the bank is legally responsible
Loss of recourse cost	Losses experienced when a third party does not meet its obligations to the bank, which are attributable to an operational mistake or event
Write-down cost	Increased expenses or a direct reduction in the value of assets due to theft, fraud, unauthorised activity, or operational errors
Loss of physical asset cost	Direct reduction in the value of physical assets due to some kind of accident
Cost to fix	Direct costs incurred to bring business

	back to operational level. Does not include enhancements to prevent problem in future
Credit losses	Increase in charge-offs due to failures of people, processes or systems
Forgone income	Lost income or opportunities for revenue. Decrease in product profitability
Business interruption	Inability to process work for an extended period of time
Insurance recoveries	Recoveries of operational losses through insurance relationships
Other recoveries	Recoveries of operational losses due to other means (vendor charge-backs, legal action, fraud recoveries, etc).
Credit recoveries	Recoveries of credit losses through collection efforts
Soft effects	Check off if event had reputation/brand, quality, business interruption effect
Causal categorisation	What were primary causes that drove the event to occur?
Process	In what process did event occur?
Credit Recoveries	Recoveries of credit losses

Key decisions related to data capture are:

❑ *Definitions of dates* Typically, events have up to four dates: start, end, detection and valuation. For many events, these dates may be the same. Valuation date is intended to record when the event was valued and when the P&L impact occurred. Some events could have material impacts over multiple periods. Capturing multiple valuation dates or separate dates for each effect is an additional level of sophistication. One key decision is what date to use when performing trend reporting. We usually want all the effects of one event to be recorded together, so as to not dilute the impact. Valuation date is the most common date selected, since reporting ties to accounting impact. Use of other dates, like end date, tie in better to when something actually occurred but creates potential problems in reporting, because when events are detected after they have "ended", it results in changes to historical data that has already been reported.

❑ *Types of events* A record status can indicate what type of event is being captured. Most are loss events or near misses. An open issue status simply means the event has been recorded but is not complete and therefore should not yet be included in reporting. Aggregate events are one way to capture high-frequency, low-impact events where individual events might be below the threshold (eg, frauds), but the aggregate impact is material. This provides a means to get the aggregate data into the total costs of operational risk in a cost-efficient manner. Aggregate events should not be used in the same manner as individual events in capital modelling.

❑ *Tracking of recoveries* Recoveries are recorded separately from the original loss incurred. This permits separate analysis of efficiency of recovery and also the cost/benefit of alternate recovery strategies. Recording recoveries separately is particularly important if loss data is used in capital modelling. For example, insurance coverage can change over time. If the recoveries are recorded separately in the database, one can model actual coverage and predict recoveries and not worry about historical data reflecting a different level of coverage.

❑ *Recording causes* It is often beneficial to record the causes that contributed to an event. These can happen multiple times for any one event.

❑ *Splitting losses* Some losses can be attributed to multiple units. This can occur if they are split between two units, or if they occur in one central unit and are then attributable to multiple lines of business. Advanced systems can track these splits for reporting, while linking the event together as one event for purposes of capital modelling.

❑ *Tracking of resolution* Some organisations want to see not only the events, but evidence that causes were corrected to prevent re-occurrence.

Process execution

Execution involves the detection, collection, validation and reporting of events. This should be performed in a timely fashion, providing reasonable assurance of the completeness of data collection and accuracy of the process.

The process starts with where and how to *detect* the event. For example, a detection method could be a process error, systems, failure, law suit or supplier failure. Next we *record* the event. The information to be recorded was already discussed in a previous section. There may be a *recovery* process to restore operations, correct customer information, recover costs or other relevant actions to recover from the event. For example, any impact to customers may require correction, systems might have to be restored, or equipment might have to be purchased. Then events are *valued and closed*. Following guidelines on event valuation, the amount of loss, when applicable, is determined. Often there is an approval process in which events are reviewed by business area management or risk officers for accuracy prior to being finalised in the database and submitted to the central Operational Risk Management (ORM) group.

The next step is to *Submit to ORM* the events. This can include the submission of individual events or bulk submissions of events collected by central groups. The ORM group should perform a quality control function over all events, checking the coding of risk category and effects, reviewing descriptions and checking valuations. On a periodic basis the ORM group can report back to the business areas all the events they have captured related to each business area. This step acts as a check that all events have been captured and the business areas *approve* the event list, attesting that the list is complete and accurate to the best of their knowledge. The ORM group can then *report* the summary results to business area management and on an aggregated basis to executive management. Sample reports are described later in this chapter.

Monitoring and control

Lastly, there is an ongoing process for *monitoring and control*. These are the steps to ensure that the event collection process has long-term integrity and is thorough and accurate.

The first step in monitoring and control is analysis by the ORM group. ORM can review the profiles of data over time to ensure consistency in the classification and collection of event data. Analysing data by loss category, event, time and value can provide insights as to the thoroughness of the process. Trend analysis is a better tool than assessing absolute amounts. Missing data or changes in profile over time can point out changing data collection patterns. There is always a question as to whether missing data means issues with the data collection process or improvements in operational risk management resulting in fewer events. With good communications across the company, a level of confidence in the results can be obtained. A few examples of monitoring analyses are:

❑ How do the number of events reported (by business area and risk category) change over time?
❑ What is the profile of events by value (by business area and risk category)? Are there any ranges of values that are missing? Is the distribution the expected shape?
❑ What is the number and value of events by business area? Are they proportional to business area size, or can differences be explained?
❑ What is the profile of number and value of events by risk category? Are they consistent over time, or can variations be explained?
❑ How does the profile of actual events compare to self-assessments? Are there any risks identified in the self-assessments with no resulting events? If not, are we confident in our processes to detect and record these events, or have they just not occurred? If self-assessments can predict an expected loss, how does that compare with the actual loss history? Are any types of events missing from the data?

An additional potential control is Internal Audit. They should be testing whether the event collection process is being followed and whether all events are recorded in a timely fashion and valued consistently. It is assumed here the Audit is independent from the Operational Risk unit. They can include event collection as one of the checkpoints in every audit performed on business areas.

Ongoing training and communication helps reinforce the process. There are always new people getting involved in the process. A few suggestions on training are:

❑ Provide a regular training program for new people involved in the process.
❑ Have policies, related training material and latest updates available on internal websites.
❑ Provide a periodic conference call for event collection participants. This is an interdisciplinary group including operations, audit, risk management and any other related parties. Discussion

items could include any updates to the process or technology, questions on the collection process, discussions of underlying trends and findings in the data, lessons learned and best practices and case studies on categorisation and valuation.

Reconciliations with the general ledger is another form of control. In theory, events can be captured in a loss database and then reconciled to the ledger. This is difficult in practice. It requires separate general ledger accounts, usually by risk category, and the process requires comprehensive procedures to book operational events to these accounts. In addition, there are often challenges with data integrity, potential duplication of events with the event database, events with multiple effects/recoveries having multiple ledger entries, and therefore matching the ledger entries with the event database. Transactions from trading rooms that normally are reflected in income accounts are difficult to segregate in separate ledger accounts. One strategy is to require events that require external payments to pass through the database in order to have approval for payment. This assures that events do get captured. Some events with consistent accounting can be extracted from the ledger into the loss database.

Another type of monitoring is internal benchmarking. Loss rates by category can be compared across business areas and variations explained. With the evolution of loss consortia, more and more external benchmarks will also be available.

Lastly, there is requirement for ongoing senior management involvement. It is senior management's review of the data and resulting actions that creates the culture for the importance of event collection. Employees must feel that the effort is worth it and that the information is being acted upon. Hence, it is imperative that the ORM group leverages these data so that the business units would find it valuable and worthwhile to collect them. Linking quality of data (or implementation of the whole risk management process) into performance measures is always a helpful reinforcement.

ROLES AND RESPONSIBILITIES

Given the discussion of standards and the collection process, it is helpful to summarise the typical roles and responsibilities of business areas and the central operational risk group, as they relate to event data.

PANEL 5 ROLES AND RESPONSIBILITIES

Business areas usually have the responsibility for the detection, recording, valuation and approval of significant Operational Events ("events"). Business area heads are responsible for implementing a process to ensure that significant events are collected in a timely and accurate manner. This responsibility is designed to provide the business with assurance that events are:

❑ detected and recorded in a timely manner;
❑ valued in an accurate and consistent format;
❑ reported to ORM in an accurate and timely manner; and
❑ considered in the overall assessment of the existing control environment.

Specific responsibilities of the business areas include:

❑ *Identifying events* Identify potential events that can occur within their processes and document the controls in place to detect these events.
❑ *Establishing formal responsibility for recording of events* Identify employees directly responsible for collecting specific events, categories of events, or events occurring within a defined process or business area. These employees must be trained in the use of operational event collection methodologies and tools.
❑ *Reporting events in an accurate and timely manner* Events should be captured within the policy timeframe for discovery, regardless of the amount of information that is available. Events should be updated with all required information and closed shortly after the final resolution of the issue.
❑ *Ensuring appropriate access to data* Ensure access to this information is controlled and only employees with a "need to know" profile have access to confidential details of losses or consolidated loss information.
❑ *Consistent valuation* Identify standard costs to be used in the valuation of events whose actual cost is not readily available or cost effective to determine. These costs must be reviewed and updated on an annual basis, or when standard costs have changed significantly.
❑ *Attestation of loss experience* Business areas are responsible for providing ORM with the assurance that the losses recorded for the business area are accurate and complete.
❑ *Incorporating loss experience into risk management practices* Business areas are responsible for considering the impact of loss events on existing control environment and risk ratings.

The central Operational Risk Management (ORM) department is responsible for providing the business areas with the tools and methodologies necessary to collect events in an accurate and timely manner. ORM will be responsible for providing basic reporting to the business areas and interpretive reporting to the institution and its risk committees.

Specific responsibilities of the ORM group include:

❏ *Facilitation of periodic collection process* The ORM department is responsible for the coordination of the collection process for operational events. This includes scheduling the collection activities, tracking participation and completion, data quality reviews, and addressing any issues that may hinder the collection efforts.

❏ *Development and maintenance of the event collection methodology* The ORM department is responsible for creating and maintaining a methodology that facilitates the timely, accurate and complete collection of operational events by business areas. This includes enhancing the methodology as new guidance or best practices are identified.

❏ *Facilitation of data sharing* The ORM department shall control distribution of event data in a manner that encourages cross-area learning while ensuring data are used by employees with a "need to know".

❏ *Development and ownership of enabling technology* The ORM department is responsible for developing and maintaining a system to support business areas in the collection, reporting and analysis of operational loss events.

❏ *Guidance in the application of the event collection Methodology and Tools* The ORM department is responsible for providing guidance to business areas in the correct application of the event collection methodology.

❏ *Reporting and analysis for operational events* The ORM department is responsible for providing stakeholders the information regarding their loss experience that is necessary to properly manage operational risk. This includes regular reporting and analysis of loss experience and relevant trends. Events reported to ORM in local currencies will be translated to for reporting purposes at the budgeted exchange rate at the time of valuation.

❏ *Ensuring appropriate access to data* The ORM department is responsible for ensuring that access to events is controlled and that only employees with a "need to know" have access to confidential details of losses or consolidated loss information.

❏ *Maintaining subject matter expertise* The ORM department is responsible for building and maintaining subject matter expertise regarding event collection. This expertise will be used to enhance methodologies and tools in support of improved risk management within the institution.

CREATING A SUPPORTIVE RISK CULTURE

A supportive risk culture is an important component of any event collection effort. When we are basically asking the organisation to share its mistakes, we must create a positive environment to assure long term success. Key success factors for creating this environment are:

❑ Treat all events as opportunities to improve. The discussion has to be focused on what happened and how can we prevent it from happening again.

❑ Don't shoot the messenger. Wherever possible, events occurring should not be cause for disciplinary actions but as a means for action to prevent harmful events from occurring in the future.

❑ Have different groups perform investigations and collect events. Assuming that ORM collects events, if a post-mortem or investigation is necessary, have a different group (eg, audit or security) investigate as a follow up.

❑ Make reporting anonymous. Eliminate any names from event descriptions, reports and discussions.

❑ Provide value to the business areas. This is not just an exercise in senior management reporting and capital calculation. Make sure reports and benchmarks are provided to business areas to help them improve their own risk management. If the process is perceived to have little value, the business areas will not support the work.

❑ Keep it simple. Make sure the reporting requirements are quick and simple to prepare and have appropriate technology support.

PANEL 6 REPORTING THE RESULTS

The objectives of management reporting are to *inform* management about their operational risk experience, *trigger actions* and *resource allocations* where necessary, and *assure* management about the *effectiveness* of the risk management process. Reporting packages have two primary constituencies: business area management, who will see primarily events related to their own areas, and executive management, who will see aggregate information from across the institution. Executive management would likely include the Risk Management department, Audit, senior risk committees and the Board of Directors. A stylised report depicted in Figure 3, with sample illustrations,

---

Figure 3 Top risks

#	Mega unit	Event description	Settlement date	Primary event category	Corresponding self-assessment risk	Top 30 risk	Actual net loss	ORSA est for
1	Auto lending	Event 101	xx/xx/03	Employment practices and workplace safety	Risk 1	N	Confidential	$X,XXX
2	International	Event 203	xx/xx/03	Execution, delivery and process management	Risk 2	N	$X,XXX	$X,XXX
3	IT	Event 151	xx/xx/03	Execution, delivery and process management	Risk 32	N	$X,XXX	$X,XXX
4	Staff functions	Event 139	xx/xx/03	System failures	Not-Identified in self-assessment	Y	$X,XXX	$X,XXX
5	Mortgage lending	Event 122	xx/xx/03	System failures	Risk 100	N	$X,XXX	$X,XXX
6	Corporate banking	Event 133	xx/xx/03	Execution, delivery and process management	Risk 51	N	$X,XXX	$X,XXX
7	Corporate banking	Event 148	xx/xx/03	System failures	Risk 400	Y	$X,XXX	$X,XXX
8	IT	Event 178	xx/xx/03	Damage to physical assets	Risk 323	N	$X,XXX	$X,XXX
9	International	Event 198	xx/xx/03	Clients, products and business practices	Risk 323	N	$X,XXX	$X,XXX
10	Corporate banking	Event 129	xx/xx/03	Execution, delivery and process management	Risk 32	N	$X,XXX	$X,XXX

All US$,000

provides an example of a standard, periodic event reporting package. Reports of these kinds could be produced at either the line of business or the corporate level. There are many opportunities to drill down information into alternate or more detailed views, and additional data to support risk analyses are often produced. These reports are starting points to work with:

❑ *Top risks* A listing of the largest risks that have occurred in the reporting period. The purpose is to inform management of risk exposures and trigger additional mitigation actions if necessary. As Figure 3 illustrates, it typically includes the date, business area, amount and description. Additional data could include whether or not the risk was identified in the self-assessment process and whether mitigating actions are or have been taken to prevent the event from occurring again.

❑ *Historical level and trends* A report of total events over time. The purpose is to raise awareness of the cost of operational risk and assess whether overall risk management performance is improving or declining. Figure 4 shows an example of reporting events by quarter, in dollars and number of events. Events over a certain threshold – for example US$5 million – are reported separately as "extreme events". The diamonds indicate the number of events, reported against the scale on the right side. Inevitably there are a few very large events that throw off all trend analysis. Analysing trends of smaller events only offers a more sound statistical analysis. In addition, if the graph were shown to scale, including large losses, the data in most quarters could be so small as make the graphic valueless.

❑ *Level and trends by event types* This is a period over period profile of events by risk category. The purpose is to further analyse sources

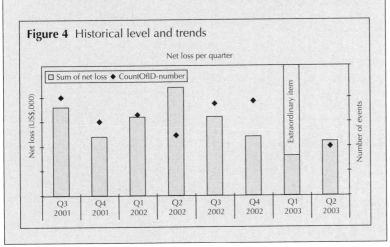

Figure 4 Historical level and trends

463

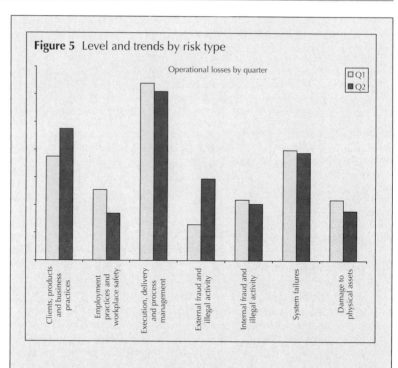

Figure 5 Level and trends by risk type

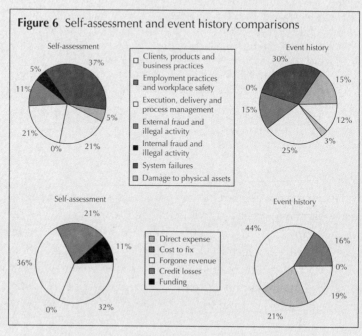

Figure 6 Self-assessment and event history comparisons

Figure 7 Data quality analysis

Data quality by business area

Business	Clients, products and business practices	Employment practices and workplace safety	Execution, delivery and process management	External fraud and illegal activity	Internal fraud and illegal activity	System failures
Auto lending						
International						
IT						
Staff functions						
Mortgage lending						
Corporate banking						
Branch banking						
Revolving consumer credit						
Small business						
Overall						

of events and understand if there are any indicative trends that might instigate further mitigation. The example in Figure 5 shows it in a bar chart format.

❑ *Level and trends by effect type* This is similar to the previous report, but by effect type. Again, the purpose is to analyse trends.

❑ *Reconciling to self-assessments* The purpose is to compare the risk profile in the self-assessment process to that conveyed by loss data. Differences can point to missing risks, missing data or mis-estimates of risk severity. Figure 6 illustrates profile comparisons by risk category and effect.

❑ *Data quality analysis* The purpose is to report on the perceived level of data quality. One hopes that weak areas will be addressed. This provides some perspective on the reliance placed on the reported data, and it also can be used to initiate requests for resource support for any lagging areas. Figure 7 illustrates an example with a rating assigned by the Risk Management department.

SUMMARY

Internal event databases are now standard practice for sound operational risk management practices. While there is broad guidance from regulators, the details of a collection process and related processes must be determined individually by each institution. A sound event collection, analysis, and reporting process should lead to lower overall losses and increased awareness of operational risk. Moreover it should provide critical inputs to operational risk capital models.

1   Basel Committee on Banking Supervision, Bank for International Settlements (2002). Sound practices for the management and supervision of operational risk. July.

2   Basel Committee on Banking Supervision, Bank for International Settlements (2003). The New Basel Capital Accord, consultative document. July.

3   BIS (2003). Supervisory guidance on operational risk, advanced measurement approaches for regulatory capital, July 2.

18

Insurance and Operational Risk

John Thirlwell
Operational Risk Research Forum

INTRODUCTION

The possibility of allowing insurance as a mitigant to the operational risk charge has been under discussion for some years. It was first highlighted in the Basel Committee's Consultation Paper of January 2001 (see Basel Committee on Banking Supervision, 2001), in which the committee indicated that they would be working with the industry on insurance and other risk-mitigation techniques. The key was to ensure that techniques would result in risk reduction and transfer rather than the exchange of one risk with another. In April 2001, as part of this dialogue, the Operational Risk Research Forum (ORRF) submitted a paper from its Insurance Working Group to the Basel Committee (see "Insurance as a mitigant for operational risk", 2001). A further paper was submitted jointly by the Industry Technical Working Group and Basel Accord Insurance Working Group (see Basel Accord Insurance Working Group, 2002) in May 2002. At that time and since, members of both the banking and insurance industry have made representations to the Basel Committee's Risk Management Group to explain the rationale for allowing insurance.

The principal arguments in favour highlighted the use of insurance both commercially and privately as a means of accepted risk management – the length of experience both industries have with specialist products, such as the bankers' blanket bond (originating in policies developed in the 19th century), as well as policies for directors' and officers' liability, unauthorised trading and computer crime. Parallels were also drawn with the acceptability of credit derivatives and other instruments as mitigants for capital relating to credit risk.

Regulators' concerns concentrated mainly on the certainty of payment (as demonstrated by the financial strength of the insurer), speed of payment (given that the need was to replace capital) and the terms of individual policies (both their diversity of coverage and technical considerations such as the ability of the insurer to cancel). There was also a major concern about the size of the insurance industry in relation to that of the banking industry. It has been suggested, for instance, that the total global capital of the general insurance market is less than that of Citigroup and, therefore, its capacity to absorb the major events for which regulators and bankers had expected insurance to cover capital needs is also diminished. Much depends, of course, of where insurance is perceived to appear on the risk-protection spectrum. In rough terms, it is usually seen as picking up risks somewhere between attritional (or expected) and catastrophic (however defined). This is rather imprecise, but then much depends on the premiums being offered for the risks being taken or laid off.

The banking industry was heartened, therefore, when the European Commission, in the second consultation paper on its proposed new capital directive (see European Commission, 2002), indicated that it was prepared to consider insurance as a mitigant for each of the three operational risk approaches, *basic* (BIA), *standardised* (STA) and *advanced* (AMA). These hopes were then somewhat diminished by Basel's QIS3 (see Basel Committee on Banking Supervision, 2002), in which insurance was recognised as a mitigant only for banks adopting the AMA.

The rationale for this restriction was that the BIA and STA were essentially not risk-sensitive, whereas the AMA was, so that it was difficult to understand why regulators should allow a risk-sensitive reduction to a non-risk-sensitive charge. The insurance industry naturally sees things differently. It has made the point, for instance, that those banks that will not be adopting the AMA, but inevitably purchase insurance as part of their normal risk management process, are probably less likely to have a capital base that will be able to sustain the abnormal or catastrophic losses that their insurance programmes are designed to cover.[1] Lack of recognition may even lead them to reduce, or at least not increase, their cover, a somewhat perverse outcome.

However, it appears that this will be where the game stops for the foreseeable future. In its third consultation paper, published in July 2003 (see European Commission, 2003), the European Commission Services also restrict recognition to the AMA. Given that the US regulators will be implementing only the AMA, it appears that this particular battle has been lost. At least the regulators agreed (Basel, EC and US) on the criteria that they will expect (or are debating) to enable insurance to be recognised (see "US and EU approaches" below). Discussion of these criteria forms the basis of this chapter.

The 20% cap on recognition of insurance as a mitigant

One immediate issue that has caused some degree of concern is the 20% limit that has been placed on the extent to which insurance can be recognised as a mitigant of the capital charge.[2]

The need for a cap has not, to date, been explained by regulators. Perhaps the cap helps to limit the degree of risk transfer from banking to insurance that might otherwise occur. It also helps to limit the possibility of moral hazard that might occur if banks were allowed to buy substantial cover and so reduce their capital. This, however, is unlikely, since the costs of acquiring the cover would almost certainly exceed the capital benefit achieved.

For their part banks have argued against the cap on the basis that, within the AMA, it is up to them to assess their risk exposure and the value of the insurance they buy. If they believe that the saving is worth the costs involved and they can justify this to their supervisor, they should be allowed to. They have also suggested that a 20% cap provides them with little incentive to take out insurance. Given that operational risk is meant to be approximately 12% of total capital, a cap of 20% represents 2.4% of regulatory capital against which must be offset the insurance premiums involved. Even for a large bank, this can emerge as a relatively small net gain. However, it is fair to add that the debate should be about risk management rather than capital management.

Not surprisingly, the insurance industry has argued against the cap in its responses to the Basel consultation. Aon Professional

Risks is concerned that there is no scope for review of the limit and also makes the point that recognition of insurance is already built into economic capital models and that supervisors, using Pillar 2, can review a bank's capital adequacy and make appropriate adjustments. It therefore argues against a permanent number at this stage. Marsh Inc argues that there are areas of operational risk that will not be insured and that, overall, it is unlikely that banks will claim "an excessive capital credit for insurance". They also asked their subsidiary, Mercer Oliver Wyman, to model the output of the Basel Committee's Loss Data Collection Exercise (2002). The result was "not inconsistent with a world in which insurance mitigates a substantial portion of Unexpected Loss and in which economic capital is reduced by even as much as 20 to 40%".

A bank's ability to take advantage of its insurance as a mitigant of its capital charge depends on a number of criteria relating to the insurer or the insurance policies involved.[3] We shall consider these criteria in the sections to follow.

QUALIFYING CRITERIA
Single-A claims-paying rating
The first criterion lays down that the insurance provider should have "a minimum claims paying rating of [single] A (or equivalent)". The ratings market for insurers is essentially dominated by four firms, A.M.Best, Fitch Ratings, Moody's and Standard & Poor's. Unfortunately, their definition of an A rating differs. While Moody's A rating denotes "ability to meet senior policyholder obligations", A.M.Best's A/A− rating denotes "strong ability to meet ongoing policyholder obligations". It is also worth noting that whereas Lloyd's of London, the leading international specialist market underwriting financial institutions, has a claims-paying rating of A, its financial-strength rating, depending on the agency concerned, is either A or A−.

The wide availability of high-quality capacity is obviously fundamental to the viability of an operational-risk market. However, in the current economic environment, and given the tendency for ratings to be downgraded rather than upgraded over recent years, it is possible that the problem of concentration, which is always a factor given the capacity of the insurance market, could be exacerbated over time. It would also be necessary to factor this into regulatory requirements. It is not clear what happens if an insurer is downgraded during the term of the insurance contract – or in later years, given the long-tail liability nature of the operational-risk insurance classes being covered. Insurers insure for risks occurring or arising during the term of the insurance contract, even if a claim is made years later.

One solution might be to allow "cut-through options" to higher-rated reinsurers who would provide protection at the front end for policies written by lower-rated direct insurers. Reinsurers would have to be persuaded to take a greater credit risk on companies ceding risk in this way. This could well drive up direct reinsurance costs, but it would at least reduce reliance on what might become a dwindling band of direct insurers.

"Cut-through" is a technique well known to the insurance industry and is already in use in many overseas markets to overcome weaknesses in local insurance markets in territories where there is a legal obligation to buy insurance locally. It has the benefit of clearly tying the insurance back to the "global master" insurance contract and so ensuring a clear contractual relationship between the client bank, insurer and reinsurer.

Claims-paying ability is, of course, fundamental to the availability of a particular insurer's name in these circumstances. This is a longer-term rating that reflects the possibility of claims having to be met some years down the road. It could be argued, though, that in making its assessment of the value of the relevant insurance cover for capital mitigation purposes, the insured bank or firm should, in addition, reflect the credit quality of the insurer (ie, financial strength in addition to claims-paying rating) and that recognition should be given for the discounted present value of claims, which will itself depend on a number of factors, some of which are reflected below.

Policy term

The third Basel consultative paper (CP3) suggests an initial policy term of no less than one year and prescribes that haircuts should be applied to residual terms of less than one year, reaching a full 100% haircut for policies with a residual term of 90 days or fewer.

This is a rather strange requirement, which appears to ignore a fundamental principle of insurance: that claims will be met if they occur within the term of the policy, whether that is on the first or 365th day of a 12-month policy. Policies do not depreciate in value as they reach maturity, other than in cases where a claim has been made and, according to the terms of the policy, this may limit the residual value of the policy until it is renewed. Given also that most policies are for 12 months, it seems to imply that all policies will begin to lose value from the day of inception.

An alternative reading is that the regulators are trying to establish terms of longer than 12 months as the normal policy. Multi-year policies are by no means unusual and, at an earlier stage of the cycle when the market was soft, were freely negotiated. History has shown, however, that locking in a policy for periods greater than one year has often caused problems. Clients who were locked in when the market began to fall reneged on their commitment, often by not paying subsequent instalment premiums; in addition, where insurers were locked in at the bottom of a soft cycle, losses caused more damage than would otherwise have happened. So there is now reluctance by both the direct market and the reinsurance market to be locked in for such a long period. Another problem with multi-year commitments is that the insurer would often find itself locked in also to terms that had become inappropriate long before the end of the contract.

It is possible that short-term policies could bring the risk of uncertainty and volatility, but frequent changes of insurer are not the market norm. Changing a bank's insurance programme and provider is not undertaken lightly and is rather different from changing, say, your motor insurance. If regulators have serious concerns on this score, 18 months might work as an acceptable compromise. In addition, under the Lloyd's accounting system, it is permissible for 18-month policies to be wholly recognised in one policy year of account, rather than being apportioned across two years. However, it would be preferable to stay with 12 months as the standard and recognise that the policy does not deteriorate with age. Longer terms might also not be welcomed by the insurance regulators, who are in some countries the same bodies as the banking regulators!

Cancellation and non-renewal periods
This subject leads neatly to the related one of cancellation and non-renewal periods. CP3 is open on this point, merely prescribing that

the policy should have "a minimum notice period for cancellation and non-renewal". In a related footnote the committee indicates that it will be discussing with the industry a definition of the minimum threshold.[4]

The principal issue here is that the insured must have a reasonable time in which to put in place alternative cover if the insurer wishes to cancel in mid-term or at expiry through non-renewal. In practice, the risk is therefore more one of renewal than cancellation. But the insurance underwriter also has rights. There are, therefore, automatic cancellation provisions for non-payment of premium or fraudulent misrepresentation. It is also reasonable that the respective cancellation rights of insurer and insured should be roughly equivalent. Comments on this issue are, of course, written against a background where it is business practice not to cancel a policy unless there is a very good reason to do so.

Cancellation periods vary with classes of business but are usually 30 to 60 days. Recognising the difficulty of seeking alternative cover in the event of cancellation or non-renewal, it could be that 90 days will suffice. Of course, there should not be a regulatory concern over firms' choosing not to renew, since presumably they would do this only once alternative cover was in place. It might therefore be reasonable to prescribe that, where renewal has not been agreed within 90 days of expiry, some haircut might be appropriate. But this need not be 100%, since it is assumed that renewal will be achieved and in any case cover is maintained in accordance with the terms of the policy up to the time of expiry.

Even at the point of expiry it could be argued that a 100% haircut is not absolutely essential. It is a practical reality of the market for extended cover to be made available, subject to appropriate conditions and payment of an appropriate premium, while negotiations continue. Recognition of this flexibility needs to be retained.

Exclusions for regulatory action

A further criterion for acceptance is that the policy should have "no exclusions or limitations based upon regulatory action". One problem here is that it is difficult to know what exactly is meant by the term "regulatory action". Is it intended to cover only the actions of financial-sector regulators? Are all fines and penalties included or is there a distinction between those that are incurred through administrative failure or incompetence and those that are incurred through acts that are criminal or akin to being so? As a topical example, would the penalties imposed by the Securities Exchange Commission (SEC) in the recent settlement reached with major investment firms in the US over the relationship between their research and corporate finance departments be covered by the exclusion?

Insurance policies already regularly exclude payment or reimbursement of a fine or government penalty and/or related costs (which is another issue). It is against public policy in some jurisdictions for insurers to insure against such liabilities. Market abuse, money laundering and laddering are good examples where exclusions are proper from both the insurer's and a public policy point of view.

Taking a wider view, there is a standard exclusion for punitive and exemplary damages, as well as standard "regulatory" exclusions, such as those imposed in the US in respect of violations of the Racketeer Influenced and Corrupt Organization Act (1961), Securities Act (1933) as amended, the Securities Exchange Act (1934) and the Employee Retirement Income Security Act (1974).

Plainly, certain exclusions are necessary. A blanket ban on them would seem to be unreasonable and contrary to public policy.

Exclusions for the receivership or liquidation of a failed bank

Similarly, Basel suggests that there should be no exclusions "for the receiver or liquidator of a failed bank". It is difficult to understand the rationale for this, since such exclusions are standard, although they relate to the period after appointment.

The effect of receivership or liquidation is to terminate the contract at the date of appointment. This applies, *inter alia*, to bankers' blanket bonds, directors' and officers' liability policies, professional liability policies and those covering unauthorised trading. While cover for "ongoing" acts ceases, termination does not affect cover for acts committed before that date, which fall within the terms of the policy. It is also normal practice for the policy to allow a period of discovery for the receiver or liquidator to lodge claims arising from acts occurring on or before the date of appointment. Similar clauses may also extend termination to instances where the assured ceases to be authorised to conduct business within the regulated environment.

The reasoning behind all of this is that appointment breaks the commercial basis of the contract. One consequence of this is that, in practice, it is also standard procedure for liquidators to appoint a new broker. The liquidator represents different interests from those of the previous owners and may wish to reserve the right to act against former advisers.

SPEED OF PAYMENT

It is interesting that this issue, which initially was one of the regulators' key concerns, has disappeared from view. Given that insurance is likely to be of most use in the case of major events, and in that context would be a replacement for liquidity as well as capital, this is surprising.

It could be, though, that regulators have accepted that, fundamentally, insurance is a contract of indemnity in which the claimant must prove the loss. This principle cannot be changed, whether we are dealing with residential home or bank insurance. It may also be that, if the insurer has a strong enough claims-paying ability, regulators would be prepared to stand behind the threatened bank in some way until payment was made. Interestingly, the Loss Data Collection Exercise showed (with caveats about the quality of data) that, where insurance claims were made, recoveries were effected in 79.7% of cases within 12 months (81.8% in the case of claims in excess of US $1 million), thus debunking one myth about insurers and perhaps encouraging regulators to believe that the payment issue is not so great as might at first have been thought.

When this issue has been discussed in the past, there have often been suggestions that insurers should, perhaps, pay first and then adjust later. This was a feature of SwissRe's FIORI product. This means, though, that, by the time reimbursement may be required, the bank concerned may not have the ability to do so. The credit risk would be reversed from the norm, where the insured is exposed to the insurer, to a situation where the insurer is reliant on the insured for payment. Such a process would also affect the liquidity of insurers, another risk that would itself have to be compensated, either through restrictions in cover or in higher premiums.

MAPPING INSURANCE COVERAGE TO OPERATIONAL RISK EXPOSURE

The Basel proposal requires firms to map their insurance coverage "explicitly" to the "actual operational risk loss exposure of the institution". This requirement is presumably intended in part to ensure that only that part of the insurance related to operational risk is considered, and not insurances extraneous to a bank's banking activities. Of itself, the requirement should not present too much difficulty. The problem is disaggregating from the overall operational risk exposure assessment those elements that are not covered, either because of accepted exclusions or because certain risks are not recognised as insurable perils. There will, inevitably, be gaps and these may well affect operational risks that are "soft" and exposure to them less capable of assessment. The extent of insurable (and insured) risks, however, is not the only element of a policy that may lead to a haircut from the overall capital figure that is being mitigated.

DISCOUNTS AND HAIRCUTS

The Basel proposal contains a specific requirement that banks, in recognising insurance within the AMA, should apply discounts or haircuts in respect of:

❑ the residual term of the policy (but see "Policy term");
❑ a policy's cancellation and non-renewal terms (see "Cancellation and non-renewal periods"); and
❑ the uncertainty of payment as well as mismatches in coverage of insurance policies (see "Speed of payment" and "Mapping insurance coverage to operational risk exposure").[5]

Uncertainty of payment relates as much to the likely timing of the payment as to the strength of the insurer and its claims-paying ability. Although the paper has concentrated on a minimum claims-paying rating of single A, consideration may have to be given about having a sliding scale of haircuts so that an AAA insurer (or reinsurer under a "look-through" arrangement) would justify little or no haircut, while a single-A firm would require some allowance to be made. This will apply to both claims-paying ability and financial strength.

Leading on from this, and related to the payment issue, is the need for banks to assess the speed of payment and estimate the value of the claim, discounted over time (see "Single-A claims-paying ability").

The question of haircuts also introduces other components that will have to be assessed to evaluate the risk covered by an insurance policy. While CP3 talks of mapping coverage to operational risks, it does not mention that, even if a particular risk is covered, exclusions and policy terms and conditions will also have to be taken into account.

Another key component of the policy will be the deductible (or excess) that applies. When the European Commission tabled earlier proposals for allowing insurance under the basic and standardised approaches, it suggested two approaches, one premium-based and the other limit-based. The premium-based approach was probably always going to have to be dropped because of its perversity. The worse a bank performed (and the more claims it made), the higher its premiums and the greater its relief against capital. The limit-based method was at least intuitively on the right lines in that it examined the insured gap between the deductible and the limit of the policy.

While banks may be able to make individual assessments on the extent to which they recognise insurance, it is probable that the methodologies and haircuts will be as varied as the banks and policies involved. This will present regulators with a considerable challenge in implementation.

THIRD PARTIES AND CAPTIVES

The Basel papers have always stated that insurance should be through a third party, but have recognised that banks may choose to use captives. In that case, "the exposure has to be laid off to an independent third party entity, for example through re-insurance, that meets the eligibility criteria".[6]

There can be little argument with the general proposition that, from a consolidated point of view, insurance through a captive represents no transfer of risk that can justify a reduction in the overall capital charge. However, where a captive holds an independent rating of single A or above and the insurance is placed on an arm's-length basis, or where the captive is adequately ring-fenced, there could be an argument that this would also justify an element of recognition. It is probably true, after all, that use of a captive will better enable a bank to "map" insurance coverage to its operational risks and that a captive may be a more prompt payer than third-party insurers. Internally, the use of a captive may also be an effective means for risk management to allocate insurance costs more directly to the appropriate business unit and thus improve evaluation of operational risks. So use of captives is to be encouraged.

Introducing a cut-through to the reinsurance market is, of course, the reasonable way for captives to be used and for the cover they provide to be recognised fully in terms of capital mitigation. As was mentioned above (see "Single-A claims-paying rating"), the use of a cut-through arrangement is important in ensuring that the cover provided by the reinsurer matches the insurance offered by the captive. If it does not, appropriate adjustments will have to be made to its evaluated cover.

DISCLOSURE UNDER PILLAR 3

Disclosure of operational-risk information under the proposals for Pillar 3 is relatively light compared with that being proposed for credit risk. This reflects banks' sensitivities to the publication of internal management information, especially regarding losses or other failures, which does not appear in the public domain and which could be open to misinterpretation in assessing the overall levels of control within a particular firm.

The only quantitative disclosure required by Basel in relation to operational risk concerns the use of insurance by AMA banks. The requirement is for banks that wish to use insurance to reduce their capital charge to provide the overall operational-risk capital charge before and after any reduction for insurance.[7]

US AND EU APPROACHES

The whole debate about the use of insurance to mitigate the capital charge is one that has struggled for some time – and continues to struggle – with the many technical issues surrounding insurance. These revolve primarily around the indemnity nature of the insurance contract and a perception that payment of claims is a relatively long process (although the Loss Data Collection Exercise gave some comfort on that score).

Many regulators were concerned at both the terms under which insurance could be recognised on an acceptable and relatively consistent basis and the capacity of the insurance industry to accept the transfers of risk that might be involved.

Against this were the arguments that the insurance industry was already carrying these risks, which were unlikely to increase dramatically, and that, if regulators could spell out their concerns about the nature of policies being written, the insurance market would be incentivised to accommodate them in revised policy wordings and possibly in revised practices, although the fundamental nature of the contract would have to remain.

But regulators also sent out mixed messages. While these concerns were being expressed, which now appear to have been allayed, the EU, in its various consultation papers, appeared to be very positive on the question of insurance, in that it looked as if it would allow recognition for all three approaches: basic, standardised and advanced. This presumably recognised that insurance was a good risk management tool that was widely used by all banks and should be encouraged. It could be argued that it should be especially encouraged among non-AMA banks, which, almost by definition, were likely to have thinner capital resources with which to withstand a major shock. Against that view was the argument that, since the BIA and STA were essentially not risk-sensitive and intended to represent minimum capital for relatively unsophisticated institutions, it was perverse to allow the capital charge to be offset by a risk-sensitive instrument such as insurance.

The net result of these debates is that the latest paper from the European Commission Services now restricts insurance recognition to the AMA, in precisely the same terms as Basel, while, of course, the US regulators are limiting application of the new Basel Accord to the advanced approaches.

Looking at the detail of the current proposals from the US and EU is instructive. (See Panel 1 for a comparison of the Basel and EU viewpoints regarding the standardised approach.) The US regulators, for instance, in their Advance Notice of Proposed Rulemaking (ANPR)[8] place insurance within an overall section concerned with risk mitigation, for which there will be a total cap on mitigation of 20%. The paper acknowledges the possibility of securities products and other capital market instruments being developed but, since none have been developed to date, they are excluded from consideration, leaving insurance as the subject of the section.

The fundamental criteria identified by the US regulators are the same as Basel, including the need for policies to have an initial term of one year and for the "haircut" adjustment to be decreased to take account of a residual term of less than one year. The criteria set out a test to establish that the insurance policy is "sufficiently capital-like" to qualify for recognition. In addition, a few words of guidance are offered. First, the institution must demonstrate that the policies concerned have a good record of timely payouts – if not, they must be excluded. Secondly, firms must show that the policy would actually be used in the event of a loss. The example is given that the deductible must not be so high that the policy would be unlikely ever be called on. Finally, captives are to be recognised only where the risk has been transferred to "an unaffiliated reinsurer".

INSURANCE AND OTHER RISK MANAGEMENT TECHNIQUES

Now that insurance recognition has been restricted to the AMA, one final question remains, which is why insurance should be singled out as a risk management technique that can lead to a reduction (subject to a specific cap) in the capital charge? If the AMA is about self-assessment, subject to regulatory adjustment through Pillar 2, there is little reason why a bank should not include recognition of insurance in its assessment, just as it does for the quality of its internal controls and for the business environment in which it finds itself. Indeed, it is difficult to see how it can avoid doing so. If the capital charge is to be shown gross and net of insurance, it is tempting to ask why not gross and net of internal controls, or as varied by differing scenario analyses. Insurance is but one aspect of good risk management. Perhaps, after all the battles for recognition, we should be grateful for its conclusion and consider the future.

CONCLUSION

Insurance cannot be a perfect transfer of operational risk. Current insurance products do not wholly match the whole gamut of operational risks. Coverage varies with each policy, although many terms and conditions will be common. Issues such as policy term, cancellation and renewal have been raised by regulators and discussed above. It would probably be helpful if a number of these issues could be resolved by the creation of a more "Basel-friendly" product than those currently available. It would also be helpful if dialogue continued so that regulators could understand more clearly the nature of the insurance market and its products and ensure that the final proposals reflected that.

There is also the question of the capacity (both depth and quality) of the insurance market to accept the scale of risk transfer that may emerge as banks develop their use of insurance, prompted in part by regulatory criteria. Already there is evidence that insurance buying is moving into the domain of risk management, where its value can be better assessed against the risks being covered. It could be that all of this will lead to new entities being developed that can better match the need, always assuming, of course, that requirements will change as dramatically as some commentators have suggested.

The Basel proposals have undoubtedly caused a re-evaluation of the role of insurance and the policies being offered. Depending on the final outcome of the accord and related legislation, it could be that the terms of policies, the risks covered and the payment process in place in 2007 are very different from those obtaining now.

PANEL 1 THE STANDARDISED APPROACH – COMPARING BASEL AND EU

The qualifying criteria for the Standardised Approach (STA) from the Basel Committee run to nearly two pages (see Basel Committee on Banking Supervision, 2003a, paragraphs 620–5). By contrast, the European Commission Services paper (see European Commission Internal Market, 2003) deals with the issue in one paragraph of 11 lines, which is itself a reduction of a few lines from the text that appeared in the working document published in November 2002.

There are probably two reasons for this, the first being fundamental, and the second leading from the first. The fundamental reason is that the EC is planning to implement its new directive across all 10,000 banks and investment firms in the EU, whereas the Basel Accord was designed primarily for internationally active banks. This then drives the second reason, which reflects the different approaches of the two groups – even though EU representatives are in the majority on the Basel Committee. It would appear that the EU regulators wish both to recognise the diversity of institutions within their jurisdiction and to encourage movement through the spectrum of approaches. The Basel Committee appears to have taken the line that it is important for standards to be as high as possible, so that the STA should not be regarded as a marginally more sophisticated basic approach, but should represent a genuine advance in the quality of risk management.

In essence, the qualifying criteria for the STA within the Basel paper are not much different from the qualitative standards for the advanced measurement approach (AMA), with the significant difference that whereas the text relating to the STA talks of "assessment", that relating to the AMA talks of "measurement". They represent, therefore, a relatively detailed set of criteria, which differs from the more general approach adopted by the EU. It may be helpful to explore these differences in more detail.

Operational risk management function

The first requirement of the Basel paper is that the bank shall have an operational risk management function with clear responsibilities assigned to it. The paper then goes on to detail the function's responsibilities, which include codifying firm-level policies, as well as designing and implementing the bank's assessment methodology and its risk-reporting system.

Interestingly, the requirement for an independent function is not specified at all by the EU, although there is a need for a "well-documented … management system" for operational risk. What is meant by a "management system" is not spelled out. What is clear, though, is that the EC recognises that many firms that wish to adopt the STA will not have a separate operational risk function, but will manage the risk through a variety of other functions within, perhaps, risk management, audit or compliance and/or through business units.

Operational loss data

Here the two papers have something in common in that they both call for the tracking of operational risk data, including "material losses". The Basel paper, however, insists that this tracking be applied by business line. It also goes on to specify the type of people who should receive reports of operational risk exposures and material losses. They are "business unit management, senior management, and to the board of directors". (See Panel 2 for a brief discussion regarding the use of external loss databases.)

Assessment and reporting

Basel has always been keen that the operational risk-assessment system should be "closely integrated" into the risk management processes of the bank. It explains that this will place assessment at the heart of a bank's monitoring, control, reporting and risk-analysis processes.

The EC, however, merely asks that there shall be a "well-documented assessment system", together with a system of "management reporting" that provides operational risk reports to "relevant functions" within the institution. It is not clear who the "relevant functions" might be. Presumably they cannot be as broad as those functions mentioned by Basel, since the EC avoids the use of the word "board", partly reflecting the differing legal structures that exist in the EU.

On the other hand, both are in agreement that procedures should be in place to ensure that appropriate action is taken in the light of the reports received.

Validation and audit

A similar divergence is apparent with validation (not mentioned at all by the EC) and audit. The EC merely requires that the assessment and management system shall be "subject to regular independent review". Basel asks the same. In addition, though, it looks for "validation" of the processes and system and then goes further when it requires that the assessment system, "including the internal validation processes", should be regularly reviewed by external auditors and supervisors.

It is difficult to understand how, or indeed why, operational risk management processes can be "validated" in this way, when they are not contributing to the capital charge, which will be derived purely from the set formulae relating to gross income by business line. Supervisors will inevitably assess them as part of Pillar 2 reviews, so that hardly needs spelling out. Quite where external auditors fit in is difficult to understand.

Incentives for good behaviour

The Basel papers have changed over time. Specific references to pay and pricing in connection with the STA have now gone. But there remains a small curiosity: that "the bank must have techniques for creating incentives to improve the management of operational risk throughout the firm". Is this another way of saying that pay and bonuses should be linked to good operational risk performance, or good operational risk management performance, which may not be the same thing? Or is this a hint that incentives should be provided via differing internal or economic capital assessments. If so, and even ignoring the subjective nature of economic capital assessments of operational risk, this can only have short-term use, since, if the bank finally gets its act together, there will be little scope for deciding that one unit is managing its operational risk significantly better than another. One major bank has already discovered this result of using economic capital as a stick and carrot.

Conclusion
It has to be assumed that both sets of regulators (who in any case overlap in their membership) are seeking to achieve the same ends. It would be helpful, though, if they could use language that in some cases is extremely prescriptive, given the diverse nature of the target audience – or is overly opaque in enabling banks to understand the requirements more fully? That both versions differ so radically only adds to the confusion banks face in trying to understand how they are expected to implement the requirements of such a non-risk sensitive approach as the STA.

References for panel 1
Basel Committee on Banking Supervision, 2003a, *The New Basel Capital Accord*, Consultative Document (Basel: Bank for International Settlements), April.

European Commission, 2002, Working Document of the Commission Services on Capital Requirements for Credit Institutions and Investment Firms, November.

European Commission Internal Market, 2003, "Capital Requirements for Banks and Investment Firms", third Consultation Paper, Annex H-3, July.

PANEL 2 OPERATIONAL LOSSES – EXTERNAL DATA
Introduction
The use of external data has remained a constant of regulators' requirements for the AMA.

The latest requirements of the Basel Committee[9] spell out that data may be from public and/or pooled data sources and should include:

❑ actual loss amounts;
❑ information on the scale of business operations where the event occurred; and
❑ information on the causes and circumstances of the loss events, or other information that would help in assessing the relevance of the loss event.

Banks must also document the methodologies used to determine their use of external data, usually in the context of a capital model or self-assessment process, including how it may be adjusted to ensure its relevance to the bank concerned.

Interestingly, the EU is not prescriptive about the details of the data that must be captured.[10] It does, however, ask firms to document the methodologies used to incorporate the data in its measurement system.

The US regulators, as a standard, stipulate that institutions should have "policies and procedures that provide for the use of external loss data in the operational risk framework".[11] In their explanatory notes, however, they go beyond Basel in outlining the information components which they wish to be captured in relation to each loss:

❏ amount;
❏ description;
❏ event type category;
❏ event date; and
❏ adjustments to the loss amount (ie, through recoveries, insurance settlements etc) to the extent known …

… and, which is interesting, "sufficient information about the reporting institution to facilitate comparison to its own organization".

The variety of requirements, especially where they are prescriptive, obviously presents difficulties of implementation for banks. The requirements, though, present difficulties also for data providers such as pooled or public data sources. And finally, even if much of the core information is available, there are difficulties of interpretation which should be recognised.

Core loss event details
Loss event amount
Subject to honest reporting all round, there should be little problem with capturing the amount of loss. There may, however, be a difference between the amount reported publicly and the actual loss or cost experienced by an institution. It is interesting, with respect to amount, that regulators leave it to firms to decide what is relevant, ie, there is no minimum threshold, in contrast with their strong steers with regard to internal data. This recognises the current paucity of external data sources and the differing standards that apply to them.

Loss event type
Event type should not present a difficulty on the face of it, but even this can be open to interpretation and is where the availability of a "description" of the loss event, or "information on its cause and circumstances" is vital. Not every loss is clear-cut, even if a firm is using the more detailed classifications contained both in the Basel event type taxonomy (below Level 1) or those used by the leading pooled-data consortia. (Incidentally, it is difficult to see how any

database can be of use in risk management if it restricts itself to the seven basic event types.) Without the background information, it is not possible to be certain about categorisation. The background information also helps firms to assess the relevance of a loss to their own institution. To that extent, the use of loss categories, without supporting information, is of little or no use.

Loss event date

The requirement for the loss event date also appears fairly simple. But how should losses be categorised that result from a sequence of events. What date should be ascribed, for instance, to the Barings or Allfirst losses? Some data pools state that the relevant date is the date when the loss is "recognised" within the institution. This is generally a fixed and final date, which has the merit of being applied consistently. The date when a loss occurred is also of relevance. Neither date, though, would reflect the cumulative development of losses, such as the ones highlighted above. This particular aspect highlights the fact that external data will be more helpful in analysing the severity rather than the frequency of loss events.

There are other losses where the cumulative amount varies over time, either because recoveries are achieved or because further losses come to light. The US regulators' Advance Notice of Proposed Rulemaking (ANPR) is right to highlight this and the need to capture this aspect, when it is available.

Scaling

Finally, we come to information about the reporting institution that facilitates comparison to its own organisation and, in addition, in the more prescriptive phrase in the Basel paper, "information on the scale of business operations where the event occurred". It is difficult to understand what is required here or whether it can easily be provided. It could be that the regulators are looking for comparators such as "global bank", "investment bank", "regional bank", "retail consumer bank", and so forth. This may be relevant at a superficial level, but will not be especially helpful for users. Individual banks within a category will vary in many ways, whether by scale of operations, quality of controls, geographical spread or location or a number of other factors.

The need, or certainly the wish, to effect comparisons within peer groups, is nevertheless a real one and one that would add value. It is probably more relevant, though, to identify the business line in which the loss occurred, which should be evident from a reasonable loss description. Business line provides a more direct comparison. The additional comparative factor will then be either qualitative or quantitative. On the qualitative side, does the peer group share similar markets, or even market shares? Does it share common control cultures? Does it share common regulators, and so common regulatory standards? On the quantitative side, we come to the issue that has bedevilled operational risk discussions for some time.

First, it is difficult to know what are the appropriate scaling factors that are relevant to each loss category and/or type of business or institution to enable a meaningful comparison to be made. The choice ranges from asset size, to transaction volume (number and/or amount), to staff numbers and so on. Even if a scaling factor can be identified, or at least agreed, there is then the difficulty of deciding how to scale. There is certainly no straight correlation between size of business and size of loss. If Bank A is twice the size of Bank B (however measured), it will not have losses twice the size, either individually or in aggregate, of the other. Nor will a loss in Bank B be equivalent to a loss of twice the size in Bank A. The same applies to business units.

Comparisons with other banks are important from a benchmarking point of view. They lie at the heart of the reasons for using external data. But, as with many things involving operational risk, this is not an exact science. It is interesting that, because of this considerable imprecision, the banks contributing to the BBA's GOLD database decided not to pursue the scaling route. But other consortia do, on a confidential basis. So, while few would argue with the regulators' aim, achieving it is possible probably only in a general sense. Scaling, therefore, comes with significant health warnings. But there are others surrounding the use of external data.

Caveats surrounding the use of external data
Completeness
The first major caveat is the obvious one that the data are only as good as those providing them. Loss event recognition and loss data capture are still imperfect in most institutions, if only because losses cannot be derived automatically from the transaction reporting system. There is heavy reliance on "manual" reporting (and re-reporting) of losses. STP does not apply, so the scope for variations, even when a loss has been captured, is real. In addition, some losses may not be reported for good legal or similar reasons, such as the terms of an insurance settlement or where, to avoid legal discovery, provisions for potential losses may not be recorded until the conclusion of litigation, even though the rules of a database demand that losses be reported as soon as they occur. All the issues surrounding the completeness of internal data capture are magnified when it comes to external data and the inevitable external disclosure involved.

Consistency
Accuracy and consistency of reporting is another issue that is a serious problem for individual firms, as has been suggested above, but again

is exacerbated in the external arena. An effective data pool demands consistent definitions and a rigorous validation process, both within each reporting institution and at the aggregate database level. More so in the case of "public" data, whose evaluation and validation are extremely difficult.

Confidentiality

One issue that can restrict the information available from external (and therefore effectively public) data is the need to respect individual banks' confidentiality and to ensure that data are anonymous.

In the case of a data consortium, its size and nature will determine whether certain data fields may or may not be admissible. A good example would be the ability to quote the country in which a loss took place, if this was a country where only one of the consortium participants was a major player. One solution to this is to ask participants to report on all fields, but to report only on those fields where there is "critical mass", however defined. This at least means that the reporting systems and protocols are in place for when the consortium expands and more fields become reportable. Another solution that could be applied to the "country" problem is to use larger regions or continents, again until the consortium has grown.

In the case of public data, the fundamental problem is the extent to which the information reported bears any relation to the truth, as regards both amount and cause. There may well be reasons, not just ones of reputation or public perception, why it is in a bank's interests for true amounts not to be divulged, or indeed why it would be dangerous to reveal the precise reasons why a particular loss had been incurred. Unless a user is able to make appropriate enquiries, public data acquired through the media must be treated with considerable caution. Having said which, it all adds to the sum of knowledge. The Ludwig report on the Allfirst affair provided banks with a valuable checklist against which to measure themselves and their procedures and controls.[12]

Uncommon cultures

Finally, and fundamentally, each bank has its own risk management and control culture. Banks do not have common levels of control. Nor do they have similar quality of control. Some may have decided to reduce the level of control for certain risks, either because of their perception of the cost-benefit involved or for competitive motives.

Conclusion

External loss data provide a wealth of information with which to assess risk exposure and increases the information that would be available to a firm if it drew solely on its own experience. As the ANPR states, it can inform a bank's understanding of industry experience, its scenario analysis and provide a benchmark for its own internal data. But, for the reasons given above, it comes with significant limitations and health warnings that should be recognised by both regulators and regulated.

1   Response and submission to the Basel Committee on Banking Supervision CP3 (2003) on issues relating to the use and recognition of insurance in the calculation of the operational risk capital requirements for banks under the proposed Capital Accord (Talbot Underwriting Ltd) July.
2   CP3, para 637.
3   CP3, para 638.
4   CP3, footnote 94, page 129.
5   CP3, para 639.
6   CP3, para 638.
7   CP3, Part 4, Table 12.
8   Advance Notice of Proposed Rulemaking, Attachment 3 (Supervisory Guidance on Operational Risk Advanced measurement Approaches for Regulatory Capital), IX Risk Mitigation, July 2003.
9   The New Basel Capital Accord, Basel Committee on Banking Supervision (April 2003), para 634.
10 Capital requirements for banks and investment firms, 2003, Commission Services' third consultation paper, Annex H-4, 1.2.3, July.
11 Advance Notice of Proposed Rulemaking, Attachment 3, 2003, Supervisory Guidance on Operational Risk Advanced Measurement Approaches for Regulatory Capital, ("ANPR"), S20, July.
12 Report to the Board of Directors of Allied Irish Bank PLC, Allfirst Financial Inc and Allfirst concerning currency trading losses (submitted by Promontory Financial Group and Wachtell, Lipton, Rosen and Katz), March 12, 2002.

BIBLIOGRAPHY

Basel Accord Insurance Working Group, 2002, "Insurance and Operational Risk", submission to the Risk Management Group on issues relating to the recognition of the benefits of insurance and the impact on the operational risk capital requirement (Industry Technical Working Group), May.

Basel Committee on Banking Supervision, 2001, *The New Basel Capital Accord,* Consultative Document (Basel: Bank for International Settlements), January.

Basel Committee on Banking Supervision, 2002, Quantitative Impact Study 3 (Basel: Bank for International Settlements) October.

Basel Committee on Banking Supervision, 2003a, *The New Basel Capital Accord,* consultative document (Basel: Bank for International Settlements), April.

Basel Committee on Banking Supervision, 2003b, "Advance Notice of Proposed Rulemaking", 2003, Attachment 3, Supervisory Guidance on Operational Risk Advanced Measurement Approaches for Regulatory Capital, *Risk Mitigation* IX, July (Washington: US Federal Reserve Board).

European Commission, 2002, Working Document of the Commission Services on capital requirements for credit institutions and investment firms, November.

European Commission, 2003a, "Capital Requirements for Banks and Investment Firms", third Consultation Paper, Annex H-3, July.

European Commission, 2003b, "Review of capital Requirements for Banks and Investments Firms", July.

Insurance as a Mitigant for Operational Risk, 2001, Report Submitted to the Basel Committee on Banking Supervision (Industry Working Group of the Operational Risk Research Forum), April.

Index